Portrait of an Eighth-Century Gentleman

Handbook of Oriental Studies

Handbuch der Orientalistik

SECTION ONE

The Near and Middle East

Edited by

Maribel Fierro (*Madrid*)
M. Şükrü Hanioğlu (*Princeton*)
Renata Holod (*University of Pennsylvania*)
Florian Schwarz (*Vienna*)

VOLUME 141

The titles published in this series are listed at *brill.com/ho1*

Portrait of an Eighth-Century Gentleman

Khālid ibn Ṣafwān in History and Literature

By

Jaakko Hämeen-Anttila

BRILL

LEIDEN | BOSTON

Cover illustration: Copyright Mithra Kamalam. Drawing inspired by a tenth-century bowl from Eastern Iran at the National Museum of Scotland (A.1976.317).

The Library of Congress Cataloging-in-Publication Data is available online at http://catalog.loc.gov

Typeface for the Latin, Greek, and Cyrillic scripts: "Brill". See and download: brill.com/brill-typeface.

ISSN 0169-9423
ISBN 978-90-04-43396-0 (hardback)
ISBN 978-90-04-43397-7 (e-book)

This book is printed on acid-free paper and produced in a sustainable manner.

Printed by Printforce, the Netherlands

Contents

Preface

Few people have been considered worth a monograph in Classical Arabic studies. Usually these have been major figures of politics, religion, science, or literature.

This is with good reason. Not only are major figures often more interesting than minor ones, but they are also better documented, especially when it comes to the Umayyad period. To write a book-length study on, e.g., the *rajaz* poet Dukayn al-Rājiz (d. 105/723) would be difficult. The poet is of some interest, but the little that is known about him can be easily put into a brief journal article (cf. Hämeen-Anttila 2013a).

However, there is a crucial difference between central and more marginal characters of early Islamic history and culture. The images of the former have undergone conscious modification when they have been filtered through successive layers of writings and rewritings and are, thus, wrought with source critical problems. In order to understand the life and roles of al-Ḥusayn, al-Ḥajjāj, or the Caliph ʿAbd al-Malik, we have to dig through layers of Shiite, ʿAbbāsid, and later histories that have consciously modified and reinterpreted Umayyad history. This has led to misrepresentations that aim at relating the events in a way that fits later ideological frameworks and partisan views.

Stories about minor characters are less prone to conscious manipulation. They have, obviously, also undergone changes during transmission but there is no strong hidden agenda behind these changes. Rather, they follow general patterns of change in oral and literary transmission. Thus, they can be used as case studies for the change and development of historical and literary material in Arabic literature from the late Umayyad period until the ninth and tenth centuries, when much of the material had been codified, and later. Many stories are attested in a great number of sources, and the individual sources show differences ranging from minor changes in vocabulary to a complete restructuring of the whole story. In such cases, later versions can be compared with earlier ones, which offers us a possibility to study the development of Arabic historical and literary material relatively undisturbed by partisan biases and to analyse the mechanisms of "natural" change that they reveal. These may then be used in more controversial cases to discern between natural changes in the transmission process and ideologically motivated, conscious changes.

There is also a manageable amount of material related to minor figures, so as to allow a survey of the whole corpus, taking into account every single story about them and every bit of evidence for their life and activities, enabling us to draw a full picture of how they were seen by later writers in all the various genres of literature and history.

Franz Rosenthal's monograph *Humor in Early Islam* (1956) is a rather solitary exception to the trend of concentrating on major figures, taking as its subject a rather unimportant comic figure from mid-eight century Medina, Ashʿab, reported to have been alive until at least 154/771, about whose historical life we know little and who is occasionally used as a literary character in later *adab* literature. Although Rosenthal's collection is far from a complete survey of all available Ashʿab stories, it took an important step towards comprehensive analysis of material around one character.

It was Rosenthal's book that originally, many years ago, inspired me to start collecting materials on another rather evasive, yet this time indisputably historical figure, Khālid ibn Ṣafwān (d. 135/752), who later became a literary character and whose encounter with Umm Salama, the Caliph al-Saffāḥ's wife, had already caught my attention in the late 1980s. Khālid's uncertain position in historiography is well symbolised by al-Ṭabarī and al-Balādhurī. While the former does not even mention him in his *Taʾrīkh*, the latter dedicates a long chapter to him in his *Ansāb*.

But who was this Khālid ibn Ṣafwān, whom I assume many of my readers will not remember having ever come across? In his own time, Khālid ibn Ṣafwān was an orator of some importance and a wit, whose sayings were remembered and transmitted. He was also part of the late Umayyad Basran tribal nobility, who was on close terms with the high and the mighty and even met at least one Umayyad and one ʿAbbāsid Caliph, although his encounters with them and other notables were later exaggerated.

In later literature, the historical Khālid is buried under various strata of literary embellishment. Stories about him tend to become anecdotes. In some early sources Khālid is said to have been a miser, and late sources contain many anecdotes about him to illustrate this. His eloquence was unanimously admired, and in literary sources we find him improvising *bon mots* in various situations – often, though, the same saying may be found attributed to others, too. Khālid is also reported to have been a misogynist, although a more detailed analysis shows this to be a probable misunderstanding based on his ascetic sayings, many of which are misogynistic for modern sensibilities, but in their own context exhibit a general distrust of wordly life rather than of women in particular. In any case, his comments became favourite material for literature on women.

In this process, we see Khālid becoming a centre of crystallisation for various kinds of anecdotes. It is well known that figures famous for a feature tend to absorb stories originally told of other, less well-known characters. A story about a wine-drinking poet will soon be found featuring Abū Nuwās, and an Umayyad witticism becomes easily attributed to Khālid.

While Khālid is represented as a character in many anecdotes, in others we find his own sayings, or at least sayings claimed to be transcripts of what he had said. Here the question of authenticity is extremely acute, but even though the texts cannot, as such, be taken as specimens of Umayyad style they may well contain traces of early rhetorics.

The present monograph is an attempt to unravel the development of Khālid's figure from a historical person into a literary character. The primary aim is not so much to get to know the real, historical Khālid – there is little that can be known about him – but to understand the mechanisms of change in early Arabic historical and literary texts.

The basis of the book is formed by a translation of all material that can be found about Khālid, mainly from Arabic sources, but in a few cases also from Persian ones, where he is occasionally mentioned. Our main source is al-Balādhurī's *Ansāb* VII/1: 55–88, which contains 115 items on Khālid, mainly anecdotes about, and sayings and parts of speeches by, him. This can be supplemented by some 200 other stories about him, made up partly of variant versions of the stories found in the *Ansāb*, partly of completely new ones, scattered all around Arabic literature, from lexicographical works and commentaries on poetry to humorous collections of *nawādir*. Counting together all the versions and attestations of Khālid stories they run into thousands.

The first Part of the book, Chapters 1 and 2, contains a study of this material. Chapter 1, "Khālid ibn Ṣafwān as a Historical Character," introduces the reader to the historical context Khālid lived in, discusses the main sources on him, both lost and extant, and analyses what little we can know about his life before literary embellishment started creating new versions of him. This chapter also gives an overview of his family line from the eponymous father of the Ahtamites, al-Ahtam, until the generation following Khālid, after which we gradually loose sight of Khālid's relatives, who sink into insignificance after the family having enjoyed some fame for more than six generations. The first chapter ends with a glance at the later fame of Khālid himself.

Chapter 2, "Khālid ibn Ṣafwān and Early Arabic Prose," first outlines the Umayyad literary context and then proceeds to study Khālid as a character, before discussing the various genres his sayings and stories about him belong to, with special attention paid to the mechanics of the anecdote. This chapter also discusses some sample cases of anecdotes in more detail, focusing on their gradual growth and on how the longer anecdotes work.

Some of the anecdotes about Khālid are among the most developed pieces of Classical Arabic prose literature and a careful analysis of all the extant variants in some cases shows us clearly how an anecdote has been built by successive generations of mainly anonymous authors. A major aim of this book is to contribute to our understanding of early Classical Arabic prose literature and its development.

Chapters 3–5 form the second Part of the book, containing all Khālid stories in translation, giving first the stories in al-Balādhurī, *Ansāb* VII/1: 55–88 (numbered B1–B115) in Chapter 3. The rest of the stories are translated in Chapter 4 (numbered A1–A108), and a handful of stories that I consider clearly misattributed, but still worth being translated for the reader to see, come in Chapter 5 (numbered C1–C3). The chapters contain an annotated translation of the stories with necessary commentaries, given partly in notes and partly in a separate section coming after the translations of all the variant versions of a story and full lists of attestations. When a variant differs considerably from the main version, it has been translated separately after the main version and marked by a, b, c, etc. (e.g., B7, B7a, B7b). Minor differences have been selectively noted. All the translations are mine, even when an existing translation is mentioned for reference.

The source of the translated version in Chapters 4 and 5 (A and C stories), as well as of the variant versions of B stories in Chapter 3, is given immediately after the story in brackets. In Chapter 3 (B stories) the source of all the main versions is al-Balādhurī, *Ansāb* VII/1: 55–88. Here I have not referred to the pagination of al-Balādhurī's work, but the stories should be relatively easy to find from the edition of the Arabic text. To facilitate this even further, I have added Source References on p. 265, which help locate the stories in the *Ansāb*. Other attestations of the story in all three chapters are given after the main source.

In Chapter 3, the stories are given in the order of the original source, al-Balādhurī's *Ansāb*. In Chapter 4, they are collected under nine different headings, to give similar stories as a bunch. The classification could have been done in several different ways, as many stories share features of several groups.

When possible, people mentioned in the stories have been identified either in the notes, commentary, or the study, except for those mentioned in the *isnād*, who have only sparingly been identified. In cases where the last link of the *isnād* also takes part in the story itself or is an eyewitness to the event, he (never she) is identified.

I have usually given dates in both *Hijrī* and AD calendars (*Hijrī*/AD), but in referring to centuries and decades I have usually only given the AD date to avoid unnecessarily complicated dates (thus, e.g., "early eighth century," instead of "late first/early eighth century"). When the same date is repeated soon after, I have only given the *Hijrī* date, as the reader should have no difficulties in finding the AD date a few lines earlier. Within the stories, I have added the AD date to the few cases which give the *Hijrī* date.

I have discussed parts of the material of this book in earlier articles and book chapters (Hämeen-Anttila 1993a, 1994, 2009, 2013b, and 2017).

I wish to thank Dr Maria Pakkala (Helsinki) for her help with some of the stories in Chapter 3, which we read together in Helsinki in 2015, as well as for helping me to acquire some less easily available sources. I also wish to thank Mr Sam Mills, MA (Edinburgh), for proofreading the manuscript and polishing my English, as well as helping me with the genealogical diagrams in Chapter 1.4. Finally, I wish to thank Sukaina Husain, MSc (Edinburgh), and Mithra K, MVA (Baroda), for designing and executing the lovely cover image.

Jaakko Hämeen-Anttila
Edinburgh, 28 February, 2020

PART 1

Study

CHAPTER 1

Khālid ibn Ṣafwān as a Historical Character

1.1 Historical Context

Khālid ibn Ṣafwān's life covers a period of rapid transformation in Arab society and the newly born Islamic Empire. Khālid seems to have died in 135/752 in an advanced age.[1] If we take his advanced age to mean that he was 70 or 80 (lunar) years old when he died, this would date his birth to around 55/675 or 65/685. He would, thus, have lived his youth in an Empire secured for the Umayyads by the Caliph ʿAbd al-Malik (r. 65–86/685–705) after the second *fitna*, of which he may, or may not, have had memories. He would then have lived through the heydays of the Marwānids to see their grip on power gradually weaken in internal strifes and local rebellions before the ʿAbbāsids finally overturned their rule and the Islamic Empire entered into a new period under a new dynasty – not that Khālid would have been present to see the consolidation of their power, so for him the 740s would hardly have ended in a clear-cut change of dynasties. Who would have known in 135/752 that the ʿAbbāsids were there to stay for a long time?

During Khālid's adult life, the old tribal system was losing its importance. During the Conquests, the Caliphs relied on tribal armies, which fought under their separate leaders, instead of forming one Caliphal army. Well into the eighth century, though, the tribal leaders retained a lot of power, but when Khālid becomes fully visible in around 110/728, they were being superceded by a bureaucracy that took care of the matters of the Empire in a much more systematic way under the eyes of the Caliph.

Obviously the change did not take place overnight, but the tribal system, with its division into Southern and Northern Arabs, gradually lost importance. Whereas originally the system of stipends (*jāʾiza*) had brought wealth and influence to tribal leaders, later the system turned them and their descendants into a salaried nobility that was dependent on the Caliph and his *dīwān*. Thus, it comes as no surprise that Khālid is not depicted as a powerful tribal nobleman, like his fathers may well have been, but a wit, orator, and, at most, companion of the Caliphs and their Governors.

Since the early conquests, the tribes had been settled in a number of new towns. In Iraq, Basra and Kufa were the main centres before the founding of

1 See Chapter 1.3.2.

DOI:10.1163/9789004433977_002

Baghdad in 145/762, a decade after Khālid's death. Thus, it is not a surprise that we meet Khālid in Basra and other towns, rather than in the desert. As we know from later sources, both cities were flourishing cultural centres, where much of the old Arabic lore, such as poems and stories, proverbs and genealogy, and lexical rarities and grammatical curiosities, were collected, organised, and codified.

Religious material was also collected at the time, with the first life of the Prophet Muḥammad being compiled by Ibn Isḥāq (d. 150/767) and *ḥadīth* collections rapidly growing from private notebooks to a public culture of lectures and published books. About these more formal aspects of religious activity we hear next to nothing in the stories about Khālid, though.

Instead of settling among the conquered population in their age-old cities, the early conquerors had usually built separate towns for themselves. Basra was established as a military camp, and although by Khālid's time it had lost its exclusively Islamic character, it must still have been a more strongly Islamic city than, e.g., Damascus. This is reflected in Khālid stories, which rarely present non-Muslim characters. Partly, of course, this is also a class question and a matter of literary taste: the tribal nobility will have had more contacts with each other than with the new converts or those who remained Christian or Jewish, while the Umayyad story corpus in general, not only the Khālid corpus, keeps up an illusion of a much purer Bedouin Arab context than would probably have been the case in real life. Non-Muslims have few, usually comic, roles in this literature.

While the administration took care of the new Empire, there were also those who were disappointed by change from an early community of Believers into subjects of the Caliph and tax-payers of a Late Antique Empire. In addition to numerous rebellions towards the end of the Umayyad period, there was also a more peaceful counter-current. While until 135/752 it is too early to speak of a Sufi movement, which started to find its form only some decades later, ascetic and pietist movements were rife. Of the nascent Shiism we hear nothing in the anecdotes, and Kufa was, indeed, more prone to early Shiism than Basra. On the other hand, perhaps the leading pietist of the Umayyad period, al-Ḥasan al-Baṣrī lived in Basra and died there in 110/728. He had numerous disciples and followers, and his lectures were attended by a multitude of people, Khālid included.

This is the world in which the historical Khālid ibn Ṣafwān al-Tamīmī al-Ahtamī al-Baṣrī lived and interacted with other orators, courtiers, poets, pietists, governors, and Caliphs, not forgetting slave girls, Bedouins, matchmakers, and misers.

1.2 Sources

1.2.1 *Lost Sources*

Although not even once mentioned by al-Ṭabarī in his *Taʾrīkh*, Khālid ibn Ṣafwān was famous in the 8th–10th centuries and stories about him circulated widely. He was also the subject of at least two monographs, both later lost as was so much of early ʿAbbāsid literature in general. The first was compiled by the Basran (and later Baghdadi) historian Abū l-Ḥasan ʿAlī ibn Muḥammad al-Qurashī al-Madāʾinī, who probably died in 228/842–843.[2] The famous Basran historian was an important transmitter of historical material for later generations in his more than 200 treatises, only two of which have been preserved, *Kitāb al-Taʿāzī* and *Kitāb Murdifāt Quraysh*.[3]

It was probably his role as a local historian that made al-Madāʾinī interested in Khālid ibn Ṣafwān: even though al-Ṭabarī ignored Khālid, Khālid did have some local importance and, moreover, he seems to have been a colourful person without whom the local history of Basra would not have been complete.

Our main bibliographical source for al-Madāʾinī's books is the list in Ibn al-Nadīm's *Fihrist*, which mentions *Kitāb Khālid ibn Ṣafwān*.[4] The book does not seem to be mentioned by anyone else, except by Yāqūt and al-Ṣafadī, who copy their information from the *Fihrist*.[5] Besides the evidence of these bio- and bibliographical sources, the fact that the book did at one point exist, whether in the form of a published and fixed text or more amorphous lecture notes,[6] is further guaranteed by the numerous stories about Khālid transmitted on al-Madāʾinī's authority, especially in al-Balādhurī's *Ansāb*, but also in many other sources, partly independent of al-Balādhurī.[7]

Al-Balādhurī's (d. 279/892) *Ansāb* contains 115 stories, a large number of which probably derive from al-Madāʾinī, and his monograph on Khālid.[8]

2 See Lindstedt (2013); Werkmeister (1983): 397–406.
3 Lindstedt (2012–14): 245 = (2013) I: 9.
4 Ibn al-Nadīm, *Fihrist*, pp. 113–117, here p. 116. See also Lindstedt (2012–14): 251 = (2013) I: 15.
5 Yāqūt, *Irshād* IV: 226; al-Ṣafadī, *Wāfī* XXII: 46.
6 Cf. Schoeler (2002) and (2006).
7 Al-Balādhurī, *Ansāb* VII/1: 55–88.
8 Al-Balādhurī, *Ansāb* VII/1: 55–88. It is not possible to say how many exactly, as al-Balādhurī shares the common habit of quoting anecdotes beginning with an anonymous *qāla*, which often, but not necessarily always, refers to the authority in the previous anecdote. Al-Madāʾinī is mentioned by name as an authority in only 20 anecdotes of *Ansāb* VII/1: 55–88. In a further 11 cases he is given as the authority in other sources, including only anecdotes not found in *Ansāb* VII/1: 55–88, or not given there on the authority of al-Madāʾinī.

Al-Balādhurī certainly supplemented the material by stories received from other sources, including al-Madāʾinī's other monographs.

The material in *Ansāb* VII/1: 55–88, is vaguely organised according to topics, which may already have been the case in al-Madāʾinī's monograph. Thus, e.g., B17 and B19–B22 concern miserliness, *bukhl*, B89–B92 discuss (mostly Bedouin) eloquence, and B94–B97 contain eulogies, with B94 tying the topic up with B89–B92. On the other hand, some stories in the *Ansāb* that feature wide apart from each other belong together or are fragments of the same story and in a few cases could even be considered variants of each other. Thus, e.g., B40 is similar to the beginning of B98. The former is quoted without any indication of the source of the story, while the latter is reported on the authority of al-Haytham (ibn ʿAdī, d. 206/821 or somewhat later). It is possible that the duplication arises from al-Balādhurī's use of al-Madāʾinī's monograph as his main source with secondary sources excerpted later and added at the end of the passage. B40a, a variant of B40, is related on the authority of al-Madāʾinī in al-Iṣfahānī's *Aghānī*, which makes it probable that al-Balādhurī received B40 from al-Madāʾinī's book. Finding B40 there, al-Balādhurī included it in his work, but coming across B98 in some other source he included it, too, as it was much longer than B40. It is very common that authors of the period first excerpted their main source, adding material from their secondary sources at the end of the chapter or passage.[9]

It seems that al-Balādhurī received the material directly from al-Madāʾinī through oral transmission. At least, the first story, B6, he quotes on al-Madāʾinī's authority is introduced by *ḥaddathanā ʿAlī ibn Muḥammad ibn ʿAbdallāh al-Madāʾinī*, and al-Balādhurī seems to make a clear distinction between *qāla* "he said" and *ḥaddatha* "he narrated," using the former for material he received indirectly, the latter for material he received directly.[10]

Al-Madāʾinī was not only interested in Khālid but in many other subjects, too, in several of which he could have come across Khālid stories. Hence, not all Khālid stories transmitted on his authority need to come from his Khālid monograph. Among his lost books there is a *Kitāb Akhbār al-Saffāḥ*, and a *Kitāb Mufākharat ahl al-Baṣra wa-ahl al-Kūfa*,[11] both of which may well have contained Khālid material, not to mention occasional Khālid stories in his other books. He was, e.g., interested in collecting stories about incorrect

9 Cf., e.g., Hämeen-Anttila (1993b): 79–88.

10 In later stories al-Balādhurī uses the expression *al-Madāʾinī qāla*, but this should not be taken as implying indirect transmission, as *qāla* here refers back to *ḥaddathanā ... al-Madāʾinī* in B6.

11 See Lindstedt (2012–14): 247, 259 = (2013) I: 12, 22.

speech (*laḥn*) in Umayyad courts,[12] and as Khālid later became (in)famous for his *laḥns*, he may well have been mentioned in this regard.

Al-Jāḥiẓ (d. 255/868) criticises al-Madā'inī and other historians for lack of comprehensiveness when it comes to early ʿAbbāsids.[13] They only codified "little from much" (*qalīlan min kathīr*), says al-Jāḥiẓ, and this seems corroborated by the Khālid material we find in various sources, but never transmitted on al-Madā'inī's authority. It is, of course, impossible to assess how much of the material from al-Madā'inī ended up in al-Balādhurī's text and how many of the stories transmitted there anonymously could derive from al-Madā'inī.

Al-Jāḥiẓ is also an important witness for the existence of a separate monograph on Khālid in the late ninth century. He tells us that "there is a book on the *kalām* (sayings) of Khālid, which is in circulation in the hands of the booksellers (*al-warrāqīn*)."[14] The other known author of a book on Khālid, al-Jalūdī, seems to have died in 332/944 and is, thus, too late to have been the author of the book al-Jāḥiẓ refers to. More probably, al-Jāḥiẓ refers to al-Madā'inī's work, as we have no information about further Khālid monographs, and despite his local fame Khālid was probably not important enough to be the subject of very many books.

Ibn Qutayba (d. 276/889) may also refer to a monograph on Khālid. When he narrates his first Khālid story in the *ʿUyūn* he refers to his source as "in the stories of Khālid ibn Ṣafwān" (*fī akhbār Khālid ibn Ṣafwān*).[15] This may refer to a monograph titled *Akhbār Khālid ibn Ṣafwān*, presumably by al-Madā'inī, many of whose books were titled *Kitāb Akhbār so-and-so*, or at least circulated under such a title:[16] again, al-Jalūdī is too late to come into question. The expression could also be a general reference to stories about Khālid, but this is made improbable by the conspicuously large number of Khālid stories Ibn Qutayba quotes in several of his books, which shows that he had an easy access to them, further implying that they were available to him through one book.[17] Moreover, some are unique, not attested elsewhere in Arabic literature, which

12 Cf. one anecdote in al-Jāḥiẓ, *Bayān* III: 240.

13 Al-Jāḥiẓ, *Bayān* III: 366.

14 Al-Jāḥiẓ, *Bayān* I: 340. In *Bayān* I: 317–318, al-Jāḥiẓ also mentions that people have memorised and repeatedly quote Khālid and Shabīb ibn Shayba's *kalām* (*yaḥfaẓuhu l-nās wa-yadūru ʿalā alsinatihim min kalāmihimā*).

15 Ibn Qutayba, *ʿUyūn* I: 78 (B40).

16 Cf. Lindstedt (2012–14): 247–248 = (2013) I: 11–12 (24 titles).

17 Ibn Qutayba quotes stories B4, B10, B12, B23, B25, B29, B30, B33, B37, B38, B40, B42, B49, B56, B59, B75, B80, B81, B101, B104, B108, B111, in a form similar to that in al-Balādhurī, *Ansāb* VII/1: 55–88, as well as nos. B63a, B70a, A3, A6, A21, A53, A63, A64, A70, and A103. These are found in his *ʿUyūn*, *Maʿārif*, *Shiʿr*, and *Gharīb*. The presence of stories not found in al-Balādhurī, *Ansāb* VII/1: 55–88, makes it probable that Ibn Qutayba did not pick them from al-Balādhurī's work but received them from another source, possibly this

further supports the conclusion that they come from a lost Khālid monograph, rather than from separate anecdotes within other collections. A story found in a single volume of stories was more likely to be ignored by later scholars than a story that had already started circulating in literature.

Neither al-Jāḥiẓ nor Ibn Qutayba identifies the author of such a book on Khālid, but it is a reasonable assumption that they are referring to al-Madāʾinī's work, which would thus have been in rather wide circulation at the end of the ninth century. While Khālid stories continue circulating *en masse* in later literature, we have little unequivocal evidence that later authors would have been using al-Madāʾinī's monograph, rather than quoting the stories through al-Jāḥiẓ, Ibn Qutayba, al-Balādhurī, and other early authors. Even the few stories later transmitted on al-Madāʾinī's authority may well derive from intermediate sources despite quoting al-Madāʾinī as their authority.[18]

The other lost book on Khālid was composed by another Basran historian, al-Jalūdī, or al-Julūdī,[19] whose *Kitāb Akhbār Khālid ibn Ṣafwān* is mentioned by Ibn al-Nadīm.[20] Our main sources on al-Jalūdī are Shiite biographical dictionaries.[21] Al-Najāshī (d. after 463/1071) mentions ʿAbd al-ʿAzīz ibn Yaḥyā ibn ʿĪsā al-Jalūdī al-Azdī al-Baṣrī Abū Aḥmad and calls him "the learned man of Basra and its historian" (*shaykh al-Baṣra wa-akhbāriyyuhā*), which fits well with his interest in Khālid.[22] He is also said to have been a companion of Abū Jaʿfar (al-Shaykh al-Ṣadūq, b. after 305/917, d. 381/991) (*min aṣḥāb Abī Jaʿfar*).[23] Al-Najāshī gives a long list of books on Shiite topics by al-Jalūdī, but also mentions several *adab* works towards the end of his list. Besides *Kitāb Akhbār Khālid ibn Ṣafwān*, he mentions *Akhbār al-ʿAjjāj*, *Akhbār Ruʾba ibn al-ʿAjjāj*, *Akhbār al-Farazdaq*, *Akhbār Abī Nuwās*, *Akhbār al-Furs*, as well as *Akhbār al-ʿArab wa'l-Furs*. He says that these titles were mainly taken from various booklists, *fihrists*, but that some he had seen. It would, thus, seem that at least parts

monograph on Khālid. Obviously, we must again assume a number of secondary sources beside his main source.

18 Al-Madāʾinī is given as the (at least seemingly) immediate authority in B40b, A19, A21, and A49, as well as in a number of cases where it is probable that the later author derived the story from al-Balādhurī and assumed that the latter's anonymous *qāla* referred back to al-Madāʾinī.

19 I wish to thank Dr Ilkka Lindstedt for his assistance in searching for sources on al-Jalūdī's life. Al-Jalūdī's biography is resumed in *GAS* VIII: 106, and he is often mentioned in passing in *GAS* II, see the Index to that volume.

20 Ibn al-Nadīm, *Fihrist*, p. 128.

21 In addition, see al-Khaṭīb, *Taʾrīkh Baghdād* I: 25 (in an *isnād*).

22 Al-Najāshī, *Rijāl*, pp. 231–234 (no. 640).

23 Al-Najāshī, too, was Abū Jaʿfar's student.

of the voluminous oeuvre of al-Jalūdī were lost rather early. Al-Najāshī ends the article by giving an *ijāza* going for all of his books back to the author himself.[24]

The other biographical source for al-Jalūdī is brief. Al-Ṭūsī (d. 459/1066 or a year later) mentions him in his *Fihrist*, as ʿAbd al-ʿAzīz ibn Yaḥyā ibn Aḥmad ibn ʿĪsā al-Jalūdī al-Azdī Abū Aḥmad, telling us that he was from Basra and belonged to Imāmīs.[25] Al-Ṭūsī gives both vocalisations, al-Jalūdī and al-Julūdī, but prefers the former. He also mentions a variant reading al-Jalwadī. Al-Ṭūsī has a date for al-Jalūdī's death, giving it as Monday, 17th of Dhū l-Ḥijja 332/10th of August 944. He mentions that al-Jalūdī had written many books, but only gives two examples of his religious works, not mentioning any of the *adab* compilations by title.

Al-Jalūdī's *Akhbār al-Farazdaq*,[26] not known to Ibn al-Nadīm, is mentioned by al-Najāshī,[27] and quoted by ʿAlī ibn Ḥamza al-Baṣrī (d. 375/985) in *al-Tanbīh ʿalā aghlāṭ al-ruwāh* in the section on the mistakes by Abū Ziyād al-Kilābī.[28] Ibn al-Nadīm does, however, know a *Kitāb Akhbār al-Farazdaq* by al-Madāʾinī,[29] which raises the question whether al-Jalūdī may, in general, have used al-Madāʾinī's works to compose his *adab* monographs on their basis, which in Khālid's case would mean that al-Madāʾinī's stories may have formed the basis of his selection. This might also explain his almost complete absence from later literature. If his work was merely an elaboration of al-Madāʾinī's, later authors may well have quoted the famous historian instead of the rather unknown Shiite author, assuming that the latter gave al-Madāʾinī as an authority in the work.

Al-Jalūdī is quoted as an authority in our material only once. A44 comes from al-Jalūdī, the *isnād* leading back to Khālid's cousin Shabīb ibn Shayba through two intermediaries.[30] Although later authors were less keen on naming their 10th-century sources than on name-dropping earlier authorities, one might still assume that those who tend to quote a full *isnād* for their stories, like Ibn ʿAsākir, would at least occasionally mention al-Jalūdī, had his book been widely circulating. It would certainly seem that his book on Khālid, as

---

24 < Abū ʿAbdallāh ibn Hadiyya < Jaʿfar ibn Muḥammad < ʿAbd al-ʿAzīz.

25 Al-Ṭūsī, *Fihrist*, pp. 183–184 (no. 393).

26 Note that, as in the case of Ibn Qutayba's *Akhbār Khālid ibn Ṣafwān*, discussed above, it is not quite certain whether or not this should be taken as a book title or, in a more general sense, as "stories about al-Farazdaq."

27 Al-Najāshī, *Rijāl*, p. 234.

28 From there the quotation was copied to ʿAbd al-Qādir al-Baghdādī's *Khizāna* IX: 221. On Abū Ziyād al-Kilābī, see *GAS* IV: 331–332.

29 Ibn al-Nadīm, *Fihrist*, p. 116. Cf. Lindstedt (2012–14): 248 = (2013) I: 12.

30 < Muḥammad ibn Zakariyyā < Mahdī ibn Sābiq < Shabīb.

well as probably all his other *adab* books, never enjoyed a wide circulation. His Khālid book at least left almost no traces in literature.

1.2.2 *Existing Stories*

Most biographical sources on Khālid, such as al-Ṣafadī's *Wāfī*, are relatively brief, and only a few are more extensive. Yāqūt's *Irshād* contains a good selection of stories about him, but the most extensive collection after al-Balādhurī's *Ansāb* with its 115 stories, is Ibn ʿAsākir's *Taʾrīkh* with some 55 stories or variants, of which Ibn Manẓūr repeats 30 in his *Mukhtaṣar*. Ibn al-ʿAdīm's *Bughya*, mainly dependent on Ibn ʿAsākir, gives 36 stories.[31] Elsewhere, there are minor blocks of Khālid stories. Al-Sharīshī's *Sharḥ* contains six stories, and al-Jāḥiẓ devotes two pages to Khālid in his *Bayān*.[32] Al-Murtaḍā's *Amālī* features a small collection of stories, mainly about Khālid's *bukhl*.[33]

In addition, individual stories about and sayings and speeches by Khālid are found scattered in almost all Arabic *adab* collections, many historical works, major lexicographical compilations,[34] some Sufi anthologies, and occasionally even Persian works, either in translation or in the original.[35] In all, I have been able to locate 223 stories and sayings, with a large number of variants to several of these, bringing the total number of translated stories and sayings up to 270.

While religious and philological material is often quoted either with full *isnāds* or at least with an *isnād* bringing the reader to the ultimate source or the most important intermediate source, this is not the case with *adab* in general and Khālid stories in particular. Thus, we cannot get an exact picture of the circulation of these stories, except as far as they appear in books.[36]

Ibn ʿAsākir, and largely following him Ibn al-ʿAdīm, are the major exceptions to this, both giving extensive *isnāds* for most of their stories. While 27 of the stories narrated by al-Balādhurī in *Ansāb* VII/1: 55–88, and their variants elsewhere, mention al-Madāʾinī as their authority, it is conspicuous that only

31 Al-Ṣafadī, *Wāfī* XIII: 254–255; Yāqūt, *Irshād* III: 274–280; al-Balādhurī, *Ansāb* VII/1: 55–88; Ibn ʿAsākir, *Taʾrīkh* XVI: 94–117; Ibn Manẓūr, *Mukhtaṣar* VII: 353–365; Ibn al-ʿAdīm, *Bughya* VII: 49–76.

32 Al-Sharīshī, *Sharḥ* IV: 134–135 (commentary to al-Ḥarīrī's *al-Maqāma al-Bakriyya*, 43.); al-Jāḥiẓ, *Bayān* I: 339–340.

33 Al-Murtaḍā, *Amālī* II: 261–263. The first two of al-Murtaḍā's stories explicitly come from al-Balādhurī, and as all the ten stories are found in al-Balādhurī, *Ansāb* VII/1: 55–88, it seems obvious that al-Murtaḍā received all his Khālid stories from this source.

34 As the lexica usually circulate the same material under the same lemma I have systematically indicated the occurrence of stories only in Ibn Manẓūr's *Lisān*.

35 In translation, e.g., ʿAwfī, *Jawāmiʿ*, B38, B60, A94. In the original, e.g., Nakhshabī, *Gulrīz*, B75, A65.

36 For the use of *isnād* in *adab* literature, see Chapter 2.7.

four of the other stories do so.[37] Partly, of course, this is due to lack of any indication of source in most cases. However, the discrepancy between variants of the al-Balādhurī stories, where al-Madā'inī is referred to, and the other stories, where he is usually not, might be taken to imply that a large number of the other stories do not derive from al-Madā'inī. Further, this would imply that al-Balādhurī has quoted a good number of the stories that were there in al-Madā'inī's monograph – otherwise, one would expect that more authors would have quoted al-Madā'inī as their authority for stories not found in al-Balādhurī.

The *isnāds* of Ibn ʿAsākir, Ibn al-ʿAdīm, and a few others show that some early collectors were interested in Khālid. Most conspicuously, the Basran al-Aṣmaʿī (b. 122/740, d. 213/828) is quoted as the (or an) authority for 24 stories, almost as often as al-Madā'inī.[38] Although he was a favourite authority and later almost anything could be attached to his name, including popular *sīras* and folktales, in *adab* literature the attributions were not completely wild, and it is evident that he was interested in Khālid ibn Ṣafwān, whom he might just have seen as a child.

Although not as prominently present, the Kufan-born historian from Wāsiṭ, al-Haytham ibn ʿAdī (d. 206/821 or somewhat later), is adduced as the authority 9 times.[39] The third recurrent authority is Shabīb ibn Shayba, Khālid's younger cousin, who is given as the authority 7 times.[40] His son ʿAbd al-Ṣamad ibn Shabīb is given as an authority in A78 and A79.

ʿAbd al-Ṣamad ibn Shabīb is otherwise little known.[41] In A78, he is the informant of al-Aṣmaʿī, which shows that al-Aṣmaʿī collected materials from family tradition – it is unfortunate that al-Aṣmaʿī is usually quoted as the last, or only,

37 I.e., A19, A21, A42, and A49. Al-Madā'inī is quoted as an authority in 27 stories in Chapter 3. I have excluded cases where an anonymous *qāla* refers to the authority given in the preceding story (e.g., B7, referring back to B6), but included cases where al-Balādhurī does not refer to al-Madā'inī, but one of the variant stories or the attestations of the main version does. Al-Madā'inī is referred to as an authority in the following stories: B6, B7, B9, B16, B21, B24–B25, B27–B30, B40–B42, B47–B48, B51, B53–B55, B60, B67, B81–B83, B87, B101, B106.

38 B7a, B8a, B9b, B12, B23, B33, B41, B43, B45, B49, B51, B56, B91a, B103; A42, A48, A52, A62, A64, A78, A80a, A83, A93, A105 (cf. also B83). For al-Aṣmaʿī, see *GAS* VIII: 71–76.

39 B9, B25, B27, B38, B51, B81, B82, B98; A69. For al-Haytham, see *GAS* I: 272 and Leder (1991).

40 B11c, B38, B40a, B45a; A24, A44, A95.

41 Cf. Ibn al-Kalbī, *Jamhara*, table 76 and below, Chapter 1.4. This obscurity of ʿAbd al-Ṣamad also makes the *isnād* where he is mentioned reliable: one may forge an *isnād*, but this is not done using obscure, almost unknown persons. Thus, a piece of philological *adab* may easily become later attributed to the famous al-Aṣmaʿī, but its later attribution to the almost unknown ʿAbd al-Ṣamad is highly improbable.

link in the *isnād*, so we cannot ascertain whether he used the family tradition more extensively. As Shabīb ibn Shayba (d. around 170/786) is the usual transmitter from Khālid, it is possible that his son only transmitted the material after his father's death, i.e., at least three decades after the death of Khālid.

ʿAbdallāh ibn Shabīb, given as the authority in A70, may be another, otherwise unknown son of Shabīb. In this story, though, Ibn ʿAsākir gives variant *isnāds* where ʿAbdallāh is called ʿAbdallāh ibn Shabīb al-Makkī. His identity, thus, remains unclear.

A further character, often associated with Khālid and also transmitting stories about him to later collectors, was Ḥafṣ ibn Muʿāwiya ibn ʿAmr al-Ghalābī, whom we meet in five stories,[42] himself a Basran orator of at least minor fame, as he made it to al-Jāḥiẓ's *Bayān*, although only with a brief mention.[43]

1.3 Life and Political Importance

1.3.1 *Historicity of the Stories*

In studying the historical Khālid ibn Ṣafwān our first obstacle is the lack of reliable historical sources. Existing biographical dictionaries are rather sketchy when it comes to Khālid's life. Few sources give any details, and most articles consist of individual sayings and speeches of Khālid, as well as stories about him, but with little context and few pieces of biographical information. Thus, it is only by the analysis of the whole corpus that we can start drawing a more accurate picture of Khālid and his life.

Khālid himself wrote nothing and there is nothing to indicate that he would have been literate.[44] Unlike his contemporaries, ʿAbd al-Ḥamīd ibn Yaḥyā (d. 132/750) and Ibn al-Muqaffaʿ (d. ca. 139/756), Khālid left no written legacy. Some speeches ascribed to him, or their fragments, have been preserved in

42 B25, B42, B50, B55, and B79.

43 Al-Jāḥiẓ, *Bayān* I: 354.

44 In the corpus that has been preserved Khālid is never depicted reading or writing anything. The only exception to this comes in a very late story, B99b. His younger cousin Shabīb ibn Shayba is, however, occasionally implied to have been literate, see, e.g., an anecdote in al-Balādhurī, *Ansāb* VII/1: 90, where his servant girl brings him a dish of paper for food, saying that it is the sole commodity in the house. The difference between the two may well be symptomatic of the diffusion of literacy among the tribal aristocracy in general. Khālid's two contemporaries of non-Arab background, ʿAbd al-Ḥamīd ibn Yaḥyā and Ibn al-Muqaffaʿ, were fully literate while Khālid may have represented the last illiterate generation of tribal nobility.

later sources, but their initially oral transmission makes the question of authenticity particularly difficult.[45]

Many anecdotes seem to talk about Khālid's life. However, it is dubious whether these stories contain information about the historical Khālid or not. Some are stereotypical anecdotes (e.g., many of the miser stories) where the use of Khālid's name seems more or less fortuitous. In a few cases, we may follow the growth of a fictitious story from anecdotes which derive from the earliest sources and purport to, and perhaps do, contain historical information.

One reason for the dearth of early historical sources on Khālid relates to his political significance or the lack thereof. The Ahtamite family was an important actor in tribal politics, and Khālid's father, Ṣafwān, is once even mentioned as the leader of Banū Tamīm in Basra.[46] In any case, his father was an influential, as well as wealthy, figure. Khālid is said to have inherited this position from his father, and stories about him present him as a close companion to several Caliphs (including the ʿAbbāsid Abū l-ʿAbbās al-Saffāḥ). This tallies well with the fact that al-Balādhurī dedicates over 30 pages to him. Reading al-Balādhurī, Khālid seems an important person.

Al-Ṭabarī (d. 314/923), however, does not mention Khālid at all in his *Taʾrīkh*. Also in other sources, al-Balādhurī included, Khālid is usually not described as the confidant of Caliphs and governors, nor is he often represented as advising them on political matters. The stories about him revolve more around the roles he has as a literary character even when he is presented socialising with the high and the mighty of the Empire.[47] Did, then, Khālid have political importance? Whence the discrepancy between al-Balādhurī and al-Ṭabarī, the former dedicating so much space to him, the latter ignoring him, despite the fact that al-Ṭabarī used some of al-Madāʾinī's works as his sources and perhaps knew al-Balādhurī's work?[48]

The latter question is perhaps the easier to answer. Al-Balādhurī and al-Ṭabarī had different aims. Al-Balādhurī concentrates on individuals and writes their histories. Khālid was undoubtedly famous in his time and, hence, merited a place in the *Ansāb*.[49] Al-Ṭabarī, however, was writing a history of the Empire. For him, persons who influenced the destinies of the Islamic Empire

45 Cf. Chapter 2.7.
46 B4, but cf. Chapter 1.4.
47 Cf. Chapter 2.2.
48 For al-Ṭabarī's sources, see Rotter (1974).
49 Al-Balādhurī's lack of interest in politics may also be seen in the fact that Khālid's more important ancestors receive much less attention than their oratorically gifted descendant, whose political influence must have been less than his fathers'. Al-Balādhurī was more interested in the aristocracy than in history as such: with good reason, Borrut (2010):

were of prime importance. Persons of lesser influence were dispensable even when they were colourful, picturesque, and reasonably famous. Why, exactly, Khālid came to be ignored to the extent that his name is not even once mentioned in this huge book is of course a question which is not easily answered and it must partly be a coincidence: thousands of names of minor characters crop up once or twice in the *Taʾrīkh*, although they had little influence on the vagaries of the Empire.

But what, then, was Khālid's role in local Basran politics? Obviously, tribal politics decreased in importance in the late Umayyad period so that men like Khālid were undoubtedly less influential than their predecessors had been. Yet he was obviously not without some significance. B3 says this explicitly ("he was powerful and wealthy"), but in later literature his literary roles dominate his image and define the apolitical contexts in which he is spoken of. Yet they occasionally imply that he had political importance, at least on a local level.

The most important sources for the political role of Khālid are Wakīʿ's *Akhbār* and al-Balādhurī's *Ansāb*. Now and then, these early sources show Khālid involved in tribal politics. A19, from Wakīʿ's *Akhbār*, mentions Khālid as the spokesman of his clan in a disagreement between them and the family of al-Qāsim ibn Sulaymān in the year 102/721, thus presenting him as involved in local politics. In this story he does not have an occasion to show off his oratorical talents, which may be why al-Balādhurī, if he knew the story, did not include it in his work.

In A14, from al-Balādhurī's *Ansāb*, Khālid is depicted as running away to avoid giving the *bayʿa*, ritual hand clasp equal to a pledge of allegiance, which implies that he was important enough for the new governor to insist on receiving it. When it comes to Khālid's military role, we have a single anecdote, B110, from al-Balādhurī's *Ansāb*, staging him as a *ghāzī*. This is mentioned only to give the background for Khālid's witticism, so that we learn nothing more about his possible military role, but from other sources we know that several of his relatives took part in military operations.[50] A35, however, depicts him as disliking the sword.

Khālid's political relevance is never the reason for telling a story in an *adab* source, but may sometimes almost accidentally become visible. Thus, while explaining a proverb Abū Hilāl al-ʿAskarī presents Khālid as political advisor to the governor of Basra, Sufyān ibn Muʿāwiya al-Muhallabī (A18), and in A27 the exchange of words between Khālid and a Bedouin is the reason for telling

---

120, calls al-Balādhurī's *Ansāb* "le chant du cygne des *ašrāf*." For al-Balādhurī's relation to *adab*, see Hasson (1999).

50 Cf. Chapter 1.4.

a story which briefly mentions that Khālid was giving a public speech concerning a peace agreement. One searches in vain for a mention of Khālid in al-Ṭabarī's *Taʾrīkh*, where the same incident is told from another viewpoint and without any reference to Khālid.[51]

A story involving Khālid in politics probably gained admission to later sources only if Khālid exhibited his oratorical talents in it and even then the political setting was dispensable or could be briefly given as background or could even be substituted by another background story that the author thought better fitted Khālid's saying.

This may clearly be seen by studying the various versions of three closely interrelated stories, B7, B108, and B9b. Through this, we may also understand the kinds of changes that were made in Khālid stories and that resulted in a probably distorted image of him as an entertaining eccentric rather than a tribal nobleman of at least some political weight. The stories are among the most frequently quoted Khālid stories. They describe him in connection with Bilāl ibn abī Burda, the judge and chief of police (*shurṭa*) of Basra.[52] The story is often told in contexts focusing on Bilāl, not Khālid.

Al-Balādhurī supplies us with three versions of what is basically one story, all on the authority of al-Madāʾinī.[53] The first reads:

> He (al-Madāʾinī) said: Bilāl ibn abī Burda had ordered Khālid to be whipped and imprisoned because he had heard that when he had taken office Khālid had said:
>
> A summer cloud that will soon disperse.
>
> Bilāl had said: "By God, it will not disperse ere it hits him with a downpour!"

The implicit context, or the informing drive, of the story is provided by the two previous anecdotes, B5 and B6, which speak about slandering and getting unnecessarily mixed up with things.[54] Obviously, the anecdote is to be seen in this light: Khālid slandered Bilāl and got mixed up with things he did not need to be concerned with, to his own disadvantage. The story itself is stripped of all background and distilled to mere witticisms. Why Khālid should have said what he did is not explained, nor does the reader miss this information.

51 Al-Ṭabarī, *Taʾrīkh* III/1: 21–23/XXVII: 143–145.

52 See Crone (1980): 147 (no. 85), with further references, as well as al-Ṣafadī, *Wāfī* X: 278–279.

53 B7, B108, B9b.

54 The organisation of the material may be deliberate, but it may also be subconscious. Yet for the reader the context seems clear enough. Khālid was also famous (cf. Ibn Khallikān, *Wafayāt* III: 12) for his blunders, *hafawāt*, some of the anecdotes about him finding their way into al-Ṣābiʾ, *Hafawāt*.

The historical context is simply irrelevant. Such a mechanism must have been at work often enough, stripping Khālid of his importance and leaving him as an Umayyad wit of no political significance.

The second story in al-Balādhurī, B108, gives a more elaborate version of the incident. According to this account an anonymous man had taken Khālid to court, and Bilāl judged in favour of the man. This incited Khālid to quote the hemistich, making it a personal response to what Khālid would have felt to be an injustice he had suffered. The third version, B9b, implies that the hemistich was quoted by Khālid as a spontaneous comment when Bilāl took office (*lammā waliya Bilāl qāla Khālid* …). Here again, the reason for what triggered the saying is left unexplained.

Other versions further elaborate the story. Wakīʿ has an impressive *isnād* for his version of B9b, partly through Khālid's Minqarī clan, and he dates the event to the beginning of Bilāl's office in Basra.[55] Even more unambiguously the date is given by al-Tawḥīdī.[56] In both, Khālid's comment is completely unmotivated.

A radically different version is told by al-Mubarrad (B7b). According to him, Khālid used to come to Bilāl to tell him stories, but he often made grammatical mistakes (*yalḥan*). Bilāl reprimanded him for this in plain words. Later, Khālid studied grammar (*iʿrāb*). When he was old and blind and heard someone riding by he used to ask who it was, and if it was Bilāl, he quoted the hemistich.[57] Thus, we may see that the background for the saying is freely invented by different authors according to their taste.

Al-Jāḥiẓ further complicates the situation.[58] He tells the same story about Ibn Shubruma and Ṭāriq, the chief of police (*ṣāḥib shuraṭ*) of Khālid ibn ʿAbdallāh al-Qasrī. Such reattributed stories, or wandering stories to borrow a useful term from *rubāʿī* studies, are by no means rare and in many cases it is impossible to say which version is the oldest, let alone the original.[59]

The versions are contradictory, and this contradiction seems already to be present in the earliest source, al-Madāʾinī, two of whose versions date the incident to the time when Bilāl took office and the third contextualises it as the result of a lawsuit tried by Bilāl. In each, the "summer cloud" episode is

55 Wakīʿ, *Akhbār*, pp. 247–248: *lammā waliya Bilāl ibn abī Burda al-Baṣra balagha dhālika Khālid ibn Ṣafwān fa-qāla.*

56 Al-Tawḥīdī, *Baṣāʾir* I: 99, no. 280: *qadima Bilāl ibn abī Burda al-Baṣra amīran fa-qāla Khālid ibn Ṣafwān.*

57 Al-Jāḥiẓ, *Bayān* III: 146. In addition, one might mention B9, where a different saying by Khālid is given as the cause of their falling out. In this version, Bilāl lets tribal noblemen wait too long for an audience and they murmur, Khālid among them.

58 See commentary to B7.

59 See Chapter 2.5.3.

transmitted not because it would shed light on Khālid's role in Basran politics but because of the witticisms it contains. The actual cause of the incident is irrelevant for the entertainment value of the story and its cause has, accordingly, either been left out or freely invented in the various versions. The background stories are not there to offer historical information concerning the event but to set the scene for the witticisms. The invariable core of the anecdote is the hemistich quoted by Khālid, the reply by Bilāl, and the antagonism between the two. All else is irrelevant, freely inventible, and, hence, devoid of historical value.

The antagonism between the two is condensed into a single comic incident.[60] The reason for the conflict is Khālid's personal grudge against Bilāl (losing a lawsuit or having been rudely reprimanded for his grammatical mistakes) or his unsolicited use of wit on an ill-chosen occasion. No political reasons are hinted at in any of these anecdotes. Yet Bilāl was appointed by the Yemeni Khālid al-Qasrī, whose whole period of governorship is characterised by appointments of Yemeni subgovernors.[61] The tribe of Tamīm is also shown in conflict with Bilāl in other sources,[62] and Khālid, as a Tamīmī nobleman, may for this reason have had tense relations with the pro-Yemeni *qāḍī*. Such tribal tensions may well have been behind the antagonism between Bilāl and Khālid, not merely a haphazard witticism that might have enraged Bilāl.

The corpus of Khālid stories highlights the importance of a detailed analysis before anecdotal material can be used for historical studies. Stories have been attributed to Khālid which in the earliest sources were told about his ancestors or other persons; others have been freely invented, sometimes turning the situation upside down; and still others have been divested of their historical content. In each case, the later source, as it stands, is of little value before we have put the version it offers into its rightful place in the literary historical tradition. The writing of Umayyad history begins with a deconstruction of ʿAbbāsid literary sources. The Khālid material provides a useful case study, which may elucidate more general tendencies in historical and *adab* sources of the early ʿAbbāsid period.

60 In some other anecdotes, the tense relations between the two also surface, but the reason for this tenseness is either not given or the quotation of the hemistich is seen to have been the origin of the antagonism.

61 Cf. Crone (1980): 146–149, and Leder (1990).

62 In, e.g., Ibn Nubāta, *Sarḥ*, pp. 391–392, there is an anecdote about al-Farazdaq, where Bilāl, being the Emir of Basra, takes sides in a boast by the Yemenis against the Tamīm.

1.3.2 *The Historical Khālid*

To have some idea of the historical Khālid, let us start by having a look at the meagre information from biographical dictionaries and similar texts. Al-Balādhurī is remarkably well informed about Khālid, so he presents a natural starting point for our study.

Al-Balādhurī gives Khālid's genealogy up to the ancestor of the subtribe, Minqar (B1), mentions his eloquence and his talent in oratory (B3) and that he was an excellent storyteller (*min … aḥdathihim*, B3), this last point obviously referring to the narration of historical *akhbār*,[63] rather than Prophetic *ḥadīths* or popular stories for entertainment. He does mention that Khālid was both powerful and wealthy (B3), but it is only his father Ṣafwān, whom al-Balādhurī labels as the tribal leader of Banū Tamīm (B4), not Khālid himself.

Bibliographical dictionaries and articles dedicated to Khālid tend to pick up a few famous names to which they link Khālid. Thus, Ibn ʿAsākir specifically mentions his relations to the Caliphs ʿUmar ibn ʿAbd al-ʿAzīz (r. 99–101/717–720) and Hishām ibn ʿAbd al-Malik (r. 105–125/724–743).[64] Yāqūt mentions Hishām and Khālid al-Qasrī (d. 126/743), governor of Iraq, but not ʿUmar ibn ʿAbd al-ʿAzīz.[65] Al-Ṣafadī calls Khālid one of the most eloquent Arabs and even dubs him *faṣīḥ al-ʿArab* which, though, does not seem to have been in common use and may well be al-Ṣafadī's own invention.[66] He also mentions that he took part in embassies to ʿUmar ibn ʿAbd al-ʿAzīz and Hishām. Khālid's close ties with the latter Caliph are well known, but he seems to owe his reputation of having admonished the former to a confusion between him and his ancestor ʿAbdallāh ibn al-Ahtam (see below). Unfortunately, al-Ṣafadī selects A9 as one of the few anecdotes which he narrates, thus cementing – possibly wrongly and somewhat anachronistically – Khālid as a companion of ʿUmar ibn ʿAbd al-ʿAzīz.

To evaluate the potential authenticity of Khālid's contacts with these and other Umayyad and early ʿAbbāsid characters, we have to go through the whole corpus with some care.

The following chronology shows the main datable events in the Khālid stories. Italicised items are of dubious historicity, while the remaining ones have some claim of reflecting historical events, at least in the sense that Khālid may have met these people, even though the exact reports of the meetings may be

63 See Chapter 3.2.2.
64 Ibn ʿAsākir, *Taʾrīkh* XVI: 94.
65 Yāqūt, *Irshād* III: 274.
66 Al-Ṣafadī, *Wāfī* XIII: 255.

fictitious.[67] Three key dates have been marked in boldface: 110, which is the date of the death of al-Ḥasan al-Baṣrī and also the date Bilāl ibn abī Burda became the *qāḍī* of Basra; 120, when the latter resigned from the position of *qāḍī*; and 135 when Khālid died, according to Yāqūt.

72 addresses Umayya ibn ʿAbdallāh
83–95 meets al-Ḥajjāj
99–101 meets ʿUmar ibn ʿAbd al-ʿAzīz
?? father Ṣafwān dies
?? goes on pilgrimage, son dies
102 meets Yazīd ibn al-Muhallab
102 lawsuit against the family of al-Qāsim
105–125 meets Hishām ibn ʿAbd al-Malik several times
110 al-Ḥasan dies, Bilāl's *qāḍīship* begins
between 110–120 meets Bilāl several times
120 end of Bilāl's *qāḍīship*
120 visits Yūsuf ibn ʿUmar
before 121 meets Maslama several times
129–132 meets Yazīd ibn ʿUmar
after 131 meets al-Saffāḥ several times
132 meets Sufyān
ca. 132 meets Abū l-Jahm
after 132? meets Rawḥ
after 133? meets Sulaymān ibn ʿAlī
135 Khālid dies (according to Yāqūt)
meets al-Mahdī (r. 158–169)

Khālid is reported to have died at an advanced age,[68] and Yāqūt places his death in 135/752.[69] If we take his advanced age to mean that he was some 70 or 80 (lunar) years old when he died, then his birth should date to around 55/675 or 65/685. B14, discussed below, would suggest a birth date around 70/689.

The dated and datable events will now be studied in some detail. The earliest datable event comes in B41, where Khālid addresses Umayya ibn ʿAbdallāh ibn Khālid al-Asīd after the latter had fled from Abū Fudayk and come to Basra. The battle of Bahrain was won by Abū Fudayk against Umayya in 72/691 and

---

67 Likewise, while some of the meetings with, e.g., al-Saffāḥ may well be historical, others can be proven to be fictitious.

68 Ibn Qutayba, *Maʿārif*, p. 404.

69 Yāqūt, *Irshād* III: 280.

Abū Fudayk died the next year. The story seems surprisingly early, as Khālid is better documented as an orator only several decades later. Abū Hilāl al-ʿAskarī offers the key to the problem.[70] In a story ultimately coming from Abū ʿUbayda, al-ʿAskarī narrates the same story about Ṣafwān ibn ʿAbdallāh ibn al-Ahtam, further defining him as "the father of Khālid ibn Ṣafwān." Ibn Qutayba goes a step further and features ʿAbdallāh ibn al-Ahtam in the same role.[71] As Khālid later became by far the most famous member of the family, this can be seen as a case of upgrading the characters:[72] instead of the somewhat obscure Ṣafwān ibn ʿAbdallāh ibn al-Ahtam or his father, Khālid has been selected in most versions as the famous Ahtamite to address Umayya ibn ʿAbdallāh. Thus, it would seem improbable that the older versions of the story featured Khālid.

It is worth pointing out that the upgrading seems already to have taken place in the work of al-Madāʾinī, as the parallel tradition shows,[73] less than a century after the death of Khālid and, moreover, codified in the work of a usually reliable historian.

A number of stories bring Khālid and the famous al-Ḥajjāj (d. 95/714) together, but all of these turn out to be dubious. A61a is merely a variant of A61, with an anonymous interlocutor, and perhaps also of B44, B44a, B44b, and B44c, all of which have much later, or anonymous, interlocutors. B52 is a variant of the much better documented B82, which features al-Saffāḥ instead of al-Ḥajjāj. B106 lets Khālid comment on al-Ḥajjāj, not claiming the two had met, and A15 may also be interpreted as Khālid commenting on something that had happened in the past.

In B81a (cf. also B81b) Khālid is depicted in the company of ʿAbd al-Malik (r. 65–86/685–705) and al-Ḥajjāj after the latter had won Dayr al-Jamājim (83/702).[74] Variants, though, mention Hishām ibn ʿAbd al-Malik and Maslama instead. In B81, al-Aḥnaf ibn Qays and Abū Bakr al-Hudhalī are also present, which, again, is anachronistic as al-Aḥnaf was already dead by 83/702.[75] Al-Zubayr ibn Bakkār relates a speech by al-Ḥajjāj after Dayr al-Jamājim, with

70 Abū Hilāl al-ʿAskarī, *Dīwān*, pp. 1047–1048.

71 Ibn Qutayba, *ʿUyūn* I: 295.

72 Cf. Chapter 2.5.3.

73 See al-Washshāʾ, *Fāḍil*, pp. 92–93, discussed under B41.

74 Also the Kufan Muḥammad ibn ʿUmayr ibn ʿUṭārid (for whom, see Crone 1980: 122) is mentioned in this story.

75 For al-Aḥnaf, see *EI2*, s.v. (Charles Pellat). Al-Aḥnaf was a Tamīmī, who in 67/686 evicted al-Mukhtār from Basra and died soon after at an advanced age. ʿAbdallāh ibn abī Sulaymān Abū Bakr al-Hudhalī was an early *qāṣṣ* (for *quṣṣāṣ*, see Armstrong 2017), but this may also anachronistically refer to Sulmā ibn ʿAbdallāh Abū Bakr al-Hudhalī (d. 159/775), on whom see *EI2*, "al-Madāʾinī" (U. Sezgin). He is also mentioned in A1. Van Ess (1991–97) II: 291, further mentions a grammarian by the same name.

Khālid in the audience and has Khālid later narrate it to Muḥammad ibn Sallām.[76] As Khālid has no role in this story, he could well have been present as a young man, but it is less probable that he could have had any major role at the time. It is also quite possible that Khālid may have transmitted the story without having been in the audience when the speech was delivered and that later sources have modified the story, making Khālid a first-hand witness for something he only transmitted.

Thus, the documentation of meetings between Khālid and al-Ḥajjāj is rather poor, and it would seem safer not to assume Khālid to have been in any direct contact with al-Ḥajjāj.

As noted above, Ibn ʿAsākir specifically mentions Khālid's relation to ʿUmar ibn ʿAbd al-ʿAzīz (r. 99–101/717–720), but the stories give little evidence for this.[77] In only three, A9, A10, and A11, Khālid is represented as being in the company of ʿUmar ibn ʿAbd al-ʿAzīz, and al-Balādhurī, who obviously had al-Madāʾinī's monograph on Khālid at hand, does not mention the earlier Caliph at all.

Khālid, possibly over thirty at the time, could well have visited the Caliph as his family belonged to the tribal aristocracy. However, other, and older, members of the Ahtamite family are more commonly represented as having met ʿUmar ibn ʿAbd al-ʿAzīz. The confusion between Khālid and his great-grand-uncle is best seen in a long admonition to ʿUmar ibn ʿAbd al-ʿAzīz by ʿAbdallāh ibn ʿAbdallāh ibn al-Ahtam, which al-Jāḥiẓ transmits on the authority of Khālid ibn Ṣafwān,[78] but Ibn ʿAbd al-Ḥakam attributes the admonition to Khālid himself.[79] Ibn al-Jawzī attributes it merely to Ibn al-Ahtam, thus using the general name of the family.[80] Immediately after this, Ibn al-Jawzī refers to a long sermon (*mawʿiẓa*) by ʿAbdallāh ibn al-Ahtam to ʿUmar ibn ʿAbd al-ʿAzīz,[81] narrating only ʿUmar's reaction to it, not the sermon itself, which may well have been a variant of the sermon variously attributed to Khālid and other members of the family. Ibn ʿAsākir transmits the same story attributed

76 Al-Zubayr ibn Bakkār, *Muwaffaqiyyāt*, pp. 96–97 (no. 39).

77 Ibn ʿAsākir, *Taʾrīkh* XVI: 94. Van Ess (1991–97) II: 243, accepts as historical stories connecting Khālid with ʿUmar ibn ʿAbd al-ʿAzīz.

78 Al-Jāḥiẓ, *Bayān* II: 117–120 < Abū l-Ḥasan [al-Madāʾinī] < Yaḥyā ibn Saʿīd < Ibn Kharrabūdh al-Bakrī < Khālid ibn Ṣafwān. For Yaḥyā ibn Saʿīd (d. 144/761), see *Bayān* II: 262, note 5. As Yaḥyā was a teacher of Shuʿba, himself one of al-Madāʾinī's teachers (see Lindstedt 2013 I: 3 = 2012–14: 237), the identification of Abū l-Ḥasan as al-Madāʾinī seems confirmed. For Maʿrūf ibn Kharrabūdh, see *Bayān* II: 117, note 9.

79 Ibn ʿAbd al-Ḥakam, *Khalīfa*, pp. 111–114.

80 Ibn al-Jawzī, *Sīra*, pp. 136–137 < Muḥammad ibn Yazīd ibn Ḥandīs < Sufyān ibn ʿUyayna.

81 Ibn al-Jawzī, *Sīra*, pp. 137–138 < Dāʾūd ibn Muḥabbar < al-Mubārak ibn Fuḍāla.

to ʿAbdallāh ibn al-Ahtam with an *isnād* ending in Khālid ibn Maʿdān,[82] thus making it less obvious that Khālid ibn Ṣafwān has any role at all in this story, even as a transmitter.

Whoever the final transmitter of the story is and whether the protagonist is ʿAbdallāh ibn al-Ahtam or ʿAbdallāh ibn ʿAbdallāh ibn al-Ahtam, it seems much more probable that ʿUmar ibn ʿAbd al-ʿAzīz would have been admonished by an older Ahtamite than by the still relatively young Khālid. Likewise, it seems improbable that a later transmitter would have replaced Khālid by ʿAbdallāh ibn al-Ahtam, rather than the other way round, as Khālid soon became the most famous member of the family. It is even possible that *all* stories connecting Khālid with ʿUmar should be seen in this light. In some cases expressions such as Ibn al-Ahtam, later interpreted as a reference to Khālid, may have caused the confusion.

A further potential cause of confusion is that according to al-Jāḥiẓ Khālid was among the orators who gave speeches in front of ʿAbdallāh ibn ʿUmar ibn ʿAbd al-ʿAzīz, the governor of Iraq.[83] The other orators mentioned are Wāṣil ibn ʿAṭāʾ, Shabīb ibn Shayba, and al-Faḍl ibn ʿĪsā al-Raqāshī.[84] Van Ess, who discusses this passage, dates this between 126/744 when ʿAbdallāh was appointed governor and 129/746–7 until which time he held the office, presumably at the beginning of his governorship when the representatives of Basra came to greet him in Wāsiṭ.[85] The famous father ʿUmar ibn ʿAbd al-ʿAzīz may have found his way into A9, A10, and A11, instead of the less famous son ʿAbdallāh, if the three stories are historical in the first place.

Thus, it would seem that all events featuring Khālid during or before the Caliphate of ʿUmar ibn ʿAbd al-ʿAzīz (r. 99–101/717–720) have to be considered dubious. Coming to the third decade of the eighth century, things start to change, though.

---

82 Ibn ʿAsākir, *Taʾrīkh* XXVII: 107–109 < Yaḥyā ibn Saʿīd al-Umawī < Maʿrūf ibn Kharrabūdh al-Bakrī < Khālid ibn Maʿdān. For Khālid ibn Maʿdān (d. 104/722), see Borrut (2010): 42–43.

83 Al-Jāḥiẓ, *Bayān* I: 24. See also Pellat (1953): 280.

84 On the last-mentioned, see van Ess (1991–97) II: 167–174. Hesitantly, van Ess sets his death before 140/757.

85 Van Ess (1991–97) II: 241–244. In II: 244, van Ess draws attention to the fact that it is not explicitly said that "the both Khālids" attended and wonders how both Khālid and Shabīb, close relatives, could have attended the same event. Van Ess also mentions that the version of al-Balādhurī does not mention Wāṣil's speech defect with R. One does remain rather hesitant as it comes to Wāṣil's famous speech without R, which does sound rather too manneristic for Wāṣil's time, but I do not find Khālid's and Shabīb's simultaneous presence too problematic as such.

Even though al-Ḥasan al-Baṣrī (d. 110/728)[86] is somewhat earlier than the best documented acquaintances of Khālid, he is rather solidly presented as having known Khālid. The earliest credible date for a Khālid story comes in A19, which tells us how the family of al-Qāsim ibn Sulaymān, or Salīm, and Khālid ibn Ṣafwān quarrelled, adding that they accepted al-Ḥasan (al-Baṣrī) as arbitrator. Then, in 102/721, Mūsā ibn Anas wrote to ʿUmar ibn Yazīd ibn ʿUmayr, who was the chief of police (see B6). Mūsā was the *qāḍī* of Basra ca. 103–105/722–724.[87]

This might imply that Khālid was already the head of the family, his father having died. The story dates this to 102/721, providing us with the first relatively certain date for Khālid. Here, as he is also in B2, al-Ḥasan is introduced as a senior character looking at the affairs of a relatively young Khālid, and in B4, which actually does not introduce Khālid himself at all, al-Ḥasan has the role of witnessing the testament of Khālid's father.

These are the only three stories that directly link Khālid to al-Ḥasan. In a number of other stories,[88] Khālid narrates his reminiscences of al-Ḥasan, clearly implying this to take place much later, but also explicitly suggesting Khālid to have known al-Ḥasan. Khālid's relation to ʿAmr ibn ʿUbayd (d. 144/761), one of al-Ḥasan's students, belongs to a later period.[89]

If we further combine B22, in which Khālid goes on pilgrimage, and B22a, in which al-Ḥasan al-Baṣrī comments on Khālid's words on his son, then technically this would date Khālid's pilgrimage to before al-Ḥasan's death (110/728). However, the evidence here is anecdotal, so no firm conclusions can be drawn.

Khālid is also mentioned in connection with Yazīd ibn al-Muhallab, governor of Basra in 96–99/715–718 and 101–102/720–721. Yazīd ibn al-Muhallab rose in revolt against Yazīd II (r. 101–105/720–724) and was killed in 102/721. In A13 Khālid escapes from Basra and meets him in Wāsiṭ,[90] and in A14 Yazīd summons al-Faḍl ibn ʿAbd al-Raḥmān ibn al-ʿAbbās ibn Rabīʿa ibn al-Ḥārith ibn

86 See *EI3*, s.v. (N.D. Mourad).

87 Pellat (1953): 289 – Pellat hesitates on the start date of Mūsā's office, and this anecdote implies that he was the *qāḍī* already in 102/721.

88 B109, A34, A62.

89 See A101, A106. For ʿAmr ibn ʿUbayd, see *EI2*, s.v. (W.M. Watt), *EI3* (N.D. Mourad), and van Ess (1991–97) II: 280–310. Khālid is also, rather surprisingly, mentioned as a contemporary of ʿAmr in Ibn al-Murtaḍā, *Bāb*, p. 25. This source also proves that the ʿAmr ibn ʿUbayd Khālid knew was the famous theologian, who was a *mawlā* of the Tamīm. B83, however, seems to refer to another ʿAmr ibn ʿUbayd, see Commentary to B83.

90 Khālid also transmits a speech given by Yazīd ibn al-Muhallab in Wāsiṭ, see al-Jāḥiẓ, *Bayān* I: 292–293.

ʿAbd al-Muṭṭalib ibn Hāshim,[91] who paid homage to him, while ʿAbd al-Wāḥid from among the sons of ʿĀmir ibn Kurayz and Khālid ran away. A44 is anecdotal and could easily be misattributed. A45 depicts Khālid in easy relations with Yazīd ibn al-Muhallab. Even though the evidence is far from overwhelming, it seems reasonable to assume that the two did, indeed, meet each other. In B44a, Khālid is depicted as meeting Maslama ibn ʿAbd al-Malik after the defeat of Yazīd ibn al-Muhallab in 102/721.

By 110–120/728–738, Khālid is quite securely attested. His meetings with Bilāl ibn abī Burda are too many and too detailed for it to be suspected that the two would not also have met in reality, especially as Bilāl is not a towering figure in later literature. Bilāl ibn abī Burda was the *qāḍī* and the chief of police (*shurṭa*) in Basra, but much less famous than his father Abū Burda al-Ashʿarī (d. 103/721 or the following year), the *qāḍī* of Kufa.[92] Bilāl was appointed by Khālid al-Qasrī and stayed in office for ten years, 110–120/728–738.[93]

Several stories connect Khālid with another influential character, Khālid ibn ʿAbdallāh al-Qasrī. Khālid seems to have been on good terms with his namesake, and, e.g., Yāqūt mentions that he used to accompany him (A4). Khālid al-Qasrī was appointed to various positions in Iraq from 105/723 or 106/724 onward and he remained there until he fell from favour in 120/738 and was imprisoned until his execution in 126/743 by Yūsuf ibn ʿUmar.[94] The stories connect Khālid ibn Ṣafwān with him both when he was in power and when imprisoned.

Khālid's close relation to Hishām ibn ʿAbd al-Malik (r. 105–125/724–743) may be exaggerated, even though it seems to be borne out by several stories connecting the two. Here, however, one must tread with some care, as it turns out that in only two cases (B38 and A4) is the connection between the two devoid of textual problems. B44c, B45a, and B81a would seem to make this connection, too, but in all cases the more reliable source, al-Balādhurī, lacks this direct connection, having Maslama, not Hishām, ibn ʿAbd al-Malik as Khālid's interlocutor in B44 and B45, and leaving the interlocutor anonymous in B81. Furthermore, al-Balādhurī does make the two speak together in B69, but the saying in B69 is not attributed to Khālid in other sources, and elsewhere it is attributed to ʿAbdallāh ibn al-Ahtam admonishing ʿUmar ibn ʿAbd al-ʿAzīz. Thus, there is some evidence for a closer relationship between Khālid and Hishām,

91 For ʿAbd al-Raḥmān Ibn ʿAyyāsh [sic] ibn Rabīʿa ibn al-Ḥārith ibn ʿAbd al-Muṭṭalib, see al-Zubayrī, *Nasab*, p. 88.

92 *EI3*, s.v. Abū Burda (N. Tsafrir – J. Schacht).

93 Al-Ṣafadī, *Wāfī* x: 279.

94 *EI2*, s.v. (G. Hawting); Leder (1990).

but the evidence is far too meagre to allow us to see Khālid as a close companion of Hishām, even though the two most probably did meet.

Khālid is often associated with the first ʿAbbāsid Caliph, Abū l-ʿAbbās al-Saffāḥ. Al-Jāḥiẓ begins his "article" on Khālid by associating him with al-Saffāḥ and even counting him among the Caliph's nightly companions (*summār*) and those of whom he had a high opinion (*ahl al-manzila ʿindahu*).[95] Likewise, Ibn Qutayba summarises Khālid's life in this way: "His (Ṣafwān's) son, Khālid, lived long (*ʿummira*) until he conversed with (*ḥādatha*) Abū l-ʿAbbās. Khālid was an eloquent and clear orator, but avaricious and prone to divorce."[96]

Al-Masʿūdī mentions Khālid as one of al-Saffāḥ's nightly companions and mainly associates him with tribal debates (*mufākhara*) between Southern and Northern Arabs. Unfortunately, al-Masʿūdī reserved most of this material for his now lost books *Akhbār al-zamān* and *Awsaṭ* and, hence, did not deem it necessary to duplicate all this in the *Murūj*.[97]

Whereas Khālid's relations with the Umayyad Caliphs have turned out to be based on a much more meagre evidence than usually thought, his relation to the first ʿAbbāsid Caliph is stronger. Al-Balādhurī has eight items connecting the two,[98] but even here it is appropriate to note that most of these items are, in fact, repetitions of what may well have been one single narrative of tribal *mufākhara* that has become fragmented and transformed into slightly different versions. Furthermore, B24 resembles B25, which has Ḥafṣ ibn Muʿāwiya al-Ghalābī as Khālid's interlocutor, instead of Abū l-ʿAbbās, which makes it probable that B24 is only an upgraded version of B25. In addition, we only have two more anecdotes, which connect Khālid and Abū l-ʿAbbās, namely A1, which derives from elsewhere in al-Balādhurī's *Ansāb*, and A24, which was, and perhaps is, a deservedly famous story and is repeated in a large number of sources, but which can definitely be shown to have been composed of several unrelated anecdotes none of which originally featured the Caliph.[99]

Thus, there is some evidence for the relations between Khālid and Abū l-ʿAbbās, but not enough to claim any kind of special intimacy between them. It goes without saying, though, that lack of evidence is not, as such, evidence for a lack of intimacy between them.

---

95 Al-Jāḥiẓ, *Bayān* I: 339.

96 Ibn Qutayba, *Maʿārif*, p. 404.

97 Al-Masʿūdī, *Murūj* §2350. On the other hand, in comparing his two extant works, the *Murūj* and the *Tanbīh*, it is evident that al-Masʿūdī often claims more than can be substantiated, so we should not exaggerate the amount of material on Khālid and Abū l-ʿAbbās he may have had at hand.

98 B24, B37, B53, B67, B82, B86, B101, B102.

99 See Chapter 2.5.1.

Few of the Khālid stories are datable with any exactness, but most of the characters that are mentioned in connection with him date to the early to mid-eighth century. As famous characters are often connected with each other without any historical legitimation, it is the lesser characters that are crucial in setting Khālid in a time, place, and social position, rather than the Caliphs, whose connections with Khālid are in many cases of dubious historicity, resulting from the tradition's habit of letting roughly contemporaneous famous characters meet and interact with each other.

In B45a, Khālid speaks with al-ʿAbbās ibn al-Walīd ibn ʿAbd al-Malik in al-Ruṣāfa during Hishām's Caliphate. Al-Ṭabarī mentions al-ʿAbbās' presence in al-Ruṣāfa only after the death of Hishām in 125/742–3,[100] but it is quite conceivable that he visited the town, Hishām's virtual capital, also during the latter's Caliphate. In one variant version, though, Khālid's interlocutor is Muʿāwiya ibn Hishām, not al-ʿAbbās ibn al-Walīd.

In A20, Khālid is shown in the company of (Saʿīd ibn al-Walīd) al-Abrash al-Kalbī, who seems to have had a great influence over the Caliph Hishām, especially towards the end of his rule.[101]

Two stories, A103 and A104, describe Khālid meeting al-Aʿmash (d. 147 or 148/764–765), a famous Kufan traditionist,[102] and A104 explicitly locates the meeting in Kufa, when Khālid was travelling through it.

Khālid is only rarely represented in the company of poets, and no poetry has been attributed to him.[103] There seems to be an indubitable connection between al-Farazdaq (d. in Basra ca. 112/730) and both Khālid, whom al-Farazdaq satirises in a short poem (A46), and his brother, Nuʿaym, who also receives mention in the poet's *Dīwān* (see B2).[104]

The two other great Umayyad poets, al-Akhṭal (d. ca. 92/710) and Jarīr (d. ca. 113/731) are mentioned only once, in a story where Khālid compares the merits of the three poets in their and Hishām ibn ʿAbd al-Malik's presence before Hishām became Caliph (A4). Such stories of comparing the merits of poets, sometimes in their presence, are very common and they deserve little credence. It would not have been impossible for young Khālid to have met

100 Al-Ṭabarī, *Taʾrīkh* II: 1751–1752/XXVI: 100–101.

101 See Hillenbrand (1989) (Index, s.v. al-Abrash).

102 *EI3*, s.v. (G.H.A. Juynboll).

103 For the confusion between him and Khālid al-Qannāṣ, see Chapter 2.4.

104 In addition, al-Farazdaq satirises the Ahtamites and, more specifically, an ʿAbdallāh among them, identified by the prose explanation as "ʿAbdallāh ibn Ṣafwān, the brother of Khālid ibn Ṣafwān." This, however, would be the only reference to such a brother of Khālid's, and the identity of this Ahtamite ʿAbdallāh remains uncertain. Further, al-Farazdaq satirises Banū Minqar in yet another poem of his (*Dīwān*, ed. al-Ṣāwī, pp. 571–573).

al-Akhṭal, but it somewhat strains credibility to assume that he had a position of *arbiter elegantiae* as early as 92/710 or, indeed, earlier, especially as this is a role that is not commonly attributed to him in the first place. Also the fact that these are *the* three Umayyad poets makes this sound very much a literary fiction, not to mention the lack of any signs of Khālid having being a poet, a transmitter of poetry, or in any other way working with poetry.[105] A variant version[106] drops the beginning and the end of the story, thus getting rid of the anachronistic encounter with the poets themselves and changing this to a later piece of literary criticism. This variant adds a further, more concise discussion of the "ten poets." Even though not anachronistic, this version does not command much more credibility than A4.

An encounter with Abū Nukhayla (d. 147/764)[107] is mentioned in only one anecdote (B83b, B83c), but as he was a relatively obscure *rajaz* poet and was known to have visited the Caliph al-Saffāḥ, it might be more credible: the more famous the person is the more commonly he is later credited with meeting other celebrities of the time. There remains one *caveat*, though. Abū Nukhayla is reported to have been a friend of Shabīb ibn Shayba,[108] so Khālid's presence could well be due to an upgrading of the less well-known Shabīb.

An even more obscure person is Durust ibn Ribāṭ al-Fuqaymī, with whom Khālid features in B16 and B70. A very minor poet,[109] whose year of death seems to be unknown, is elsewhere represented in a few stories together with the same characters with whom Khālid often interacted. Thus, e.g., al-Jāḥiẓ, narrating on the authority of al-Aṣmaʿī, describes him as visiting Bilāl ibn abī Burda, when the latter was imprisoned, and elsewhere in the *Bayān*, quotes invective verses on him by al-Farazdaq.[110]

In B14, Khālid comes into contact with Rawḥ ibn Ḥātim, who is depicted in the story (especially clearly in B14a) as a young man meeting an older, venerable gentleman. As our earliest references to Rawḥ in historical literature seem to date from 132/749,[111] the story may have to be situated close to this year. In this story, Rawḥ refers to Khālid being over sixty. There is no reason to assume that this is strictly accurate, but if we assume it to be so and further assume that "over sixty" means 60–65 and that the meeting took place around 132, then Khālid's year of birth would be around 67–72. Even though there are

105 Cf. Chapter 2.4.
106 See A4, commentary.
107 See *GAS* II: 465.
108 See Commentary to B83.
109 See al-Fīrūzābādī, *Qāmūs* II: 170, s.v. DRST, who mentions him briefly.
110 Al-Jāḥiẓ, *Bayān* II: 166 (> al-Ābī, *Nathr* II: 192), *Bayān* II: 284.
111 See commentary to B14.

numerous ifs in this, a birth date around 70/689 would fit most of the datable stories that we have reason to consider potentially authentic.

In A12, the recently appointed governor of Basra, Sufyān ibn Muʿāwiya sends for Khālid. Sufyān was appointed in 132/750, and the meeting should be dated to this year.

In a number of stories Khālid is represented in the company of Sulaymān ibn ʿAlī.[112] In al-Mubarrad's version of B102, one of these occasions is explicitly dated to the time when Sulaymān was the governor of Basra (133–139/751–756),[113] which would be the latest datable event in Khālid's life, some obvious anachronisms apart.

As far as I can see, only Yāqūt gives the exact date of Khālid's death, namely 135/752.[114] Al-Dhahabī explicitly mentions that he has not been able to find his date of death.[115] Although Yāqūt is often unreliable with dates, Khālid must have died around this time, as there are no reliable stories involving any datable events or persons after this time.

All in all, rather few Khālid stories are blatantly anachronistic. This, unfortunately, does not vouchsafe their historicity, as the transmitters of these stories and the authors who took them into their compilations were generally well acquainted with the history of the period and could easily set Khālid in a context which rings true, whether or not the story is historical.

In one late story, A94, transmitted by ʿAwfī (d. after 630/1232),[116] Khālid is connected with the Caliph al-Mahdī (r. 158–169/775–785). The blatant anachronism is most probably due to Khālid being a much less prominent character in Persian literature of the late 12th, early 13th century, so that the compiler and his source did not see the anachronism in setting Khālid at the time of al-Mahdī.[117] His cousin Shabīb ibn Shayba, though, is sometimes connected with this Caliph,[118] so it is possible that he and Khālid have been confused with each other in this story.

Thus, we see Khālid well acquainted with the higher echelons of Basran society towards the mid-eighth century. His intimate connections with Caliphs

112 B11a, B11b, B13, B102, B115, A17.

113 Pellat (1953): 280.

114 Yāqūt, *Irshād* III: 280.

115 Al-Dhahabī, *Siyar* VI: 226.

116 ʿAwfī, *Jawāmiʿ* I/2: 76–77 (no. 62). For ʿAwfī, see *EIr*, s.v. (J. Matīnī).

117 Interestingly enough, in B101, al-Jāḥiẓ, *Ḥayawān* VI: 152, offers a variant where the Caliph is also al-Mahdī. Al-Jāḥiẓ was hardly unaware of the anachronism, so the passage is either a slip of the pen or due to later copyists. It would perhaps be overenthusiastic to read this as a rare remnant of the title *al-Mahdī* having been used by several Umayyad and early ʿAbbāsid Caliphs, see *EI2*, s.v. (W. Madelung).

118 See Chapter 1.4.

have been exaggerated, but he probably did meet both Hishām ibn ʿAbd al-Malik and Abū l-ʿAbbās al-Saffāḥ, being thus one of the many Umayyad courtiers who were welcomed by the early ʿAbbāsids as well.[119] When it comes to governors and *qāḍīs*, Khālid seems to have been on more relaxed terms with them and his acquaintances seem also to have included ascetics and proto-Sufis.[120] The relations with Basran poets would be of little surprise, but the evidence is very meagre and of the type that is unfortunately prone to later fabrications: all too many people are described as commenting on famous poets' verses in their very presence.

Geographically, Khālid's life seems to have been mainly restricted to Basra, although every now and then he features in Kufa, Wāsiṭ, and al-Ruṣāfa, and his pilgrimage to Mecca is also mentioned, though not very securely documented.

1.4 Genealogy and Family

Khālid belonged to the aristocracy of Banū Minqar, a subtribe of the powerful Tamīm. The family's descent from Bedouin ancestors seems strong enough, despite occasional attempts to throw doubt on their lineage, as well as on Khālid himself (B9 and A46). It is obvious, though, that the further back we go, the more legendary the biographical information becomes.

Ibn ʿAsākir, and following him Ibn al-ʿAdīm, begin their articles on Khālid by giving his full *nasab* reaching back to Maʿadd ibn ʿAdnān, the legendary ancestor of the Northern Arabs: Khālid ibn Ṣafwān ibn ʿAbdallāh ibn ʿAmr ibn al-Ahtam (also know as Sinān) ibn Sumayy ibn Sinān ibn Khālid ibn Minqar ibn Asad ibn Muqāʿis (also know as al-Ḥārith) ibn ʿAmr ibn Kaʿb ibn Saʿd[121] ibn Zayd-Manāt ibn Tamīm ibn Murr ibn Udd ibn Ṭābikha ibn Ilyās ibn Muḍar ibn Nizār ibn Maʿadd ibn ʿAdnān Abū Ṣafwān al-Tamīmī al-Minqarī al-Ahtamī al-Baṣrī.[122]

---

119 The continuity between the Umayyads and the ʿAbbāsids is often underestimated, but lately emphasised by, e.g., Borrut (2010): 336–337.

120 For al-Ḥasan al-Baṣrī, see above. For other early pious Muslims whom Khālid is said to have met, see B107.

121 Ibn ʿAsākir reads Saʿīd, but Ibn al-ʿAdīm has the correct form Saʿd. For Saʿd ibn Zayd-Manāt, see, e.g., Ibn Qutayba, *Maʿārif*, p. 76.

122 Ibn ʿAsākir, *Taʾrīkh* XVI: 94; Ibn al-ʿAdīm, *Bughya* VII: 49. The whole article of Ibn al-ʿAdīm, *Bughya* (VII: 49–76) is heavily dependant on Ibn ʿAsākir. There are a number of other Khālids, who should not be confused with our Khālid. Thus, e.g., Ibn ʿAsākir, *Taʾrīkh* LIV: 131, mentions a Khālid ibn Ṣafwān al-Makhzūmī, also know as al-ʿAṭṭāf. Al-Jāḥiẓ, *Bayān* I: 336, mentions a Khālid ibn Salama al-Makhzūmī *al-khaṭīb*.

The immediate genealogy of Khālid from Minqar downwards is given by al-Balādhurī in B1 on the authority of al-Kalbī as Khālid ibn Ṣafwān ibn ʿAbdallāh ibn ʿAmr ibn al-Ahtam (i.e., Sinān) ibn Sumayy ibn Sinān ibn Khālid ibn Minqar. Al-Balādhurī also mentions a variant genealogy dropping ʿAmr, which makes Khālid the son of Ṣafwān ibn ʿAbdallāh ibn al-Ahtam, but al-Balādhurī prefers the genealogy of al-Kalbī. Al-Jāḥiẓ and Ibn Qutayba give this shorter genealogy for Khālid.[123] Ibn Manẓūr lists as his *nisbas*: al-Tamīmī al-Minqarī al-Ahtamī al-Baṣrī.[124] The place of Khālid's family within a wider context of Tamīmīs may be conveniently seen in Ibn al-Kalbī, *Jamhara*, table 76.[125]

According to al-Jāḥiẓ the tribes of Iyād and Tamīm were specifically talented in oratory, more so than other Arabs. To prove his point, he relates that the Prophet himself transmitted sayings by Quss ibn Sāʿida (al-Iyādī) and then relates the well-known story of the Prophet commenting on ʿAmr ibn al-Ahtam's oratorical talents by saying that "there is magic in some oratory" (*inna min al-bayāni la-siḥran*). He further mentions how Muʿāwiya had said that Tamīm had been given wisdom and elegance of expression (*maʿa riqqati ḥawāshī l-kalim*).[126] Closer to Khālid himself, Qays ibn ʿĀṣim al-Minqarī glorifies in a poem the oratorical talents of Banū Minqar,[127] and al-Jāḥiẓ gives an impressive list of famous orators belonging to Banū Minqar. Reading al-Jāḥiẓ's *Bayān*, this aspect of the family reigns supreme.[128]

The information from the pre-Islamic period and the lifetime of the Prophet Muḥammad is problematic, as always, and, moreover, hardly relevant in a study on Khālid. We tread on a more secure ground with the early Islamic Empire. Ibn Nubāta dates the ascendance of the Ahtamites (Banū l-Ahtam) to the times of the Caliph ʿUmar (r. 13–23/634–644).[129] The family was influential enough to be known as the Ahtamites, *al-Ahātim*, in, e.g., a verse by al-Farazdaq.[130] *Āl*

---

123 Al-Jāḥiẓ, *Bayān* I: 355–356; Ibn Qutayba, *Maʿārif*, pp. 403–404. Ibn Qutayba repeats this in *Shiʿr*, p. 402, adding that the family of al-Ahtam were orators.

124 Ibn Manẓūr, *Mukhtaṣar* VII: 353. Sources that agree with al-Balādhurī, but are mostly less comprehensive, include Abū ʿUbayd, *Nasab*, p. 239; Ibn Khallikān, *Wafayāt* VI: 182; Ibn Mākūlā, *Ikmāl* IV: 447; and Ibn Rustah, *Aʿlāq*, p. 206. Note that the lack of reference to a biography on Shabīb seems to indicate that Shabīb's biography in *Wafayāt* II: 458–460 (MS Ṣ, but not found in the other manuscripts), may be by a later hand, not Ibn Khallikān himself.

125 For the family, see al-Balādhurī, *Ansāb* VII/1: 49–94, van Ess (1991–97) II: 26, and Eisener (1987): 26, n. 87, 95.

126 Al-Jāḥiẓ, *Bayān* I: 52–53, 54.

127 Al-Jāḥiẓ, *Bayān* I: 218–219.

128 Al-Jāḥiẓ, *Bayān* I: 355–356.

129 Ibn Nubāta, *Sarḥ*, p. 149.

130 Ibn Qutayba, *Faḍl*, p. 10; al-Farazdaq, *Dīwān*, p. 613.

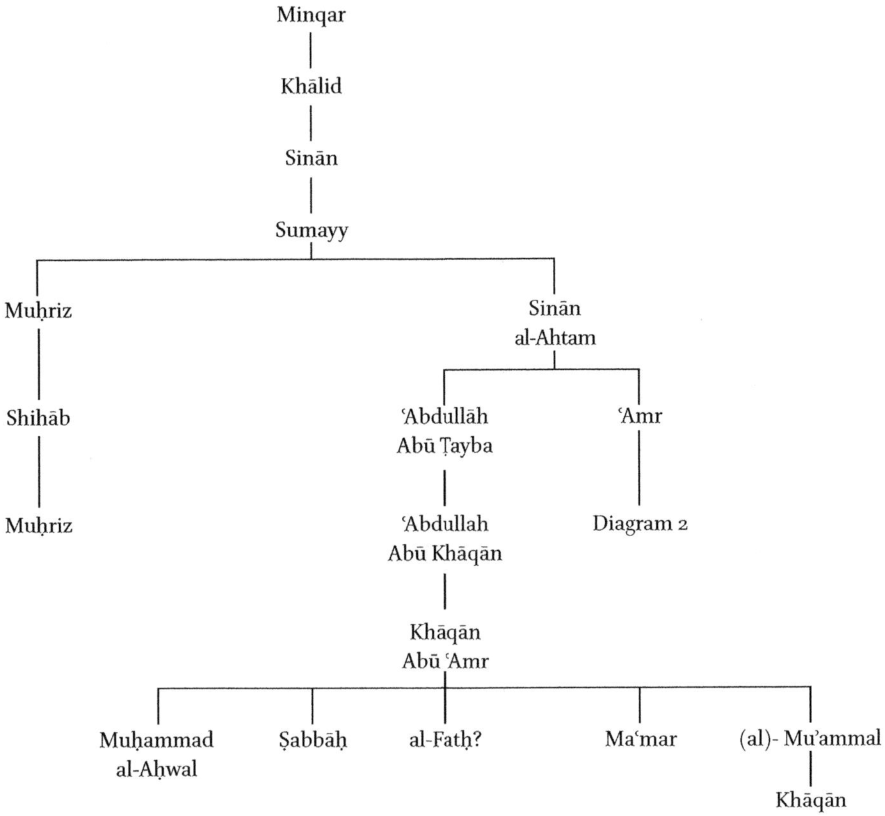

DIAGRAM 1

al-Ahtam are also mentioned in a poem by al-Laʿīn al-Minqarī.[131] Ibn Rustah uses a shortened form al-Ahtamīn to denote Khālid's extended family.[132] This, of course, may be a scribal error for al-Ahtamiyyīn.

The following three diagrams are primarily based on al-Balādhurī, *Ansāb* VII/1: 49–94, where the biographies of Khālid and some of his relatives are given. Information on names and genealogies culled from al-Balādhurī, *Ansāb* VII/1: 55–88, has not been supported by references to avoid an unnecessary volume of notes, as the information will be easily found in Chapter 3 (B1–B115). Information from other sources has been referenced in notes. The genealogy above Sinān al-Ahtam will not be discussed.

131 Al-Jāḥiẓ, *Bayān* III: 323–324. For Munāzil ibn Rabīʿa, who is said to have received his cognomen al-Laʿīn from the Caliph ʿUmar, see al-Jāḥiẓ, *Bayān* III: 323, note 5. In the verses quoted by al-Jāḥiẓ he refers to Jarīr and al-Farazdaq.

132 Ibn Rustah, *Aʿlāq*, p. 206.

1.4.1.1 Sinān al-Ahtam

The great-great-grandfather of Khālid, Sinān al-Ahtam Abū Mālik, is said to have received his nickname *al-Ahtam* "the One without front teeth" after Qays ibn ʿĀṣim al-Minqarī had hit him with his bow and broken his teeth (*hatama famahu*).[133] Ibn Khallikān mentions a competing version, according to which al-Ahtam lost his central incisors in the battle of al-Kulāb.[134]

A dubious story of al-Ahtam's impure descent is told, e.g., by Ibn Rustah, according to whom Sumayy ibn Sinān claimed as his part of the spoil taken from al-Ḥīra a pregnant slave girl, who, after a few days, gave birth to al-Ahtam. Later, when Banū Tamīm sent an embassy to the Prophet, Qays ibn ʿĀṣim blamed al-Ahtam for his supposedly impure descent.[135] Our sources are too few to make much of this, but it might be noted that genealogy was a fluid concept at the time and such adoptions could well have happened.

1.4.1.2 ʿAmr ibn al-Ahtam

The first really famous ancestor Khālid had was his great-grandfather ʿAmr ibn al-Ahtam (d. 57/676).[136] In a great many sources, ʿAmr is said to have met the Prophet Muḥammad.[137] His witty remark invited the often-quoted comment from the Prophet: *inna min al-bayāni la-siḥran wa-inna min al-shiʿri la-ḥukman*, "there is magic in some oratory and wisdom in some poetry."[138]

The stories about the Prophet are notoriously problematic from a source critical point of view, and the historicity of this particular story is very much open to doubt, especially as we find more or less the same story featuring an anonymous Ibn al-Ahtam (obviously here with the meaning "a member of Banū Ahtam") and ʿUmar ibn ʿAbd al-ʿAzīz, ending in ʿUmar saying: *inna min al-bayāni mā fīhi siḥr*.[139] Neither need be of any historical value, but as a narrative this version may well be earlier, and the changing of ʿUmar ibn ʿAbd al-ʿAzīz to the Prophet would then be a typical example of upgrading the story's interlocutors.[140]

---

133 Ibn Qutayba, *Maʿārif*, pp. 403–404; Ibn Khallikān, *Wafayāt* III: 12. Cf. also Ibn Rustah, *Aʿlāq*, p. 206, al-Ḥuṣrī, *Zahr*, p. 39, and Ibn Manẓūr, *Mukhtaṣar* VII: 353. For ʿAmr in general, see also al-Jāḥiẓ, *Bayān* I: 349, and ps.-al-Jāḥiẓ, *Maḥāsin*, pp. 22–23.

134 Ibn Khallikān, *Wafayāt* III: 12. For the battle of al-Kulāb, see Lyall (1906).

135 Ibn Rustah, *Aʿlāq*, p. 206.

136 See *EI2*, s.v. (J. Wensinck – Ch. Pellat).

137 E.g., al-Balādhurī, *Ansāb* VII/1: 50–52. Cf. al-Jāḥiẓ, *Bayān* I: 349.

138 For a slightly different version quoted in al-Jāḥiẓ, *Bayān* I: 52–53, see above.

139 Al-Balādhurī, *Ansāb* VII/1: 89.

140 See Chapter 2.5.3.

According to other stories, ʿAmr was sent by al-Ḥakam ibn abī l-ʿĀṣ to ʿUmar ibn al-Khaṭṭāb to bring the message of the capture of Rāshahr. In pre-Islamic times he was nicknamed al-Mukaḥḥal, "the One embellished with *kuḥl*," because of his beauty,[141] a theme that may give some added flavour to the stories about the less striking appearance of Khālid himself (cf. B29).

ʿAmr is also reckoned by al-Balādhurī among the poets of Tamīm.[142] Al-Ābī shows him in the role of *arbiter elegantiae* (cf. Khālid in A4) by letting him answer a question concerning the poet al-Zibriqān,[143] put to him by the Prophet.[144] Ibn Nubāta depicts him speaking to the Prophet *pro et contra*, again something that we encounter in the anecdotes about Khālid, too.[145] Al-Jāḥiẓ classifies him as one of the orators of Banū Tamīm and speaks highly about him both as a poet and an orator: "his poetry is like clothes that are shown to kings for them to take what they want and there was none among the desert-living Arabs at his time who would have been more eloquent than he."[146] Al-Jāḥiẓ classifies ʿAmr as being among the few who were able to combine poetry and oratory.[147] He also tells a story of how, in the presence of ʿUmar ibn al-Khaṭṭāb, Qasāma ibn Zuhayr judged ʿAmr's speech elegant and his poetry better than a verse by ʿAdī ibn Zayd. ʿAmr's importance as a tribal leader is also made clear by, e.g., Ibn Nubāta.[148] Al-Waṭwāṭ mentions that ʿAmr followed the prophetess Sajāḥi for some time, which fits with A3, where Khālid transmits some historical material on Sajāḥi's muezzin.[149]

Whatever the individual historicity of these stories, Khālid's great-grandfather was seen as a major figure in early Islamic times. Before following the family line down from ʿAmr ibn al-Ahtam, let us take a look at another family line, which was of some importance.

1.4.1.3 ʿAbdallāh ibn al-Ahtam

Al-Ahtam's other famous son was ʿAbdallāh. Al-Jāḥiẓ tells how, according to Suḥaym ibn Ḥafṣ, ʿĀṣim ibn ʿAbdallāh ibn Yazīd al-Hilālī and ʿAbdallāh ibn

141 Al-Balādhurī, *Ansāb* VII/1: 51; al-Jāḥiẓ, *Bayān* I: 355.

142 See *GAS* II: 199–200.

143 See *GAS* II: 200–201.

144 Al-Ābī, *Nathr* VI: 45.

145 Ibn Nubāta, *Sarḥ*, p. 148. For Khālid, see Chapter 2.6.

146 Al-Jāḥiẓ, *Bayān* I: 355: *innamā shiʿruhu ḥulalun munashsharatun bayna aydī l-mulūki taʾkhudhu minhu mā shāʾat wa-lam yakun fī bādiyati l-ʿarabi fī zamānihi akhṭaba minhu.*

147 Al-Jāḥiẓ, *Bayān* I: 45.

148 Ibn Nubāta, *Sarḥ*, pp. 148–151.

149 Al-Waṭwāṭ, *Ghurar*, p. 268.

al-Ahtam delivered speeches in front of ʿUmar ibn Hubayra[150] and ʿAbdallāh ibn Hubayra, and they preferred ʿĀṣim to Ibn al-Ahtam.[151] Someone commented on this, saying: "vinegar may be sour (in comparison to wine), yet it is not (mere) water."[152] Al-Jāḥiẓ also describes Ibn al-Ahtam as an orator who delivered sermons or speeches in front of mighty people and participated in embassies (*dhā maqāmāt wa-wifādāt*). Al-Jāḥiẓ further tells how ʿAbdallāh[153] answered the speech by Ziyād in Basra when the latter had arrived there as the governor appointed by Muʿāwiya.[154]

1.4.1.4 ʿAbdallāh ibn ʿAbdallāh

This ʿAbdallāh's son, also named ʿAbdallāh, was appointed by Qutayba ibn Muslim as governor of Marw.[155] After falling out of favour, he is said by al-Balādhurī to have become a petty merchant in Syria until the ascent of Sulaymān ibn ʿAbd al-Malik, when he again showed his oratorical talents. Al-Jāḥiẓ tells us that he governed Khurāsān and accompanied embassies to Caliphs and delivered speeches (*khaṭaba*) in front of kings, i.e., Umayyad Caliphs.[156]

Ibn ʿAsākir seems to mean this ʿAbdallāh in an article titled ʿAbdallāh ibn al-Ahtam Abū Maʿmar, as ʿAbdallāh ibn ʿAbdallāh ibn al-Ahtam would seem better to fit, chronologically, the information he gives.[157] According to Ibn ʿAsākir, ʿAbdallāh went (*wafada*) to Sulaymān ibn ʿAbd al-Malik as a messenger of Yazīd ibn al-Muhallab, and ʿAbdallāh ibn ʿAyyāsh al-Hamdānī transmitted (stories or *ḥadīths*: *ḥakā*) from him. He is also reported to have exhorted ʿUmar ibn ʿAbd al-ʿAzīz. Ibn ʿAsākir mentions him as a poet, who went to Isfahan to panegyrise ʿAttāb ibn Warqāʾ.[158] He also relates a story about him on his death bed mentioning a chest full of money (100,000 [dirhams]) of which he had neither paid the *zakāt* nor had he given any of it to relatives, keeping it instead as a reserve in case of hard times.[159] When this was told to al-Ḥasan [al-Baṣrī], the latter used it as an example in an improvised sermon.[160] This shows the

150 ʿUmar served under several Umayyads in various roles from 77/696 until his death in 132/749. See Crone (1980): 107.
151 Al-Jāḥiẓ, *Bayān* I: 355.
152 *Al-khall ḥāmiḍ wa-lam yakun māʾ*.
153 Or Ṣafwān, see note 2. Cf. also al-Jāḥiẓ, *Bayān* II: 175.
154 Al-Jāḥiẓ, *Bayān* II: 65.
155 Al-Balādhurī, *Ansāb* VII/1: 54–55.
156 Al-Jāḥiẓ, *Bayān* I: 355. See also al-Balādhurī, *Ansāb* VII/1: 92–93, and al-Jāḥiẓ, *Bayān* II: 173.
157 Ibn ʿAsākir, *Taʾrīkh* XXVII: 107–110.
158 Ibn ʿAsākir, *Taʾrīkh* XXVII: 109–110. For ʿAttāb ibn Warqāʾ, cf. Crone (1980): 112–113.
159 Ibn ʿAsākir, *Taʾrīkh* XXVII: 110.
160 For a similar story featuring Khālid's father and al-Ḥasan, cf. B4 and below.

motif of miserliness, which we will later find more prominent in the anecdotes about Khālid.[161]

1.4.1.5 Khāqān ibn ʿAbdallāh

ʿAbdallāh's son Khāqān ruled Maysān for Saʿīd ibn Daʿlaj.[162] Al-Jāḥiẓ calls this Khāqān also ʿAbdallāh, making him thus ʿAbdallāh ibn ʿAbdallāh ibn ʿAbdallāh.[163] Elsewhere, he quotes verses by Abū l-Ṭurūq al-Ḍabbī and Makkī ibn Sawāda al-Burjumī on Khāqān ibn ʿAbdallāh (ibn ʿAbdallāh)[164] ibn al-Ahtam.[165]

1.4.1.6 Ṣab(b)āḥ ibn Khāqān

Ṣab(b)āḥ ibn Khāqān does not seem to have been too famous.[166] Ṣabbāḥ ibn Khāqān al-Minqarī is mentioned in Abū Nuwās' *Dīwān*. According to a story attached to one of his poems, Abū Nuwās, as a young man, met Ṣabbāḥ and others in Basra. The poem, which mentions Ibn Khāqān and qualifies him as "noble on both father's and mother's side" (*al-najīb al-abawayni*) was, according to this story, Abū Nuwās' firstborn.[167]

Al-Jāḥiẓ tells us that Ṣabbāḥ was "knowledgeable, eloquent, wise, and strong, and he knew many narratives (*riwāya*). In addition, he was generous, patient, and ready to suffer for truth, helping his friends and standing up for the rights of his neighbour."[168]

Ṣabbāḥ ibn Khāqān further appears in an *isnād* in al-Qālī's *Amālī* (B37) leading to Ḥammād ibn Isḥāq, transmitting from his father, and this further from his paternal uncle Ṣabbāḥ ibn Khāqān.[169] Ḥammād was the son of the famous musician Isḥāq al-Mawṣilī, whose family roots go back to a Persian origin,[170] but the expression "paternal uncle" may either have been loosely used or Ṣabbāḥ may have been Isḥāq's early protector.

1.4.1.7 Muḥammad, Maʿmar, and Mu'ammal, Sons of Khāqān

According to al-Jāḥiẓ, Muḥammad ibn Khāqān al-Aḥwal was one of the orators of Banū Tamīm. Al-Jāḥiẓ had seen him and heard him speak. Maʿmar is said

161 See Chapter 2.2.2.
162 Al-Balādhurī, *Ansāb* VII/1: 93. For Saʿīd, who disappears from our sources after 164/780, see Kennedy (1990): 70, note 188.
163 Al-Jāḥiẓ, *Bayān* I: 355.
164 Either al-Jāḥiẓ here shortens the genealogy or there may be a mistake.
165 Al-Jāḥiẓ, *Bayān* III: 322–323.
166 Al-Balādhurī, *Ansāb* VII/1: 93.
167 Abū Nuwās, *Dīwān* II: 92–93.
168 Al-Jāḥiẓ, *Bayān* I: 356.
169 Al-Qālī, *Amālī* I: 213.
170 See *EI2*, s.v. Ibrāhīm al-Mawṣilī (J.W. Fück).

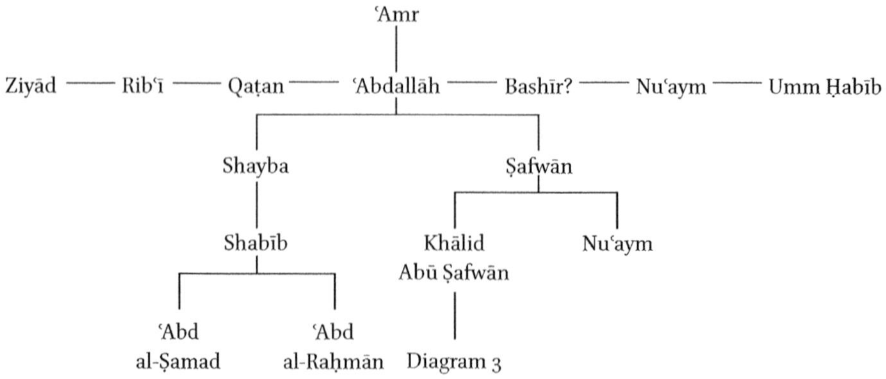

DIAGRAM 2

to have taken part in embassies, which implies that he, too, was of some local importance. A third brother, Mu'ammal, or al-Mu'ammal, is again classified by al-Jāḥiẓ as one of the orators of Banū Tamīm.[171] He quotes Abū l-Zubayr as saying that he never saw an orator of the city (*min khuṭabā' al-amṣār*) more like an orator of the desert than al-Mu'ammal. The latter's son, Khāqān, is also mentioned by al-Jāḥiẓ.[172]

Al-Fatḥ ibn Khāqān is mentioned by Ibn 'Abdrabbih in a list of five *laḥḥāns*, along with Khālid, his father, Khāqān, and al-Walīd ibn 'Abd al-Malik.[173] It is possible that the first four belong to the same family, which would mean that al-Fatḥ should be added to the sons of Khāqān.

A more distant relative of Khālid's, Muḥriz, is known to have been killed in the battle of Marj 'Adhrā'.[174]

Khālid's great-grandfather 'Amr ibn al-Ahtam had six sons and one daughter known by name. Several of the sons were known as warriors.

1.4.1.8 The Children of 'Amr ibn al-Ahtam

Qaṭan was considered a valiant knight (*fāris shujā'*). He was imprisoned by 'Abdallāh ibn Khāzim in Khurāsān and later killed in the latter's court.[175] Rib'ī was one of the heroes of Tamīm (*min rijāl Banī Tamīm*) and an important man, and Ziyād was a poet and a horseman, who invaded al-Sind under Ḥarrī ibn Ḥarrī al-Bāhilī or the latter's son, 'Abd al-Raḥmān.[176]

---

171 Al-Jāḥiẓ, *Bayān* I: 355.
172 Al-Jāḥiẓ in *Bayān* I: 356.
173 Ibn 'Abdrabbih, *'Iqd* II: 478.
174 Al-Balādhurī, *Ansāb* VII/1: 93.
175 Al-Balādhurī, *Ansāb* VII/1: 52–53.
176 Al-Balādhurī, *Ansāb* VII/1: 53.

Bashīr and Nuʿaym are rather shadowy characters. Even the name of Bashīr Abū l-Ziqāq, or Abū Bashīr, is uncertain. His cousin ʿAbdallāh ibn ʿAbdallāh ibn al-Ahtam having escaped from Qutayba ibn Muslim's reach, Bashīr was killed instead of him in Khurāsān, even though Bashīr had been antagonistic towards his cousin.[177] Nuʿaym was satirised by ʿAbd al-Raḥmān, son of Ḥassān ibn Thābit.[178] Finally, the only daughter known by name, Umm Ḥabīb, was married to the grandson of the Prophet, al-Ḥasan ibn ʿAlī, but, according to al-Balādhurī, the marriage proved short-lived. Al-Ḥasan had married Umm Ḥabīb on the presupposition that she would be as beautiful as her brother Nuʿaym was. This proved not to be so, and al-Ḥasan divorced her.[179] Al-Ḥasan's marriages need not always be historically true, but the story provides evidence for the prestige the family was supposed to have enjoyed in early Islamic times.

1.4.1.9 ʿAbdallāh ibn ʿAmr and Shayba ibn ʿAbdallāh

This leaves us with the sixth son, Khālid's grandfather ʿAbdallāh. Ibn Manẓūr calls Khālid's grandfather ʿAbd al-Raḥmān,[180] but this seems a mere error. Little is known of this ʿAbdallāh, except that he had at least two sons, Ṣafwān and Shayba. The scarcity of information on ʿAbdallāh may imply that he died relatively young, and Khālid's father Ṣafwān may have succeeded him at an early age as the head of at least this family line. ʿAbdallāh's other son, Shayba, is again little known.[181] He was killed, along with some of his relatives, by Qutayba ibn Muslim.[182]

1.4.1.10 Shabīb ibn Shayba and His Sons

Shayba's son, Shabīb ibn Shayba ibn ʿAbdallāh ibn ʿAmr ibn al-Ahtam[183] al-Minqarī al-Tamīmī al-Baṣrī Abū Maʿmar, is, besides Khālid, the only truly famous later member of Banū l-Ahtam if we are to judge by later literature where dozens of anecdotes are told about him. Major clusters of these may be found in various sources.[184]

---

177 Al-Balādhurī, *Ansāb* VII/1: 53–54.

178 Al-Balādhurī, *Ansāb* VII/1: 52.

179 Al-Balādhurī, *Ansāb* VII/1: 52.

180 Ibn Manẓūr, *Mukhtaṣar* VII: 353.

181 His name is occasionally misspelled as *Shabba*. Where the mistake is obvious, this has been silently corrected.

182 Al-Balādhurī, *Ansāb* VII/1: 55.

183 Thus according to al-Balādhurī, *Ansāb* VII/1: 89–90. Al-Jāḥiẓ, *Bayān* I: 355, calls him Shabīb ibn Shayba ibn ʿAbdallāh ibn ʿAbdallāh ibn al-Ahtam. This variant is also mentioned, and rejected, by al-Balādhurī.

184 See, e.g., al-Balādhurī, *Ansāb* VII/1: 89–92, and al-Jāḥiẓ, *Bayān* I: 112–113, 295, 351–352, and 355–356. For his life, see Werkmeister (1983): 385–387. Cf. al-Sāmarrāʾī (2001).

There is some vacillation between Khālid and Shabīb in the anecdotes, the same story being told of, or saying transmitted from, both (cf., e.g., B49 and B49a). Shabīb is also occasionally quoted as transmitting stories about Khālid.[185] Khālid was the more famous of the two,[186] and Shabīb and Khālid are occasionally called "the two Khālids," using the name of the more famous of the two for the pair of them.[187] For Shabīb's appreciative evaluation of his older relative, see A39.

Shabīb lived in Basra, and he often figures in Khālid stories, sometimes mentioned as his neighbour (e.g., B49). When Baghdad had been established in 145/762, Shabīb moved there.[188] He seems to have been well connected with high authorities from very early on. According to Ibn ʿAbdrabbih he made a pilgrimage to Mecca in 125/743 where he met the future Caliph al-Manṣūr.[189]

During the Caliphate of al-Manṣūr (136–158/754–775), i.e., only after Khālid's death, Shabīb moved from Basra to the newly-established Baghdad where he was favoured both by this Caliph and his successor, al-Mahdī (158–169/775–785).[190] Several anecdotes, both in al-Balādhurī, *Ansāb*, and elsewhere,[191] connect him with the Caliph al-Mahdī. Al-Ṭabarī, who does not mention Khālid in his book, mentions Shabīb twice, once in connection with al-Manṣūr in 158/775[192] and once offering condolecences to al-Mahdī in 169/785 for the death of his daughter.[193]

Shabīb may have had some political influence already under the Umayyads. Al-Jāḥiẓ depicts him trying to obtain a pardon for the tribe al-Azd from Salm ibn Qutayba, governor of Basra 132/749 and 145–146/763–764.[194] In A18, though, Khālid is presented in a similar role, which makes it unclear, which of the two used his influence or, indeed, whether both did so.

---

185 See Chapter 1.2.2.

186 Note also that Yāqūt, in his short note on Shabīb in *Irshād* III: 407, defines Shabīb as "the companion of Khālid" (*ṣāḥib Khālid*). Likewise, al-Ḥuṣrī, *Zahr*, p. 953, explicitly ranks Khālid higher than Shabīb.

187 E.g., al-Jāḥiẓ, *Bayān* I: 24 (a verse by Bashshār ibn Burd, discussed below, Chapter 1.5).

188 Cf. Ibn al-Khaṭīb, *Taʾrīkh Baghdād* IX: 275.

189 Ibn ʿAbdrabbih, *ʿIqd* V: 106–110. Cf. also Werkmeister (1983): 386, and *ʿIqd* III: 467–468.

190 Cf. Werkmeister (1983): 385.

191 E.g., Ibn ʿAbdrabbih, *ʿIqd* III: 165.

192 Al-Ṭabarī, *Taʾrīkh* III: 430/XXIX: 134. The text reads Shabīb ibn Shabba, which has led Kennedy wrongly to assume that he might be an otherwise unknown brother of ʿUmar ibn Shabba, see Kennedy (1990): 134, note 450.

193 Al-Ṭabarī, *Taʾrīkh* III: 544/XXIX: 264.

194 Al-Jāḥiẓ, *Bayān* I: 390. For Salm, see Crone (1980): 137, and Pellat (1953): 280–281. Pellat, p. 280, claims Salm to have died in 145/762–3, but on the next page says that his second governorship continued until the next year.

Shabīb was also known as a transmitter of *ḥadīths*, here in the sense of traditions of the Prophet.[195] In a story related by al-Balādhurī, Ibn al-Mubārak (d. 181/797) ("or someone else") quotes *ḥadīths* from him, and when asked how he transmits *ḥadīths* from a man who accompanied rulers and pleased them,[196] Ibn al-Mubārak defends Shabīb's reputation by saying that he had nobility and virtue (*muruwwa*) and would thus not lie when it came to *ḥadīths*.[197]

Yāqūt calls Shabīb a narrator of historical stories (*akhbārī*) and a poet, besides being, of course, an orator and an *adīb*.[198] As Yāqūt seems to be the only one who considers Shabīb to have been a poet and as we do not find any verses attributed to him in literature it is probable that this is only an unsubstantiated guess.

Shabīb had also some direct political importance, in addition to his potential influence on Caliphs as their courtier. According to al-Balādhurī, he was appointed to a position in al-Ahwāz for some time under ʿAbdallāh ibn ʿUmar ibn ʿAbd al-ʿAzīz.[199] Al-Balādhurī seems to have received at least some of his information about Shabīb from al-Madāʾinī.

Werkmeister assumes Shabīb to have died around 170/786.[200] In his short article on Shabīb, Yāqūt claims him to have died only after 200/816,[201] which seems improbable. As Yāqūt often takes death dates out of thin air, this is most probably only a guess, and there do not seem to be any stories that would connect Shabīb with persons or events towards the end of the second century AH.

Shabīb's two sons, ʿAbd al-Raḥmān and ʿAbd al-Ṣamad are scarcely known. The former, like his uncle Nuʿaym, had a reputation for excessive drinking,[202] but he is also quoted for a wise saying of his on the definition of three types of love.[203] The other son is known from Ibn al-Kalbī, *Jamhara*, table 76, and he also appears as a transmitter of Khālid stories in A78 and A79.[204]

1.4.1.11 Ṣafwān ibn ʿAbdallāh and His Sons

Khālid's father, Ṣafwān, was married to Arwā bint Sulaym. Sulaym was a *mawlā* of Ziyād ibn abī Sufyān, which explains the references to ignoble descent

---

195 Werkmeister (1983): 385.
196 *Yajrī maʿahum fīmā yurīdūn.*
197 Al-Balādhurī, *Ansāb* VII/1: 92.
198 Yāqūt, *Irshād* III: 407.
199 Al-Balādhurī, *Ansāb* VII/1: 90.
200 Werkmeister (1983): 385. Werkmeister, in fact, gives 170/768, but the AD date is a simple mistake for 786.
201 Yāqūt, *Irshād* III: 407.
202 Al-Balādhurī, *Ansāb* VII/1: 93.
203 Shams al-Khilāfa, *Ādāb*, p. 59.
204 See Chapter 2.2.

sometimes directed at Khālid, in addition to the rumours concerning ʿAmr ibn al-Ahtam. Al-Jāḥiẓ describes Ṣafwān as an orator and leader (*khaṭīb raʾīs*).[205] According to B4, Ṣafwān led the tribe of Tamīm "in the days of Masʿūd," which would appear to refer to Masʿūd ibn ʿAmr, the Azdī leader of a revolt in Basra in 64/683–684, even though the early date makes this uncertain, not to mention the fact that it is usually Ibn al-Ḥārith who is said to have led the Tamīmīs during this time. On the other hand, if the story of al-Ḥasan al-Baṣrī rebuking him when Ṣafwān was on his death bed is authentic, then Ṣafwān should have died prior to 110/728, which makes it within the limits of possibility that he could already in 64 have been old enough to be the leader of his tribe. In C2, though, Ṣafwān is presented in the company of al-Aḥnaf, who died soon after 67/686. In this story, Ṣafwān is still a young man, who is rebuked by his father.[206] This makes it difficult to claim that already in 64 he could have been leading the Tamīmīs, even temporarily, even though otherwise it would be convenient to assume that he took over the leadership from his father rather early.

Ibn Qutayba also tells us that Ṣafwān was an orator and that he died a rich man in Basra. Ibn Qutayba tells us that he left an inheritance of 120,000 dirhams, which, he said, he had put aside for "vicissitudes of time, tyranny of rulers, and boasting to relatives."[207] Al-Ḥasan al-Baṣrī (d. 110/728) rebuked him, saying: "You leave it to those who will not praise you and yourself go to meet Him who does not forgive you."[208] Above, though, we have already come across a similar story about ʿAbdallāh ibn ʿAbdallāh ibn al-Ahtam, which lessens the story's claim for historicity: al-Ḥasan hardly took it upon himself to be there to scold all Ahtamites at their death scene.

In the *Naqāʾiḍ*, Abū ʿUbayda Ṣafwān ibn al-Ahtam seems to be a reference to Khālid's father.[209] Ṣafwān and his son Khālid, are sometimes confused with each other in literature.[210]

One of Ṣafwān's sons, Nuʿaym, is only known for having been infamous for drinking wine, for which he was satirised by al-Farazdaq. The other son, Khālid Abū Ṣafwān, is the focus of this book.

---

205 Al-Jāḥiẓ, *Bayān* I: 355.

206 Note that there is some confusion in this story, see commentary to C2.

207 Ibn Qutayba, *Maʿārif*, pp. 403–404 (*ʿaḍḍ al-zamān wa-jafwat al-sulṭān wa-mubāhāt al-ʿashīra*).

208 *Khallaftahā li-man lā yaḥmaduka wa-taqdamu ʿalā man lā yaʿdhiruka*, cf. B4.

209 Abū ʿUbayda, *Naqāʾiḍ*, p. 751 (line 9).

210 E.g, B10, B11a, and al-Jāḥiẓ, *Bighāl* II: 218.

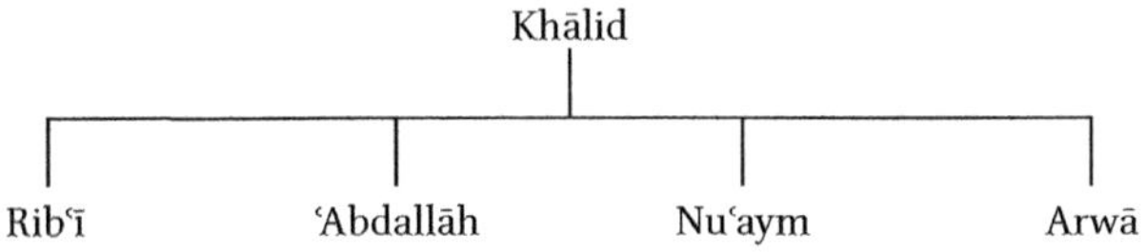

DIAGRAM 3

1.4.1.12 Khālid ibn Ṣafwān's Children

Four of Khālid's children are known by name, or five, if we take his *kunya*, Abū Ṣafwān, literally and assume the existence of an otherwise unknown son Ṣafwān. Ribʿī was killed by the "blacks" (*sūdān*) in Basra during the days of Sawwār ibn ʿAbdallāh.[211] Descendants of Ribʿī still lived at al-Balādhurī's (or his source's?) time in Basra.[212] An Ibn al-Ribʿī is mentioned by Abū Nuwās in a poem together with [Ṣabbāḥ] ibn Khāqān,[213] which might refer to a grandson of Khālid's, although, as we have seen, Khālid's son was not the only Ahtamite to bear the name Ribʿī.

ʿAbdallāh, also known as al-Mamrūr because he was afflicted (*muṣāb*), died in Basra.[214] Nuʿaym, namesake of an uncle of his, cf. above, is mentioned in A49. There the story is told together with a variant version using the name Abū l-Ḥuṣayn, which may have been Nuʿaym's *kunya*. A daughter Arwā is only known from al-Balādhurī's *Ansāb*.[215]

After Khālid's children, the family fades from our sight, having been involved in Islamic politics and oratory for more than two hundred years.

1.5 Khālid's Later Fame

Khālid ibn Ṣafwān remained, for a long time, one of the paragons of early Arabic oratory and it is easy to find very appreciative comments on him in biographical dictionaries and *adab* works throughout centuries. Thus, al-Jāḥiẓ (d. 255/869) was impressed by Khālid, praising him lavishly as an orator. According to him, Khālid is one of the orators who are famous among the ordinary learned people, *ʿāmma*, and have precedence over others in the opinion of the connoisseurs, *khawāṣṣ*.[216] Al-Jāḥiẓ further gives Khālid as an example

211 *Qāḍī* of Basra in 138–144/755–761 and 147–157/764–774, see Pellat (1953): 290.
212 Al-Balādhurī, *Ansāb* VII/1: 89.
213 Abū Nuwās, *Dīwān* II: 92.
214 Al-Balādhurī, *Ansāb* VII/1: 89, 93.
215 Al-Balādhurī, *Ansāb* VII/1: 72.
216 Al-Jāḥiẓ, *Bayān* I: 339.

of someone who quickly understood the point in a pithy saying.[217] Likewise, al-Murtaḍā (d. 436/1044) says that Khālid was famous for his eloquence, *balāgha*, and beautiful expressions, *ḥusn al-ʿibāra*.[218]

Al-Sharīshī (d. 619/1222) declares Khālid to have excelled in both praising something and blaming it.[219] Al-Sharīshī, though, refers to what he had written in *Sharḥ* I: 75–76, where, in fact, it is ʿAmr ibn al-Ahtam who shines in the *maḥāsin wa-masāwī* in the presence of the Prophet Muḥammad. Obviously, al-Sharīshī thinks that the skill ran in the family.

Yāqūt (d. 626/1229) introduces Khālid as one of the eloquent Arabs and their orators, adding that he was a prolific transmitter of stories (*rāwiya li'l-akhbār*),[220] and Ibn Khallikān (d. 681/1282) states that he and Shabīb ibn Shayba were famous for their "fluency, eloquence, and oratory."[221]

Perhaps the strongest proof of Khālid's fame, in addition to his ubiquitous presence in *adab* literature, comes in the list of common sayings in Ibn al-Shajarī's (d. 542/1148) *Amālī*.[222] In the list of these sayings, Ibn al-Shajarī gives "I met a Khālid ibn Ṣafwān in eloquence,"[223] making Khālid the paragon of eloquence, just as Ḥātim al-Ṭāʾī was the paragon of generosity ("a Ḥātim in generosity") and al-Nābigha that of poetic skill ("an al-Nābigha in poetry"), etc. His list of famous names is very similar to that of al-Kāmil al-Khwārizmī (d. after 510/1117),[224] who, in a letter to a scribe, uses Khālid's name as a symbol for eloquence.[225]

Further high praise for Khālid comes in a verse by Abū Tammām (d. 231/845), who lauded the poet ʿAlī ibn al-Jahm (d. 249/863),[226] saying that if he believed in the stars, he would say that ʿAlī has attained to the shape of Mercury and that if ʿAlī had lived earlier, he, Abū Tammām, would believe that Khālid's eloquence derived from ʿAlī's expressions:[227]

---

217 Al-Jāḥiẓ, *Ḥayawān* I: 91.
218 Al-Murtaḍā, *Amālī* II: 262.
219 Al-Sharīsh, *Sharḥ* IV: 135. In the edition, there is a misprint here, reading Khālid ibn Ṣarwān.
220 Yāqūt, *Irshād* III: 274.
221 Ibn Khallikān, *Wafayāt* VI: 182 (*faṣāḥa*, *balāgha*, and *khiṭāba*).
222 Ibn al-Shajarī, *Amālī* I: 121.
223 *Laqītu Khālid ibn Ṣafwān balāghatan.*
224 See Hämeen-Anttila (2002): 433–434.
225 See Ibn Ḥamdūn, *Tadhkira* VI: 403 (*wa-qamaʿtu fī l-faṣāḥa Khālid ibn Ṣafwān*).
226 See *EI2*, s.v. (H.A.R. Gibb).
227 Al-Ḥuṣrī, *Zahr*, p. 953 = *Dīwān*, pp. 86–87 (in reverse order and with variants).

law kuntu yawman bi'l-nujūmi muṣaddiqan /
la-zaʿamtu annaka nilta shakla ʿUṭāridī
aw qaddamatka l-sinnu khiltu bi-annahū /
min lafẓika shtuqqat balāghatu Khālidī

Khālid was especially famous for his ability to extemporise and, even when a speech drew out, to keep consistent. Al-Jāḥiẓ puts this succinctly: "He was the best of people to remember the beginning of his speech and the keenest to keep in mind what he had already said."[228] Speaking about B101, al-Jāḥiẓ opines that it shows what a great memoriser (*al-rāwiya al-ḥāfiẓ*) Khālid was and adds that if he did not premeditate his words but extemporised the saying, then there is no one in the world to equal him. If the Yemeni interlocutor of Khālid had spoken a whole year with the tongue of Saḥbān Wāʾil, Khālid would have dumbfounded him with his brief but pithy remark.[229]

Before al-Jāḥiẓ, the Basran poet Makkī ibn Sawāda had put the same idea in verse:[230]

He knows how to reveal words, well trained,
remembering what he has conferred, word by word.

He surpasses the greatest men in every assembly,
let it be the orator Saḥbān, or Daghfal.

When he improvises, you will see the others
like male bustards, who perceive a hawk.

In a verse quoted by al-Jāḥiẓ,[231] Bashshār ibn Burd (d. 167/783) considers Wāṣil ibn ʿAṭāʾ (d. 131/748) greater than Khālid as orator, but this, too, is an indirect way of affirming Khālid's exalted position as an orator: Wāṣil was *even* greater than Khālid (and a number of other great orators Bashshār mentions).[232]

228 Al-Jāḥiẓ, *Bayān* I: 339.

229 This is quoted on the authority of al-Jāḥiẓ's nephew, Yamūt ibn al-Muzarraʿ (d. ca. 303/915) in al-Ḥuṣrī, *Zahr*, pp. 872–873, and Abū Hilāl al-ʿAskarī, *Dīwān*, p. 333.

230 Al-Jāḥiẓ, *Bayān* I: 339–340. The same verses are quoted by al-Ḥuṣrī, *Zahr*, p. 954; al-Marzubānī, *Muʿjam* I: 543; and Ibn al-Sarrāj, *Jawāhir*, p. 618 (vv. 1+3, attributed to Bakr ibn Sawāda). Abū l-Ṭāhir al-Baghdādī, *Qānūn*, pp. 55–56, seems to quote this from al-Jāḥiẓ. For Saḥbān, who died towards the beginning of the eighth century, see *EI2*, s.v. (T. Fahd). Short biographies of Daghfal and Saḥbān are given, e.g., in al-Ḥuṣrī, *Zahr*, pp. 954–955.

231 Al-Jāḥiẓ, *Bayān* I: 24. The verses are taken from there to Bashshār's *Dīwān* IV: 79.

232 Cf. Yāqūt, *Irshād* V: 567, and Ibn al-Murtaḍā, *Bāb dhikr al-Muʿtazila*, pp. 18–19 (quoting al-Jāḥiẓ). Qutbuddin (2019): 208, takes Bashshār's verses to disparage Khālid and the

Shabīb ibn Shayba is often compared with his elder relative, and the unanimous opinion is that Khālid was the greater of the two. Thus, al-Ḥuṣrī says that Shabīb used to be compared (*yushabbah*) with Khālid, but that Khālid was of higher merit in all matters, both among the learned and the ordinary (literate) people (*fī l-khāṣṣa wa'l-ʿāmma*).[233]

Somewhat surprisingly, Khālid's ascetic sayings, such as B9 and A9, also owned him a place in Sufi literature, and we encounter stories about him in some Sufi books, cf., especially, A9.

---

others, but this misses the point: it is not their inferiority that is discussed but Wāṣil's superiority.

233 Al-Ḥuṣrī, *Zahr*, p. 953.

CHAPTER 2

Khālid ibn Ṣafwān and Early Arabic Prose

2.1 Linguistic and Literary Context

In Chapter 1.1 we have seen that the world in which Khālid ibn Ṣafwān lived was undergoing profound changes. During the early eighth century Classical Arabic language and written literature were also in their formative period.

Linguistically, there was a major process going on during Khālid's lifetime. The conquests had brought Arab tribes into close contact both with each other and with speakers of other languages. Even though the conquering armies kept for some time their tribal identities, even when settling down, the speakers of various dialects began to interact with each other more closely than they had done on the Peninsula. At this time the various pre-Islamic dialects will have been influenced by the interaction between tribes originally from different parts of the Arabian Peninsula and neighbouring areas.

Before the conquests, the Arabs of the Peninsula had for centuries been open to foreign linguistic influence, but settling close to the indigenous population in Egypt, Syria, and Iraq intensified these contacts. In Iraq, the local population mainly spoke various forms of Aramaic, and their influence on the language of the conquerors, which is still to be seen in present-day Iraqi sedentary dialects, will have been great by the time Khālid was active. Likewise, Persian contributed a large number of loanwords to Arabic from this period onward.

All this expedited the change from Old Arabic to New Arabic, with the spoken dialect of the townspeople soon becoming different from the language of their Bedouin forefathers, the sedentary population of the Arabian Peninsula, and the contemporary Bedouins, who retained their old life style.[1]

The change in spoken language coincided with, and perhaps caused, the formation and codification of a literary language, Classical Arabic. Philologists started collecting Old Arabic materials – both lexicographical and grammatical – from the Bedouins, which in the end led to the formation of "correct," normative Arabic. This process was still ongoing during Khālid's time, who lived, it should be emphasised, before the final definition of what was to be considered Classical Arabic. Thus, the great lexicographer and grammarian, al-Khalīl ibn Aḥmad was born in 100/718 and died somewhere between

1 For the development of language, see Fück (1950): 4–47, and Versteegh (1997): 37–73. For early lexicography, see Baalbaki (2014): 1–61.

 | DOI:10.1163/9789004433977_003

160/777 and 175/791.[2] His work was seminal in creating a system for codifying Arabic vocabulary. The father of Arabic grammar, Sībawayhi, seems to have been born a couple of years after Khālid's death, perhaps around 140/757, and to have died in 180/796,[3] almost half a century after Khālid.

Neither al-Khalīl ibn Aḥmad nor Sībawayhi were the first to be interested in lexicography and grammar, but symbolically they situate Khālid in a period immediately before the final codification of Classical Arabic grammar and lexicon. Many of the stories present Khālid as a natural speaker of Old Arabic, meaning here the idealised Bedouin form of language, who used forms alien to the later rules of Classical Arabic (*laḥn*). According to one story, B7b, Khālid was driven to learn grammar (or grammatical inflection, *iʿrāb*) in a mosque, which, most probably, is not a historical account, though, but a later fabrication. After the generation of Khālid, Classical Arabic was taught as a learned form of language to speakers of a newer form of the same language, New Arabic.

Hand in hand with the interest in "pure" Arabic language went an interest in the tribal past of the Arabs. It was somewhat later that authors started writing proper books on topics such as genealogy, tribal warfare (*ayyām al-ʿarab*), and Bedouin sayings and proverbs, but the roots of all these can already be seen in the activities of the early eighth century, and many of the informants used by the authors of the early monographs were Khālid's contemporaries.[4]

When looking for people who still retained or remembered the Bedouin past, Arab scholars, many of them of non-Arab background, often went to the desert to live among the Bedouin and collect materials from them, either by observation or active questioning, both methods strongly attested in philological literature. Probably an even more common method was to interview Bedouins coming to the town. In Basra, the single most important meeting place of the Bedouins and the philologists, as well as other townspeople, was al-Mirbad, a market place located just outside of the town proper.[5] It is slightly surprising that the place name is only found once (B11b) in the Khālid corpus.[6]

Some Bedouin informants stayed rather permanently in towns and became what is usually called "learned Bedouins," linguistic informants, as well as authors in their own right. Although Khālid was not a regularly used authority on pure language and Arab lore, he is occasionally quoted as such (cf., e.g., A30

---

2 *GAS* VIII: 51–52.

3 *GAS* IX: 51–52.

4 Cf. relevant parts of the *GAS*, although its author, Fuat Sezgin, is usually too ready to accept the existence of conspicuously early works, which most scholars would usually take as legendary. For *ayyām al-ʿarab*, see Toral-Niehoff (2014b).

5 *EI2*, s.v. (Ch. Pellat).

6 For A42, see note 956 to the translation.

and A31), showing that he was still considered to retain some natural knowledge of pure Arabic and Bedouin life.

While some worked on the Arab past, others turned to the study of Iran and its past. The little-known Jabala ibn Sālim and his much more famous colleague Ibn al-Muqaffaʿ (d. ca. 139/756) and other, mainly anonymous authors had started translating Middle Persian texts already during Khālid's lifetime, and it is quite possible that Khālid knew especially Ibn al-Muqaffaʿ.[7] He is also credited with transmitting Persian lore, although this is not fully substantiated in the anecdotes.[8]

The Islamic Empire had to some extent been literate in Arabic from the beginning and more specifically so since the 690s when Arabic gained ground as the language of administration at different paces in various parts of the Empire. During Khālid's lifetime, however, Arabic prose literature was still mainly oral, and few literary texts had been produced in writing.

The formative period of Arabic prose literature coincided with the change of dynasty from the Umayyads to the ʿAbbāsids in the mid-8th century. Among the very first *adab* books one finds Ibn al-Muqaffaʿ's own texts, closely following the model of his translations from Middle Persian, and the treatises of ʿAbd al-Ḥamīd ibn Yaḥyā, who died in 132/750, just a few years before Khālid. Ibn al-Muqaffaʿ's texts, as will later be seen, exhibit some striking similarities and even passages identical with sayings attributed to Khālid.

While little was written, at least in a form intended for publication, Arabic oral prose flourished: oratory (*khiṭāba*) was still more prominent than writing (*kitāba*). Later, the oral lore of the Umayyad period was codified, and we find in ʿAbbāsid literature thousands and thousands of pages of text that purports to derive from Umayyad *literati*, but with major text critical problems.

Specimens of Umayyad oral prose in ʿAbbāsid books may not be authentic, yet they probably reflect, at least to some extent, contemporary oral literature and may give us an idea of what was being composed and transmitted at the time. Thus, there is no question that oratory was a central skill for anybody who wanted to make a name for himself, and al-Jāḥiẓ's *Bayān* is a monument to those who managed to do so, at least temporarily – many of the names in the *Bayān* became obscure rather soon and disappear from later works. The role of this oral prose in the development of written prose has not been much studied.[9] An obvious reason for this is that the problems of authenticity and transmission are very acute and sometimes create insurmountable problems.

7 Cf. Chapter 2.3.1.

8 See Chapter 2.4.

9 For early Arabic oratory, see Qutbuddin (2019). For *khuṭbas* in general, see Dähne (2001). For al-Ḥajjāj's speeches, see Klasova (2018).

Other much favoured genres were sayings, proverbs, and maxims, which were both collected and compiled. Genuine Bedouin sayings, or sayings purporting to be such, were eagerly collected, and orators and, perhaps a bit later, writers both used Bedouin proverbs and coined new ones. Ibn al-Muqaffaʿ and other translators added the pre-Islamic Persian tradition of *andarz*, wisdom literature, to the selection of texts that soon became familiar to the learned.

Oratory was an art performed both formally (sermons; formal speeches in front of the Caliph, etc.) and informally, sometimes extemporised. The same seems to have been true for other contemporary genres. Tribal boasting, *mufākhara*, had a political side as long as tribal affiliation had meaning in political questions, but it also became a diatribe for persons who were probably not that serious in their debates.[10]

Closely akin to tribal boasting was the concept of *maḥāsin wa-masāwī* ("good and bad qualities"). This concept is reflected in manifold ways. It was one of the tropes of an orator to be able to elaborate in both positive and negative terms on a given topic, sometimes within the same speech. Compilers of books were also eager to include in their compilations stories that, read together, became *maḥāsin wa-masāwī*.[11]

Alongside collecting speeches and maxims by orators and others, the ninth-century compilers also collected stories about orators and other interesting and/or influential persons of both pre- and early Islamic times. Although few of the earliest collections have been preserved, we know from Ibn al-Nadīm's *Fihrist* and other sources that a large number of collections on a variety of topics were compiled from the late eighth century onward. These included stories about a person or a town, a profession or a characteristic, whether authentic reminiscences of days gone by or fictitious attempts to create a credible past.

Once such anecdotes had entered written tradition they rarely exited. The same material was circulated from one anthology to another, so that it is often possible to trace the vagaries of a story for a millennium, from ninth-century collections till nineteenth-century ones. There was no idea of intellectual copyright: good stories were freely reused, either as such or modified to match the individual taste of the compiler or his generation. The anecdotes formed a living mass that took ever new expressions and the same anecdote could find its way into very different contexts. As late collections could draw on the earliest

10 Later, literary debate, *munāẓara*, became a much-favoured genre, but its origins do not seem to go back to Umayyad times, or at least we have no evidence to show they did. We can follow the development of the genre only later, from ʿAbbāsid times onward, see Hämeen-Anttila (2014).

11 For the genre, see Geries (1977).

ones, there is usually no linear development to be seen, and a late source may well contain an early version of a story.

While most of this material either was historical or claimed to be so, there were also a large number of stories about characters, rather than individuals, and these laid no claim for historicity. Misers and fools, slavegirls and prostitutes, Bedouins and judges lead an anonymous and ahistorical life in the collections, some stories going back to the time of Khālid.

In addition to secular oral literature, there was also a strong religious current of oral stories in the Umayyad period. Israelite stories (*al-Isrāʾīliyyāt*) contained narratives about previous prophets that were not accepted as authentic *ḥadīths*, and prophet stories (*qiṣaṣ al-anbiyāʾ*), narrated by professional storytellers, *quṣṣāṣ*, added to the pool of religious narratives. While the Khālid corpus does not contain any of these, some of Khālid's speeches would fall into the genre of *maqāmāt al-ʿulamāʾ*, sermons preached in front of mighty people to drive through to them the religious truths and their importance (cf. especially B38).

Thus, while the period is not well documented and the source critical problems are considerable, oral prose literature was flourishing and it is one of the tasks of the scholar to try and tease some authentic, or nearly authentic, material out of the huge ocean of stories that claim to go back to the Umayyad period.

2.2 Khālid as a Literary Character

In some stories Khālid may be seen as an author, who produces textual units, such as sayings and speeches, that can be appreciated as literary productions of his. In others he is clearly a character rather than an author in his own right. In this chapter, some of his roles as a character will be studied.

Stories about Khālid may be organised in a number of ways, and there will always be some overlap between the groups. A story about Khālid's eloquent misogynism may contain themes of misogynism, eloquence, and asceticism, as well as present him as a courtier in the presence of mighty rulers. Consequently, it could be grouped under any of these three or four headings.

In some stories Khālid takes on the role of historian and storyteller,[12] while in others he is depicted in various roles as a courtier and companion of Caliphs and governors.[13] In some of these, he is involved in debates, which often

12 Studied in Chapter 2.4.

13 Cf. Chapter 1.3.2.

develop into *maḥāsin wa-masāwī* stories with Khālid and his opponent debating the merits of two tribes or towns.[14]

Most Khālid anecdotes, however, can be grouped under one of five headings. Chapter 2.2.1 will study Khālid as a *laḥḥān* and linguistic authority, Chapter 2.2.2 as a miser, Chapter 2.2.3 as a misogynist, Chapter 2.2.4 as an ascetic, and, finally, Chapter 2.2.5 as an orator and wit.

In later literature, Khālid was mainly seen through these five roles. Some sources tell amusing stories about his avarice, some concentrate on his relation with women, while others present him showing off his eloquence. Whereas some sources provide us with a wide variety of Khālid stories, others give a more limited view of him. Reading al-Jāḥiẓ's *Bukhalāʾ* we only meet the miser, but reading the same author's *Bayān* Khālid the orator is much more prominent. While it is not impossible to combine all these roles in one person (a linguistic authority and orator may well be a miser, misogynist, and ascetic), yet it is clear that whatever historicity there is in these anecdotes, it is buried deep under layers of storytelling.

2.2.1 Laḥḥān *and Linguistic Authority*

While Khālid is usually described in the stories as a witty character, he is also presented as a *laḥḥān*. The term *laḥḥān* is ambiguous, though. Its most common meaning refers to "making many grammatical mistakes," but going through the various uses of the term *laḥn* in Classical Arabic Manfred Ullmann (1979) has shown that, in addition to linguistic mistakes, the term may also refer to a manner of speech, use of Old Arabic dialect, or allusion. Ullmann also mentions the semantic field of melody,[15] irrelevant in the present context, except perhaps for A29 (Khālid ibn Ṣafwān used to say: If one occupies oneself with searching for a *laḥn* and looking for a rhyme, one forgets the argument), which might refer to melodious speech, although more probably it refers to the manner of speech.

In the sense of speaking an Old Arabic dialect Ullmann mentions expressions such as *laḥn Quraysh* and *laḥana l-rajul idhā takallama bi-lughatihi* ("man speaks in *laḥn* when he speaks his [Old Arabic] dialect"),[16] expressions which highlight a difference from standard forms of Arabic – in many cases an anachronistic concept, as Classical Arabic was only defined in the early ʿAbbāsid period – and do not have any negative connotations. The earliest documented cases of *laḥn* as a clearly negative term (linguistic mistake) are no earlier than

14 Studied in Chapter 2.6.
15 Ullmann (1979): 12.
16 Ullmann (1979): 12–13.

the late first/early second century AH.[17] In most of the Khālid anecdotes the word has this meaning, but it is quite possible that in at least some cases it may originally have been used in the earlier sense of speaking an Old Arabic dialect. Other stories may have been created only later when *laḥn* had already acquired its later standard meaning of making mistakes, and we cannot exclude the possibility that Khālid's fame for his *laḥn* may have been reinterpreted to refer to mistakes rather than a manner of speaking.

Whatever the meaning of *laḥn* and *laḥḥān* during his lifetime, later Khālid became one of the stereotype *laḥḥāns*, in the sense of a speaker making grammatical mistakes, and he found his way onto several lists of famous *laḥḥāns*. Abū ʿUbayda, as quoted by Ibn ʿAbdrabbih gives a list of five famous *laḥḥāns*, mentioning Khālid and his father, Khāqān, al-Fatḥ ibn Khāqān, and al-Walīd ibn ʿAbd al-Malik.[18] The first four belong to the same family, implying that *laḥn* was a family heritage among them. In another part of the same book, though, Abū ʿUbayda is quoted for a slightly different list, this time including Khālid's father Ṣafwān instead of Khālid himself, Khāqān, and Khāqān's son Mu'ammal, instead of al-Fatḥ, thus listing three Ahtamites.[19]

As far as history is concerned, Khālid's use of language may have deviated from what started to be considered as correct Arabic either because he retained features of Old Arabic dialects that came to be considered impure or because his speech was affected by changes from Old Arabic to New Arabic. In any case, it may well be that Khālid represented the last generation that learned a language close to Old Arabic naturally and not as a taught language.

In some stories, this discrepancy between rules taught at school and the natural ability to speak Arabic comes to the fore. Thus, B35 mentions that Khālid made mistakes (*yalḥan*) in his speech. When his interlocutor suggests taking a look at grammar (*naḥw*), Khālid refuses with the reason that it would interfere with his natural speech, his Arabness (*iʿrāb*). In a similar story (B7b) Khālid ends up taking grammar lessons in a mosque.

While in many stories Khālid defends himself and his way of speaking Arabic, in others he admits the superiority of the Bedouins, who have retained the purity of their language, not being contaminated by the corrupt language of towns and villages – this, of course, does not quite match the real linguistic history of Arabic, but it became early on a topos in *adab* and philological literature that even contemporary Bedouins retained their Old Arabic language

17 Ullmann (1979): 22–23.

18 Ibn ʿAbdrabbih, *ʿIqd* II: 478.

19 Ibn ʿAbdrabbih, *ʿIqd* III: 415. Al-Jāḥiẓ, *Bayān* II: 220, lists Khālid al-Qasrī, Khālid ibn Ṣafwān, and ʿĪsā ibn al-Mudawwar as three eloquent *laḥḥāns*.

form in its pristine purity. Thus, in B74 Khālid accepts his inferiority in front of genuine speakers of contemporary Bedouin dialects.

In contrast to the claims that Khālid was a *laḥḥān*, in some stories the purity of his language is defended. According to al-Jāḥiẓ, none of Khālid's (and Shabīb ibn Shayba's) expressions were ever imputed as non-Arabic.[20] This matches well the fact that, despite being blamed for *laḥns* Khālid was also considered a linguistic authority in a number of stories. Some of his lexical rarities are quoted in dictionaries on his authority (e.g., B22b), using his saying as evidence for the correct use of the word.

In A31, Khālid is also quoted as an authority for Bedouin lore concerning the system of winds, *anwāʾ*, among speakers of pure Arabic. In al-Bukhārī's *Taʾrīkh*, Khālid is briefly quoted for the meaning of the word *farʿa*.[21]

This role of an authority or informant is, though, only occasional, and Khālid is found as an authority only rarely in the dictionaries, most probably because his family had been sedentarised for some generations and represented the urban tribal aristocracy, while philologists in general favoured Bedouins as authorities. In *adab* literature, Khālid is seen as a *laḥḥān*, rather than a linguistic authority.

2.2.2 *Miser*

In addition to being a famous *laḥḥān*, Khālid also made it onto the list of the four Arab misers, together with the poets al-Ḥuṭayʾa (d. after 41/661) and Ḥumayd al-Arqaṭ (d. probably in the 80s/700s) and the grammarian Abū l-Aswad al-Duʾalī (d. 69/688).[22]

As we have already seen,[23] some of his older relatives were also accused of being misers, so this seems to be a topos in description of Basran Tamīmīs. This is confirmed in a saying by al-Ḥasan al-Baṣrī, who takes Khālid's stinginess as a sign of him being a trueborn Tamīmī (B22a).

---

20 Al-Jāḥiẓ, *Bayān* I: 318. Al-Jāḥiẓ's expression (*wa-mā aʿlamu anna aḥadan wallada lahumā ḥarfan wāḥidan*), though, is open to another interpretation, too. I take it to derive from *wallada* "to call somebody/something *muwallad* (halfbreed, not truly Arabic)," but one could also derive it from the meaning "to generate," i.e., to attribute words to another person.

21 Al-Bukhārī, *Taʾrīkh* III: 156 (1.2.536 < Zayd ibn ʿAlī < Ibn ʿAbbās < Qutayba).

22 Yāqūt, *Irshād* III: 267 (an article on Ḥumayd al-Arqaṭ, on the authority of Abū ʿUbayda – note that the same Abū ʿUbayda labels several of Khālid's family as *laḥḥāns*, cf. Chapter 2.2.1); al-Salawī, *Kawkab*, 39; Ibn Ḥamdūn, *Tadhkira* II: 318 (no. 819); al-Marzubānī, *Nūr*, p. 146; al-Nuwayrī, *Nihāya* III: 297; and al-Ibshīhī, *Mustaṭraf* I: 171. Cf. also Pellat (1953): 148, and B3, B83a, and A52, as well as al-Zubaydī, *Ṭabaqāt*, p. 107.

23 Chapter 1.4.

Khālid's *bukhl* earned him a place in al-Jāḥiẓ's *Bukhalāʾ* and al-Khaṭīb al-Baghdādī's book by the same title. Al-Murtaḍā gives a short collection of seven *bukhl* stories after three Khālid stories on other topics, thus introducing Khālid to his readers primarily as a miser.[24]

In one story (B21), Khālid is even made to acknowledge that he is a miser, inviting friends passing by to join him to discuss withholding. The anecdote is very much in the tenour of al-Jāḥiẓ's *Bukhalāʾ* and, despite coming from al-Madāʾinī, sounds very literary. The large number of *bukhl* stories in al-Balādhurī, presumably many of them coming from al-Madāʾinī's collection, shows this to be a topic that was attached to Khālid's name rather early.

In another, B80, Khālid seems to be proudly proclaiming that he will only offer "chilled water and weighty words" for those visiting him, and in B111 he proposes to a woman, but at the same time tells her that there will be no way to his dirhams and dinars. In A35, he explains why he is not the lord of his people despite his eloquence: "I withhold my property from them and I dislike the sword." Besides being a miser, Khālid almost proudly dismisses all military prowess.

B113, though, lists dowry as a special case where Khālid was generous, besides giving presents to relatives, and buying bananas. The anecdote does not give a very stingy characterisation of Khālid. Likewise, in A72 (cf. A96) he appears propagating generosity, at least to one's friends, and in A106 even more so. As Khālid ibn Ṣafwān is more a literary creation than a historical person, no consistency is to be expected from him.

In Arabic literature on misers, food and money feature prominently on the list of things misers are shown specifically to be attached to.[25] Both topics are also prominent in Khālid anecdotes.

In Khālid's case, money is the most common object of unsound attachment. At its strongest this is expressed in B60 and its variant B60a, where Khālid addresses his coins in terms of an almost parental tenderness.[26] Similarly, in B17, Khālid mentions his unwillingness to part with his dirhams, but this story is also partly ascetic in tone.[27]

In B39, Khālid considers a single dirham as a suitable donation, since a Muslim's bloodmoney is merely single dirhams piled one above the other. B85 is similar to B39, Khālid only giving a *dānaq* to a beggar belonging to his own tribe. He defends his behaviour by saying that if all his Tamīmī relatives would

---

24 Al-Murtaḍā, *Amālī* II: 261–263. The *bukhl* stories are B60, B85, B39, B17, B77, B19, and B20.

25 See, e.g., Malti-Douglas (1985).

26 Cf. also B59.

27 See Chapter 2.2.4.

give the same, the beggar would be a rich man. These two stories are variations of the same idea, a certain kind of *reductio ad absurdum*: affluence can be divided into minimal units of little value themselves, which, turning the tables, gives gravity to every penny because riches are nothing more than pennies piled one above the other.

In A66, Khālid advises his son to keep to his money and his religion, which implicitly puts the two on an equal standing and gives money an almost sacred importance. In B77, Khālid says that he would prefer a son fond of wine to one fond of meat, because wine is not always available, whereas meat is. While not making it explicit, the story implies that for Khālid religious reputation spoilt by drinking wine is a lesser harm than spending money to purchase meat, thus turning the societal norms upside down and putting money above religion in importance. Al-Murtaḍā quotes this anecdote among others on *bukhl*, showing that the aspect of *bukhl* in this anecdote did not go unnoticed by Mediaeval scholars.[28]

A more general attachment to wealth is seen in B22, one of the most popular stories about Khālid's *bukhl*. The story has several variants, but its core is the witty ending, where Khālid says that his son, or his allowance, is quicker "to destroy [his] property than are moths in wool in summer!" (B22a). Here the focus is on the linguistic play on words that sound similar and result in a tongue twister (*al-sūs fī l-ṣūf fī l-ṣayf*) rather than *bukhl* itself. It is worth noting how freely the background story that leads to the witty end has again been modified. B22 tells how, going on pilgrimage, Khālid leaves his son in charge of his properties. When returning he notices that a considerable sum has been spent. In B22a, Khālid in general defends his policy of giving only a small allowance to his son,[29] while no context is given for B22b.

Similar to this is another popular story, A53, where Khālid defends himself for not spending some of his considerable wealth because "Time is vaster than my fortune." In both stories, the focus is on elegant expressions, and although Khālid does take on the role of miser, this is of secondary importance, while the real gist lies in his eloquent way of putting his ideas into words.

Miserliness with food is another common theme of *bukhl* in Classical Arabic literature,[30] but it is less prominent than money in the Khālid corpus. At first sight, B42, where Khālid first praises cheese but on learning that there is none in the house readily changes his opinion and disparages it, would not seem to belong to *bukhl* stories at all. The anecdote does, indeed, belong to *maḥāsin*

28 Al-Murtaḍā, *Amālī* II: 263.
29 For this, cf. B93.
30 See Malti-Douglas (1985): 67–72.

wa-masāwī, but it also implies *bukhl*, as Khālid is shown to be fond of the cheep food stuff, yet reluctant to have it bought for him. The variant B42a makes the *bukhl* aspect clear, by beginning with an explicit mention of Khālid having been a famous miser and bringing into the scene a guest, a Bedouin, who often appears in the role of a guest, or party crasher, *ṭufaylī*, in *bukhl* stories. This makes the timely lack of more cheese welcome to Khālid, who is exempted by it from his duty as the host to provide more food to the guest.

B43 is a variant of the same idea, Khālid again speaking both for and against cheese, but here the *bukhl* aspect is almost completely sidelined, and the anecdote concentrates on the *maḥāsin wa-masāwī*, Khālid's ability to extemporise on both the pros and cons of cheese. This story can better be compared with those where Khālid's opinion of riding swift horses changes depending on whether or not he is riding one (e.g., B110a).

A very typical *bukhl* story is B58, where Khālid refuses to give a banana (in the variant B58a a plum, a fruit of even less value) to the servant who had fetched him some, on the pretext that the servant would already have eaten from the load. This is a typical feature of *bukhl* stories:[31] it would have been customary to show some generosity toward the servant, and Khālid's words aim at doing away with this expectation by referring to a (real or imagined) sharing of the food by the servant on his own, thus releaving Khālid from being dutybound to act his role. Moreover, Khālid shows his stinginess, perhaps subconsciously, by saying that he would have given *one* banana/plum to the servant.

Perhaps also B19, where Khālid defines wealth, should be taken as a *bukhl* story, as it is in stark contrast to Bedouin ideals of generosity and lack of interest in wealth, which to Khālid seems of central importance. Likewise, B20 (Khālid used to say: It is better to have a neighbour who you fear may break into your house than to have a merchant as your neighbour because the latter will always be ready to lend you money and to write a promissory note) sounds suspiciously close to miserliness, even though it could also be taken as sound advice in money matters. Either way, it is clearly built on the same model as B77, discussed above, and highlights the importance of money.

B79 contains another topos of *bukhl* literature, food that is described in detail but that never materialises or if it does, as in this case, is taken away before the guest has had time to eat, or to eat enough. Stereotypical are also A51 and its variant A51a, where Khālid himself eats chicken but only gives olives to his guest. It is also chicken in A52 which Khālid refuses to share with his surprise guest. In this story, even he himself indulges in chicken only after a doctor's insistence, showing that he is stingy not only to his guests but to himself as well.

---

31 Cf. Malti-Douglas (1985): 72–78.

B78 (Someone said to Khālid: "I love you." Khālid replied: "Why should you not? You are not my cousin, nor my neighbour, nor sharing the same profession.") is better taken as a case of misanthropy, rather than *bukhl*, but it may also have a hint of *bukhl*, as it, in a sense, idealises relations that have no close ties, which would create an obligation of generosity.

Miserly themes are also often found in connection with misogyny and asceticism, which are discussed in the next two subchapters.

2.2.3 *Misogynist*

Despite the presence of some female authors, Classical Arabic literature is a product of a patriarchal society, where attitudes towards women significantly differed from modern ones. Negative attitudes towards women can be found as such, but they are also topoi of *bukhl* and asceticism. The former, because women are seen as an economic liability and marriage means added expenses, especially if the wife is, or the wives are, free, and the latter, because women are often seen (from a male view point) as earthly goods and pleasures that turn a man's mind away from the Hereafter that is what really matters.

Within the Khālid corpus, there are a relatively large number of stories about Khālid and women. Even though Khālid is not particularly strongly seen as a misogynist, all the three kinds of negative attitudes towards women can be found in the corpus.

B16, which was later ingenuously used for creating A24,[32] is a short speech by Khālid against marrying. In its original form, it reads as a piece of ascetic advice, telling us that women should be shunned and the final sentence (also circulating independently as B12) emphasises this ascetic trend. As B16 advises against taking wives, but does not say anything about slave girls, it could also be read in the light of *bukhl*, as free women caused more expenses than slavegirls and as Khālid is also known for his predilection for slave girls (B25, B112). Nothing in the story itself, though, suggests such a reading, which only becomes possible in the light of other Khālid stories.[33]

B103 shows Khālid as "a divorcing man," who obviously easily got weary of his wives, seemingly without reason,[34] and B104 shows him enjoying his life having divorced all his wives. These stories exhibit Khālid in a clearly misogynistic light, as themes of *bukhl* and asceticism are absent from these stories, at least in the form they now have: Khālid enjoys divorcing women as such, being

32 See Chapter 2.5.1.

33 Cf. also B61.

34 This is also implied in B111.

just happy to get rid of them, not because that would save money or help him to think of the Hereafter.

In addition to the anecdotes presenting Khālid as misogynist, we also meet him in the opposite role, as an orator describing ideal wives[35] and pleasures of marriage (A24, first part of the story).[36] As many of these anecdotes are unhistorical, there is no reason to try and explain away the contradictions in the material. The role reserved for women in these anecdotes is again alien to modern sensibility, women being seen from a distinctly and exclusively male viewpoint.

2.2.4 *Ascetic*

Perhaps the most surprising role Khālid takes in the stories is that of an ascetic. A late Persian source, ʿAwfī's *Jawāmiʿ*, goes as far as to say that "Khālid-e Ṣafwān was one of the ascetics and pious men of his time" (A94), but the author only has a vague idea of who Khālid was, as can be seen from his setting him at the time of the Caliph al-Mahdī in this story.

This fame results from several sayings and speeches in which Khālid assumes a religious role. There is no clear evidence that these would date from towards the end – or some other period – of his life, and it is quite possible that either the historical or the fictitious Khālid merely responds to the expectations of the audience in producing religious exhortation to those in high positions. In A8, he himself puts this into words by saying: "I have promised to God that when I am alone with a king, I will always remind him of God, He is noble and mighty."

Khālid's asceticism is sometimes a matter of interpretation or point of view. Many stories in which he appears as a miser or a misogynist contain ascetic elements:[37] both misogynists and ascetics vociferated against marriage and both misers and ascetics avoided expensive dishes.

A good example of the unclear border of asceticism and *bukhl* can be seen in comparing B12 with B16. B12 is clearly an ascetic saying, perhaps Khālid's most famous one, and there is nothing in it to hint at miserliness: "I spent the whole night wishing for things, fulfilling the green ocean with red gold. Yet of all that, I only need two loaves of bread, two jugs (of water), and two old rags."

While B12, thus, is a typical piece of ascetic advice, which could be put into the mouth of almost any early Islamic ascetic or later Sufi, in B16 it comes as the punch line after a misogynistic rant against women and marriage. Thus,

35 B23, B24, B25, B27.

36 See Chapter 2.5.1.

37 See Chapters 2.2.2 and 2.2.3.

B16 vacillates between the themes of misogyny and asceticism, with themes of *bukhl* coming up in the advice against marrying four wives as they make a man penniless.

Typically, Khālid is depicted as preaching abstinence in short sayings. Often these are addressed to his son, which is a topos in Arabic literature. In B105 and even more so in B105a, Khālid advises his son to lead pious life and detach himself from the world, and in A47 he is asked about a son of his and replies: "He spares me my earthly troubles and leaves me free to think of my hereafter." Here, Khālid almost appears as a recluse, which, obviously, does not match the other information we have concerning his life.

In B14, Khālid is depicted as an old man who preaches abstinence from the world to others (the sermon being only mentioned, not quoted), but later admits that he himself should withdraw from it as well. B106 has him meet with some pious people and first blame them for coming to the door of an Emir and later praising them, thematically coming close to B14a.

While not openly ascetic, the saying B18 ("Satan, with his perfidy and snares deceives us by obscurities and attacks us with lust. When he has wearied us by deception, he comes back and attacks") is strongly religious and strengthens the ascetic image of Khālid, otherwise somewhat incongruous with most of the stories. One may also take B32 and B84, against jesting, as signs of religious avoidance of (coarse) humour.[38]

Sometimes, as in B17 (Khālid said: By God, I am not happy to spend a dirham except for knocking at the gate of Paradise or buying bananas) there is an ascetic undertone in an anecdote the focus of which seems to be elsewhere. In this case, the comic preference for bananas (cf. B58) makes this a comic rather than serious anecdote and it also relates to *bukhl* stories.[39]

Some of Khālid's longer sermons, which belong to the genre of *maqāmāt al-ʿulamāʾ*, contain exhortations and advise the addressee to turn away from earthly pleasures. The most famous of these, B38, later found its way even to the *Thousand and One Nights* and fully matches the conventions of the *maqāmāt al-ʿulamāʾ* genre. As we have very few complete speeches attributed to Khālid, it is difficult to assess whether or not they could stylistically be his, but it would seem more circumspect to assume that they, B38 included, are later elaborations of, at most, an original nucleus.[40]

---

38 In B87, Khālid advises against making fun, but on slightly different grounds.

39 Cf. B113.

40 For an overview of Khālid's sermons and speeches, see Chapter 2.7.

2.2.5 *On Eloquence*

While Khālid's sayings and his speeches give us a view on how he used – or was thought to have used – rhetorical features,[41] he is also often depicted as commenting on eloquence and defining it.

Many anecdotes emphasise the importance of being eloquent. Thus A32 insists on always being eloquent and training one's oratory talents:

> You will not be truly eloquent until you address your black slave girl during a dark night in an urgent matter in the same way as you would speak in the council of your tribe. The tongue is a member which you have to train. If you neglect it, it will grow weak, just as you strengthen your hand by exercise and your body by lifting stones and other weights. It is like your feet, which will walk when you have accustomed them to walk.

While there is no reason to assume that this particular saying is any more historical than the others, it may well reflect the late Umayyad, early ʿAbbāsid attitudes toward oratory. While orators certainly prepared their major speeches, it stands to reason that a constant preoccupation with oratory will also have given them the ability to extemporise when necessary.[42]

Arabic anecdotes, both in the Khālid corpus and more generally, tend to focus on spontaneous shows of wit and oratorical talent, instead of informing us of how the orators prepared for their speeches. However, if taken literally, A45 shows that Khālid did prepare at least some of his speeches – one of the rare cases where premeditation instead of spontaneity is mentioned. In this story, the face of a beautiful slave girl makes him forget his plans, even though in the end his natural eloquence saves the day and results in a concise remark that worked at least as well as the longer speech he had prepared would have done.

In A29, Khālid seems to speak against focusing on the technical issues in a speech at the cost of the content, which can be interpreted as referring to extemporised speech: "If one occupies oneself with searching for a *laḥn* and looking for a rhyme, one forgets the argument."

Al-Jāḥiẓ's *Bayān* is a monument for the high appreciation of oratory in early Islamic (as well as pre-Islamic) society, and the sayings of Khālid are in

41 These will be discussed in Chapter 2.3, while the present chapter focuses on the contents of Khālid's sayings on eloquence and related subjects.

42 This is a feature well known in, e.g., oral storytellers, who are able to re-create stories based on the large number of formulaic expressions they master by heart. In some cases, singers of runes that only use one metric pattern, like the Finnish singers of *Kalevala*, are known to have started, unconsciously, using the metre in their free, everyday speech.

agreement with this. In B26, Khālid even defines the human being through his ability to speak: "What would a man be without tongue but a loose-running beast or a painted picture?" As is well known, the ability to speak was considered a distinctive feature of the human being by Greek philosophers, but Khālid's saying obviously refers not so much to the ability to speak as such but to eloquence. A57 makes this rather explicit by saying that people who cannot express themselves eloquently are mere riffraff.[43] For Khālid, eloquence was a merit comparable to beauty: these two are what make a man excellent.[44]

While in A32, Khālid is made to emphasise constant eloquence as the way to become a good orator, A105 shows him disdaining being eloquent in an unworthy situation, and A37 makes him say that when addressing an ignoramus he does not apologise for his incapacity, i.e., he does not even endeavour to speak eloquently. While several definitions of eloquence emphasise conciseness, this also clearly shows that a certain level of education was needed to understand, or at least appreciate, a good piece of oratory.

Both the Khālid corpus and Arabic *adab* literature in general contain a large number of pithy definitions of what makes a saying or sermon eloquent. These definitions usually concentrate on the verbal form of the speech, but in B15 Khālid, extolling a man for his eloquence, also points to his sedate performance when speaking, before emphasising his ability to grasp "the tail of an argument when its head has gone before," i.e., being able to give a coherent speech from the beginning to the end, a feat he himself is said to have mastered.[45]

B94 gives a brief depiction of the performative aspects of giving a speech, as Khālid describes a man who has passed away:

> By God, he was a great speaker, with a swift tongue, easy flow, and ample words. The root of his tongue was firm and its sides fine. He had nimble lips, his mouth never dried, and his mind was wide. He made few gestures, but good allusions. He was of sweet character and beautiful grace. He was quiet or loquacious (as need be), he healed the mange, treated the sores, and hit the mark. He was not babbling in his speech nor scanty in his manliness (…).

43 A91, a poisonous description of merchants, shows the haughtiness of Khālid, historical or imagined, as a member of tribal aristocracy, towards merchants, one point being the latters' inability to speak (correctly or well).

44 Cf. B33, B33a, B89, as well as B63 and its variants.

45 Cf. Chapter 1.5.

Perhaps the most noteworthy part of this long eulogy is the reference to "few gestures;" obviously, Khālid considers the power of the plain word more central than any gesticulation during the speech.

In an often-repeated saying (B66 and variants)[46] Khālid defines eloquence as ability to be concise and hit the mark instead of speaking in a long-winded manner ("Eloquence lies not in an easy tongue and a lot of blabbering, but in hitting the mark and getting at the right argument"). Such brevity is a recurrent theme in defining eloquence in Classical Arabic literature and one finds dozens, if not hundreds, of sayings to that effect by a variety of eloquent speakers. A101 gives an example of such conciseness that Khālid – or Shabīb – admired, and in A34 Khālid shows his admiration of one pithy saying by al-Ḥasan al-Baṣrī. Despite this conciseness, Khālid is also depicted as being very fond of speaking (A41), but in A33 he defends himself against such claims: "I give long speeches for two reasons: either when speaking briefly would not avail or in order to exercise my tongue. Holding your tongue will make you tongue-tied."

The power of eloquence is reflected in B54 and even more explicitly in B54a, where Khālid is depicted literally killing a man by his crushing eloquence – in the variant B54b this merely leads to the voluntary exile of his opponent, the ʿAbdarī. No wonder Khālid defined eloquence as one's best intercessor and one's most effective weapon (A76).

While he himself is often described as not always considering carefully what he was saying, in B29 Khālid is annoyed at an imprecise use of words by his wife, who had, seemingly offhand, called him beautiful (*jamīl*) instead of sweet (*ḥulw*), as he admits lacking the pillar, the robe, and the cloak of beauty, which are then defined.

The stories represent Khālid as occasionally falling into *laḥn*,[47] but he also makes a point of true eloquence being natural Arabness, whereas grammar that has to be learned hampers it (B35). Related to this, Khālid clearly gives precedence to Bedouin speakers of "pure" Arabic and sees non-Arabs as the root cause of the corruption of language, a standard attitude in Arabic *adab* literature. Thus, despite being himself a great orator, he cedes the place of honour in oratory to Bedouins, with whom he, as a town-dweller, cannot compete.[48] B91 and even more so B91a show him, however, jealous of other (professional) speakers.

On the other hand, in B90 Khālid condemns excessive use of strange Bedouin vocabulary, as he also condemns "defective village language," by

46 Cf. also A36 and A38.

47 Cf. Chapter 2.2.1.

48 Cf. B74, B92, A27.

which he obviously means the impure Arabic that has been affected by non-Arabic, presumably Aramaic, substrate languages. This anecdote also provides one of the longest descriptions of eloquence in the corpus: true eloquence is

> such that its elements are noble and its meanings intricate, sweet in the speakers' mouth, pleasing to the hearers and when years pass it only grows in beauty. Transmitters pick it up and travellers acquire it, and it is like the treasures of famous verse and stories you cannot forget.

In a more comic tone, he is shown in A25 making fun of a man who tries, with poor results, to sound eloquent but obviously lacks a good command of proper Old Arabic, which leads him to produce a sentence, which is an odd mixture of slightly arcane vocabulary paired with a gross grammatical mistake. A26 ridicules non-Arabs discussing Arabic grammar, and one may well assume that this would have been Khālid's take on Sībawayhi, had the two ever met.

2.3 Stories and their Rhetorical Features

This chapter will discuss the rhetorical features in the sayings and speeches of Khālid. Chapter 2.3.1 discusses the contents of these sayings and Chapter 2.5 analyses the anecdotes, which are, strictly speaking, stories about Khālid rather than stories by him, although they almost always contain sayings by him and are sometimes narrated by him. Finally, Chapter 2.7 briefly studies Khālid's speeches and sermons.

In Khālid's sayings,[49] *sajʿ* only plays a minor role, whereas parallelism is more widely used, which matches what we know about early Arabic prose.[50] Khālid does, however, use occasional rhymes. Most often this happens either in his maxims or in his longer speeches in front of the Caliph or other high officials, but even these speeches are for the most part unrhymed and the rhyme rarely extends further than a single pair. It is possible that compilers have both favoured in their selection rhymed passages following later taste and added more rhyming into his speeches. Thus, the historical Khālid may have used even less rhymes than the corpus would suggest.

The preponderance of *sajʿ* in some versions against others may be exemplified by two versions of A24 (*Khālid and Umm Salama*),[51] the one by al-Masʿūdī

49 In this chapter, I use Khālid as shorthand for "what was ascribed to Khālid."
50 See Horst (1987): 221–227; Beeston (1983): 180–185.
51 For this anecdote, see Chapter 2.5.1.

(d. 345/956), the other by al-Bayhaqī (d. early fourth/tenth century). Although the authors are roughly contemporaneous, al-Bayhaqī clearly represents a more developed version. There are three arguments in favour of this: B16, which has been used to create A24[52] and is an early version as it comes from al-Madā'inī's book (through al-Balādhurī), is much closer in style to al-Mas'ūdī's version than to al-Bayhaqī's; secondly, al-Bayhaqī's version is much rarer than al-Mas'ūdī's, which is closer to most of the other versions. Although a wide distribution does not, as such, prove earlier provenance, it makes it in any case probable. Thirdly, al-Mas'ūdī's version resembles in its style texts that we know to derive genuinely from the Umayyad and early 'Abbāsid periods.

The proliferation of *saj'* in al-Bayhaqī's version may be seen in comparing the same passage from Khālid's second speech in three different versions. The oldest of these is certainly B16, which has later been used to build A24:

> lā tazawwaj wāḥidatan fa-taḥīḍa idhā ḥāḍat wa-tunfasa idhā nufisat wa-ta'ūda idhā 'ādat wa-tazūra idhā zārat wa-tamraḍa idhā mariḍat. wa-lā tazawwaj **ithnayn** fa-takūna bayna **sharrayn** wa-lā tazawwaj thalāthan fa-takūna bayna thalāth athāfī wa-lā tazawwaj arba'an fa-yujfirnaka wa-yuhrimnaka wa-yuflisnaka.
>
> Do not take one wife, because when she menstruates, you menstruate with her, and when she lies in childbed, you will be there, too. When she visits someone or travels away or is sick, it is the same with you. Do not take two wives because then you will be between two evils. Do not take three wives because then you will be (as a cauldron boiling) upon three stones. Do not take four wives because they will exhaust you (sexually) and make you old and penniless.

Rhyme has been indicated in boldface. As can be seen it is only attested once and in a position where it may easily be spontaneous: the dual ending *-ayn* is prone to recur when speaking of two items. Whether spontaneous or deliberate, it is a weak rhyme consisting of one morpheme (dual ending) being repeated.

In al-Mas'ūdī's version of A24,[53] this reads (only Khālid's relevant lines are given, while his interlocutor's lines have been omitted, but this does not affect the rhyming):

---

52 See Chapter 2.5.1.
53 Al-Mas'ūdī, *Murūj* §2330.

> aʿlamtuka anna l-ʿarab ishtaqqat ism al-ḍarra min al-ḍarr wa-anna aḥadahum lam yakun ʿindahu min al-nisāʾ akthar min wāḥidatin illa kāna fī l-jahd (…) wa-akhbartuka anna l-thalāth min al-nisāʾ ka-athāfī l-qidr taghlī ʿalayhinna (…) wa-akhbartuka anna l-arbaʿ min al-nisāʾ sharr majmūʿ li-ṣāḥibihinna yushayyibnahu wa-yuhrimnahu wa-yusqimnahu.
>
> I told you that the Arabs of the olden days derived the word *ḍarra*, 'second wife,' from *ḍarr*, 'harm.' None of them took more than one wife without getting into trouble. (…) Moreover, I told you that three wives are like the three stones on which the cauldron boils, and you, too. (…) And I told you that four wives are the sum of all evil combined for their husband: they turn his hair grey and make him senile and sick.

Although the passage has otherwise undergone substantial restructuring (to begin with, having been made into a dialogue instead of the original monologue), al-Masʿūdī, or his source, avoids, or ignores, *sajʿ* throughout.[54]

Al-Bayhaqī, *Maḥāsin*, p. 421, on the contrary, reads:

> inna l-ʿarab ishtaqqat ism al-ḍarr min ism al-ḍarratayn wa-inna **l-ḍarāʾir** sharru **l-dhakhāʾir** waʾl-imāʾ āfat al-manāzil wa-lam yajmaʿ rajulun bayna **mraʾatayn** illā kāna bayna **jamratayn** tuḥriquhu wāḥidatun **bi-nārihā** wa-tulḥiquhā ukhrā **bi-sharārihā** (…) wa-akhbartuka anna l-thalāth idhā jtamaʿna kunna kaʾl-athāfī l-muḥriqa wa-anna l-arbaʿ yataghāyarna fa-lā yaṣbirna wa-yataʿālayna wa-lā **yahwayna** wa-in uʿṭīna lam **yarḍayna**.
>
> The Arabs derived the word *ḍarr*, 'harm,' from *ḍarra*, 'second wife.' Second wives are the worst of possessions and slave girls are the ruin of the house. No man has taken more than one wife without ending up between two firebrands, the one burning him with its fire, the other throwing its sparks at him (…) And I told you that three wives are like three burning hot stones and four are jealous to each other and without patience, haughty and unloving, and even when they are given, they will not be satisfied.

Although still a far cry from later, heavily ornamented prose, the role of *sajʿ* has clearly grown in this version.

---

54 As *sajʿ* almost never consists of units of single (orthographic) words immediately following each other, *yushayyibnahu wa-yuhrimnahu wa-yusqimnahu* cannot be taken as a series of rhymes.

The same tendency is to be seen throughout the story when comparing the versions of al-Masʿūdī and al-Bayhaqī. Thus, e.g., whereas al-Masʿūdī writes: *anna ʿindaka rayḥānatan min al-rayāḥīn* ("you have with you one of these flowers"), al-Bayhaqī has: *ʿindaka rayḥānat al-**rayāḥīn** wa-sayyidat nisāʾ **al-ʿālamīn*** ("you have with you the flower of flowers and the lady of all the women in the whole world"), thus producing the rhyme by adding a rhyming sentence to the presumably unrhymed original.

We may find similar variation in rhythm and rhyming in comparing B60 with its variant versions, B60 presumably representing an old version, although al-Madāʾinī is not explicitly given as the source for the story in al-Balādhurī's *Ansāb*. However, some of the parallel sources do derive this from al-Madāʾinī. Here the punchline, Khālid's tender address to a dirham, reads: *la-ṭāla mā ghawwarta fī l-bilād wa-anjadta ammā wa'llāhi la-uṭīlanna **ḍajʿatak** wa-la-udīmanna **ṣarʿatak*** ("you have travelled long days in various countries and on highlands. Now, by God, I will make you lie down and repose for a long time"). This version uses parallelism and one case of rhyme, but the rhythm is much stronger in, e.g., the version of al-Zamakhsharī (B60a): *yā ʿayyār kam **taʿīr** wa-kam taṭūfu **wa-taṭīr** la-uṭīlanna ḍajʿatak* ("O vagrant, for how long have you been travelling far and wide! I will make you lie down for a long time"). Al-Nuwayrī (B60) gives a different variant: *ṭālamā sirta fī l-bilād ammā wa'llāhi la-uṭīlanna ḥabsaka wa-la-udīmanna labthaka* ("you have travelled long days in various countries. Now, by God, I will make long your detention and prolongate your stay"). Here, the rhyme has been given up or, perhaps more correctly, has been replaced by a less strict one *ḥabsak/labthak*. The three versions also show how freely the exact words of Khālid are being changed while keeping the general meaning.

Against this background A4, which we have already seen to be of suspicious authenticity for quite different reasons,[55] also stands out as having been composed in a different style:

> ammā aʿẓamuhum **fakhran** wa-abʿaduhum **dhikran** wa-aḥsanuhum **ʿudhran** wa-ashadduhum **mayalan** wa-aqalluhum **ghazalan** wa-aḥlāhum **ʿalalan** al-ṭāmī idhā **zakhar** wa'l-**ḥāmī** idhā **zaʾar** wa'l-**sāmī** idhā **khaṭar** alladhī in **hadar qāl** wa-in **khaṭar ṣāl** al-faṣīḥu l-**lisān** al-ṭawīlu l-ʿ**inān** fa'l-Farazdaq.
>
> The greatest of them in *fakhr* is al-Farazdaq. His fame travels widest and he is the best when apologising, but he is the most tilted of them, the least in love poetry, but again the sweetest in giving a second draught, a

55 See Chapter 1.3.2.

> torrent when he overflows, fiercely hot when he rages, lofty when he is parading. When he bellows he says the right thing and in a serious moment he assaults. He speaks correctly and holds long reins.

The intricate net of rhymes, short clauses, and strong rhythm make it difficult to accept this as even remotely reflective of Umayyad rhetorics.

While longer series of rhymes are lacking in the earliest layers of Khālid stories, parallelism is strongly present. A typical example comes from B33: *raḥima llāhu abāka kāna yaqrī l-ʿayna jamālan waʾl-samʿa bayānan* ("God bless your father! He used to feast the eye with his beauty and the ear with his eloquence"). The parallelism of eye/ear is strengthened by the identical morphological structure, which leads to phonetic similarity, though not rhyme, between *l-ʿayna* and *l-samʿa*, as well as between *jamālan* and *bayānan*. In A56, we have a contrasting parallelism between two words and their counterparts: *anbatatʾhu l-ṭāʿa wa-ḥaṣadatʾhu l-maʿṣiya* ("Obedience made him grow and disobedience reaped him").

While *sajʿ* only plays a minor role in Khālid's sayings and his speeches, description (*waṣf*) is central to them. This is especially true in longer speeches, where description is prominent. This may mark the greater care put into composing these speeches, whether by Khālid or by later authors who have composed them or elaborated on the material they had at hand. Women and wives are described in ornate language in several stories[56] and food is described in equally eloquent ways.[57] We also find numerous descriptions of nature,[58] and the tribal and town *mufākharas* are full of descriptive passages, as are Khālid's prose panegyrics (e.g., B94).[59]

Much attention is given to witty sayings that are presented as having been extemporised. Al-Jāḥiẓ is reported by al-Ḥuṣrī to have admired Khālid's ready reply to a Southern Arab's tribal boast, which Khālid devastated by his brief reply: "But what should I say to people who weave clothes, train monkeys, and tan hides? A hoopoe led the way to them and a rat drowned them" (see Commentary to B101). The saying contains few tropes and is in rather unelaborated language (*wa-mā aqūlu li-qawm innamā hum bayna nāsij burd wa-sāʾis qird wa-dābigh jild, dalla ʿalayhim hudʾhud wa-gharraqatʾhum faʾra*), and its strength lies in the spontaneous wit, which, moreover, does not invite a reply,

56 B24, B25, B27, A24.

57 B79, B81, A42, A43, A44.

58 B38, B81, A42.

59 See Chapter 2.6.

thus marking the end of discussion without giving the opponent any chance to reply.

As brevity and conciseness are often highlighted as crucial to eloquence by both Khālid and others[60] it will come as no surprise that Khālid is shown to be able to condense his sayings to a minimum when needed[61] and to admire the same ability in others.[62]

Figura etymologica is also amply used in the stories, mostly in blame. Thus, in B9 Khālid attacks the imprisoned Bilāl by playing with the etymology of his, and his ancestors', names: Bilāl's grandfather Abū Mūsā al-Ashʿarī (d. ca. 48/668)[63] is claimed by Khālid to have received his *kunya* not from any son of his but from his razor (*mūsā*),[64] which implies him to have worked in the very low manual profession of barber. In B54, Khālid ruins the reputation of an ʿAbdarī by drawing down his ancestors, ʿAbd al-Dār having, according to Khālid, received his name from being a house (*dār*) slave (*ʿabd*) of Quraysh, while the Northern Arabs had hit his ancestors on head (*amma*), bridled them (*khazama*), and overcome them (*jamaḥa*), playing with the etymogies of Umayya, Makhzūm, and Jumaḥ,[65] which leaves in shadow the ʿAbdarī's weak attempt to disparage Khālid through the etymology of his, and his ancestors', names, mainly with Qurʾānic allusions: Khālid is implied eternally to remain (*khālid*, Q 47:15) in Hell, being a barren rock (*ṣafwān*, Q 2:264), and descending from a toothless (*ahtam*) ancestor. Qurʾānic references are also used in plenty without word plays (e.g., B30, B38, B53), which would imply a good command of the Qurʾānic text, but the authenticity of such sayings is, of course, open to doubt, so that we cannot say much about Khālid's real religiosity or knowledge of the Qurʾān.

These stories also reverbarate with ancient tribal history, which is understandable in the context of tribal *mufākhara* as it necessitates a good knowledge

60 See Chapter 2.2.5.

61 E.g., B45, B46, B69.

62 B46 al-Aḥnaf; A34 al-Ḥasan al-Baṣrī; A101 ʿAmr ibn ʿUbayd.

63 See *EI3*, s.v. (M. Lecker).

64 In B9a, Bilāl chastises Khālid for his mother's name, ʿAfra, which he implies, quoting a verse by Qays ibn ʿĀṣim, to be related to *ʿifirra*, "malignant; foul; crafty" (see Lane 1863–93, s.v. *ʿfr*).

65 B54a further develops the series of etymologies. For a similar series of etymological wordplays, see Ibn Ḥamdūn, *Tadhkira* VIII: 18 (no. 15), where the Caliph meets a man, who, step by step, identifies himself as Shihāb ibn Jamra from Banū l-Ḥuraqa and Banū Ḍimār, living in Ḥarrat Laylā and heading for Laẓā – all words etymologically connected with the semantic field of "fire."

of tribal history, a point where Khālid is said to have excelled.[66] The *ubi sunt* motive is also sometimes used by Khālid (B38, B97).

The use of *figura etymologica* is not restricted to personal names. In B10a Khālid dismisses asses as mounts, using the etymological connection between *ʿayr* "wild ass" and *ʿār* "shame," further strengthening this with a reference to Q 31: 19, where the voice of asses is said to be the most unpleasant voice. In A24, he further connects the word *ḍarra* "co-wife" with *ḍarr* "damage; harm."

2.3.1 *Maxims and Punch Lines*

As Chapter 2.5 will show, in some cases we can see how anecdotes have been modified during their transmission and how the present forms of the story are demonstrably much later than Khālid. We also have good reason to assume that the same is mostly the case even when this cannot be proven.

However, when studying the variants of an anecdote, one very often notes the persistance of the witty (often concluding) remark of the protagonist, the punchline: while the surrounding story may drastically change, the core sentence is often transmitted in a fixed form in all, or most, sources. This, obviously, does not prove that the sayings as such come from the historical Khālid, but it, at least, shows that certain parts of the story are more resistant to change than other parts and, hence, potentially older than the surrounding prose narrative, in some cases perhaps even close to authentic.

The same phenomenon is to be seen even in literary works quoting other literary works. These, too, tend to modify the narrative parts that outline the background situation and then quote the punchline(s) verbatim.[67]

On the other hand, maxims, even more so than anecdotes, have a tendency to be attributed to several suitable characters, so that we can speak of wandering maxims.[68] Thus, e.g., B5 ("Truthfulness is laudable except in the case of a slanderer, who is the worse the truer he is") is attributed to both Khālid and Ibn Shubruma. While the saying may have been transmitted more or less intact, as far as its verbal form goes, it has been reattributed to at least one of the two.

Khālid's maxims are quoted either separately or as parts of an anecdote, sometimes the same saying appearing in both ways in different sources. In some cases, it is clear that there once was a background story and although some sayings could have been coined just as sayings, this would seem rather

66 See Chapter 2.4.

67 For an example showing how al-Thaʿālibī quotes al-Ṭabarī, cf. Hämeen-Anttila (2018a): 52–54.

68 Cf. Chapter 2.5.3.

improbable and we may assume that most, if not all, of Khālid's sayings are either extracted from a speech of his or taken from an anecdote, whether authentic or of a later date.

B26 ("What would a man be without tongue but a loose-running beast or a painted picture?") may stand as an example of a saying which has no context and the original context of which is not obvious. Whereas religious sayings could come from a sermon, here the original context, if there was such, is more difficult to gauge, although a general discussion on rhetoric between Khālid and other courtiers and orators is always a possibility, as is religious admonition, God being the One to endow humankind with the ability to speak. There are several such uncontextualised sayings on rhetoric and oratory in the corpus (e.g., B66: "Eloquence lies not in an easy tongue and a lot of blabbering, but in hitting the mark and getting at the right argument").

This particular saying B26 may well refer to Aristotle's definition of man as a rational being, where *logikos* was translated as *nāṭiqa* "rational; speaking." Khālid never refers to the Greek sciences that had started being translated towards the end of the Umayyad period and there is no reason to assume that he would have been familiar with the Greek philosophical tradition, so the Aristotelian allusion, if such it is, must have been picked by him from other sources, if the saying is authentic.

B6 ("Bashīr got mixed with things out of ignorance. He miscarried in them, neither being able to endure them patiently nor getting determinedly out of them") also lacks context, being a character definition of a rather obscure Basran Bashīr ibn ʿUbaydallāh. To grasp the full impact of the saying, one should know the background story. Likewise, B7 ("A summer cloud that will soon disperse") needs a background, which is given in B7a and B7b. In a saying similar to B6, B15 (Khālid extolled a man, saying among other things: "I have never seen one more sedate in gushing forth (his words) or having a deeper well or being firmer in grasping the tail of an argument when its head has gone before or more discerning of *ubna* and *waṣma*"), the need for the context has been eliminated by leaving the person described anonymous, so that instead of being an individual he has become a type, a representative of a larger category, and Khālid's laudatory words are not bound to one individual, but are given as a model of eloquent panegyrics.

Some sayings are general in character and could have been coined as sayings in the first place, although they may equally well come from a longer speech or an anecdote. Hence, B5 (cf. above) and B28 ("If manliness were easy to carry and light to bear, the base would not leave an inch of it for the noble. Yet it is heavy to bear and formidable to carry. Hence, the noble have taken it on themselves, but the base have turned away from it") are able to stand alone.

Not all contextless sayings are of a general character. B17 ("By God, I am not happy to spend a dirham except for knocking at the gate of Paradise or buying bananas") and its parallel B113 ("There are three things in which I am not sparing with my dirhams: dower for women, presents for relatives, and buying bananas") are rather specific to Khālid, who, if we are to trust these sayings, had a marked predilection for bananas, but the sayings themselves are quoted without any context. B18 ("Satan, with his perfidy and snares deceives us by obscurities and attacks us with lust. When he has wearied us by deception, he comes back and attacks") could well stand by itself, even though it could also be a passage detached from, e.g., a sermon. B31 ("Khālid once said of a man: He really is a man whom God has made extraordinary by nature and whose behaviour He has set upright. Whom wealth makes haughty and immoderate, him does it leave and lower") could refer to a particular man, as implied by the minimal context given by al-Balādhurī, but it could equally well come from a sermon and concern the exemplary man.

In a few cases, Khālid's sayings have found their way into collections of proverbs. Thus, the core of B22a ("The thirty dirhams are quicker to destroy my property than are moths in wool in summer") is found in a number of these. In al-Maydānī's *Majmaʿ*, virtually the same saying is given anonymously, and it is, of course, possible that, like in B7, Khālid has merely quoted a proverb and made it famous by his quotation.[69]

In a few cases, Khālid's witticism is created by a well-timed quotation, rather than a phrase coined by him. One of the most common sayings of his is the comment "a summer cloud that will soon disperse" on Bilāl ibn abī Burda.[70] The quotation comes from a poem, probably by ʿImrān ibn Ḥiṭṭān (d. 84/703), and it is only the timing of the saying, and Bilāl's equally witty reply, that make it a favourite among *adab* authors. In B30, both Khālid and al-Farazdaq quote the Qurʾān in a witty and allegedly improvised discussion.

The unadorned B8 is a showcase of how one saying may be served both with and without context. In B8, we merely have a devastating comment on Bilāl: "Justice in the house of Bilāl is rarer than red sulphur in the house of Abū l-Zard al-Ḥanafī." In B8a, some general context is provided for the saying, and in B9a we have an exact context for the saying, with a long story of what happened afterwards. The saying is only found in a few sources, which is probably not because it would not have been appreciated as such, but because this Abū l-Zard was completely obscure for later readers, as he remains for us, too. In this, and many other cases, we have no way of deciding whether the long

69 Al-Maydānī, *Majmaʿ* II: 462.
70 B7, B9b, B9c, B108.

version (B9a) is the original and B8 and B8a its fragments or whether B9a is built by combining different sayings and anecdotes to produce a longer and more coherent story, as in the case of A24.[71]

Likewise, the witticism of B36 does not depend on it being ornate – as a matter of fact, it lacks the slightest ornamentation – but on being an instantaneous reply to a verse propagating trying one's best when one thinks himself capable of something ("When your soul tells you that you are capable / of taking what other men hold, then try!") – a veritable pep talk of the eighth century. Khālid's dry reply is simply: "Nay, by God, but call it a lie!" This may gain added piquancy if the reader knows that, in fact, the verse is usually transmitted in the form suggested by Khālid.[72]

B23, B24, B25, and B25a (descriptions of an ideal wife) show a clear family resemblance, with the short B23 finding close paralleles in both B24 and B25, but the latter two otherwise differing from each other in the exact words, although more or less coinciding on a general level. Whereas B23 is given without any context, as Khālid's opinion on whom to marry, B24 and B25 are fully contextualised, the former as a dialogue between Khālid and the Caliph Abū l-ʿAbbās, the latter as a dialogue between Khālid and the first-person narrator of this version, Ḥafṣ ibn Muʿāwiya al-Ghalābī. B25a has only a very general context, Khālid speaking to an anonymous male matchmaker. In B25 and B25a Khālid's interlocutor gets the last word, which throws a comic light on Khālid's speech, while in B23 and B24 his speech seems to be supposed to be taken at face value, as an ornate description of an ideal woman. The high position of the interlocutor in B24 makes it probable that the story has been upgraded.

The flexibility of Khālid stories may also be seen in B10, B10a, and B10b. B10, potentially the oldest version as it goes back to al-Madāʾinī's monograph on Khālid, serves us an eloquent description of a donkey with minimal context, the general Abū l-Jahm (ibn ʿAṭiyya) seeing Khālid riding a donkey and asking him why he is doing so. In B10b, Khālid's interlocutor is an anonymous Basran nobleman. In B10a, we have a change of interlocutor to ʿAlī ibn al-Jahm ibn abī Ḥudhayfa, which may be a corruption of Abū Jahm ibn Ḥudhayfa al-ʿAdawī, which is how al-Sharīshī understood this, calling the interlocutor ʿAlī ibn al-Jahm al-ʿAdawī, and the story has now changed into a *maḥāsin wa-masāwī* story with Khālid first blaming Ibn al-Jahm for riding a donkey and then defending himself when riding the same donkey.[73]

71 For A24, see Chapter 2.5.1.

72 See commentary to B36.

73 Al-Sharīshī, *Sharḥ* IV: 135.

Likewise, in B11 one can see the gradual contextualisation of a saying, assuming again that al-Balādhurī's version, possibly going back to al-Madā'inī, represents the oldest layer. B11, a saying by Khālid on various riding animals, is given without any context. In B11a (< al-Jāḥiẓ), the saying is preceded by a brief dialogue between Khālid and Sulaymān ibn ʿAlī, who asks Khālid why he rides a donkey, and Khālid's saying is given as an answer to Sulaymān's question. A location (al-Mirbad) is added in B11b (< al-Tawḥīdī).

B11c (< Ibn ʿAsākir) is given with an *isnād* leading back to Shabīb ibn Shayba, which gives some grounds for taking this as an early version. In it, Shabīb is the interlocutor of Khālid and the whole story is told as a series of questions by Shabīb and answers by Khālid ("How about X?" "They are for Y"). Thus, we either have a saying that has been changed into a dialogue, or a dialogue in which the questions have been deleted in order to create a more dense text.

In a similar way, we have in B12 ("I spent the whole night wishing for things, fulfilling the green ocean with red gold. Yet of all that, I only need two loaves of bread, two jugs (of water), and two old rags") a contextless saying, which in B16 has become the end of a short dialogue between Khālid and his interlocutor, or the other way round.

The contextless sayings find one of their closest parallels in the works of Ibn al-Muqaffaʿ, some of the individual sayings of whose *Kitāb al-Adab* (or *al-Ādāb*) *al-kabīr* find very close parallels in Khālid's sayings, the main difference between the two being that Khālid's sayings are transmitted separately, while Ibn al-Muqaffaʿ's *Adab* combines his into chapters.

As a matter of fact, there may well have been a historical link between Khālid and Ibn al-Muqaffaʿ. Banū l-Ahtam are known to have had relations to Ibn al-Muqaffaʿ, one of the leading intellectuals of the Late Umayyad period,[74] and even though Khālid himself is not said to have known Ibn al-Muqaffaʿ his cousin Shabīb ibn Shayba is sometimes mentioned in connection with him.[75]

Against this background it is interesting to note that Ibn al-Muqaffaʿ's *Adab* shares several sayings with the Khālid corpus. A72 shows that there is, without the slightest doubt, a genetic link between Ibn al-Muqaffaʿ's *Adab* and the Khālid corpus:

> ibdhil li-ṣadīqika mālaka wa-li-maʿrifatika bishraka wa-taḥiyyataka wa-li'l-ʿāmmati rifdaka wa-ḥusna maḥḍarika wa-li-ʿaduwwika ʿadlaka wa-ḍnan bi-dīnika wa-ʿirḍika ʿan kull aḥad. (A72)

74 See van Ess (1991–97) II: 26, 243.

75 E.g., al-Balādhurī, *Ansāb* VII/1: 91, and Ibn ʿAbdrabbih, *ʿIqd* III: 324–325.

> Be generous with your property to your friends, with your joyful countenance and greeting to your acquaintances, with your help and friendly appearance to common people, and with your justness to your enemies, but be stingy with your religion and reputation to each and everyone!
>
> ibdhil li-ṣadīqika damaka wa-mālaka wa-li-maʿrifatika rifdaka wa-maḥḍaraka wa-li'l-ʿāmmati bishraka wa-taḥannunaka wa-li-ʿaduwwika ʿadlaka wa-inṣāfaka wa-ḍnan bi-dīnika wa-ʿirḍika ʿan kull aḥad.
>
> *Adab*, p. 65

As the comparison shows, the differences between the two are a couple of additions in the *Adab* (or omissions in the Khālid corpus) and some slight changes in the order of the phrases.[76] The near identical phrasing cannot be accidental but there must be a genetic link between the two.

The same goes for A80a and *Adab*, p. 50:

> in sa'ala l-wālī rajulan ghayraka fa-lā takun anta l-mujīb fa-inna dhālika khiffa bi'l-sā'il wa'l-mas'ūl (A80a)
>
> When a governor asks someone else than you, do not answer him yourself. That would be slighting both the one who asks and the one who is asked.
>
> idhā sa'ala l-wālī ghayraka fa-lā takūnanna anta l-mujīb ʿanhu fa-inna stilābaka l-kalām khiffa bika wa-stikhfāf minka bi'l-mas'ūl wa-bi'l-sā'il
>
> *Adab*, p. 50

There are also less marked, yet still clear similarities between several other sayings of Khālid and Ibn al-Muqaffaʿ's *Adab*.[77]

Excluding the possibility of a common source as an unnecessary complication, as Khālid and Ibn al-Muqaffaʿ were contemporaries in the same town and quite possibly knew each other, one of the texts must have borrowed these sayings from the other. As the textual tradition of the Khālid corpus, and of these particular sayings, is less solid than the transmission of the *Adab*, it would seem more probable that these sayings have strayed from Ibn al-Muqaffaʿ's

---

76 Note that *taḥiyya* and *taḥannun* are only orthographic variants, with *taḥiyya* clearly making better sense. On the other hand, the reading *damaka wa-mālaka* in the *Adab* seems superior to A72's *mālaka*, as the other objects of the imperatives come in pairs.

77 Cf. A78 and *Adab*, p. 35; A79 and *Adab*, p. 36, and A82 and *Adab*, pp. 60–62.

books over the years and been reattributed to Khālid. However, the possibility cannot be excluded that Ibn al-Muqaffaʿ received material orally from the Basran wit and appropriated some of his sayings inserting them into his written collection of wisdom sayings. Thus, it remains possible that Khālid is the author of these sayings. The historical Khālid could also have quoted sayings coined by Ibn al-Muqaffaʿ.

Some of these sayings have *isnāds* that may shed some more light on the relations of the texts. A72 is only preceded by an anonymous *qāla*, but this most probably refers back to an earlier saying on the same page, A80a, where the *isnād* ends with < al-Aṣmaʿī < al-ʿAlāʾ ibn Jarīr.[78] A78 has in Ibn ʿAsākir's *Taʾrīkh* an *isnād* ending in < al-Aṣmaʿī < ʿAbd al-Ṣamad ibn Shabīb,[79] and A79 has in the same source an *isnād* ending in < ʿAbd al-Ṣamad ibn Shabīb, with no mention of al-Aṣmaʿī. Thus, if we trust the *isnāds*, four of the five cases are transmitted through al-Aṣmaʿī,[80] and two of these further through a son of Shabīb ibn Shayba, which would speak in favour of an early attribution of these sayings to Khālid, which, of course, does not prove that they would not have been taken into his sayings early on or even been borrowed by Khālid himself from Ibn al-Muqaffaʿ.

2.4 Khālid as Storyteller and Transmitter of Poetry

Although Khālid is best documented as an orator, a wit, and a literary character, he also had some fame as a storyteller and historian. Thus, e.g., Ibn ʿAsākir mentions that Khālid was famous for "transmission of stories" (*riwāyat al-akhbār*) and used to sit together with Hishām ibn ʿAbd al-Malik and Khālid ibn Yazīd (sic) al-Qasrī.[81] Al-Raqīq al-Qayrawānī further claims Khālid to have been on very intimate terms with al-Saffāḥ, because of his vast repertoire of stories (*li-… kathrat riwāyatihi*), again showing Khālid as a storyteller or transmitter

78 A Basran historian and traditionist, transmitting material in, e.g., al-Iṣfahānī, *Aghānī* VII: 39, 63–64, 172, and al-Ṭabarī, *Taʾrīkh* II: 1251/ XXIII: 198.

79 Ibn ʿAsākir, *Taʾrīkh* XVI: 111.

80 A72, A78, A80a, A82.

81 Ibn ʿAsākir, *Taʾrīkh* XVI: 94 (> Ibn al-ʿAdīm, *Bughya* VII: 75). Ibn al-ʿAdīm, *Bughya* VII: 49, locates the meeting(s) with Hishām at al-Ruṣāfa. Cf. further al-Ṣafadī, *Wāfī* XIII: 255. Khālid ibn Yazīd al-Qasrī is probably a mistake for Khālid ibn ʿAbdallāh al-Qasrī, possibly inspired by Khālid ibn Yazīd ibn al-Muhallab. While Khālid ibn Ṣafwān meets Yazīd ibn al-Muhallab in several anecdotes (cf. Index of personal names), the latter's son Khālid is otherwise not attested in the corpus. Yazīd ibn Khālid ibn ʿAbdallāh al-Qasrī is only mentioned in passing in B40a and, being a less well-known character, is probably not intended here.

of historical material.[82] Al-Ḥuṣrī mentions that Khālid knew (*kāna ... ḥāfiẓan*) stories of (early) Islam and the days of the *fitan*, the days of the Caliphs, anecdotes (*nawādir*) concerning transmitters (*ruwāt*), and all that *ahl al-adab* are trading in (*kull mā taṣrif fīhi ahl al-adab*).[83]

In A1, the first ʿAbbāsid Caliph, Abū l-ʿAbbās, is made to say: "[w]hen we want to know something about Tamīm or Persia and the Persians (*ʿulūm Fārs wa'l-ʿajam*) we go to Khālid ibn Ṣafwān." Even though Khālid is here specifically credited with transmitting Persian lore, this is not quite substantiated in the anecdotes about him.

Discussing B101, though, al-Masʿūdī says that after his famous sentence about tanners and weavers Khālid went on to expostulate on the blame of the South Arabs, finishing with the story of how the Ethiopians conquered their country and how the Persians enslaved them.[84] Though this end to al-Masʿūdī's version may well have been freely invented, it fits Khālid's reputation as an important transmitter of historical stories.[85] The story of al-Khawarnaq, B38, which is perhaps the most commonly attested longer story about Khālid, also refers to the Persians, even though the story itself comes from Arab lore.

The first part of the Caliph's comment in A1 is, on the other hand, well documented. The preserved stories abundantly document Khālid's interest in, and knowledge of, Basran history, and especially the role of his fellow Tamīmīs in it, as well as his encounters with his contemporaries, but other parts of historical lore are only rarely transmitted on his authority. Even a case like A2 on Shabath ibn Ribʿī, Sajāḥi's muezzin, turns out to be part of the tribal lore of Tamīm, rather than a *ridda* story as such, as both Sajāḥi and Shabath were Tamīmīs.[86]

In most cases where Khālid transmits historical material, he is either taking part in the action or the focus of the story is the witty comment by Khālid, with the strictly historical material being given as the background for Khālid's saying. Al-Jāḥiẓ reports a rare case in which Khālid acts as a pure transmitter, Shabīb ibn Shayba transmitting from him a long speech (*khuṭba*) delivered in Wāsiṭ by Yazīd ibn al-Muhallab, Khālid having been an eyewitness to the event.[87]

With one exception, Khālid, while telling stories about the past, never uses an *isnād*, being more of a storyteller than a proper historian. Ibn al-ʿAdīm

---

82 Al-Raqīq al-Qayrawānī, *Quṭb*, p. 325 (a version of A24). Cf. also B3.
83 Al-Ḥuṣrī, *Zahr*, p. 954.
84 Al-Masʿūdī, *Murūj* §1257.
85 See also al-Balādhurī, *Ansāb* III: 169; al-Ḥuṣrī, *Zahr*, p. 954. Cf. also Lecker (2005): 72–73.
86 See *EI2*, s.v. Sadjāḥi (V. Vacca) and Donner (1993): 95, note 629. Al-Madā'inī wrote on the *ridda*, too, see Lindstedt (2013) I: 16 = (2012–14): 253.
87 Al-Jāḥiẓ, *Bayān* I: 292–293.

does say that Khālid transmitted from Maymūn ibn Mihrān al-Jazarī,[88] but the only example I have been able to find is a story about ʿUmar ibn al-ʿAzīz and Maymūn, narrated by the latter in Ibn ʿAsākir's *Taʾrīkh*, and transmitted by Khālid.[89] Otherwise, Maymūn's name is not found in connection with Khālid. It is probable that this transmission relation owes more to Ibn al-ʿAdīm's will to find at least one teacher of Khālid's, as listing someone's teachers and students was a standard part of a biographical article.

There is also one single mention of Khālid transmitting from Zayd ibn ʿAlī, the Prophet's great-grandson who died in 122/740.[90]

It is clear that Khālid was not a historian in the sense of some of his contemporaries, who lectured on history in mosques and, though not writing books in the same sense as later historians, yet had their lectures disseminated through students' lecture notes. Khālid resembles more the *qāṣṣ*, semipopular religious storyteller.[91]

On the other hand, Khālid himself appears in *isnāds* of later transmitters. Thus, e.g., Ibn ʿAsākir relates that Shabīb ibn Shayba transmitted stories from Khālid.[92] Ibn al-ʿAdīm adds the names of Ḥafṣ ibn Ghiyāth, Yūnus al-Naḥwī, Ibrāhīm ibn Saʿd,[93] and al-Mughīra ibn Muṭarrif as transmitters from Khālid, which would make Khālid a transmitter of historical material.[94] However, these transmitted stories are, as far as we can see, mostly about Khālid himself, not stories merely narrated by him, so he is more an authority of his own life than an informant used by historians.

The first three transmitters on Ibn al-ʿAdīm's list are attested in the *isnāds* of some stories in the Khālid corpus as first transmitters from Khālid. The fourth, however, al-Mughīra ibn Muṭarrif, is linked to Khālid only in the abovementioned passage on ʿUmar ibn al-ʿAzīz in Ibn ʿAsākir's *Taʾrīkh*,[95] here written al-Mughīra ibn al-Muẓarraf al-Wāsiṭī, so that not only a "teacher" of Khālid, but also one of his few "students" may have been taken from one single story.

88 Ibn al-ʿAdīm, *Bughya* VII: 49. Maymūn was an early historian, who died in 117/735, see *EI2*, s.v. (F. Donner), Borrut (2001): 44, and Ibn Qutayba, *Maʿārif*, pp. 448–449.

89 Ibn ʿAsākir, *Taʾrīkh* XLV: 232; also found in Ibn al-Jawzī, *Sīra*, pp. 182–183.

90 See Kohlberg (1992): 319 (no. 514) and cf. al-Bukhārī, *Taʾrīkh* III: 156, quoted in Chapter 2.2.1. For Zayd, see *EI2*, s.v. (W. Madelung).

91 For *quṣṣāṣ*, see Armstrong (2017).

92 Ibn ʿAsākir, *Taʾrīkh* XVI: 94. A clear case where Shabīb transmits from Khālid comes in al-Jāḥiẓ, *Bayān* I: 292–293, where Khālid narrates a *khuṭba* given by Yazīd ibn al-Muhallab in Wāsiṭ.

93 For Ibrāhīm ibn Saʿd, see also al-Dhahabī, *Siyar* VI: 226.

94 Ibn al-ʿAdīm, *Bughya* VII: 49.

95 Ibn ʿAsākir, *Taʾrīkh* XLV: 232. This part of the *isnād* is missing from Ibn al-Jawzī, *Sīra*, pp. 182–183.

Moreover, in al-Jāḥiẓ's *Bayān* the same al-Mughīra ibn Muṭarrif transmits from Shuʿayb ibn Ṣafwān,[96] further undermining the credibility of Khālid as a regular link in the transmission of historical information.

Khālid ibn Ṣafwān has sometimes also been seen as a minor poet, due to confusion with Khālid al-Qannāṣ. This mistake is made both by Brockelmann and Sezgin,[97] while Blachère, Ullmann, and Pellat refute the identification, as does, implicitly, al-Maymanī.[98] The identification of the two is baseless: the orator Khālid is never called "al-Qannāṣ" and there is some doubt about the name of al-Qannāṣ's father, as in al-Ṣafadī's *Wāfī* the poet is called Khālid ibn Abān Abū l-Haytham, not ibn Ṣafwān.[99] Besides, the poet's date remains unknown and, based on stylistic features, his poems should rather be dated somewhat later than Khālid ibn Ṣafwān (d. 135/752).

A52, which Sezgin refers to, does mention Khālid as a poet but only in a very offhand manner and without substantiating the claim in any way ("Al-Aṣmaʿī has said: The misers of the Arabs are four, all of them poets: al-Ḥuṭayʾa, Ḥumayd al-Arqaṭ al-Saʿdī, Abū l-Aswad al-Duʾalī and Khālid ibn Ṣafwān al-Tamīmī").[100] Yāqūt and al-Iṣfahānī give the same list (both < Abū ʿUbayda) but without claiming the four misers to have been poets.[101]

Contrary to the vague reference to Khālid as a poet, al-Mubarrad explicitly says that Khālid did not compose verses,[102] and the huge majority of the stories have no connection with poetry at all or present Khālid only as quoting verses whose author can be identified. These are never implied to be his own verses. In some cases, they remain anonymous, but there is little reason to assume that Khālid was the author of a verse he quotes merely because we cannot identify its author. Al-Marzubānī does make this mistake, though, attributing an anonymous verse to Khālid, who, in fact, seems merely to be quoting it.[103]

While there are numerous stories where the Qurʾān is quoted or alluded to, poetry seems much less prominent. Khālid does quote individual verses or

---

96 Al-Jāḥiẓ, *Bayān* II: 120. For Shuʿayb ibn Ṣafwān, see al-Jāḥiẓ, *Bayān* II: 59, note 2.

97 *GAL* S I:93; *GAS* II: 462–463. Sezgin's reference to Ibn Khallikān is wrong, and I cannot locate it in my copies of Ibn Khallikān's *Wafayāt*.

98 Blachère (1952–66): 511; Ullmann (1966): 48; *EI2*, s.v. Khālid ibn Ṣafwān (Ch. Pellat); al-Maymanī (1937): 102.

99 Al-Ṣafadī, *Wāfī* XIII: 247. Note also that the orator never has the *kunya* Abū l-Haytham.

100 From al-Marzubānī, *Nūr*, pp. 146–147 (no. 150).

101 Yāqūt, *Irshād* III: 267, and al-Iṣfahānī, *Aghānī* II: 46.

102 Al-Mubarrad, *Kāmil* II: 44 (B83a).

103 Al-Marzubānī, *Muwashshaḥ*, p. 22. The misattribution is also found in Qudāma, *Naqd*, no. 655, whereas al-Jurjānī, *Asrār*, p. 154, gives it as anonymous. Cf. also Ritter (1959): 131, note 91.

hemistichs in a number of stories,[104] but in only one, B38, is he depicted as quoting a longer excerpt from a poem, which further confirms Khālid's lack of interest in poetry. As B38 is one of the most often transmitted long speeches of Khālid, it may gain inappropriate prominence, though.

In some anecdotes, at least A99, A107, and A108, Khālid is quoting verses in a manner that does not exclude the possibility that the verses might be his own. Mostly, however, the poetic quotations are light verses that do not reflect any serious interest in poetry, and even though it cannot be proven, it remains more probable that even these cases are to be taken as Khālid quoting verses by others or a later author putting these doggerel verses into his mouth when modifying or creating a story rather than Khālid quoting any verses of his own. Even if they were his, these simple verses would not justify taking Khālid to have been a poet.

As shown in Chapter 1.3.2, Khālid is sometimes, though not often, depicted in the company of poets and once, A4, shown as giving eloquent criticism on contemporary and slightly earlier poets, but the anecdote is unique and of rather dubious authenticity.

All said, Khālid seems to be less often connected with poetry than many of his contemporaries, and there is neither reason to identify him with Khālid al-Qannāṣ nor to see him as a poet in his own right.

2.5 Anecdotes as Early ʿAbbāsid Prose

Khālid anecdotes are stories about Khālid, not stories authored by him. However, in some of them he appears as a storyteller.[105] If we take this at face value, ignoring all questions of authenticity, this would mean that in their final form these anecdotes were authored by Khālid, whether or not they narrated events that had really taken place.

This would obviously be a naive reading of the anecdotes. In some cases, as in A24,[106] we can show that the final versions where Khālid appears as the narrator are, in fact, later inventions, sometimes based on earlier materials. When Khālid appears as the first-person narrator in A24, it is merely a narrative technique adopted by the anonymous author who created this story, and the real, historical Khālid had nothing to do with the final version. It should also be

104 B7 (=B9b, B9c, B108), B9b, B38, B45a, B64, B75, B81, B87, B94, B98, B102; A5, A12, A18, A48, A49, A52, A95, A107, A108.

105 Cf. Chapter 2.4.

106 See Chapter 2.5.1.

clear that in the majority of cases where this cannot be proven it still remains the default supposition: most probably, the use of Khālid as a first-person narrator in the final form of the story is always a literary technique. Even though the story might go back to what Khālid himself had once narrated, the final form it has received is hardly from Khālid, perhaps contrary to the case of the maxims and sayings that are often in the core of the story and may, indeed, in some cases go back to Khālid more or less in the form they appear in the preserved texts.[107]

There is no evidence that Khālid ibn Ṣafwān would ever have written anything, and the stories about him do not imply him to have been literate: no letters of his are mentioned in the stories, nor do we find him reading books or even playing with dotted and undotted letters in his witty sayings: all wordplays are based on the phonetic, not orthographic, similarity of the words. The only exception to this is B99b, where Ṣāliḥ ibn Shaykh ibn ʿAmīra tells in early 217/832 a story about his grandfather. This story involves correspondence between the grandfather and Khālid about a cousin of Khālid's. This long story relates to the short stories B99 and B99a, where Khālid uses the same witty saying when speaking to his cousin (B99) or to an anonymous man. Even if we accepted the story as strictly historical, there would still remain a gap of more than 80 years between the situation where this is narrated and the event itself, so this would only tell us about ideas or vague reminiscences people of the 830s had about the literacy of people living in the first half of the eighth century.

Hence, we cannot properly speak of Khālid as an author in the strict sense of later, literary cultures. Yet, in the stories about him he is presented as giving public speeches, coining pithy sayings that remained in use as maxims, and extemporising on various topics, which give him some claim of being an oral author.

Some technical features of Khālid's sayings have already been studied.[108] As al-Balādhurī's article on Khālid[109] has some claim of representing a relatively early layer of the material, examples were primarily taken from there and only supplemented by material from other sources when necessary.

Despite Khālid not being the author of the anecdotes, the inherent literary value of some of them makes it worthwhile to study them in some detail. This chapter will study some of the anecdotes where Khālid is one of the characters. Some of these are narrated in the first person singular, but most are told in the third person. As the anecdotes have in any case most probably undergone

---

107 Cf. Chapter 2.3.1.

108 See Chapters 2.3 and 2.3.1.

109 Al-Balādhurī, *Ansāb* VII/1: 55–88.

various developments since Khālid's time, examples are also taken from later material, which sometimes exemplifies the growth and development of the anecdotes better than the versions in al-Balādhurī's *Ansāb*.

Strictly speaking, Khālid is not mentioned in a single Umayyad, or even eighth-century ʿAbbāsid, source. All information we have about him comes from later sources, which also means that the final form of the anecdotes that we can study always considerably postdates Khālid himself. This chapter will study Khālid anecdotes and their development in an attempt to see how they have changed during transmission and to understand the mechanisms of change in anecdotal literature using the Khālid corpus as a case study.

In Classical Arabic literature anecdotes (often called *nawādir*) are short, independent microunits that are not related, except often thematically, to the surrounding context, whether this be other anedotes or microunits of different genres (maxims, poetic or Qurʾānic verses, etc.). At its very shortest, an anecdote may consist of minimal context (e.g., "Khālid said") and the witty saying of the main character given as the punchline.

Mostly, anecdotes consist of only one episode, but sometimes episodes are combined with each other to produce a longer anecdote with two or three, rarely more, separate episodes.

The great majority of Khālid stories are short anecdotes consisting of one episode.[110] In most, Khālid is shown as the protagonist, but in some he is a secondary character and the limelight is on some other character. Thus, in B7, duplicated by B9 and B108, Khālid is dumbfounded after his witticism ("A summer cloud that will soon disperse") is devastatingly answered by Bilāl ibn abī Burda with "not ere it hits you with a downpour of hail," the last word (and the last action, Khālid being whipped thereafter) remaining thus with Bilāl and the expected verbal victory of Khālid turning into a complete defeat. The protagonist of this story is Bilāl, not Khālid. B8 and B8a partly duplicate the version of B9, but here the protagonist is Khālid, whose insulting comment on Bilāl is given without Bilāl having an opportunity to retaliate.

Likewise, in B30, playing with Qurʾānic quotations, it is al-Farazdaq who gets the last word, and Khālid remains a secondary character, as he also does in B40, where Khālid al-Qasrī is in the focus, and the Caliph Hishām is the one whose final eloquent comment is the punchline to which the story has been building.

---

110 Note, however, that al-Ḥuṣrī, *Zahr*, pp. 93–94, mentions long stories about/by Khālid, but adds that he will not transmit these (*wa-lam adhhab fī hādhā l-ikhtiyār ilā muṭawwalāt al-akhbār ka-aḥādīth Ibn Ṣūḥān wa-Khālid ibn Ṣafwān wa-naẓāʾirihimā*) due to the nature of his compilatory work.

In B66 ("Eloquence lies not in an easy tongue and a lot of blabbering, but in hitting the point and getting at the right argument"), Khālid defines eloquence in a contextless saying. B66a changes this, possibly through contamination with B91, into a dialogue where an anonymous person gets the final word (The Qurashī said: "Abū Ṣafwān, I am not aware of having committed any sin against you, except for sharing the same profession") and, thus, pushes Khālid into a secondary position, which completely changes the tone of the saying. In B66, Khālid's saying is given as pondered, wise speech, in B66a it becomes a jealous attempt to pull down a fellow orator. B70 also pushes Khālid into the background and lets Durust ibn Ribāṭ get the final say (Khālid said: "We have seen no place like al-Ubulla which would be closer, of a sweeter draught, or a better hideout for a servant of God." Durust ibn Ribāṭ said to this: "Why, then, are distances traversed towards Mecca?"), while B70a only gives Khālid's words and lets him enjoy the limelight. Thus, small changes in the story redefine its focal point and lead to a completely new reading.

It is usually hard and in practice impossible to prove that a certain story would be an authentic record of a moment in Khālid's life, but early and strong attestation and the presence of historical but soon forgotten characters, like Durust ibn Ribāṭ, make it probable that an anecdote has been attached to Khālid's name early on, and some such anecdotes may indeed retain memories of the historical Khālid.

It is easier to prove the contrary, namely that an anecdote in all probability does not derive from the time of Khālid himself. Chapters 2.5.1 and 2.5.2 will show how anecdotes are sometimes combined with each other and the resulting anecdote is, clearly, not authentic in any sense. In other cases, such as B60 ("When he received his stipend (*jā'iza*) Khālid used to say to dirhams: By God, you have travelled long days in various countries and on highlands. Now, by God, I will make you lie down and repose for a long time") it is difficult to understand what the real Sitz im Leben would have been, Khālid playing the role of a miser and fondly addressing his dirhams, which in the eighth century would have been contrary to all good manners expected from a man in Khālid's position. Thus, even though the anecdote is widely documented and attested in relatively early sources, it is difficult to accept that it is historical in any sense.[111]

111 The only way to defend its historicity would be to take it as ironical.

2.5.1 *Building Up Stories 1: A24* (Khālid and Umm Salama)

Among the Khālid stories told by al-Madāʾinī there are some that are of considerable length, the longest being B38 and B82. These stories are more focused on the use of language, however, than on developing narrative structures.

In the remaining part of the corpus, there are a number of other long stories, the most interesting of which is A24, a story of Khālid's encounter with the Caliph's wife, Umm Salama. Told in brief, A24 describes how when alone with him Khālid told the Caliph al-Saffāḥ about the pleasures of marrying several wives and taking concubines – the Caliph is said to have been in a monogamous relationship with Umm Salama.

When Khālid left, Umm Salama managed to force the Caliph to tell her what had happened and, enraged, sent some of her servants to beat Khālid up. Some days later, Khālid was summoned back to the Caliph and asked to repeat his earlier speech. Even though the two were again alone, Khālid soon realised that Umm Salama was overhearing them from behind a curtain and reversed the tables by severely asserting that the Caliph should be satisfied with one wife, the splendid Umm Salama. The story ends with Khālid leaving the two and Umm Salama sending him a gift.

Most of the stories in the corpus, however, are rather brief. Two such brief stories deserve our attention in the light of what later became of them when they were used to build A24. The first (B16) reads:

> < *al-Madāʾinī* < *ʿAdī ibn al-Faḍl*: Khālid said: "Do not take one wife, because when she menstruates, you menstruate with her, and when she lies in childbed, you will be there, too. When she visits someone or travels away or is sick, it is the same with you. Do not take two wives because then you will be between two evils. Do not take three wives because then you will be (as a cauldron boiling) upon three stones. Do not take four wives because then they will exhaust you (sexually) and make you old and penniless." Ibn Ribāṭ al-Fuqaymī said to him: "You have forbidden everything that God has permitted!"[112] Khālid replied: "Better than all this is (to have) two loaves, two old rags, two jugs (of water) and to worship the Merciful."[113]

The story presents Khālid as speaking against marriage in general but here he is not so much a misogynist as he is in some other stories.[114] In this anecdote

---

112 Cf. Q 66: 1.

113 Khālid's last words also circulated as a separate saying, see B12.

114 Cf. Chapter 2.2.3.

his adverse attitude towards women is explained in his final words by his piety and asceticism, which are recurrent themes in Khālid stories. Mostly, however, his frugal life style is related to his meanness, not to a nobler characteristic, and we may perhaps assume that here, too, there is at least a hint at avarice.[115]

The story is told with little context. His interlocutor, (Durust) ibn Ribāṭ al-Fuqaymī, is a little-known contemporary of Khālid. He is mentioned in a few anecdotes in connection with the same persons whom we know to have been acquainted with Khālid.[116] Thus, there is nothing inherently unhistorical in the anecdote: moving around in the same society, the two would probably have known each other. Had they not met each other, one cannot easily see what motive there would have been for connecting Khālid with a person scarcely known by later generations. Thus, we may, *a priori*, accept the story as potentially historical, even if it may have undergone changes during the period of its oral, or even literary, circulation. The sayings of Khālid are also brief enough not to tax the memory of the narrators. If Khālid did not say exactly what the anecdote claims him to have said, he may well have said something like it. And his interlocutor may well have been Ibn Ribāṭ.

As such, the saying fits well with the pithy nature of most of Khālid's sayings. We may easily conceive this piece having been received as such by al-Madāʾinī from his informant, ʿAdī ibn al-Faḍl.[117] Naturally, though, we cannot prove that it was not a fragment of a longer story, which has otherwise been lost. Yet there is no obvious reason as to why the historian al-Madāʾinī would have left out its context, especially if it originally involved a Caliph or some other well-known person.

The second noteworthy story is B24:[118]

> < *al-Madāʾinī* < *Ibrāhīm ibn al-Mubārak*: The Commander of the Believers, Abū l-ʿAbbās said to Khālid ibn Ṣafwān: "People have said so much about women! What kind of woman pleases you most?" Khālid replied: "O Commander of the Believers, I like best a woman who is neither a skinny young thing nor big and decrepit. As to her beauty, it is enough that she looks great from afar, pretty from near, her upper part a leafless palm branch and her lower part a sandhill. She shall have been nurtured

115 Note especially the last item in Khālid's speech against marrying: wives will make him penniless.

116 Al-Jāḥiẓ, *Bayān* II: 166 (> al-Ābī, *Nathr* II: 192), on the authority of al-Aṣmaʿī, mentions him having visited Bilāl ibn abī Burda when the latter was imprisoned. In *Bayān* II, 284, there is an invective verse on Ibn Ribāṭ by al-Farazdaq. Cf. Chapter 1.3.2.

117 For ʿAdī ibn al-Faḍl Abū Ḥātim al-Baṣrī (d. 171/787), see al-Ṣafadī, *Wāfī* XIX: 534.

118 Cf. also B23 and B25.

> in wealth, but then need shall have befallen her, so that wealth has educated her and poverty made humble. She shall be seductive towards her husband, but chaste towards her neighbour. When we are alone, we are people of this world, but when we are separated from each other, we are people of the world to come."

This passage is unrelated to B16. Even al-Madāʾinī's informant in this story is different from that in B16, so that we cannot easily derive the two from a larger, fragmented story. Here Khālid, on the Caliph's order, describes his dream woman in a way that is similar in tenour to his speech in A24, to which we shall soon turn, although in details the two descriptions of women have little in common.

Read together, the two anecdotes combine to make a story of *maḥāsin wa-masāwī*, or *pro et contra*, the first speaking against marriage, the second, if not expressly in its favour, then at least in a positive tone about it. Yet in al-Madāʾinī's monograph they are given separately, the only common denominator being the identity of the protagonist. The passage against marriage is contextualised as a mini-sermon to a friend of Khālid, Ibn Ribāṭ, the voluptuous description of a lady is set in the court of the Caliph al-Saffāḥ. No mention is made of the Caliph's wife, Umm Salama.

Both stories are written in elegant language but neither of them would deserve much attention as such. Completely unrelated to them, there is in the *Ṣaḥīḥ* of al-Bukhārī a *ḥadīth* (no. 4913)[119] involving another Umm Salama, one of the wives of the Prophet. This *ḥadīth*,[120] cognate with another (no. 5191), belongs to a cycle relating to, and explaining, Q 66: 1–5, the passage beginning with: "Prophet, why do you prohibit that which God has made lawful to you, in seeking to please your wives. God is forgiving and merciful."[121]

In this particular *ḥadīth*, ʿUmar ibn al-Khaṭṭāb is displayed as worried when he hears that some of the wives of the Prophet are not quiet and obedient but cause their husband trouble. He comes to learn this when his own wife meddles, as he thinks, in his business and she defends her behaviour by referring to the Prophet's homelife: times have changed with Islam and women have their say in family matters. When ʿUmar goes to see his daughter, the Prophet's wife, Ḥafṣa, he learns that the wives of the Prophet do really sometimes oppose their husband. After leaving Ḥafṣa, he next visits Umm Salama, who turns out to be a lady with firm opinions. Having heard what ʿUmar is up to, she exclaims:

---

119 *Kitāb Tafsīr al-Qurʾān, bāb Sūrat al-Taḥrīm 1–2.*

120 Studied in more detail in Akar (2006): 76.

121 The translation is based on Dawood (1956).

"You are a wonder (*ʿajaban laka*), Ibn al-Khaṭṭāb, you put your nose (*dakhalta fī*) in everything! And now you want to come between the Apostle of God and his wives!" Umm Salama makes it clear that she does not welcome any busybodies wishing to influence her husband and his relations with his wives.

Dumbfounded, ʿUmar leaves her. The rest of the *ḥadīth* need not detain us any longer, except for the end. After having been absent for a while, ʿUmar comes to see the Prophet and finds him lying on a reed mat with no cushions to soften it, so that the imprint of the reeds is clearly visible on his side. Seeing this, ʿUmar starts crying. When the Prophet asks the reason for his behaviour, he answers: "O Apostle of God, the Persian and Byzantine kings (*Kisrā wa-Qayṣar*) have all their luxuries (*fīmā humā fīhi*). You are the Apostle of God, (yet you live in such poor conditions)!" The Prophet said: "Does it not satisfy you that they have this world, but we have the next world?" Thus, the *ḥadīth* also contrasts the ascetic behaviour of the Prophet with the luxuries of earthly rulers.

With this, the *ḥadīth* comes to an end. It is explicitly related to the position of women and their behaviour towards their husbands, and it is given to explain the background of a Qurʾānic verse which asks why the Prophet prohibits that which God has made lawful to him.

That the *ḥadīth* circulated by the time of Khālid in Basra, seems to be proven by Ibn al-Jawzī, *Ādāb*, p. 67. This confirms that the elements from which this story was composed were present in Basra in the late eighth century.

An unknown author seems to have detected the similarities between the situation of al-Saffāḥ, the mighty Caliph, reputedly monogamously married to Umm Salama, and the Prophet Muḥammad, also married to an Umm Salama, whose relations with his wives were the reason for revealing a Qurʾānic verse. Likewise, this author realised that there is something similar between the behaviour of the courtier Khālid ibn Ṣafwān describing women to the Caliph and that of ʿUmar ibn al-Khaṭṭāb in his role as an outsider coming between the Prophet and his wives.

We have no way of knowing who this author was. What we do know is that some time before the middle of the tenth century a longer story *Khālid and Umm Salama* (A24) had emerged. This story involves Khālid, the Caliph al-Saffāḥ, and Umm Salama, the wife of the Caliph, and it was enthusiastically received by other literati. The earliest extant sources for this story are al-Masʿūdī's (d. 345/956) *Murūj* and al-Bayhaqī's (early fourth/tenth century) *Maḥāsin*. The two versions deviate from each other so widely that they have to be taken as independent versions, making it less probable that either of their authors would have been the first author of *Khālid and Umm Salama*. Had one of them been its first author, the other should have received the story from a written and well-known contemporary source and would perhaps have been less ready to modify it at will.[122] There is also a third version, found in Ibn Badrūn's (early sixth/twelfth century) *Sharḥ*, which can be derived from neither al-Masʿūdī nor al-Bayhaqī. Other attestations in various sources are derivable either from al-Bayhaqī or, more often, al-Masʿūdī.

Khālid and Umm Salama contains elements from the *ḥadīth* no. 4913, B16, and B24. It hardly has any historical background, as it turns up rather late and elements of it are found in other contexts in al-Madāʾinī's monograph on Khālid. In addition, one would be hard pressed to explain why the story should have been cut into pieces and one piece set in a context involving an obscure Ibn Ribāṭ. The reverse development is, of course, most understandable. *Khālid and Umm Salama* has to be considered a fictitious narrative, though based on historical sources and ascribed to historical characters. Thus, it merits analysis as an independent piece of fictitious literature, not as a historical report. That it, and similar long anecdotes, have received but little attention seems at least partly due to the anonymity of their authors: we do not know the name of the author who first created this story from various elements and we cannot even be certain whether al-Masʿūdī and al-Bayhaqī are responsible for the versions attested in their books or whether they merely put down a version they found in an earlier source.

Yet a closer look at many such long anecdotes will show that in Classical Arabic *adab* literature prose narratives do exist that have been constructed with care and that exhibit a creative, though anonymous genius. Let us study the case of *Khālid and Umm Salama* more closely. For translation, the reader is referred to Chapter 3 (A24).

Khālid and Umm Salama is a long and elaborate story in comparison to the mostly brief anecdotes in al-Balādhurī's *Ansāb*, many of which derive from al-Madāʾinī's lost work. Al-Madāʾinī was a historian, and his stories aim at reporting what he thought the historical Khālid had said or done in various situations, even though he may well have embellished or elaborated his sources. Obviously, too, al-Madāʾinī not only wanted to educate but also to entertain, these two being the cornerstones of *adab*, but he did this within the limits of historical reports. Anecdotes, witty sayings, and speeches form the material of al-Madāʾinī, and though the authenticity of the speeches may be doubted, one may easily accept that al-Madāʾinī worked more or less *bona fide*, recording what material was circulating about Khālid by his time.

---

122 Let it be added that it is immaterial whether the first author of A24 was al-Masʿūdī, al-Bayhaqī, or some anonymous author. The present analysis concentrates on how the anecdote was created and how it is structured, not on who its author was.

The anonymous author of *Khālid and Umm Salama* worked in a different way. Whereas al-Madāʾinī was a historian, our author freely created a piece of fictitious literature. He must have been aware that what he tells is not the historical truth and that he is dealing very liberally with his sources. In using the *ḥadīth* no. 4913 as his intertext and in creating a story around the figures of Khālid and Umm Salama, the wife of al-Saffāḥ, he consciously stepped outside of the historical into the fictitious. Historical material provided him with usable elements but from these he freely created a new story. His relation to his historical, or would-be historical, sources was probably the same as Shakespeare's: we are not to take Shakespeare's history plays as accurate versions of history as understood at his time but as free elaborations only vaguely based on the historical sources the author was using.

The author of *Khālid and Umm Salama* substituted the more famous protagonist, the Caliph Abū l-ʿAbbās al-Saffāḥ, for the scarcely-known Ibn Ribāṭ of B16. Incidentally, in some late versions Hārūn al-Rashīd, Lady Zubayda, and Abū Nuwās have been substituted for the original protagonists: it is a general tendency in *adab* and especially popular stories for famous characters to draw around themselves material that fits their character but originally derives from elsewhere.[123]

The author combined anecdotes that originally had nothing to do with each other. He perhaps noticed the opportunity provided by the name of the Caliph's wife being the same as that of the Prophet's, Umm Salama. He used this coincidence to play with a religious intertext, and selected Umm Salama, the wife of al-Saffāḥ, as another character for the story. The *ḥadīth* may even have inspired him to create the story in the first place.

When we turn to inspect the literary structures of, and devices used in, the story, we come across a wealth of features, beginning with subtle allusions and double-entendres and ranging to intertexts. We see that *Khālid and Umm Salama* is not a simple anecdote but an elaborate piece of literature with an intricate net of allusions and careful and subtle characterisation.

To start with, the author has selected the beginning of a speech by Khālid (B16), which in its original context is aimed against marriage in general. In *Khālid and Umm Salama* he turns the tables around: what originally was a speech against marriage is now introduced as an admonition against taking *only* one wife. This is achieved by postponing the rest of B16 to Khālid's second speech, where the further arguments of Khālid are used to create a case against marrying *more* than one wife.

---

123 Cf. Chapter 2.5.3.

The two parts of B16 have thus been separated from each other. They have been given two different foci, neither of which was found in the original. Instead of asceticism and celibacy, we find first polygamy and then monogamy exulted. The end of this latter part is close in tenour to the *maqāmāt al-ʿulamāʾ*, admonitions to persons in high positions, which are also attested in the Khālid corpus.[124] Thus, standing against a Caliph and opposing his base instincts was not unheard-of, though in the *maqāmāt al-ʿulamāʾ* it is, obviously, never the protagonist himself who kindles the flame of temptation to begin with. If we were to read *Khālid and Umm Salama* in the framework of *maqāmāt al-ʿulamāʾ*, it would sound like a parody, the same person first leading the Caliph into temptation and then criticising him for falling into it.

The protagonists of *Khālid and Umm Salama* have been given specific characterisations, which make them alive and distinct, unlike the stereotypical characters found in many anecdotes. The Caliph is described as a person wide open to influence. In the beginning, he seems to be quite satisfied with his life with just one wife, but once Khālid has had his say, the idea of polygamy begins to haunt the Caliph's mind. When she later enters, Umm Salama finds her husband "deep in thought and looking worried."[125] It seems that the ascetic feature of monogamy – when all the lovely young women would be available – is not so much al-Saffāḥ's conscious choice, as the avoidance of luxury by the Prophet is certainly to be understood to be in the *ḥadīth*, but something he has merely accepted without a second thought: the active role must have fallen to his energetic wife, Umm Salama.[126]

Once reminded of the pleasures of polygamy, al-Saffāḥ, contrary to the example set by the Prophet, whose successor as the head of the community (*khalīfa*) he was, is tempted by it. Far from being content with leaving the luxury to others and claiming the world to come as his, he wants his share of the luxury once his courtier has pointed it out for him. Ironically enough, the Caliph himself refers, though only rhetorically, to the ties between himself and the Prophet being severed ("May I be absolved …"). In fact, it is his own morally

---

124 See Chapter 2.2.4.

125 Incidentally, this resembles the beginning of the *ḥadīth* no. 4913, where the wife of ʿUmar ibn al-Khaṭṭāb comes in and finds her husband pondering on some matter of importance. When she volunteers her opinion, the story is set in motion.

126 Note that this is not a historical fact but the implicit context of the fictitious *Khālid and Umm Salama*. According to a (probably fictitious) story in al-Masʿūdī, *Murūj* §2326, al-Saffāḥ, after his recovery from temporary impotence during his wedding night with Umm Salama, swore not to marry other wives or to take concubines. Reading this in the light of A24, one might suggest that the idea was not his own but put into his head by Umm Salama.

ambivalent behaviour that absolves him, morally at least, from his relationship with the Prophet. Unknowingly, he pronounces his own verdict.

Yet even lust cannot entice the Caliph out of his passivity. He does not *do* anything in the story, except for wishing to hear the first speech again and again and uttering weak exclamations of wonder or indignation during the second speech. These exclamations, moreover, only incite Khālid to an escalating series of statements against polygamy and, in the end, to the exultation of Umm Salama along with respective criticism of the Caliph. After the first speech, the Caliph may be burning for these Basran and Kufan beauties, not to mention young concubines, yet he does not act. He does not reward his courtier, as the latter expected him to do. This is not spelled out in the story but is clearly to be inferred: it is the private army of Umm Salama that comes to see Khālid, not gift-bearers from the Caliph, and the latter, it should be emphasised, never appear on the scene, not even after the servants of Umm Salama have paid their nefarious visit to Khālid's house.

Later, the Caliph simply remains agape when Khālid impertinently lies to his face. The Caliph knows that the story went differently, but Khālid may fearlessly turn everything upside down: the Caliph does not punish him for his lies and impudence, as he should have done. He cannot push himself into any action, either rewarding or punishing the courtier.[127] And, naturally, he could not, on his own initiative, send for the belles Khālid had described.[128] His greatest feat is to send for Khālid to repeat his sweet description of girls. When at first he does not find his courtier, he can again do nothing more than send his servants to search for him, although, in fact, it was not Khālid the Caliph ultimately wanted but the beautiful girls. But to reach out for them was too much for him, at least without further incitement from Khālid.

The Caliph does not have one of the brightest minds, either. During his second speech, Khālid tries to hint at his real situation, at the same time insinuating that the behaviour of the Caliph himself is reprehensible, but the Caliph notices neither, since they are not spelled out by Khālid. In Arabic,

127 The phrase "may God kill you and put you to shame" may have yet another implication if taken literally (cf. note 904 to A24): instead of acting himself, al-Saffāḥ can only wish someone else would take the action, which in his lethargy he himself is unable to be involved in.

128 In the version of al-Bayhaqī, we have a very vivid picture of the Caliph "tapping (*yankut*) the inkwell in front of him with his pen," obviously totally absorbed in thoughts Khālid has implanted. Was he thinking of writing to his agents to procure the girls his verbose courtier had described to him? If he was, he never proceeded from thoughts to action but was waiting for Khālid to come and prompt him once more. For *yankut al-arḍ* as a sign of being absorbed in deep thought, cf., e.g., *Kalīla wa-Dimna*, p. 14.

Khālid's crucial phrase is ingeniously ambivalent. When he says "*wa-turīdu an taqtulanī*," *taqtulanī* may as well be the 2nd person masculine ("Do you want to kill me?") as the 3rd person feminine ("Do you want her to kill me?"). Khālid is making one last effort to wake up the Caliph. When this goes unnoticed, he rather openly moves over to side with Umm Salama.

In this phrase, there is also a clear allusion to Q 28: 19, where Moses is addressed by a man who fears for his life: *Yā Mūsā a-*turīdu an taqtulanī *kamā qatalta nafsan bi-l-amsi? In turīdu illā an takūna jabbāran fī l-arḍi wa-mā turīdu an takūna mina l-muṣliḥīn* ("Moses, *do you want to kill me* as you killed a person yesterday? You are surely seeking to be a tyrant in this land, not an upright man"). The subtle allusion evades the Caliph, who is not infuriated by Khālid actually insinuating that he is aspiring to become a tyrant, just as he did not realise that Khālid is desperately trying to refer to the secret presence behind the curtain. And when Umm Salama is, in the end, satisfied, and she and Khālid join forces, the Caliph can hardly do more than whine. The reader starts feeling that the Caliph in his impotence does not deserve the beautiful wives and concubines Khālid had been describing. In fact, in *Murūj* §2326, al-Masʿūdī does refer to al-Saffāḥ's reputed temporary impotence on his wedding night. Al-Saffāḥ's physical impotence is mirrored in his impotence in taking any independent action.

This can also be seen on a linguistic level. Al-Saffāḥ's lines mainly begin with weak exclamations. Out of his eleven lines in al-Masʿūdī's version, eight begin with exclamations (*wayḥaka* three times; *subḥāna llāh*; *bariʾtu*; *waylaka* twice; *mā laka qātalaka llāh*). Even the verbs used by him are usually intransitive or the subject is someone other than the Caliph (*mā ṣakka masāmiʿī*; *samiʿtu*; *waqaʿa minnī mawqiʿan*; *lam yakhriq masāmiʿī*). Umm Salama's lines, on the contrary, go directly to the point, and she uses pervasive questions, sovereign commands, and definitive statements (*la-unkiruka*; *hal ḥadatha*; *fa-mā qulta*; *ṣadaqta*; *ghayyara wa-baddala wa-naṭaqa*). Khālid is distinguished by his use of static nominal clauses, which by their nature do not express change, but describe a state.

The real Abū l-ʿAbbās al-Saffāḥ would have been quite a different person. In later literature he is generally described as brisk and active. This Abū l-ʿAbbās is described by al-Balādhurī in his *Ansāb* as follows:[129]

---

129 Al-Balādhurī, *Ansāb* III: 166 (< ʿUmar ibn Bukayr < al-Haytham < Ibn ʿAyyāsh). It is actually not relevant whether this represents the historical Caliph or not. What is important for the analysis of the story is that this represents the Caliph as the contemporaries of the redactors of this anecdote would have known him.

> Abū l-ʿAbbās was the most liberal of people. He never postponed something he had promised or left the *majlis* without fulfilling his promise.

Likewise, al-Thaʿlabī depicts him as a Caliph who rewards his entertainers and companions without the slightest delay.[130] This is the received image the audience of A24 would have had in mind and the behaviour of the Caliph here should be seen in this light. The change in his characterisation was purposefully made by the author of A24 and is, thus, highly significant: he is not using some traditional way of describing al-Saffāḥ as an inert daydreamer and weakling but is startling the reader by presenting a surprising characterisation. He is creating a character far removed from the historical person who bore the same name.[131]

Umm Salama, the Caliph's wife, on the other hand, is an active protagonist. Even before the story begins she has made her husband feel her influence and forego the pleasures of polygamy. Once she realises that there is something suspicious going on, she very determinedly first squeezes the story out of her husband and then quickly acts upon it, sending her servants with their *kāfirkūbāt* to beat the poor Khālid and to teach him a lesson. Later, when Khālid is confronted with both the Caliph – who is quite unaware of the presence of his wife – and Umm Salama, who dominates the situation from behind the curtains, Khālid knows who really is the boss in the house, or palace, and acts accordingly, giving no more than lame excuses to the Caliph. When the Caliph asks whether he calls him a liar, Khālid does not choose to answer properly but replies by asking his own question: "And do you want to kill me?" The reply is, on the surface, insolent ("well, if you don't like it, go ahead and kill me") and below the surface either again insolent (if the Caliph picks up the allusion to Moses) or a desperate call for help – which the Caliph, needless to say, does not notice. Nor does he realise that his wife is overhearing their discussion.

Here we are far from the atmosphere of the *ḥadīth* no. 4913. The *ḥadīth* grew out of an ultimatum from God (Q 66: 1–5) towards refractory wives and the well-known end of the story was the surrender of the wives to the will of God and His Prophet. When our story ends, the Caliph remains inert. Either he has not been following what happens and remains uncertain as to what is actually going on, or he is too weak to do anything when the conspiracy between Umm Salama and Khālid is laid bare before his, and the reader's, eyes.

---

130 Al-Thaʿlabī, *Tāj*, p. 40. For the identification of the author, usually quoted as ps.-al-Jāḥiẓ, see *EI2*, s.v. al-Thaʿlabī (Gr. Schoeler), and Schoeler (1980).

131 Occasionally, though, al-Saffāḥ is described in historical literature in less active terms, see Kennedy (1986): 128, so this description is not completely unique.

Khālid is right in siding with Umm Salama. Hardly has he returned home after his second speech, when Umm Salama's servants arrive, this time with gifts. Umm Salama knows how to use both the stick and the carrot. The Caliph should have done this very thing after the first speech but instead he began daydreaming. After his second speech, there is nothing for Khālid to be afraid of: no punitive expedition will be sent by the passive Caliph. Umm Salama is the active one in the palace, thus reversing the traditional roles of men and women. There were active ladies in the ʿAbbāsid palace but essentially it was a man's world. Thus, again, the author has reversed the expected situation and characterised a historical person in a novel way.[132]

Khālid, the courtier, is described as promoting his own interests. First he thinks that the Caliph is the right person to have on his side, but when he realises the power relations between him and Umm Salama, he loses no time in switching sides. He knows which way the wind blows. The Khālid of al-Madāʾinī and al-Balādhurī had been suspicious of women, finding divorce one of his greatest joys.[133] The protagonist of this story is, in the beginning, quite different, finding his pleasure in describing charming women.

On the other hand, Khālid's character is perhaps the truest to history of these three. In most sources, Khālid is described as being witty and quick to comprehend and to react; he had a way with words and loved describing things, be they women or something else. In this story, Khālid is shown meddling in business not his own and getting bettered by a woman. In many stories, he is likewise shown to lack premeditation, and this story can also be read as one of his many blunders, *hafawāt*, which is why Ibn Hilāl al-Ṣābiʾ included it in his *Hafawāt*.[134]

There is always a danger of over-interpretation but I would nevertheless like to draw attention to the parallelism in *Khālid and Umm Salama* and Q 66: 1 between the role of Khālid and that of God. What Khālid starts with is to take God's role in admonishing the Caliph to do as the Prophet was admonished to in the Qurʾānic verse. Seen in this light, the story becomes a tale of hubris. Forgetting that he cannot act towards the Caliph as God had acted towards His Prophet, Khālid goes to the Caliph to prompt him to search for female pleasures instead of prohibiting that which God has made lawful to him. This

132 This change of roles is not unusual in Arabic literature. A very similar situation is found in a short anecdote about al-Aḥnaf, Muʿāwiya, and Fākhita bint Qaraẓa in Ibn Qayyim al-Jawziyya, *Akhbār*, pp. 185–186. Here, too, a clever courtier does not hesitate to take the winner's side.

133 Cf. B103 and B104. But cf. B24 and B25, too.

134 According to Ibn Khallikān, *Wafayāt* III: 12, "Khālid was a man of many slips and he did not stop to think about what he was saying."

hubris nearly leads to a downfall, which Khālid avoids only by withdrawing to the seclusion of his house. It is only when Khālid resumes his more servile position – not vis-à-vis the Caliph but his wife – that he gets out of harm's way and is even rewarded.[135] Instead of emulating God, he meekly listens to the words from behind the curtain and obeys this "invisible tongue" (*lisān al-ghayb*). Khālid is not a god but the servant of an unseen, yet dominant character. That this was ever in the mind of the author of A24 or his Mediaeval audience is far from obvious, but it does add some piquancy to the story as we read it.[136]

The characters of the protagonists are carefully drawn and essential for understanding the story. The description of the protagonists is not, and does not aim at being, historical. The author of *Khālid and Umm Salama* is drawing a picture that does not claim to be historical and is not following the received image. He is freely using his imagination to devise a good story.

In addition to characterisation, the author is using structural devices to make his story good literature. One such feature relates to the change in point of view in the middle of the story.[137] The first part is narrated in the third person, as told by an omniscient narrator. The second part is of heightened tension and is, respectively, told in the first person singular, from Khālid's point of view. His surprise when the Bukharans arrive, his horror when he is summoned to the palace, and, finally, his realisation of the situation are all told in his own words. This makes the tension even more palpable than it would have been had the story been told, as in the first part, by an omniscient and detached narrator, who can neither be surprised nor emotionally involved.[138]

---

135 After the first part, Khālid was nearly beaten with *kāfirkūbāt*, "unbeliever-smashers" (from Persian *kūftan, kūb-* 'to smite'). Now, he is no more *kāfir*, "ungrateful" (towards Umm Salama), but a *muslim*, resigning himself to the will of Umm Salama.

136 In general, one should be careful about reading modern ideas into Mediaeval texts. There is more in these texts than meets the eye but that does not mean that we may let our interpretative mind roam freely. The reader should, thus, take this paragraph as an example of how we *might* interpret such longer and more complicated stories in Mediaeval literature but not how they necessarily *should* be interpreted.

137 Cf. Chapter 2.5.3.

138 One might also note that in the *ḥadīth* no. 4913 ʿUmar tells his story in the first person singular in the same way as Khālid tells the second part of his, and the first-person narration may have been inspired by the *ḥadīth*. There are also some further similarities between the *ḥadīth* and *Khālid and Umm Salama*: After ʿUmar has been sent away by Umm Salama, he tells us that he stayed away (*ghibtu*) from the Prophet (cf. Khālid staying away from the palace after Umm Salama's action). Later, ʿUmar is propelled into action by a knock at the door (*fa-idhā ṣāḥibī l-anṣārī yaduqq al-bāb*), in the same way that Khālid is activated by people rushing in. As such, these parallels are not conclusive but added to the other similarities, they strengthen the case for seeing here a conscious use of an intertextual relation between the two texts.

The change of viewpoint is also useful in showing the gradual growth of Khālid's understanding. It first crosses his mind that the servants might have been sent by Umm Salama but he remains uncertain of this. When he sees movement behind the curtain, the suspicion grows that Umm Salama is not only behind the curtain but behind the whole affair. The laughter from behind the curtain finally settles the question, and Khālid proceeds to the climax of his second speech, a eulogy of Umm Salama and a direct accusation of the Caliph for being lascivious.[139] To achieve this gradual movement most effectively, the author appropriately chose first-person narration.

The story is also symmetrically structured. It is basically divided into two, and the division is marked by the change of narrator in the middle. We can further divide both parts into four movements, which mirror each other:[140]

1.	Khālid comes to meet the Caliph	Khālid comes to meet the Caliph
2.	Khālid speaks to please the Caliph	Khālid speaks to please Umm Salama
3.	Khālid returns to his house	Khālid returns to his house
4.	(Nothing comes from the Caliph)	A gift comes from Umm Salama
	A punishment from Umm Salama	(No punishment from the Caliph)

The expectations of Khālid change diametrically in the two parts of the story. The first part shows him confident in his expectations of being rewarded by the Caliph, the nexus between the parts presents his disillusionment, and in the second part, he has changed his attitude. It would be too much to say that his character develops in a modern sense but there is a certain growth in his understanding. What he learns in the story is that it is Umm Salama who is to be flattered, not the weak Caliph: their real power relation becomes clear to him as the events unravel. Khālid basically remains the same throughout the narrative: this is not a story of his growth to become a new man. Yet in relation to the Caliph and Umm Salama, Khālid has changed, now knowing who it is he must beware of and please. Had there been a continuation to this anecdote, we would perhaps have met a new Khālid.

The device of creating comic tension by repeating a story in a completely different and even diametrically reversed form is also found elsewhere in

139 Incidentally, the accusation is not false: the Caliph does lust for these women, though only after Khālid has himself put the idea into his head.

140 The implied events which are not explicitly stated are given in brackets. We could also see this structure as cyclical (expectation of reward – speech – return home – close escape from being beaten – return to palace – speech – reward) but I am doubtful as to whether this would contribute anything new to the analysis and whether the author built his story with a cyclical structure in mind.

comic literature. It is closely related to the *maḥāsin wa-masāwī* genre. In a similar form it is, e.g., found in a widely attested story about a Bedouin who first tells happy news about his host's home in order to get some food, but when his wishes are frustrated, he repeats the story loading it with calamities, one surpassing the other.[141]

Thus far we have analysed al-Masʿūdī's version. Generally, al-Bayhaqī's version does not much differ from al-Masʿūdī's and one may, roughly, take the above analysis to fit both and, thus, in broad terms, the original *Khālid and Umm Salama*. Al-Bayhaqī reinterpreted the focus of the story by appropriating it into his work dedicated to *maḥāsin wa-masāwī* stories.[142] In al-Masʿūdī, the story was narrated for its comic effect. In al-Bayhaqī, the same reason, obviously, is important, but the story has been classified on the basis of the juxtaposition of Khālid's two speeches, listing, first, the good points of polygamous life and then its bad points as well. Al-Bayhaqī's version is, though, artistically clearly inferior to that of al-Masʿūdī.

Al-Bayhaqī, however, still has a predilection for historical writing. He retains the names of the protagonists and creates a story which has some historical verisimilitude: the events described in the story could have taken place, and the characters do bear a certain resemblance to the historical persons behind them. Al-Madāʾinī's Khālid had a reputation for stories connected with women and the historical al-Saffāḥ reputedly did confine himself to monogamy.[143]

The anonymous author has also not quite freed himself of history and would, perhaps, not have felt that he was working within a genre completely detached from history. Despite many embellishments and considerable freedom concerning his sources he is, after all, producing a *khabar*, a piece of historical information, and his story was later used as such. Al-Masʿūdī is a historian, though a charmingly loquacious one, and his *Murūj* is not a collection of *novelle* but, at least marginally, a historical work. Had al-Masʿūdī thought that the story was clearly unhistorical, he would probably not have included it in his *Murūj*, at least not without a word of warning.

141 See, e.g., al-Ibshīhī, *Mustaṭraf* I: 258; al-Nuwayrī, *Nihāya* III: 300–302. The story type is universal, cf. Aarne – Thompson (1961), no. 2040 ("Climax of Horrors") = Uther (2004), no. 2040, and Schwarzbaum (1962): 321–328.

142 The story could also be classified under *al-faraj baʿd al-shidda*. Al-Madāʾinī is credited (*GAS* I: 314, no. 6; Lindstedt 2012–14: 256 = 2013, I: 19) with a short text on the theme but there is nothing to suggest that the present story would have been included in this work and seeing how it is built on other stories, it clearly is of a later date.

143 One might here note a certain parallelism with the Prophet Muḥammad, who was monogamous during the life of Khadīja. The story, told by al-Masʿūdī in *Murūj* §2326, of how al-Saffāḥ came to marry Umm Salama resembles the story of the Prophet and Khadīja and may well have been modelled on it.

The original author of *Khālid and Umm Salama* was a creative writer in spite of himself. He took several Khālid anecdotes, connected these with a *ḥadīth*, and seasoned his story with allusions to the Qur'ān and other sources. He worked with his sources in much the same way as early Renaissance authors, such as Boccaccio and other authors of *novelle*.

Khālid and Umm Salama is an example of anonymous but highly developed literature and the anecdote collections and other *adab* works contain many other such long narratives, which come close to early Renaissance *novelle* in their artful use of structure and literary devices. The story of the *Weaver of Words*[144] is another example of some fame, but these stories have usually received little attention despite their merits as rare pieces of highly developed prose fiction from Mediaeval times.

Most authors worked with characters and plots which had some connection with historical persons and events, such as in *Khālid and Umm Salama*. Al-Tanūkhī (d. 384/994),[145] besides using written sources, collected oral stories from persons he knew, taking thus a step towards detaching literature from history, yet remaining within the limits of the historical or pseudohistorical. The final step in this direction was taken by al-Hamadhānī in his *maqāmas*.

Badīʿ al-Zamān al-Hamadhānī (d. 398/1008) sifted through traditional *adab* sources, as well as, perhaps, folklore, to find suitable plots for his *maqāmas*. He took the decisive step outside of history by replacing the original characters of the stories with characters he himself had created and who, thus, had no real historical basis.[146] Moreover, when he reattributed anecdotes, he left this undisguised: what he wrote was literature, not history by any standard, and he did not try to convince his readers that they were reading historical *akhbār*. His *maqāmas* also never made it into historical works, but always remained within the sphere of *adab*.

Al-Hamadhānī also combined with each other anecdotes which were originally completely unrelated and built from these multiepisodic *maqāmas* where two or more stories are narrated within one *maqāma*, the protagonists continuing their adventures from one episode to another. The author of *Khālid and Umm Salama* took a step towards this by fusing together elements taken from different sources, but he did not go beyond a single, though bipartite, episode.

144 For which, see Hämeen-Anttila (2002): 80–82, and (1998): 83–96.

145 For al-Tanūkhī's works, see, e.g., Bray (2019) and the bibliography given there on pp. 305–312.

146 On the lack of his protagonists' historicity, see Hämeen-Anttila (2002): 41–43.

As is commonly known, Medieval Arabic literature did not favour long, fictitious prose genres. In prose, it concentrated on the short and witty anecdote – basically, a *nukta* with, or without, its background story, *sālifa* – which it preferred to be historical or, at least, in a historical guise. Such stories were either based on historical events or purported to be so, the only major exception being stories that were not told about individuals but about types ("a Bedouin", "a pretty slavegirl") and which were accordingly ahistorical.

Khālid and Umm Salama, the *Weaver of Words*, and the works of al-Tanūkhī and al-Hamadhānī gradually distanced themselves from this model of literature which had directed the attention of authors towards history and away from fiction. But it is not the aim of the present chapter to follow that development any further.

2.5.2 *Building Up Stories 2: B82* (Northern Arabs vs. Southern Arabs)

Khālid ibn Ṣafwān's sayings and his speeches are often transmitted in both short and long forms, so that what in one story may be a brief saying with only minimal context is part of a long speech in another. In such cases, it would seem obvious that we either have a short saying, around which a more elaborate context has later been built, or a longer speech that has become fragmented so that only a short passage has continued circulating on its own.

In many cases, we only have either a short or long version, but in some we have both, which enables us to study the mechanisms of change in that particular case, further giving us some ground for speculation in other similar cases.

In al-Balādhurī's *Ansāb*, there is a set of four stories with clear links to each other.[147] The longest (B82) of these reads:[148]

1. They say: The Commander of the Believers Abū l-ʿAbbās summoned Ibrāhīm ibn Makhrama al-Kindī, some people from Banū l-Ḥārith ibn Kaʿb, who were maternal uncles to Abū l-ʿAbbās, and Khālid ibn Ṣafwān. They started boasting.
2. Ibn Makhrama said: "The people of Yemen are the kings of the Arabs. In the age of the Jāhiliyya, the Bedouinship and the kingship belonged to them and they passed these on as an inheritance, one mighty man inheriting from another, the latter from the former and the (now)

---

147 B52, B82, B86, B101.

148 For notes and comments, see Chapter 3 (B82). The numbering of the segments has been added for easy reference and to highlight the structure of the story. The respective structural elements have also been marked in the other stories, B52, B86, and B101. For *mufākharas* in general, see Chapter 2.6.

bygone from his ancestors. To them belonged the Nuʿmāns, the Mundhirs and the Qābūses, to them belonged ʿIyāḍ, the lord of the sea, as well as the one whose flesh was protected by bees. To them belonged the one whose body the angels washed, and the one on whose death the Throne shook. To them belonged the one spoken to by the wolf and the one who used to take every ship by force. There is nothing important that is not attributed to them, neither a fine horse nor a cutting sword, neither strong armour nor a valuable garment. When they were asked, they gave, and when a guest alighted by them, they received him hospitably. No one can vie with them nor boast to them. They are the real Arabs whilst others just want to pass as Arabs!"

3. Abū l-ʿAbbās said: "I do not think the Tamīmī will agree on this." Khālid said: "The rash fellow has erred without knowledge and spoken amiss when he boasted to Muḍar, to whom belonged the Messenger of God (may God bless him and greet him) as well as the Caliphs and the members of his family. How can he boast to Muḍar of people who ride asses, weave clothes, train monkeys, and tan hides? A hoopoe led (Solomon) to them and a rat drowned them."

4. Then he turned to al-Kindī and said: "Are you boasting of fine horses and sharp swords and strong armour? What glory is there greater than Muḥammad, the best of mankind and the most noble of the nobles? God has bestowed him graciously on both us and you. They[149] were his followers and they were known and respected because of him. To us belong the Chosen Prophet and the Accepted Caliph, the lordship and the nobility. To us belong the founded Temple, the raised roof, and the *minbar* where he preached. To us belong the Zamzam, its (Mecca's) lowlands, and the office of giving water (to pilgrims). Can anyone be equal to us? Do anyone's words reach our glory? To us belongs Ibn ʿAbbās, the learned among people, whose stories are sweet and whose sayings are followed. To us belongs the Lion of God and the Sword of God, to us belongs the Veracious One and the Distinguisher and ʿAlī ibn Abī Ṭālib (may God, He is exalted, be pleased with him). He never disbelieved in God or swerved from truth to vanity. To us belongs the man of Two Lights, the martyred ʿUthmān."

5. Then the son of al-Ahtam continued: "How about your knowledge of your people's language? What do they call fingers among you?" He (al-Kindī) replied: "*Shanātir*." Khālid asked: "What about the ear?" He replied: "*Ṣinnāra*." Khālid asked: "And the beard?" He replied:

149 I.e., the Northern Arabs.

"*Zubb*." Khālid said: "God, be He praised and exalted, has spoken 'in a clear Arabic tongue.' Yet have you heard Him say: 'Put your *shanātir* into your *ṣinnārāt*?' (cf. Q 2: 19) Or: 'Do not take me by the *zubb*?' (cf. Q 20: 94)"

6. Abū l-ʿAbbās (may God be pleased with him) said: "What have you, Yemeni, to do with the men of Muḍar?" Then he ordered Khālid to be rewarded, giving him money and property in Basra.

The structure of the story is:

1. Setting the scene;
2. the speech of the Southern Arab;
3. dialogue between Abū l-ʿAbbās and Khālid;
4. Khālid's speech;
5. dialogue between Khālid and the Southern Arab;
6. verdict by Abū l-ʿAbbās.

This story offers us a fully-fledged *mufākhara*, tribal debate, in the Caliphal court (1), with first one speaker, Ibn Makhrama al-Kindī, boasting on the Southern Arabs (2) and Khālid replying on behalf of the Northern Arabs (4), while the Caliph himself acts as the umpire and, finally, judges the contest in Khālid's favour (6). In addition to the boasts, the story includes a comical dialogue between Khālid and Ibn Makhrama (5), which takes the, more or less imagined, Southern Arabic dialect as a laughing stock, and another brief dialogue between Khālid and Abū l-ʿAbbās (3), which includes the famous saying on weaving, etc.

A few sentences similar to, but not identical with, a part of Khālid's reply (4) to Ibn Makhrama's speech in B82 are found in B52, this time with minimal context, the Southern Arab remaining anonymous and the Caliph being replaced by the famous governor al-Ḥajjāj (d. 95/714), the incident thus being dated to some 40 years earlier:

1–2. A Yemeni man boasted to Khālid at the door of al-Ḥajjāj.

5. Khālid replied: "From among us come the Prophet who was sent and the Caliph who is hoped for. Among us is the revealed (*munzal*) Book and the House towards which one prays."

In the third anecdote, B86, Khālid surprisingly takes the opposite, Southern Arab side, and the story has no Southern Arab as Khālid's interlocutor. This, again, takes place in the presence of the Caliph Abū l-ʿAbbās:

1. They say: Khālid came to Abū l-ʿAbbās, may God, He is exalted, have mercy on him. Abū l-ʿAbbās said to him: "O Khālid, how well do you know my maternal relatives?" Khālid asked: "Which of them, O Commander of the Believers? I know them all." Abū l-ʿAbbās said: "Those who are the closest to me and have the strongest claim on me, the offspring of al-Ḥārith ibn Kaʿb."
2. Khālid said: "O Commander of the Believers, they are the height of nobility and the trunk of generosity! They have features which have never been combined in any other of their people. Among their people they have the best condition and the noblest disposition. They keep their covenant best and they have the furthest aspirations. In war they are a firebrand and under duress a support. They are the heads while others are but tails." Abū l-ʿAbbās said: "How excellent you are, O son of Ṣafwān. You have well described them!"

While sharing few identical elements with the anecdotes B82 and B52, the general tenour of B86 links it to them.

The fourth anecdote (B101) takes the middle part of B82 and builds a separate story of it, giving the pithy and devastating saying about weaving, etc. at the end, the most prominent place in the story. Again, Khālid's opponent remains anonymous and the discussion takes place in Abū l-ʿAbbās' presence:

1. < *Abū l-Ḥasan al-Madāʾinī*: Khālid spent an evening at the court of the Commander of the Believers, Abū l-ʿAbbās.
2. Some people of Banū l-Ḥārith boasted, but Khālid remained silent.
3. The Commander of the Believers said to him: "O son of Ṣafwān, what is the matter? Why do you not say anything?" Khālid replied: "But these are the maternal relatives of the Commander of the Believers!" The Caliph said: "You are my paternal relative. Paternal relatives are not below maternal relatives." Khālid said: "But what should I say to people who weave clothes, train monkeys, and tan hides? A hoopoe led the way to them and a rat drowned them."
6. Abū l-ʿAbbās laughed at this.

B82 and B101 are centred on one memorable expression, the reference to "people who weave clothes," etc. This saying is brief and could well have been memorised. While in B101 it ends the discussion, in B82 it merely leads to a renewed attack by Khālid (4), which, as it happens, lessens the pungency of the saying.

B82 would seem to be a composite story.[150] Its core is formed by the speeches by Ibn Makhrama and Khālid (2, 4), which build up a nice case of tribal *mufākhara*. The middle part (3), resembling B101, intervenes in this and has all semblance of being a later addition to an earlier *mufākhara*, whichever time that derives from. Finally, the end of B82 (5) feels again extraneous to the *mufākhara* and has a different tone. While the speeches of Ibn Makhrama and Khālid are formal and serious, building on tribal and early Islamic history, the end brings notes of grotesque comic and sexual innuendos. Using bogus Southern forms and inserting them into Qur'ānic quotations is slightly risqué by itself and changing Q 20: 94 into a sentence which means "Do not take me by the penis" works on a level completely different from the two speeches.[151]

Thus, it would seem that there are at least three (or four if we include Khālid's speech in favour of the Southern Arabs) different and originally separate elements in these stories: Ibn Makhrama's speech and Khālid's reply (2, 4); Khālid's devastating comment on people who weave clothes, etc. (3); and a gross philological joke at the expense of the Southern Arabs (5).

Such freedoms were taken by authors who did not consider themselves forgers. Where there were in an anecdote good ingredients for a witty story these could be added to another one in order to create a partly fictitious longer story with no qualms of conscience. This could then be used by authors of historical or semi-historical works, such as al-Mas'ūdī's *Murūj*, the fictitious material, thus, finding its way into historical works. The real authors of these long versions remain anonymous.[152]

Partly, of course, the changes may be due to early oral transmission, which may have changed the story unknowingly. However, it is clear that even when the textual transmission was literary, similar liberties were taken without hesitation. A good example from historical literature comes from al-Tha'ālibī (d. 429/1038), who claims to be quoting al-Ṭabarī (d. 314/923), while, in fact, he rewrites the whole passage, only keeping some pithy expressions and the general run of the narrative, as the comparison of the two passages shows.[153]

---

150 In al-Balādhurī, B52, B82, and B86 are given without any authority, and B101 on the authority of al-Madā'inī. In other sources (for documentation, see Chapter 3, B82), B82 is attributed to al-Madā'inī by Ibn al-Faqīh and to al-Haytham ibn 'Adī by several sources.

151 Cf. commentary on B82.

152 Cf. Leder's "unauthored literature" (Leder 1988). The situation in historical literature and the anecdotes are very similar and the genres freely borrow from each other, so their development should always be studied in tandem.

153 Al-Tha'ālibī, *Ghurar*, pp. 26–27; al-Ṭabarī, *Ta'rīkh* I: 208/II: 8. For a detailed comparison of these passages, see Hämeen-Anttila (2018a): 52–54.

In this, al-Thaʿālibī's way of handling his written source closely resembles the way Khālid stories were freely modified, and the same can be found in, e.g., the way later authors rewrote Ibn al-Muqaffaʿ's *Kalīla wa-Dimna*.[154]

It is quite possible that we should take the punch lines in Khālid's speeches as the only part of our corpus that could have some claim of going back to the 8th century and, perhaps, to Khālid himself. All else has to be considered suspect of having been freely modified, or invented, by later authors, even when they received their material in a written form. This does not mean that early books would necessarily have been in a fluid state, though.[155] The case of the al-Ṭabarī quotation shows unequivocally that al-Thaʿālibī did not even attempt to reproduce his source exactly. The differences do not mean that al-Ṭabarī's historical work would still have been in a fluid state around 1000 AD, but that authors quoting from him did not feel themselves restrained to doing so *verbatim*.

Even a cursory look at the longer dialogues and orations by Khālid shows that they exhibit great variation in different sources, whereas many shorter sayings have been transmitted almost unchanged in scores of sources. It seems that these longer speeches are often built around a core saying that found a fixed form very early, at least in the case of those sayings that are found widely distributed as early as the ninth century. If not by Khālid, these sayings are at least specimens of mid- to late 8th-century prose.

The longer speeches and more elaborate anecdotes can and should be taken into account when writing a history of Arabic literature. We cannot just ignore Khālid's, and other orators', contributions to the development of Arabic prose style. Though perhaps not specimens of Umayyad prose in the form in which they have reached us they are specimens of early ʿAbbāsid prose and in most cases they seem to have received their form in the time before al-Jāḥiẓ's generation.

2.5.3 *Literary Technique in the Anecdotes*

The previous two chapters have studied some anecdotes and their construction in detail. The present chapter sums up some literary techniques used in the anecdotes of the Khālid corpus. The results will, though, largely hold true even for other contemporary and later anecdotes.[156]

---

154 Cf. de Blois (1990).

155 Cf. Schoeler (2006).

156 Some story collections, such as al-Tanūkhī's (d. 384/994) *Faraj*, contain more developed anecdotes and even though many of the results of the present chapter will hold true there, too, they also use additional literary techniques.

Techniques studied in this chapter include the use of *isnād*, closely related to the change of narrative voice and the use of a first-person singular narrator; creation of dialogue; upgrading of interlocutors; and the phenomenon of wandering stories, related to upgrading.

2.5.3.1 Use of Isnād

The *isnād*, or chain of transmitters, has two different uses in the anecdotes. On the one hand, it lends a sense of historicity to the stories, whether genuine or not, and on the other, it allows the characters to speak in their own voice instead of a more neutral, and less involved, voice of an omniscient narrator.

Within the stories, *isnād* is not used by Khālid himself, who does narrate old stories but almost never with an *isnād*.[157] The *isnāds* used for creating a sense of historicity in narrating stories from or about Khālid are used in two different ways. Some authors, most notably Ibn ʿAsākir and Ibn al-ʿAdīm, systematically use full *isnāds*, documenting the transmission chain from the earliest authority unto themselves. The latest links in the temporal sequence presumably indicate the real transmission chain of the anecdote, but the historicity of the early part of the chain is much more open to doubt.

More commonly the *isnād* only gives an early authority, or a brief chain of authorities, as the original source of the story, but does not aim at building a complete *isnād* from Khālid to the final author. Here the authority may be an early collector, such as al-Aṣmaʿī, or an earlier author of a book, from which the later author has taken the story.[158] The title of the book may, or may not, be mentioned. Thus, in A24 al-Kumaylī only mentions the name of the author of his source, Abū l-Faraj, but not the title of his book.[159]

This use of *isnād* could be called technical use as it aims at documenting the source from which the author has taken the story.[160] Studying such *isnāds* gives us information concerning the transmission and diffusion of a story.

From a literary point of view, the second case of *isnād* is more interesting, quoting the ultimate authority of the story in the form of Khālid himself or an eyewitness to the event, who sometimes takes part in the action. While it is possible that in some cases this is a real *isnād* in the sense of an early collector,

---

157 Cf. Chapter 2.4.

158 Cf., e.g., al-Tijānī, *Tuḥfa*, p. 176, quoting Abū l-Faraj's *Nisāʾ* and Ibn al-Kardabūs' *Iktifāʾ* as the authorities of his version of A24.

159 Al-Kumaylī, *Nuzha*, p. 691.

160 It has to be added that authors have a strong tendency to quote the ultimate, rather than the immediate, authority. Thus, when author A uses a book by B, who quotes C as his authority, A tends only to quote C as his source, bypassing B. For this in philological literature, see Hämeen-Anttila (1993b): 43.

such as al-Aṣmaʿī, having heard the story from the mouth of, e.g., Shabīb ibn Shayba, in other, perhaps most, cases the ultimate authority is given in order to create heightened tension and involvedness in the story, as when Khālid narrates in the first person singular what happened to him or an eyewitness gives a vivid tableau of an extemporised saying.

Related to this, we find a number of other technical features used for narrative effect. One of these is what I would call "fictitious hesitation." In some stories, such as B79, the narration is interrupted by the (in this case anonymous) narrator adding a variant version of what was actually said, introduced by "or he said" (*aw qāla*). It would be naive to believe that this is always a *bona fide* sign of hesitation as to the exact wording of the story, knowing how freely the stories were modified during transmission.

The clearest case comes in the purely fictitious A24.[161] In al-Bayhaqī's version, Khālid asks the Caliph to lower the curtains so that he can give him some sincere advice. Khālid's line ends with *anṣaḥuka bihi* "*with* which I advise you," after which the narrator adds *aw qāla: fīhi* "or he said: *about* which." Now, this implies great accuracy of transmission, even in minor details such as the exact preposition used by Khālid. Knowing that the story is fictitious, we can see that there is no factual basis for this fictitious hesitation.

A sudden sign of hesitation as to the exact wording is used for narrative affect, creating an illusion of exactness in a story that may well be completely fictitious in the first place.[162] Showing hesitation only at a marginal detail implies that the main storylines should be accepted as accurate. In the particular case of B79, the hesitation at the end of the story as to what happened after the intruder had left – itself a completely unnecessary addition – lends an aura of accuracy to the main part of the story.[163]

In his *The Art of Badīʿ az-zamān al-Hamadhānī as Picaresque Narrative* (1983), James T. Monroe interpreted the *isnād* of the *maqāma* as parodying

161 Cf. Chapter 2.5.1.

162 In the *isnāds* of *ḥadīths*, such hesitation may be a sign of real attempt at maximal accuracy, but especially in cases where the hesitation is expressed by the earliest links of the *isnād* it is quite possible that it is used for the very same reason, to convince the reader that otherwise the story is an accurate reproduction of what really was said or took place. Cases of fictitious hesitation may easily be found in any literature, cf., e.g., Thomas Love Peacock, *Melincourt or Sir Oran Haut-Ton* (I–II. Ed. Richard Garnett. London: Aldine House 1893) I: 119, where Desmond's story is prefaced by another fictitious character saying: "and he related to me his history, which I will tell you *as nearly as I can remember* [Italics mine, JHA], in his own words."

163 Cf. also B58a, where al-Jāḥiẓ hesitates at an unimportant detail in the story.

the *isnād* of *ḥadīths*.[164] As I have endeavoured to show elsewhere,[165] Monroe's analysis does not do justice to the *maqāmas* he studied. When it comes to anecdotes, there is no reason to assume that the *isnāds* are parodistic: from very early on, abbreviated *isnāds* had been in standard use in *adab* literature.

2.5.3.2 Change of Narrative Voice

Most of the anecdotes are told by an omniscient narrator, while some are related either by an eyewitness or by Khālid himself in the first person singular. What is more interesting is that in some stories the narrator changes midway through the story from an omniscient narrator to the first person singular.

A24 has already been discussed,[166] but the results are worth repeating here. This is an unusually complex and well-structured anecdote that uses various literary devices to create a good story. One of them is the change of narrative voice. The first part is told by an omniscient narrator, but when the plot thickens and we come to a series of breath-taking scenes where Khālid's personal safety is first threatened and he later, step by step, takes in the whole picture of what is going on, the narrator changes into the first-person singular voice of Khālid himself, thus allowing a more immediate and emotionally involved narrative. As we have seen, the anecdote contains a number of clearly premeditated and carefully executed details, and it is difficult to maintain that the change in the narrative voice was accidental.

B79 is much shorter, but there we can see a similar use of the change of narrative voice, again roughly midway through the story. Here the latter half is told by the voice of Khālid's guest, Ḥafṣ ibn Muʿāwiya. While a much less clear case than A24, there still is a similar situation of Ḥafṣ being victimised by seeing the tray full of delicious dishes being carried away never to return – or to return only after the freshness had come, according to a variant. While far from the intensity of A24, it seems probable that the change of narrative voice is also here used to allow for a more emotionally loaded narrative.

B14a uses the change of narrative voice to let the interlocutor of Khālid, Rawḥ ibn Ḥātim explain his motives by letting us inside his thoughts:

> Rawḥ has said: I respected him too much to answer and thought to myself: "He's an old man. Perhaps he wanted to startle me in order to know how I would answer him." Then I said: "(…)".

164 Monroe (1983): 20–21.
165 Hämeen-Anttila (2002): 46–48.
166 See Chapter 2.5.1.

The presumably older version, B14, lacks this change of narrative voice and does without the hesitation on the part of the young Rawḥ when upbraiding the elderly gentleman, Khālid, showing how the two changes go hand in hand.

Contrary to these three cases, in B98, the change comes early on in the story and there is no obvious reason why it takes place. It seems that here the change is purely incidental and has no literary motivation behind it.

2.5.3.3 Creation of Dialogue

In comparing variant versions of an anecdote with each other, we sometimes notice that what in one version is told as an uncontextualised saying, or short monologue, by Khālid may in another be a dialogue between Khālid and his interlocutor. Thus, e.g., in B11 Khālid describes various mounts, and no context is given for his monologue. Assuming that B11 represents an earlier form of the story, B11a and B11b develop this by creating a context (especially B11b) and producing an interlocutor, Sulaymān ibn ʿAlī, whose question acts as the prop to which the saying is attached. Obviously, we could also turn the tables and see B11 as a reduced narrative, stripped of the context and the interlocutor. The story is too short to allow us to prove which way it has developed, but it would seem to be more natural for a monologue to develop into a dialogue than vice versa.

B11c then takes further this embryonic dialogue, where Sulaymān ibn ʿAlī has only one line (and in B11a a brief command for Khālid to speak). This time the interlocutor and the first-person narrator of the incident is Shabīb ibn Shayba, who is allocated four questions, each drawing a reply from Khālid who describes four types of mounts, one in each answer.[167]

2.5.3.4 Upgrading of Interlocutors

The phenomenon which I call upgrading of interlocutors, is very common in anecdotal literature. This refers to changing the interlocutor(s) of the protagonist, or sometimes the protagonist himself, from anonymous, unknown, or less important characters into more famous and/or important ones. Thus, within the Khālid corpus, we often find versions of the same anecdote with the same protagonist but with two or more different interlocutors. In some versions, the interlocutor may be anonymous or he may be a little-known person, while in others he has become the Caliph, a governor, or someone else on the uppermost rungs of the social and administrative hierarchy or an otherwise remarkable character, such as a famous ascetic or poet.

---

167 Cf. also al-Masʿūdī's version of B16, discussed in Chapter 2.5.1.

Upgrading of the interlocutors is very common, and even in the relatively limited corpus of Khālid stories we find plenty of examples. While it is often difficult or impossible to prove which of the versions is the oldest, in some cases this is possible, and almost without exception it is the version with the high-ranking interlocutor which is the later version and the one with the low-ranking interlocutor is the earlier one.

Thus, e.g., when discussing A24, we have seen how B16, transmitted through al-Madāʾinī and, thus, in all probability a relatively early version, features an almost completely unknown Durust ibn Ribāṭ as Khālid's interlocutor, but when the definitely late A24 was compiled from a number of Khālid stories, it is no longer Ibn Ribāṭ who features in the story but the Caliph Abū l-ʿAbbās al-Saffāḥ.[168]

In most cases it is not possible to prove which of the versions is the earlier, but we may with good reason assume that upgraded versions tend in general to be later. In addition to this being provable in a number of cases (while I have not found a single case where we could prove an anecdote to have been downgraded, excluding cases of anonymous, or later forgotten, interlocutors, cf. below), it is difficult to understand a mechanism through which a famous character would be replaced by an obscure one, especially if the latter has fallen into quasi-complete oblivion in later times.

B37, a speech of congratulation to a newly appointed governor/Caliph, is another probable case of such upgrading. In the version found in al-Qālī's *Amālī*, Khālid's speech is addressed to an anonymous governor, *wālī*, whereas in al-Balādhurī, it is the first ʿAbbāsid Caliph al-Saffāḥ himself whom Khālid addresses.[169] Moreover, al-Qālī's version has a long *isnād* taking us back to Ṣab(b)āḥ ibn Khāqān, a Basran who belonged to Banū Minqar[170] and was a relative of Khālid,[171] which gives us good grounds to suggest an early date for this version.

Likewise, one may assume that B23, which contains a contextless saying on women by Khālid, would be older than B24, where a couple of sentences have grown into a longer speech and the interlocutor is again the Caliph Abū l-ʿAbbās al-Saffāḥ. Here a story with no interlocutor is in a sense upgraded from an absent interlocutor to a famous one. In cases where there is no context or the interlocutor is anonymous ("a governor," "a man"), it is also quite possible that the name of the interlocutor in an earlier version, especially if he was not

168 See Chapter 2.5.1.
169 Al-Qālī, *Amālī* I: 213.
170 Cf. al-Iṣfahānī, *Aghānī* XV: 160.
171 Cf. Chapter 1.4.

famous, may have been dropped either accidentally or as being irrelevant, so that one could also envisage a certain kind of downgrading from a known to an unknown or absent interlocutor.

B44 and its variants provide a clear case of upgrading. In B44 and B44a it is Maslama ibn ʿAbd al-Malik who asks Khālid about al-Ḥasan al-Baṣrī, while Khālid's interlocutor remains anonymous in B44b, and in B44c it is the Caliph Hishām himself who asks Khālid about al-Ḥasan. A61 and A61a, which differ only slightly from B44 and could almost be seen as its variants, show a similar upgrading, with A61 having "a Bedouin" as Khālid's interlocutor, but al-Ḥajjāj taking on this role in A61a.

It would also seem that we have a similar upgrading in B45. In B45a, the protagonist is al-ʿAbbās ibn al-Walīd ibn ʿAbd al-Malik, who has been replaced in B45 by his even more famous uncle, Maslama ibn ʿAbd al-Malik,[172] whereas in most sources it is the Caliph Hishām ibn ʿAbd al-Malik who appears as Khālid's interlocutor.

2.5.3.5 Wandering Stories

Just as interlocutors may be changed, the protagonist may also undergo changes, with the same story being attributed to a number of protagonists. The Khālid corpus includes several such "wandering stories," to borrow a term from the study of Persian *rubāʿiyāt*. This can also be seen as upgrading the protagonist, and, again, it would strongly seem that in cases of such wandering stories the more famous the protagonist the more probably we are having a later version of a story.

B10 and its variants can be taken as an example of both upgrading characters and possibly attributing the story to a better-known protagonist. In what would appear to be an early version, as it comes from al-Madāʾinī, Khālid defends his habit of riding donkeys to a rather obscure general Abū l-Jahm, and in B10b his interlocutor is merely an anonymous Basran. However, in B10a his interlocutor is ʿAlī ibn al-Jahm ibn al-Ḥudhayfa, a much better-known character. Moreover, a similar story is also found in al-Jāḥiẓ's *Bighāl*, where the interlocutors are Khālid's father and ʿAbd al-Raḥmān ibn ʿAbbās,[173] and in Ibn Qutayba's *ʿUyūn* the interlocutors are an anonymous Hāshimite and al-Faḍl ibn al-Rabīʿ.[174] While it is virtually impossible to ascertain who the original characters were and whether there is any historical truth in the story, one might assume also here that an anonymous or scarcely known character would have

172 On whom, see Borrut (2010): 229–282.
173 Al-Jāḥiẓ, *Bighāl* II: 218 (> al-Nuwayrī, *Nihāya* X: 85–86).
174 Ibn Qutayba, *ʿUyūn* I: 250.

been replaced by a better-known one. The motivation for this, though, may not be literary, but merely an attempt to make sense of the name Abū l-Jahm, unknown to some of the later compilers, who either dropped his name altogether (B10b) or "corrected" it to a person they knew (B10a).

B41 seems to be a case of reattributing a story originally told about Khālid's father, Ṣafwān, as in al-ʿAskarī's *Dīwān*, or his more distant ancestor ʿAbdallāh ibn al-Ahtam, as in Ibn Qutayba's *ʿUyūn*, to their famous son/descendant.[175] The scene is set no later than 72/691, at which time Khālid was less likely the one to speak on behalf of all Basrans than his father, the leader of Tamīm, or his even elder relative ʿAbdallāh. Even though this could theoretically be one of the first public performances of the young Khālid, this would still leave unexplained why his less well-known father/ancestor was later credited with a similar speech.

The existence of these variants can also be used to claim that the story is, if not historical, then at least relatively early. If the story had been created no earlier than close to al-Balādhurī's time, one might expect Khālid's father and ancestor to have been so obscure by the time that the creator of the story would not have chosen either of them as the protagonist in the first place. The existence of the variants is understandable only if the story has been created before Khālid had become famous, and then reattributed to him after he had done so. Thus, the most natural way to read the three variant versions is to assume that the story contains a historical core with Ṣafwān or ʿAbdallāh addressing Umayya ibn ʿAbdallāh in 72/691 or that it was invented soon after this, when Ṣafwān and ʿAbdallāh were still prominent figures among the Ahtamites and had not been pushed into shadow by Khālid's fame. Respectively, B41 would have been created, accidentally or on purpose, when Khālid had become the most famous Ahtamite, far above the other members of the family.

In Chapter 1.3.2 we have already seen numerous cases of wandering stories with Khālid or one of his ancestors as the protagonist. In most cases it would seem that Khālid's name has later replaced that of his ancestor, as the historical context of the story makes it improbable that Khālid originally featured in it. On the contrary, there are no cases where, e.g., Khālid's father Ṣafwān would appear together with mid-eighth-century characters so that one would have reason to assume that his name has replaced that of his famous son.

In only one case, A94, may Khālid have replaced a later character, as the story is set in the time of the Caliph al-Mahdī. Obviously, this could also be a simple mistake in the name of the Caliph. However that might be in this case, in general the fact that Khālid's name has not been inserted into stories

175 Al-ʿAskarī, *Dīwān*, p. 1047; Ibn Qutayba, *ʿUyūn* 1: 295.

where the protagonist was originally a later character also means that Khālid was no more at the peak of his fame as a literary character centuries later. In contrast we can see from some late variant versions of A24 how Abū Nuwās' name was used to replace that of Khālid, thus upgrading the story from Khālid to Abū Nuwās.

Sometimes the change of the main character may be accidental, and in such cases there is no reason to assume that the version with the less famous character should be the earlier. Thus, B49, where Khālid comments on his younger relative Shabīb ("Shabīb does not have secret friends nor open enemies"), is occasionally told in the reversed form, with Shabīb commenting on Khālid. In al-Jāḥiẓ's *Ḥayawān* the text runs: "Shabīb ibn Shayba was mentioned to Khālid ibn Ṣafwān, and (the latter) said" (*dhukira Shabīb ibn Shayba ʿinda Khālid ibn Ṣafwān fa-qāla*).[176] A simple deletion of *ʿinda* would cause a rearrangement of the sentence's syntax and result in an inverted sense: "Shabīb ibn Shayba mentioned Khālid ibn Ṣafwān and said" (*dhakara Shabīb ibn Shayba* [[*ʿinda*]] *Khālid ibn Ṣafwān fa-qāla*).[177]

2.6 *Mufākhara* and *maḥāsin wa-masāwī*

In Classical Arabic literature, there are three closely interrelated types of prose texts that discuss the merits and flaws of various things. Literary debates, usually called *munāẓaras*, are the most formally developed form of these, having two, or sometimes more, usually non-human protagonists listing their own merits and, often, the flaws of the other in turns, with the text usually ending in a judgement by a judge or, in later periods, a petition for the patron to decide the case.[178]

The Khālid corpus includes no such texts, even though B82 has some similarity with *munāẓaras*. The genre seems to have entered Arabic literature only some time after the death of Khālid.[179] The other two forms discussing merits and flaws are well attested in the corpus. In a *mufākhara*, two, or sometimes more, people boast on their tribe, town, or some other aspect of their life,

176 Al-Jāḥiẓ, *Ḥayawān* V: 592.

177 Similar confusions are found also elsewhere, cf., e.g., an exchange between Jesus and John the Baptist in, e.g., Ibn Kathīr, *Qiṣaṣ* II: 432, vs. al-Tawḥīdī, *Baṣāʾir* VII: 127, no. 374. See Hämeen-Anttila (1999): 72, with further references.

178 For literary debates in general, see Wagner (1962). They are often called *mufākharas*, too, so the terminology is by no means clearly defined. The term *munāẓara* is also often used for scholarly debates, for which see Forster (2017).

179 See Hämeen-Anttila (2014): 264–270.

often, but not necessarily, attacking the other, or others. Occasionally, we only find an attack on the other's/others' tribe without any boast about one's own.

In *maḥāsin wa-masāwī* one person either speaks in turns in favour of something and then against it, *pro et contra*, or two speakers share this task, one speaking in favour, the other against something, without this evolving into a boasting match as in the *mufākhara*. Even though this is how *maḥāsin wa-masāwī* are usually defined, perusing, e.g., al-Bayhaqī's *Maḥāsin* or ps.-al-Jāḥiẓ's work with the same title, one notes that very often the case is not a matter of praising and blaming the same thing, but of praising one thing and blaming its opposite. In modern analysis we might want to exclude these from the genre, but in their own, Mediaeval context they undoubtedly went under the name of *maḥāsin wa-masāwī*.

While in the literary debate there almost always is a final judgement or an appeal to the patron at the end, in the *mufākhara* this is optional, and in the *maḥāsin wa-masāwī* rare.[180]

While there were no fixed literary genres of *mufākhara* or *maḥāsin wa-masāwī* by the time of Khālid himself, it is possible to see in the corpus texts that conform to these genres as they became later defined. Thus, Khālid appears in both tribal *mufākharas* between Northern and Southern Arabs and city *mufākharas* between Basra and Kufa.[181]

In tribal *mufākharas*, Khālid usually speaks in favour of Northern Arabs (e.g., B52). In the fully developed *mufākharas* (e.g., A20) he is answered by others, who speak in favour of Southern Arabs. In some cases, we only have Khālid's boast, which may be a fragment of an otherwise lost *mufākhara*, giving us only the part showing Khālid's eloquence. Sometimes, we have variants of the same anecdote, one in the form of a *mufākhara*, the other a monologue by Khālid. Whether such a case shows fragmentation of a *mufākhara* or, on the contrary, growth of a *mufākhara* around an original core with only one speech, or saying, has to be decided case by case and often remains unsolvable. B57 introduces one descriptive sentence of Khālid's on Basra with the words "Khālid vied with some Kufans and said," which clearly shows that this is a sentence which has been, or has been thought to have been, detached from a longer *mufākhara*.

B82 is the furthest developed tribal *mufākhara* between Khālid and Southern Arabs, represented by Ibrāhīm ibn Makhrama al-Kindī. The development of this story has already been studied in detail.[182] Another long *mufākhara*

---

180 For *maḥāsin wa-masāwī* in general, see Geries (1977).

181 City *mufākharas* in B54, B54a, B54b; B70, B70a; B81, B81a, B81b; and A21. Cf. also al-Masʿūdī, *Murūj* §2350.

182 Chapter 2.5.2.

belonging to the same group of anecdotes is B101, itself clearly related to B86, with both set in the presence of the Caliph Abū l-ʿAbbās al-Saffāḥ. B101 starts with the boast of the Southern Arabs from Banū l-Ḥārith ibn Kaʿb, which is only mentioned, not reported, as the focus is on Khālid and his eloquence. Khālid is then shown tearing this to pieces with his concise disparaging of the Southern Arabs.

The third anecdote which belongs to this group, B86, brings a rather surprising twist to the story, doing away with the anonymous representatives of Banū l-Ḥārith and letting Khālid speak in their praise at the demand of the Caliph. Al-Balādhurī's version of the story has only this initial speech, but B101 and a variant version[183] make it probable that this was originally transmitted *in tandem* with Khālid's devastating criticism, which would make this version a case of *maḥāsin wa-masāwī*. While making up an excellent story and showing Khālid's quick wit and ability to extemporise – admired, according to al-Ḥuṣrī and Abū Hilāl al-ʿAskarī, by al-Jāḥiẓ – it seems probable that this is a later development, it being rather improbable that Khālid would have been prone to heap praise on Southern Arabs in the early ʿAbbāsid court, even though this cannot, of course, be excluded. More probably, though, we can again see how a speech by an anonymous Southern Arab has been reattributed to a more famous protagonist or, perhaps, invented *ex nihilo* to give piquancy to the story and to highlight Khālid's eloquence.

The tribal *mufākhara* usually concerns tribes rather than individuals, but in B54 and its variants the debate is taken onto a personal level, Khālid and an anonymous ʿAbdarī, or Qurashī, insulting each other using folk etymologies of their, and their ancestors', names.

Another subgenre of *mufākhara* in the corpus focuses on towns. In many anecdotes Khālid is presented as speaking in favour of Basra,[184] sometimes in combination with his interlocutor speaking in favour of Kufa (B81, A21), the two cities forming the standard pair of Iraqi cities in *mufākharas*. The short anecdote B70, however, contrasts Mecca with al-Ubulla, the suburb of Basra, but the story is not a fully-fledged *mufākhara*. Incidentally, the presence of the little-known Durust ibn Ribāṭ in this anecdote makes it sound more authentic than the larger number of more polished *mufākharas* between Basra and Kufa, although his presence can by no means be taken as evidence of authenticity, a term which it is always hazardous to use in the Umayyad period. The variant B70a does without Durust's intervention, which also changes the focus of the anecdote – in B70, Durust gets the last word and Khālid is implicitly shown

183 Al-Ḥuṣrī, *Zahr*, pp. 872–873.

184 B57, B81, A21, A23.

beaten by him, as it would have been difficult to counter his comment, due to the special status of Mecca in Islam.

B81 and its variants allow us a glimpse at how fragmentation or building up of stories works by dropping or adding elements to them, depending on how we look at the variant versions. B81 presents a relatively short speech by Khālid on the *maḥāsin* of Basra, without any background story (but bringing Maslama ibn ʿAbd al-Malik into the story with one short question). B81a presents a much more developed version of the story, which is now set in the (improbable)[185] context of an embassy to ʿAbd al-Malik in 83/702, with al-Ḥajjāj being present. This version has the structure of a complete town *mufākhara*, with Muḥammad ibn ʿUmayr ibn ʿUṭārid speaking in favour of Kufa, and al-Ḥajjāj and ʿAbd al-Malik giving the final verdict in favour of that town over Basra.

B81b strips the story of any reference to towns, focusing instead on Khālid's description of date palms, while yet another variant[186] sets the story in the presence of ʿAbd al-Malik without mentioning al-Ḥajjāj, and adds short, anonymous words by representatives of Mecca, Medina, and Kufa, giving only Khālid the opportunity to speak lengthily on his town, Basra.

A21,[187] set in the presence of Yazīd ibn ʿUmar ibn Hubayra, forms a rare case where Khālid's lines are abbreviated ("We have *azādh* and *maʿqilī* dates and so and so") and his opponent, the Kufan ʿAbd al-Raḥmān ibn Bashīr al-ʿIjlī, is given the main role. While telling us nothing about the possible authenticity of the story, it makes it probable that this story derives from sources that did not focus on Khālid, as in those he usually emerges victorious or is at least given full opportunity to exhibit his oratorical talent, the main aim of the book by al-Madāʾinī and, presumably, al-Jalūdī being to transmit stories of the great orator Khālid, not to show him being bested by someone else.

A44, with its delicious description of food,[188] could be converted to a *mufākhara* by attaching it more firmly to Basra and adding a further interlocutor speaking in favour of food in Kufa. However, there is no indication that A44 is a fragment of a longer story.

While Khālid may appear, based on the number of anecdotes, to have been prolific in tribal and town *mufākharas*, it should be noted that this may partly be due to the fragmentarisation of longer stories, the large number of variant versions, and the predilection of later sources for these stories. While we do often come across the topic in the corpus, it seems probable that this is not

185 See Chapter 1.3.2.

186 See commentary to B81.

187 A22 is a fragment of the same story, as shown by A23.

188 Cf. A43.

due to a great number of separate stories being transmitted early on, but to a small number of stories and different parts of them, appearing often in the sources. Thus, one can reduce them to a rather small number of earlier stories that seem to have been later fragmented and/or elaborated.

The brief anecdote B92 refers to a tension between town dwellers and desert Arabs, the latter gaining the upper hand with a Bedouin's short blame of the town dwellers after Khālid's disparaging remarks on the Bedouins. The same superiority of the Bedouins is seen in the cases where Khālid readily admits their linguistic superiority.[189] While B92 resembles a *mufākhara* it is too underdeveloped to be considered as such in its extant form.

When it comes to *maḥāsin wa-masāwī*, we find many stories where Khālid is depicted as speaking for or against something, together with variants where Khālid speaks both in favour of and against a phenomenon or where another character replies to Khālid's speech, thus creating a *maḥāsin wa-masāwī* story.

In all cases, it is usually impossible to say whether one version is older than the other, but one might surmise that it has been more common to add the second speech (or reattribute someone's speech to Khālid) to create a *maḥāsin wa-masāwī* story than the other way round. In a few cases, this seems extremely probable and, in the case of A24 and the variants of B82 this may even be proven.[190]

One case of either building-up or fragmentation can be seen in comparing B10 with B10a and B10b. While B10 and B10b only present Khālid as preferring donkeys as mounts[191] and speaking in their favour, B10a adds an initial speech by Khālid against donkeys, thus creating a *maḥāsin wa-masāwī* story – or, if we take B10a as our starting point, B10 and B10b show how a longer story, B10a, has been fragmented by dropping the first part of the story.

B27 contains a speech by Khālid in favour of older women, with an anonymous ʿAnbarī answering with a speech in favour of young girls. Read together, the two speeches again form a *maḥāsin wa-masāwī* pair, or, to be more exact, a pair of *maḥāsin* of two opposite concepts or things. Even though this was not done by later authors, the story could easily become a regular *maḥāsin wa-masāwī* by reattributing the latter speech to Khālid and composing a middle part explaining the change of Khālid's mind, as was done in the case of A24.[192]

---

189 See Chapter 2.2.1.
190 See Chapters 2.5.1 and 2.5.2.
191 Cf. also A85.
192 See Chapter 2.5.1.

B42 and B43, both containg short speeches/sayings by Khālid in favour of and against eating cheese are concise examples of *maḥāsin wa-masāwī* where the focus is on Khālid's *bukhl* and his ability to speak both for and against something.

2.7 Speeches

Khālid's fame was largely based on his speeches and orations, and this is the aspect biographers and other men of letters constantly take up and highlight in their articles and comments on Khālid.[193] It is also commonplace for authors to refer to Khālid's speeches and to quote a sentence or two from them, without reporting the whole speech. However, considered in its entirety, the corpus contains surprisingly few complete speeches by Khālid, and in only one case, B38, do we seem to have a complete formal speech by him.

In addition, one finds a number of cases in which Khālid is said to have been in a formal delegation that went to meet a Caliph or a governor and to have spoken at the occasion. B40 mentions how he came in a delegation to Hishām and then quotes an informal conversation between the two, but no formal speech of Khālid is given. In the variant version B40a, any reference to a formal occasion has been dropped and the exchange of words is given as a casual conversation between the Caliph and the courtier. We have also seen how Khālid was inserted into many such stories to replace a less known relative of his.[194]

In B40 and B40a, Khālid is represented as speaking in favour of Khālid al-Qasrī in front of the Caliph in an informal conversation. In A45, he visits Yazīd ibn al-Muhallab on a matter of an imprisoned nephew of his, with a premeditated speech, which Khālid forgets when he sees a beautiful slavegirl and the only thing he is able to say is a flattery consisting of only one well-proportioned sentence, which moves the governor to grant him his wish. We have a similar polite flattery of a few lines in B37, where the Caliph Abū l-ʿAbbās rewards Khālid for his words.

A27 refers to a further type of formal speech discussing a peace agreement. The story, however, gives little context for the situation and does not quote Khālid's speech, concentrating on other issues instead.

Many descriptive passages are given as fragments of informal speeches, and some tribal *mufākharas* fall under the umbrella of a more formal oratory of a kind. However, Khālid's formal speeches are only very rarely reported. In two

193 See Chapter 1.5.

194 See Chapter 1.3.2.

stories, A9 and A11, ʿUmar ibn ʿAbd al-ʿAzīz, most probably anachronistically, asks Khālid to admonish him, and Khālid obliges, but the reader is only given a very brief version of the admonition, its central part. In B14 he is mentioned to have admonished Rawḥ ibn Ḥātim ibn Qabīṣa ibn al-Muhallab, but his words are not reported.

Even though A8 claims that Khālid had promised God that when alone with a king, he would remind him of God, it is only B38, which reports such an admonition in detail. In this story, Khālid himself transmits his speech in front of Hishām ibn ʿAbd al-Malik. The whole story is told in elegant prose, relying more on parallelism than on rhymed prose, which could be taken as a sign of relatively early provenance. In the narrative part, it has one allusion to the Qurʾān, and the speech itself contains a lengthy (8 lines) verse quotation from ʿAdī ibn Zayd. Moreover, the story told by Khālid gives the context of the speech, explaining both the scene at the beginning of the delivery of the speech and what happened after it.

B38 falls nice and squarely within the genre of *maqāmāt al-ʿulamāʾ*, admonitions spoken by pious persons in front of Caliphs and other high-ranking persons. As the speech itself is reported by Khālid and thus given as a later reminiscence, rather than an eyewitness report, it is clear that it is at least one step distanced from its real presentation, if it ever took place. More probably, it, like all the other longer texts, has undergone further changes during transmission.

2.8 The Literary Khālid: Conclusions

Chapter 2 has shown us Khālid as a literary character in a variety of roles, studied the rhetorical features of lines attributed to him, and shown how anecdotes are developed by later authors.

Khālid ibn Ṣafwān has found next to no place in histories of Arabic literature. If "literature" is understood to refer to written literature that aims at producing single-authored, finalised works, there is good reason for this lack of interest: Khālid never produced any such work and, moreover, he may well have been illiterate, as there is no indication in the corpus of him writing anything nor is he ever depicted reading.[195]

On the other hand, Khālid was unanimously considered a great orator[196] and should, thus, earn a position in any study of Umayyad oratory and ornate

195 Cf. Chapter 1.3.1, with one late and unreliable exception.
196 Chapter 1.5.

prose. The authenticity of the transmitted speeches may be questionable, but there is no question that he did influence the genre and was looked upon as a great master of Arabic oral prose.

Khālid's role as an (oral) author has not been fully recognised. One of the few who have noticed it is Carl Brockelmann who wrote "Als Vorläufer der späteren *Adabliteraten* können Männer wie Ḫālid b. Ṣafwān (…) gelten."[197] Blachère mentions Khālid briefly in his chapter on *Art oratoire et prose littéraire*, but seems to be dubious as to the authenticity of Khālid's extant orations, seeing their polished form as speaking against their authenticity.[198] In the *Cambridge History of Arabic Literature*, Khālid is only mentioned in passing in an article on Sufi literature in the volume dedicated to ʿAbbāsid learned literature,[199] while one searches in vain for his name in the volume dedicated to Umayyad literature.[200] Finally, in her *Arabic Oration* (2019), Tahera Qutbuddin mentions Khālid a couple of times, but only in passing.[201]

There is good reason to hesitate in pronouncing any of Khālid's speeches as authentic, due specifically to the oral transmission before codification: there is no evidence for any written collections of Khālid's speeches, or even transcripts of his individual orations prior to al-Madāʾinī and even though we cannot exclude the possibility of the one-time existence of transcripts of his speeches, the lack of any sign of such a written tradition must make one hesitate before making a claim of this kind.

To what extent can we tease out any genuine information on Umayyad prose from the Khālid corpus? It is perhaps the shorter sayings that we might more easily accept as potentially closer to authentic than the long speeches. The study of the variation in the stories would also imply the same: in many cases there seems to be a relatively invariable nucleus in some of the transmitted sayings, stories, and speeches, while later authors have otherwise been very free in rephrasing them. In a few cases, we may even follow the growth of some such inauthentic speeches around nuclei that could, but need not, be authentic.[202]

The general lack of authentic material from the Umayyad period makes it also difficult to compare Khālid's speeches with contemporary material. We do have a lot of speeches reported from Umayyad and earlier orators, but their

---

197 *GAL* S I: 105.

198 Blachère (1966): 731–732.

199 Farah (1990): 59.

200 Beeston et al. (1983).

201 Qutbuddin (2019): 189, 208, 266, 556.

202 See Chapter 2.5.1.

authenticity is just as dubious as that of Khālid's speeches.[203] Instead of trying to pronounce any final judgements on the question of authenticity, my aim has been to tease out some features of sayings attributed early on to Khālid, to show how the material has developed over time, and, when possible, to point out how some later versions have developed. This, further, gives us some material that represents the earliest detectable layers of the stories, whether at Khālid's time or slightly later. Against this, we can then assess other sayings which do not seem to conform with the style of these earlier sayings.

But what about Khālid as an author in his own right? As Khālid probably never wrote or published anything, his authorship may only be seen through others transmitting from him. The speeches reported from him are all too few and too fragmentary to allow us any serious comparison, but as faithful transmission never was the aim in historical and literary texts,[204] it seems extremely improbable that, e.g., B38 would allow us to study how Khālid composed his speeches. Much more probably, it shows how early ʿAbbāsid compilers authored speeches, possibly on the basis of some authentic fragments, and attributed them to Umayyad orators.

On the other hand, the study of transmitted materials tends to show that the core expressions (e.g., witty sayings) may have been transmitted more faithfully, so that some of the brief sayings of Khālid may well contain material going back to Khālid himself, although there does not seem to be any way to prove which particular sayings might be so early as to be potentially authentic. The best one can say is that the corpus may contain authentic material of Khālid's eloquence, especially in the case of short sayings.

Much more importantly, the corpus shows how Khālid was remembered and how his sayings and speeches as well as anecdotes about him found their form in the ninth century and after. The earliest layers of preserved anecdotes will have found their form by the time al-Madāʾinī (d. 228/842) made his compilation, which would date some of the stories only some three quarters of a century later than Khālid himself. Other stories, of course, continued their development, but a large part of the corpus can, with reasonal confidence, be said to represent Arabic prose literature in the period before al-Jāḥiẓ. Though not allowing us to see Umayyad literature too clearly, the stories do show us very early ʿAbbāsid narrators at work.

---

203 Qutbuddin (2019) and Klasova (2018) are more optimistic as to the authenticity of early Islamic speeches, but I cannot share their optimism, nor do I see a strong case made for the authenticity in their works, which, however, remain valuable contributions to Arabic rhetorics as attested in later sources. For collections of purportedly Umayyad speeches, see, e.g., the beginning of vol. IV of Ibn ʿAbdrabbih's *ʿIqd*.

204 See Hämeen-Anttila (2018a): 52–56, and (2018b): 16–23.

PART 2

Translations

CHAPTER 3

Stories from al-Balādhurī, *Ansāb* VII/1: 55–88

B1 Khālid ibn Ṣafwān ibn ʿAbdallāh ibn ʿAmr ibn al-Ahtam – whose name was Sinān – ibn Sumayy ibn Sinān ibn Khālid ibn Minqar the Orator belonged to them (the descendants of ʿAmr ibn al-Ahtam). Someone other than al-Kalbī has said: He is Khālid ibn Ṣafwān ibn ʿAbdallāh ibn al-Ahtam, but the opinion of al-Kalbī is more correct.

COMMENTARY: For Khālid's genealogy, see Chapter 1.4.

B2 His brother Nuʿaym ibn Ṣafwān ibn ʿAbdallāh ibn ʿAmr ibn al-Ahtam (also belonged to them). Nuʿaym was a drinker and constantly vexed his brother Khālid. Al-Ḥasan al-Baṣrī said about them: "O wonder at these two men! They have no admonisher in themselves and no scolder sent by God to upbraid them!" Al-Farazdaq lampooned this Nuʿaym:

> O, convey my message to Nuʿaym,
> Nuʿaym ibn Ṣafwān, driven out of Banū Saʿd:
>
> You are no reciter whose readings we would recognise[1]
> nor are you among sinners the steadfast and staunch.

B3 Khālid ibn Ṣafwān was very eloquent and one of the best orators and storytellers. He was powerful and wealthy, but a miser. His *kunya* was Abū Ṣafwān. The mother of Khālid and his brother Nuʿaym was Arwā bint Sulaym, who was a *mawlā* of Ziyād ibn abī Sufyān.[2]

---

1 From a little poem of three verses, see al-Farazdaq, *Dīwān*, p. 154. The *Dīwān* recension differs slightly and has to be understood as "you are no entertainer of guests whose hospitality (*qirāt*) would be wished for." The problem with this translation is that the verbal noun of *qarā* is *qirā*, not **qirāt-*. In al-Balādhurī, with the antithetical reference to *fussāq*, the verse is probably to be understood as translated above, reading *qārī* and *qirāta* as poetic licenses for *qāriʾi* and *qirāʾata*. For *qirāt-* < *qirāʾat-*, cf., e.g., Abū Nuwās, *Dīwān* III: 44 (*Khamriyyāt* 25: 9). The third verse in the *Dīwān*, missing from al-Balādhurī, refers to Nuʿaym's origin in al-Ḥīra, cf. B9. Banū Saʿd are the sub-tribe of Tamīm to which Khālid and Nuʿaym belonged.

2 Better known as Ziyād ibn Abīhi (d. 53/673).

 | DOI:10.1163/9789004433977_004

B4 The father of Khālid, Ṣafwān, was the leader of Banū Tamīm at the time of Masʿūd. Ṣafwān was an orator, too. When he died, he bequested 120,000 (dirhams)[3] and al-Ḥasan (al-Baṣrī) was a witness to his will. Someone asked Ṣafwān: "For what purpose did you set up and collect all this wealth?" He answered: "Against the calamities of Time, against the harshness of the ruler, and for priding myself among kinsfolk." Al-Ḥasan said to this: "By God, you are leaving it to people who will not praise you while you yourself are going to meet the One who will not forgive you!"[4]

Ibn Qutayba, *Maʿārif*, pp. 403–404.

COMMENTARY: Ṣafwān, like his son Khālid, is not mentioned by al-Ṭabarī. Masʿūd ibn ʿAmr al-Azdī rebelled in Basra and died in 64/684.[5] Al-Waṭwāṭ tells a similar story about ʿAbdallāh ibn al-Ahtam and al-Ḥasan al-Baṣrī.[6]

B5 < *Hishām ibn al-Kalbī* < *"his father"*: Khālid ibn Ṣafwān said: Truthfulness is laudable except in the case of a slanderer, who is the worse the truer he is. This has also been attributed to Ibn Shubruma.[7]

B6 < *ʿAlī ibn Muḥammad ibn ʿAbdallāh al-Madāʾinī*: Khālid ibn Ṣafwān said about[8] Bashīr ibn ʿUbaydallāh ibn abī Bakra:[9] "Bashīr got mixed with things out of ignorance. He miscarried in them, neither being able to endure them patiently nor getting determinedly out of them."

B7 He (al-Madāʾinī) said: Bilāl ibn abī Burda had ordered Khālid to be whipped and imprisoned because he had heard that when he had taken office Khālid had said:

> A summer cloud that will soon disperse.

Bilāl had said: "By God, it will not disperse ere it hits him with a downpour!"

---

3 Explicitly so in Ibn Qutayba, *Maʿārif*.

4 Cf. Ibn al-Jawzī, *Ādāb*, p. 124. Al-Jāḥiẓ, *Bayān* III: 127, attributes a similar saying to Abū Ḥāzim al-Aʿraj (d. 140/757).

5 For the *fitna* of Masʿūd, see Ulrich (2007) and the primary sources mentioned there.

6 Al-Waṭwāṭ, *Ghurar*, pp. 363–364.

7 ʿAbdallāh ibn Shubruma (d. 144/761), *qāḍī* of Kufa.

8 The text reads *li-Bashīr* "to Bashīr."

9 On the Basran Bashīr, see al-Ṭabarī, *Taʾrīkh* II: 208/XVIII: 218–219, and al-Balādhurī, *Ansāb* VII/1: 382–384.

B7a < *Abū Yaʿlā Zakariyyā ibn Yaḥyā ibn Khallād al-Minqarī* < *al-Aṣmaʿī* < *ʿAlī ibn Muslim al-Bāhilī* < *Qatāda*: When he heard that Bilāl ibn abī Burda had become the governor of Basra, Khālid ibn Ṣafwān said:

> A summer cloud that will soon disperse.

Bilāl sent for Khālid and asked: "Are you the one who said 'A summer cloud that will soon disperse'? Yet, by God, it will not disperse ere it hits you with a downpour of hail!" Then he ordered him to be whipped a hundred lashes.

(Wakīʿ, *Akhbār*, pp. 247–248/II: 25); Ibn ʿAbdrabbih, *ʿIqd* IV: 36;[10] al-Tawḥīdī, *Baṣāʾir* I: 99 (no. 280); Ibn ʿAsākir, *Taʾrīkh* X: 515–516.[11]

B7b Khālid ibn Ṣafwān used to come to Bilāl ibn abī Burda to tell him stories, but he made grammatical mistakes. Exasperated by this Bilāl said: "Are you telling me stories about Caliphs but making mistakes like water-carrying women!"[12]

< *al-Tawwazī*: After that Khālid ibn Ṣafwān started going to the mosque to learn grammar (*iʿrāb*). Later he became blind. When the retinue of Bilāl rode by, Khālid used to ask: "What is this?" When he was told that it was the Emir, he used to say:

> A summer cloud that will soon disperse.

This was told to Bilāl, who sent someone to sit by Khālid and to inform him about what he said. When Bilāl once again passed by Khālid, Khālid said as he always did. This was reported to Bilāl, who came to Khālid and said: "By God, it will not disperse ere it hits you with a downpour of hail!" Then Khālid was whipped a hundred lashes. Some say that he was not whipped, but Bilāl ordered his belly to be trampled underfoot.

(al-Mubarrad, *Kāmil* II: 42–43); al-Balādhurī, *Ansāb* (ed. al-ʿAẓm) XVIII: 262–263; Ghars al-Niʿma al-Ṣābiʾ, *Hafawāt*, pp. 318–319 (no. 319); Ibn Khallikān, *Wafayāt* III: 11–12;[13] al-Ṣafadī, *Wāfī* X: 279. *Brief versions* on *laḥn*: al-Zamakhsharī, *Rabīʿ* I: 649; al-Ābī, *Nathr* V: 274.

---

10 < al-Aṣmaʿī.

11 < Abū l-Qāsim ibn al-Samarqandī < Abū l-Ḥusayn ibn al-Naqqūr and Abū Manṣūr ibn al-ʿAṭṭār < Abū Ṭāhir al-Mukhallaṣ < ʿAbdallāh ibn ʿAbd al-Raḥmān Zakariyyā ibn Yaḥyā < al-Aṣmaʿī < ʿAlī ibn Musallam al-Bāhilī < Qatāda.

12 For *saqqāyāt* as gossipers, see al-Maghribī, *Nuzha*, pp. 171–172. Al-Ābī, *Nathr* V: 274, reads erroneously *al-sittāt*.

13 < Ghars al-Niʿma Ibn al-Ṣābiʾ *fī baʿḍ taṣānīfihi*.

COMMENTARY: Cf. also B9 and B108. A similar story is told by al-Jāḥiẓ about Ibn Shubruma and Ṭāriq ibn abī Ziyād, the *ṣāḥib shuraṭ* of Khālid al-Qasrī.[14] Cf also al-Tanūkhī, *Faraj* I: 171 (no. 58):

> Abū l-Ḥasan al-Madāʾinī said in his book *Kitāb al-Faraj baʿd al-shidda wa'l-ḍīqa*: When he came across some problem (*shidda*), Ibn Shubruma used to say: "(It is but) a cloud. Then it will disperse."

Müller attributes the verse to ʿImrān ibn Ḥiṭṭān (d. 84/703).[15] For a similar story about how Sībawayhi started learning grammar, see al-Sīrāfī, *Akhbār*, pp. 43–44.

B8 Khālid used to say: Justice in the house of Bilāl is rarer than red sulphur in the house of Abū l-Zard al-Ḥanafī. Abū l-Zard al-Ḥanafī, about whom al-Farazdaq said as he did, has already been mentioned.

B8a Khālid ibn Ṣafwān used to come to Bilāl ibn abī Burda during Bilāl's governorship and visit him when he was in power, but when away from him Khālid slandered him and said: "There is no more religion in the heart of Bilāl than there are jewels in the house of Abū l-Zard al-Ḥanafī." Abū l-Zard was a penniless man.

al-Balādhurī, *Ansāb* (ed. ʿAẓm) XVIII: 264; Ibn ʿAbdrabbih, *ʿIqd* IV: 36.[16]

COMMENTARY: Cf. B7, B9a, and B108. Abū l-Zard is mentioned by al-Farazdaq, *Dīwān* (ed. al-Ṣāwī), p. 814.

B9 < *al-Madāʾinī*: Khālid ibn Ṣafwān came to Yūsuf ibn ʿUmar while Bilāl ibn abī Burda was being punished. Khālid said to Yūsuf: "May God make the Emir prosper! This here is Bilāl ibn abī Burda ibn abī Mūsā. His grandfather was a barber who took his *kunya* from his razor (*mūsā*) and married Ṭahafa bint al-Dammūn, who was black-skinned and had (but) tufts of hair. She was the mother of Abū Burda. Al-Dammūn admitted being a *mawlā* of the Emir. Bilāl's mother was his father's slavegirl, who used to go out to the market. People used

14 Al-Jāḥiẓ, *Bayān* III: 146. Cf. also, e.g., Ibn ʿAbdrabbih, *ʿIqd* III: 176, 204; al-Thaʿālibī, *Thimār*, p. 653; Ibn Qutayba, *ʿUyūn* I: 120; al-Jurjānī, *Muntakhab*, pp. 303–304; ʿAbd al-Qādir al-Baghdādī, *Ḥāshiya* II: 475.

15 Müller (1979): 85–89.

16 < al-Aṣmaʿī.

to touch her flank and Bilāl's father used to hit her on head and beat her because of a single dirham."

Bilāl answered: "My father married an Arab woman equal (in descent) to himself, but this man's father and his uncle (Shayba) fell in love with two emancipated Basran women. When their families feared that these men would cause disgrace to them, they made them marry the women. This (Khālid) is the son of Ziyād's slavegirl and his cousin (Shabīb) is the son of a slavegirl belonging to the family of Maʿmar. He dares to be insolent towards me because of three things: He is free, while I am a prisoner; the Emir is angered with me but pleased with him; he is in al-Ḥīra on his own ground, where he was born. The ground knows him and he knows it. He is like a dog, bold at the gate of his own people."

al-Ṣafadī, *Nukat*, pp. 148–149;[17] al-Mubarrad, *Kāmil* III: 342–343;[18] al-Waṭwāṭ, *Ghurar*, p. 147.[19]

B9a < (*ʿAbdallāh ibn Aḥmad ibn Ḥanbal*) < *Muḥammad ibn Ṣāliḥ al-ʿAdawī* < *Ibn Dāja*: People gathered at the door of Bilāl ibn abī Burda when he was the governor and the judge of Basra. The chamberlain (*ādhin*) kept them waiting and the sun started bearing on them. Then the chamberlain came and made them rise from the carpet and moved them over to the other side, to shade.

Someone said: "Glory be to God! Is there no piety nor abstinence from sin (*ḥaraj*)[20] here!" Khālid ibn Ṣafwān replied: "By God, *ḥaraj* is here rarer than red sulphur in the house of al-Ward al-Ḥanafī!" – He was a penniless man.

This saying reached Bilāl, who received Khālid and let him hear things. Bilāl was afraid that Khālid would slander him, so he made him swear (he would not do so). Bilāl also said: "By God, he will not come out of the prison until he brings me people who will bail him! They shall guarantee that each one will give me one thousand (dirhams) if Khālid will not come to me with them." And he did so.[21]

Later, Khālid al-Qasrī was dismissed from the governorship of Iraq. Yūsuf ibn ʿUmar was appointed governor and Khālid ibn Ṣafwān came to complain about Bilāl. Bilāl was brought in chains, and the two met in front of Yūsuf. Khālid started attacking Bilāl, who said: "O Emir, may God ennoble you! This man is arrogant because of three things: He is free, while I am a prisoner. The

17 With major variants, partly taken from B108.
18 < al-Kalbī, with variants.
19 Al-Waṭwāṭ's version follows al-Mubarrad.
20 Cf. al-Zabīdī, *Tāj* V: 480.
21 I.e., Khālid escaped, cf. B9b.

Emir is angered with me but pleased with him. He is on his ground, while I am a stranger."

When Bilāl said that he was a stranger, Khālid left the room. Yūsuf noticed this and asked: "What is the matter with him? Woe upon him! This man is from Kufa and he is from Basra and now the Kufan tells us that he is in his country! Tell me what this is about!" Someone answered: "May God kill Bilāl, how vicious he is! He referred to Khālid's (clan's) origin being in al-Ḥīra, implying that they are of suspect lineage because of their mother, ʿAfra." Then he recited the verses of Qays ibn ʿĀṣim:[22]

A ghastly dame (*ʿifirra*)[23] brought you from her country,
a Ḥīran. (It is) not as you claim.

Had I not defended you, you would have become slaves.
Her abode was al-Ḥīra and al-Saylaḥūn.[24]

(Wakīʿ, *Akhbār*, p. 256/II: 37–38)

B9b < *Abū l-Ḥasan al-Madāʾinī: When Bilāl took office, Khālid ibn Ṣafwān said*:

A summer cloud that will soon disperse.

Bilāl sent for Khālid and asked: "Are you the one who said: 'A summer cloud that will soon disperse'? By God, it will not disperse ere it hits you with a downpour of hail!" Then he ordered Khālid to be whipped a hundred lashes.

It is said that Khālid used to visit him during his reign but slandered him when away from him, saying: "There is less belief in Bilāl's heart than jewels in the house of al-Zard." Al-Zard al-Ḥanafī[25] was a penniless man. Bilāl arrested him and Khālid was afraid lest he would kill him. Bilāl said: "I will not let you go, unless ten people bail you, among them your brother Nuʿaym." They did bail him, promising that they would pay him a hundred thousand (dirhams)[26]

---

22 The verses in Wakīʿ's *Akhbār* are corrupt and they have been tacitly corrected. For the story of the mutual insults between ʿAmr ibn al-Ahtam and Qays in the presence of the Prophet after the conquest of Mecca, see Ibn Rustah, *Aʿlāq*, p. 206.

23 Read so with Ibn Rustah, *Aʿlāq*, p. 206. For the word, see Ibn Manẓūr, *Lisān* IX: 285, s.v.

24 A place between al-Ḥīra and al-Qādisiyya, see Yāqūt, *Buldān* III: 298–299. Yāqūt erroneously attributes four verses of the poem to ʿAmr ibn al-Ahtam.

25 The manuscript of Ibn ʿAsākir reads Abū Dardāʾ.

26 Explicitly so in Ibn ʿAsākir, who also adds here "except for Nuʿaym, who had no money."

if Khālid disappeared. Khālid did run away and broke covenant with them and Bilāl took a hundred thousand from them. Khālid said:

> O son of castrator (fem.) of testicles,[27] do not deem me
> weak, not able to leave the place.
> Bilāl has been granted (authority) on us in God's earth and sky
> – may God free us from him, and quickly![28]

When Yūsuf ibn ʿUmar arrested Bilāl, Khālid attacked him, saying: "May God keep the Emir! This is Bilāl ibn abī Burda ibn abī Mūsā. His grandfather was a barber, who took his *kunya* from his razor (*mūsā*). His grandmother was Ṭahafa bint Dammūn, who was black-skinned and had (but) tufts of hair. His mother was his father's slavegirl, whom he used to beat for a dirham. She used to go around in the market and her feet were like donkey's hooves. Slaves used to touch her flanks."

Bilāl replied: "You dare to speak to me (so) because the Emir is pleased with you but angered with me, and I am a stranger but you are at the door of your mansion." – That day Yūsuf was in al-Ḥīra, and Bilāl implied that Khālid derived his origin from the people of al-Ḥīra. – "Are you not Khālid ibn Ṣafwān ibn al-Ahtam, who stands on his claws?[29] You are like a dog, bold at the gate of his people. This man's father and his uncle fell in love with two emancipated Basran women. When their families feared that these men would cause disgrace to them, they made them marry the women. You are the son of Banū Ziyād's slavegirl!"

Khālid said to Yūsuf: "O Emir, this is the most stupid of all people. By God, he does not know his abode of Arabness[30] from his abode of emigration!" Bilāl replied: "Yes, I do, by God! My abode of Arabness is Yemen and my abode of emigration is Medina. But I will tell you about your abodes of Arabness and emigration: your abode of Arabness is al-Ḥīra and your abode of emigration is Basra."

---

27 For *wahṣ*, see Ibn Manẓūr, *Lisān* XV: 414, s.v.: castrating an animal by tying its testicles and then crushing them between two stones. The expression is used as an insult, cf. a verse by Jarīr on Ghassān (*Lisān* XV: 414, s.v. = *Dīwān*, p. 891, no. 21: 9).

28 Ibn ʿAsākir adds a third verse.

29 This refers to Khālid's imputedly impure lineage. See Lane (1863–93), s.vv. *burthun* and *burjuma*.

30 I.e., his origin.

(al-Balādhurī, *Ansāb*, ed. al-ʿAẓm, VII: 402–403); Wakīʿ, *Akhbār*, p. 248/II: 25;[31] Ibn ʿAsākir, *Taʾrīkh* X: 516.[32]

B9c < *Abū l-Mundhir Hishām ibn Muḥammad al-Sāʾib al-Kalbī*: Bilāl ibn abī Burda was steadfast when he was punished. For some reason Yūsuf ibn ʿUmar brought him in chains into his presence when they were in al-Ḥīra. Khālid ibn Ṣafwān rose and said to Yūsuf: "O Emir, this enemy of God, Bilāl, whipped and imprisoned me although I did not stray from the flock nor had I renounced obedience in any way." Then he turned to Bilāl and said: "Glory be to God, who has put an end to your rule, demolished your support, finished your glory, and changed your situation. By God, you kept strictly aloof, thought slightly of the nobles, and showed partisan spirit (*ʿaṣabiyya*)!"

Bilāl answered: "O Khālid, you are arrogant towards me because of three things that are for you and against me: The Emir is angered with me but pleased with you. You are free, while I am a prisoner. You are on your ground, while I am a stranger." With this he silenced Khālid. [It is said that the Ahtamites were some riffraff, who had entered Banū Minqar and traced their descent from them.][33]

The reason for Bilāl having Khālid whipped during his governorship was that he once passed by Khālid with a handsome retinue and Khālid said:

> A summer cloud that will soon disperse.

Bilāl heard this and said: "By God, it will not disperse ere it hits you with a downpour of hail!" Then he ordered Khālid to be whipped and imprisoned.

(al-Ḥuṣrī, *Zahr*, p. 935); Wakīʿ, *Akhbār*, pp. 256–257/II: 29;[34] Ibn al-Kumaylī, *Nuzha*, p. 871.

COMMENTARY: Cf. B7, B8, and B108. Wakīʿ, *Akhbār*, p. 248, gives the additional detail that as Nuʿaym had no money the 100,000 dirhams were collected from among the nine other bailsmen. Wakīʿ also presents an additional verse to the poem quoted by Khālid.

---

31 Abbreviated < Abū Yaʿlā al-Minqarī < al-Aṣmaʿī and al-ʿAlāʾ ibn al-Faḍl < "his father."

32 Abbreviated < al-Aṣmaʿī and al-ʿAlāʾ ibn al-Faḍl < "his father." This ties up with the *isnād* of B7b where the first part of this story is given with a number of *isnāds*.

33 The sentence is missing from most manuscripts. Al-Mubarrad, *Kāmil* III: 342–343, explains that the origin of the family of al-Ahtam was from al-Ḥīra and that they were a mixed lot (*ushāba*), who had joined Banū Minqar and were originally from Byzantium.

34 < Jaʿfar ibn Muḥammad al-ʿIjlī < al-Haytham ibn ʿAdī < Ibn ʿAyyāsh, with major variants. Ibn ʿAyyāsh is here given as an eyewitness to the scene.

B10 He (al-Madāʾinī) has said: Khālid passed by the general (*al-qāʾid*) Abū l-Jahm on a donkey of his. Abū l-Jahm said to him: "What's this, Khālid!" Khālid answered: "This is a wild ass from among the daughters of al-Kudād,[35] having knotted (i.e., strong) feet and sand-coloured legs. It endures hardships and brings one to the next halting place[36] and it detains me from becoming an obstinate tyrant."[37]

Ibn Qutayba, *ʿUyūn* I: 250–251; al-Tawḥīdī, *Baṣāʾir* VIII: 198 (no. 734).[38]

B10a Khālid ibn Ṣafwān came to ʿAlī ibn al-Jahm ibn abī Ḥudhayfa and found him ready for a ride. When a donkey was brought to Ibn al-Jahm, Khālid said: "Don't you know that an ass (*ʿayr*) is a shame (*ʿār*) and a donkey a disgrace? It has an ugly voice[39] and is unpleasantly unable.[40] It slips on shallow ground and tumbles in mud. It is not suitable for a hero (*faḥl*) to ride[41] nor is it a mount for a load. Its rider is loathsome and his fellow traveller looks down on him."

Ibn al-Jahm now disliked the idea of riding a donkey, dismounted, and took a horse. The donkey was given to Khālid, who mounted it. Ibn al-Jahm said to him: "Woe to you, Khālid! Do you forbid something you do yourself?" Khālid replied: "But this is a wild ass, a descendant of al-Kurbāl,[42] may God keep you! It has shiny legs and animated feet. It lets those ride who walk and brings them to mountain paths and it detains me from becoming an obstinate tyrant. If I did not know my place I would go astray and would not be among the guided!"[43]

(al-Ḥuṣrī, *Zahr*, pp. 983–984); al-Sharīshī, *Sharḥ* IV: 135;[44] al-Zamakhsharī, *Rabīʿ* IV: 401–402; Ibn Ḥamdūn, *Tadhkira* V: 255 (no. 675); al-Rāghib al-Iṣfahānī, *Muḥāḍarāt* IV: 634.

---

35 Cf. al-Farazdaq, *Dīwān*, p. 158; Ibn Manẓūr, *Lisān* IV: 432a (s.v. DHMJ), XII: 44b (s.v. KDD).

36 See Lane (1863–93), s.v. *ʿuqba*.

37 Cf. Q 11: 59 and 14: 15.

38 In al-Jāḥiẓ, *Bighāl* II: 218 (> al-Nuwayrī, *Nihāya* X: 85–86), a somewhat similar story is told about Khālid's father, Ṣafwān, and ʿAbd al-Raḥmān ibn ʿAbbās ibn Rabīʿa ibn al-Ḥārith ibn ʿAbd al-Muṭṭalib, on whom, see al-Zubayrī, *Nasab*, p. 88. Ibn Qutayba, *ʿUyūn* I: 250, narrates this as a dialogue between an anonymous Hāshimite and al-Faḍl ibn al-Rabīʿ.

39 Cf. Q 31: 19.

40 Cf. Lane (1863–93), s.v. *fawt* (*asmaʿu ṣawtan wa-arā fawtan*).

41 The expression could also be translated "for a stallion to mount."

42 The reading al-Kurbāl may have been caused by the following *al-sirbāl*, which rhymes with it. Al-Thaʿālibī, who quotes from Ḥamza, has *al-Kudār*. According to note 4 in al-Ḥuṣrī, *Zahr*, p. 983, al-Kurbāl is a district in Fārs, but the place name is not found in, e.g., Yāqūt, *Buldān*. The reading of B10, al-Kudād, is clearly superior to the others.

43 Cf. Q 6: 56.

44 The interlocutor here is ʿAlī ibn al-Jahm al-ʿAdawī.

B10b Khālid ibn Ṣafwān and al-Faḍl ibn ʿĪsā al-Raqāshī used to prefer donkeys over ponies as mounts, taking Abū Sayyāra[45] as their model. A Basran nobleman once met Khālid ibn Ṣafwān and, seeing him on a donkey, asked: "What's this for a mount?" Khālid replied: "This is a wild ass from among the daughters of al-Kudād, having sand-coloured legs, knotted (i.e., strong) feet, and thick skin. It lets those ride who walk and brings them to mountain paths. It is rarely sick and easily cured and it detains me from becoming an obstinate tyrant or one of the evil-doers.[46] Had not the donkey many benefits Abū Sayyāra would not have ridden wild asses for forty years!"

(Ḥamza, *Durra*, p. 153); al-Thaʿālibī, *Thimār*, pp. 369–370;[47] al-Maydānī, *Majmaʿ* II: 245; al-Balawī, *Alif-bāʾ* II: 492.[48]

COMMENTARY: Parts of Khālid's speech are also given by Ḥamza, al-Maydānī (*Majmaʿ* II: 246), and al-Balawī in a Bedouin's answer to a speech by al-Faḍl ibn ʿĪsā, which in these versions comes after the story about Khālid.

B10a changes the story into a *maḥāsin wa-masāwī*. Al-Zamakhsharī, al-Thaʿālibī, and Ibn Ḥamdūn[49] have first Khālid speak in favour of donkeys and then the anonymous Bedouin answer by listing their negative features (different from those in al-Ḥuṣrī's version) as a response to Khālid's words, thus dividing the *maḥāsin wa-masāwī* between two characters. This answer has then been attributed to Khālid by al-Shimshāṭī:[50]

> Khālid ibn Ṣafwān said: What a bad animal donkey is! If you let him go his way, he turns around, and if you stop him, he puts forth his yard. He is of little help but produces a lot of dung, he is slow to charge but quick to escape. You cannot use him for a woman's dowry or for bloodwit.

Al-ʿAskarī collects a number of these phrases, including the passage above, mainly attributing them to anonymous Bedouins and not mentioning Khālid.[51]

45 The pre-Islamic wise man ʿUmayla ibn al-Aʿzal ibn Khālid Abū Sayyāra was proverbial for riding his black ass for forty years, see *EI2*, s.v. (Ch. Pellat).

46 While the last phrase is not found exactly as such in the Qurʾān, it is strongly reminiscent of Qurʾānic diction.

47 < Ḥamza.

48 < Ḥamza al-Iṣbahānī, *Kitāb al-Amthāl*.

49 Al-Thaʿālibī, *Thimār*, pp. 369–370, and Ibn Ḥamdūn, *Tadhkira* V: 255.

50 Al-Shimshāṭī, *Anwār* I: 351.

51 Al-ʿAskarī, *Awāʾil*, p. 17.

B11 Khālid said: Ponies (*barādhīn*) are for elegance and calm, horses for pursuit and escape, camels for blood(money) and long journeys, mules for loads and burdens, and donkeys for leisurely and easy riding.

al-Tawḥīdī, *Imtāʿ* III: 60; al-Thaʿālibī, *Tawfīq*, p. 59 (abbreviated); al-Thaʿālibī, *Thimār*, p. 357 (no. 548, anonymous).

B11a Sulaymān ibn ʿAlī said to Khālid ibn Ṣafwān when he saw him riding a donkey: "What is this, Abū Ṣafwān?" Khālid replied: "O Emir, may God bless you, shall I tell you about riding animals?" Sulaymān said: "Do so." Khālid continued: "Camels are for carrying and riding as a counterbalance,[52] mules for loads and burdens, horses for pursuit and escape, ponies (*barādhīn*) for elegance and steady going (*waṭāʾa*), and donkeys for leisurely and convenient riding."

(al-Jāḥiẓ, *Bighāl* II: 220); Ibn al-Sarrāj, *Jawāhir*, p. 879.

B11b Khālid ibn Ṣafwān rode a donkey and passed by Sulaymān ibn ʿAlī, who was on a balcony (*manẓara*) in al-Mirbad. Sulaymān asked him: "What about horses and purebred (racers)?" Khālid replied: "May God keep the Emir! Horses are for battle, camels for burdens, riding camels (*rakāʾib*) for elegance, donkeys for loads, and asses for leisureliness."

(al-Tawḥīdī, *Baṣāʾir* III: 48, no. 125); al-Dajājī, *Safaṭ*, p. 55.

B11c *Abū Saʿd ibn al-Baghdādī < Abū Manṣūr ibn Shukrawayhi and Muḥammad ibn Aḥmad ibn ʿAlī Abū Bakr al-Simsār < Ibrāhīm ibn ʿAbdallāh ibn Muḥammad < al-Maḥāmilī Abū ʿAbdallāh < ʿAbdallāh ibn abī Saʿd < al-Ḥasan ibn ʿAlī ibn Manṣūr < Muḥammad ibn Saʿīd al-Rāzī < Muḥammad ibn Ḥumayd < ʿAbd al-Raḥmān ibn Maghrāʾ < Shabīb ibn Shayba*: I met Khālid ibn Ṣafwān, who was riding a donkey of his, and said to him: "Abū Ṣafwān, how about swift horses?" He replied: "They are for pursueing and escaping, and I'm neither pursuing nor escaping." "I continued: "How about ponies?" He replied: "They are for those who make haste and hurry, but I am neither making haste nor hurrying." I asked: "How about mules?" He replied: "They are for loads and burdens, and I have neither the one nor the other." I asked him: "So what do you do with this donkey of yours?" He replied: "I ride leisurely, approaching slowly, and when I want to, I visit a dear friend on it."

(Ibn ʿAsākir, *Taʾrīkh* XVI: 111); Ibn al-ʿAdīm, *Bughya* VII: 65–66.[53]

---

52 See Lane (1863–93), s.v. ZML.

53 < Abū Naṣr al-Qāḍī < ʿAlī ibn abī Muḥammad < Abū Saʿd ibn al-Baghdādī < Abū Manṣūr ibn Shukrawayhi and Muḥammad ibn Aḥmad ibn ʿAlī Abū Bakr al-Simsār < Ibrāhīm

COMMENTARY: Cf. Q 16: 8, which refers to God having created horses, mules, and asses for men to ride. In B13 Khālid is again speaking with Sulaymān, which either is a pure coincidence, as it well may be, or a sign that originally (in the work of-Madāʾinī?) there was a short cluster of stories here involving Sulaymān.

B12 Khālid said: I spent the whole night wishing for things, fulfilling[54] the green ocean with red gold. Yet of all that, I only need two loaves of bread, two jugs (of water), and two old rags.

al-Jāḥiẓ, *Bayān* III: 164; Ibn Qutayba, *ʿUyūn* II: 396; Ibn abī l-Ḥadīd, *Sharḥ* II: 423; al-Ābī, *Nathr* VII: 134; Ibn ʿAsākir, *Taʾrīkh* XVI: 113;[55] Ibn al-ʿAdīm, *Bughya* VII: 63;[56] Ibn Manẓūr, *Mukhtaṣar* VII: 364.

COMMENTARY: The expression *dhū ṭimrayn* is frequently used in reference to ascetics.[57] The saying also belongs to a longer story, see B16. The "two old rags" is a topos, which one also finds in, e.g., some of the death bed verses by Muʿāwiya.[58]

B13 Sulaymān ibn ʿAlī once mentioned that a man wished to be appointed to some office. Khālid said: "By God, even if he were appointed to Suwayqat al-Baḥrayn,[59] he could not run it. He also combines this (inability) with base descent, bad manners, and lack of inherited property (*nashab*)."

B14 They say that one day Khālid ibn Ṣafwān met Rawḥ ibn Ḥātim ibn Qabīṣa ibn al-Muhallab.[60] Khālid spoke about the world and preached

---

ibn ʿAbdallāh ibn Muḥammad < al-Maḥāmilī Abū ʿAbdallāh < ʿAbdallāh ibn abī Saʿd < al-Ḥasan ibn ʿAlī ibn Manṣūr < Muḥammad ibn Saʿīd al-Rāzī < Muḥammad ibn Ḥumayd < ʿAbd al-Raḥmān ibn Maghrāʾ < Shabīb ibn Shayba.

54 In most versions *ḥattā kabastu*.

55 < Abū l-Qāsim ʿAlī ibn Ibrāhīm < Abū l-Ḥasan al-Muqriʾ < Abū Muḥammad al-Ḥasan ibn Ismāʿīl < Aḥmad ibn Marwān < Aḥmad ibn Dāʾūd < al-Māzinī < al-Aṣmaʿī.

56 < Abū l-Ḥasan Muḥammad ibn Aḥmad ibn ʿAlī < Abū l-Maʿālī ʿAbdallāh ibn Ṣābir < Rashaʾ ibn Naẓīf < al-Ḥasan ibn Ismāʿīl < Aḥmad ibn Marwān < Aḥmad ibn Dāʾūd < al-Māzinī < al-Aṣmaʿī.

57 Cf., e.g., al-Jāḥiẓ, *Bayān* III: 277 (in a *ḥadīth*). For its use in *ḥadīths*, see Wensinck (1992) IV: 27.

58 See Ibn ʿAbdrabbih, *ʿIqd* III: 232.

59 Literally "the little market of Bahrain."

60 Rawḥ ibn Ḥātim ibn Qabīṣa Abū Khalaf is first mentioned in 132/749 in connection with the siege of Wāsiṭ in the army of al-Saffāḥ. Later, he was the chamberlain (*ḥājib*) of al-Manṣūr. In 159/776 he became the governor of al-Sind. In 166/782 he was the governor

abstinence from it. Then he said to Rawḥ ibn Ḥātim: "O Abū Khalaf, despite all your nobility and importance and the worldly things God has given you, I can see you seeking worldly things ever so much!" Rawḥ answered him: "O Abū Ṣafwān, the only thing that makes me desirous of the world is that whenever I, a young man, visit someone's door, I find you there before me, though you are above sixty and not much is left for you." Khālid replied: "By God, if so you say, then I have lost the splendour of my face, the sword of my backbone, and the passion of my heart. More than this that you see, I need calm and comfort, a tidy house, a vessel of perfume (*naḍūḥ*), and a drawn curtain."

B14a < *al-Ḥakam al-Aʿrābī*[61] < *Rawḥ ibn Ḥātim*: When I was standing at the door of one of the governors of Basra, Khālid ibn Ṣafwān came, looked at me, and said: "Young man (*yā bna akhī*), by God, I never come to a governor's door, morning or noon, without seeing you standing there! Do you so much love worldly things and covet them?"

Rawḥ has said: I respected him too much to answer and thought to myself: "He's an old man (*huwa ʿamm*). Perhaps he wanted to startle me in order to know how I would answer him." Then I said: "By God, O uncle, is there not enough quest for worldly things from your side when you see me standing here?" He laughed and said: "Young man, if so you say, then the lustre of my face and the brilliance of my eyesight have gone and the time of ailments is drawing close. By God, there never was a time in our lives when we did not prefer this world to the next. It just ever seems to evade us[62] as it keeps running away from us."

(al-Tawḥīdī, *Baṣāʾir* IX: 23–24, no. 60); al-Tawḥīdī, *Baṣāʾir* V: 171 (no. 573);[63] Ibn ʿAsākir, *Taʾrīkh* XVIII: 234–235;[64] al-Qālī, *Amālī* II: 197.[65]

---

of Basra, and finally from 171/787 onward he was the governor of Ifrīqiya. He died in 174/791, forty years after Khālid. See *EI2*, s.v. (M. Talbi).

61 In *Baṣāʾir* V: 171, Ibn al-Aʿrābī.

62 This sentence has been translated from Ibn ʿAsākir (*thumma lā tazdādu lanā illā takhalliyan*). *Baṣāʾir* IX: 23–24, reads *thumma mā nazdādu lahā illā taḥalliyan* and *Baṣāʾir* V: 171, *fa-mā tazdādu ʿindanā illā taḥalliyan*.

63 < Ibn al-Aʿrābī.

64 In an article on Rawḥ, with variants < Abū Muḥammad ʿAbdallāh ibn Aḥmad ibn Naṣr and Abū l-Ḥasan ʿAlī ibn Barakāt ibn Ṭāhir < Abū Bakr al-Khaṭīb < Abū l-Ḥusayn ibn Bishrān < Abū ʿAlī ibn Ṣafwān < Abū Bakr ibn abī l-Dunyā < al-ʿAbbās ibn Hishām ibn Muḥammad < "his father."

65 Only the last two sentences, with variants < Abū ʿUmar < Abū l-ʿAbbās < Ibn al-Aʿrābī. The *isnād* is attached to the previous article, this being introduced by "with the same *isnād*."

COMMENTARY: The two versions given by al-Tawḥīdī have slight differences. Some of the differences connect *Baṣāʾir* V: 171 with al-Balādhurī's version.

B15 Khālid extolled a man, saying among other things: "I have never seen one more sedate in gushing forth (his words) or having a deeper well or being firmer in grasping the tail of an argument when its head has gone before or more discerning of *ubna* and *waṣma*."[66]

al-Tawḥīdī, *Baṣāʾir* I: 62 (no. 166);[67] Ibn Manẓūr, *Lisān* XV: 320 (s.v. WṢM); al-Zabīdī, *Tāj* XXXIV: 54–55.[68]

B16 < *al-Madāʾinī* < *ʿAdī ibn al-Faḍl*: Khālid said: "Do not take one wife, because when she menstruates, you menstruate with her, and when she lies in childbed, you will be there, too.[69] When she visits someone or travels away or is sick, it is the same with you. Do not take two wives because then you will be between two evils.[70] Do not take three wives because then you will be (as a cauldron boiling) upon three stones. Do not take four wives because they will exhaust you (sexually)[71] and make you old and penniless." Ibn Ribāṭ al-Fuqaymī said to him: "You have forbidden everything that God has permitted!" Khālid replied: "Better than all this is (to have) two loaves, two old rags, two jugs (of water), and to worship the Merciful."

ps.-al-Jāḥiẓ, *Maḥāsin*, p. 221; Ibn ʿAsākir, *Taʾrīkh* XVI: 111–112;[72] al-Sharīshī, *Sharḥ* IV: 134.

COMMENTARY: Cf. B12. This story is fully discussed under A24 and in Chapter 2.5.1. Ibn ʿAsākir prefaces it as follows:[73]

66 Both words denote certain types of speech defects.

67 < Ibn al-Aʿrābī.

68 The story is also mentioned, but not told, in Ibn Manẓūr, *Lisān* I: 52 (s.v. ʾBN).

69 I.e., when she is ritually impure, you remain without sex. Al-Sharīshī adds "and (only) when she is pure, you are pure."

70 Ps.-al-Jāḥiẓ has *fa-taqaʿa fīmā bayna l-jamratayn* which may have been inspired by *sharar* "sparks" and would go well with the following *athāfī*. Al-Sharīshī reads *taqaʿu bayna ḍarratayn*, which is clearly a mistake for *jamratayn*. The interlocutor in ps.-al-Jāḥiẓ's and al-Sharīshī's version is an anonymous man.

71 Lane (1863–93), s.v. *jafara*.

72 < Abū l-Qāsim al-Shaḥḥāmī < Abū Aḥmad ʿAbd al-Raḥmān ibn Isḥāq al-ʿĀmirī < Abū ʿAmr Aḥmad ibn abī l-Furātī < Abū Mūsā ʿImrān ibn Mūsā < Abū l-Ḥasan Muḥammad ibn Muḥammad ibn abī l-Jalāb when he came to ʿUthmān al-Ḥumrī < Jaʿfar ibn Sawād.

73 Ibn ʿAsākir, *Taʾrīkh* XVI: 111–112. Cf. also al-Sharīshī, *Sharḥ* IV: 134.

> A man came to Khālid ibn Ṣafwān, who asked him: "Are you married?" The man replied he was not, and Khālid said: "Then marry." After a while he said: "Do not marry!" The man asked why not, and Khālid said, etc.

The story about Khālid is very similar to a saying attributed to an anonymous Bedouin in al-Rāghib, *Muḥāḍarāt* III: 202.[74]

B17 Khālid said: By God, I am not happy to spend a dirham except for knocking at the gate of Paradise or buying bananas.

al-Murtaḍā, *Amālī* II: 262; al-Khaṭīb al-Baghdādī, *Bukhalāʾ*, p. 259; Ibn ʿAsākir, *Taʾrīkh* XVI: 115; Ibn Manẓūr, *Mukhtaṣar* VII: 364.

COMMENTARY: In Ibn ʿAsākir, Ibn Manẓūr, and al-Khaṭīb, B17 is combined with B39. Cf. also B113.

B18 Khālid said: Satan, with his perfidy and snares (*manāṣib ḥibālihi*) deceives us by obscurities and attacks us with lust. When he has wearied us by deception, he returns to attack.

B19 Khālid used to say: Whose wealth is sufficient is neither rich nor poor, because when a misfortune falls upon him, it will destroy his sufficiency. Whose wealth is below sufficiency is poor and whose wealth is above sufficiency is rich.

al-Murtaḍā, *Amālī* II: 263.

B20 Khālid used to say: It is better to have a neighbour, who you fear may break into your house, than to have a merchant as your neighbour because the latter will always be ready to lend you money and to write a promissory note.

al-Murtaḍā, *Amālī* II: 263.

COMMENTARY: Cf. the action of the merchant in *al-Maqāma al-Maḍīriyya* by al-Hamadhānī.[75]

B21 < *al-Madāʾinī* < *ʿAbdallāh ibn Salm*: Once a man belonging to the family of al-Muhallab and another belonging to the family of al-Musabbiḥ ibn al-Ḥawārī al-ʿAtakī, both of whom were misers, went by Khālid('s house).

---

74 Cf. also the previous anecdote in al-Rāghib, *Muḥāḍarāt* III: 201.

75 Al-Hamadhānī, *Maqāmāt*, pp. 129–131.

Khālid said to them: "Come and sit down and let us tell stories about withholding. By God, that is harder than freely giving!"

COMMENTARY: Withholding is harder than giving because the code of behaviour necessitates giving and a miser has to think hard to avoid meeting the demand without seeming to do so.[76] For the famous aristocratic family of the Muhallabids, see *EI2*, s.v. (P. Crone), and for the aristocratic family of al-Musabbiḥ, see Crone (1980): 121.

B22 He (al-Madāʾinī) said: Once Khālid went on pilgrimage and left his son Ribʿī in charge of his property. When Khālid came back, Ribʿī had spent a considerable sum. Khālid said: "I put Ribʿī in charge of my property, but, by God, he was quicker (to destroy) it than are moths in wool in summer!"

B22a Someone asked Khālid ibn Ṣafwān: "How is your son?" He replied: "He is the lord of the young men of his people in both wit and *adab*." He was asked: "How much do you give him a month?" Khālid replied: "Thirty dirhams." The other said: "What can he do with a mere thirty dirhams! Why don't you give him more? You profit thirty thousand." Khālid replied: "The thirty dirhams are quicker to destroy my property than are moths in wool in summer!"

When Khālid's words were related to him al-Ḥasan said: "I stand witness that Khālid is a trueborn Tamīmī!"[77]

(Ḥamza al-Iṣfahānī, *Durra*, p. 35); al-Maydānī, *Majmaʿ* I: 149 (no. 412); al-Thaʿālibī, *Thimār*, p. 679; al-Thaʿālibī, *Tamaththul*, p. 589;[78] Abū Hilāl al-ʿAskarī, *Jamhara* I: 201 (no. 249);[79] al-Ābī, *Nathr* III: 290;[80] al-Zamakhsharī, *Mustaqṣā* I: 6 (no. 8).

B22b *ākal min al-sūs*: It is said that Khālid ibn Ṣafwān said to his son Ribʿī: "My son, you are quicker to destroy my property than are moths in wool in summer! By God, you will not prosper this year, nor the next (*qāb*), nor the

76 Cf. Malti-Douglas (1985): 72–78 (hospitality anecdotes).

77 Al-Maydānī adds the explanation "al-Ḥasan said this because Tamīmīs are known for their avarice and greed."

78 Both the *Thimār* and the *Tamaththul* only give Khālid's last phrase, and al-Thaʿālibī tacitly changes *al-thalāthūn* to *la-thalāthūn*, since he does not give the preceeding discussion which legitimises the determined article. In the *Thimār*, al-Thaʿālibī deems this the most eloquent comparison with moths. In the *Tamaththul*, the text has been wrongly emended on the basis of one manuscript.

79 Abbreviated, but the basic elements (the allowance of an anonymous son; the proverb) are present.

80 Abbreviated, as in al-ʿAskarī, *Jamhara*, and using the expression *la-aʿbath* for *la-asraʿ* in almost all other versions.

one after that (*qubāqib*)!" – This is like you say: "You will not prosper today nor tomorrow nor the day after that."

(al-Qālī, *Afʿal*, p. 22). *Latter part only*: Ibn ʿAbbād, *Muḥīṭ* V: 215, 430;[81] Ibn Manẓūr, *Lisān* XI: 8 (s.v. QBB); al-Azharī, *Tahdhīb* VIII: 299; al-Ṣaghānī, *Takmila* I: 234; *Kitāb al-ʿAyn* V: 29; al-Fīrūzābādī, *Qāmūs* III: 547 (s.v. QBB); al-Zabīdī, *Tāj* III: 512; al-Balawī, *Alif-bāʾ* II: 436.

COMMENTARY: Ibn ʿAbbād, Ibn Manẓūr, and the lexicographical tradition in general give the respective names of the years in the sequence *al-ʿām – qābil – qābb – qubāqib – muqabqib*. This seems to contain some fantastical formations of the lexicographers. Ibn Manẓūr also adds, on the authority of Ibn Barrī, from Ibn Sīda: *unẓur qābb bi-hādhā l-maʿnā*, with explanations. He also adds (from Ibn Sīda) al-Aṣmaʿī as the authority of this story and lets him conclude: "They (the Arabs) do not know anything past this," i.e., any word denoting further years.

The saying *asraʿu min al-sūs*(*fī l-ṣūfi fī l-ṣayf*) is often found as an anonymous proverb.[82] Whether Khālid originated this proverb, cannot be said, but he did make it popular. The variant versions seem to have joined this with B93, q.v.[83]

Ibn Durayd narrates this saying from an anonymous Bedouin concerning his son's daily allowance of one *dānaq*.[84] That this is basically the same story is shown by the presence of the two key elements, the allowance of a son and the proverb, though here Bedouinised to "*al-ʿuthth fī l-ṣūf fī l-ṣayf*."

Abū Bakr al-Khwārizmī uses the saying to blame a governor (*ʿāmil*): "a moth in silk in summertime is merely a well-doer in comparison to him."[85] Abū l-Qāsim al-Wāsānī inserted this into a poem of his.[86] Similar expressions are found widely in literature.[87]

B23 Khālid ibn Ṣafwān used to say: If one wishes to marry, let him take a woman who is noble among her people, but herself humble, whom wealth has

81 Here only *al-ʿām – qābil – qabāʾil*.

82 E.g., *Kitāb al-ʿAyn* II: 231–232; al-Ābī, *Nathr* VI: 192; al-Maydānī, *Majmaʿ* II: 462 (no. 2804). In al-Maydānī, *Majmaʿ*, *afsad*, instead of *asraʿ*.

83 See also Kraemer (1961): 281, note 1.

84 Ibn Durayd, *Jamhara*, p. 83.

85 Quoted in al-Thaʿālibī, *Yatīma* IV: 203.

86 Quoted in al-Thaʿālibī, *Yatīma* I: 342.

87 E.g., al-Hamadhānī, *Maqāmāt*, pp. 317–318 (*inna l-karam asraʿ fī l-māl min al-sūs* = *Rasāʾil*, p. 394), al-Jurjānī, *Muntakhab*, p. 409 (*al-ʿiyāl sūs al-māl*).

educated but poverty subjugated, who is chaste to her neighbour but seductive to her husband.

Ibn Qutayba, *ʿUyūn* IV: 6; Ibn ʿAsākir, *Taʾrīkh* XVI: 108:[88] Ibn ʿAsākir, *Taʾrīkh* XVI: 112 (variants); Ibn al-ʿAdīm, *Bughya* VII: 66;[89] Ibn Manẓūr, *Mukhtaṣar* VII: 362; al-Zamakhsharī, *Rabīʿ* IV: 292;[90] al-Suyūṭī, *Shaqāʾiq*, p. 88 (from the *Rabīʿ*).[91]

COMMENTARY: B24 and B25 are closely related to B23. Ibn Manẓūr repeats the story later.[92] Al-Sharīshī attributes the words *al-ʿazīzatu fī qawmihā l-dhalīlatu fī nafsihā* to an anonymous Bedouin, but this comes in the middle of a block of Khālid stories.[93] Ibn Nubāta quotes Qays ibn Zuhayr asking the tribe of al-Namir ibn Qāsiṭ for a woman "whom wealth has educated but poverty subjugated."[94] For the antithesis between *adhilla* and *aʿizza*, cf. also Q 5: 54.

B24 < *al-Madāʾinī* < *Ibrāhīm ibn al-Mubārak*: The Commander of the Believers, Abū l-ʿAbbās said to Khālid ibn Ṣafwān: "People have said so much about women! What kind of woman pleases you most?" Khālid replied: "O Commander of the Believers, I like best a woman who is neither a skinny young thing nor big and decrepit.[95] As to her beauty, it is enough that she looks great from afar, pretty from near, her upper part a leafless palm branch and her lower part a sandhill. She shall have been nurtured in wealth, but then need shall have befallen her, so that wealth has educated her and poverty made humble. She shall be seductive towards her husband, but chaste towards her neighbour.

---

88 < Ibrāhīm ibn Isḥāq al-Ziyād[ī] < al-Aṣmaʿī.

89 < Abū l-Ḥasan Muḥammad ibn Aḥmad < Abū l-Maʿālī ibn Ṣābir < Abū l-Qāsim ʿAlī ibn Ibrāhīm < Rashaʾ ibn Naẓīf < al-Ḥasan ibn Ismāʿīl < Aḥmad ibn Marwān < Ibrāhīm ibn Isḥāq < al-Ziyādī < al-Aṣmaʿī.

90 Only the sentence *ḥaṣān fī jārihā mājina ʿalā baʿlihā*. Just above this passage al-Zamakhsharī quotes another anecdote where al-Ḥajjāj asks Ibn al-Qirriyya (on whom, see Ibn Qutayba, *Maʿārif*, p. 404, and *EI2*, s.v. [Ch. Pellat]) to describe a woman he would best love. Ibn al-Qirriyya answers with phrases some of which are identical to those of B24. Al-Suyūṭī, *Shaqāʾiq*, p. 92, quotes the same passage from the *Rabīʿ*.

91 Al-Suyūṭī elaborates on the theme, taking as his starting point the word *ʿurub*, used of Houris in Q 56: 37, and quoting from Ibn ʿAsākir's *Taʾrīkh* (p. 82) the words of Isḥāq ibn ʿAbdallāh ibn al-Ḥārith al-Nawfalī in the presence of Bilāl ibn abī Burda, as well as three *ḥadīths* (pp. 87–88, 97).

92 Ibn Manẓūr, *Mukhtaṣar* VII: 363, note 1.

93 Al-Sharīshī, *Sharḥ* IV: 134.

94 Ibn Nubāta, *Sarḥ*, p. 139.

95 Cf. the *ḥadīth* of Ibn ʿUmar, quoted in Ibn Manẓūr, *Lisān* XI: 47a (s.v. QḤM): *ibghinī khādiman lā yakūnu qaḥman fāniyan wa-lā ṣaghīran ḍaraʿan*.

When we are alone, we are people of this world, but when we are separated from each other, we are people of the world to come."

Ibn Ḥamdūn, *Tadhkira* V: 310 (no. 829); Ibn ʿAbdrabbih, *ʿIqd* VI: 107; al-Ābī, *Nathr* VI: 48.

COMMENTARY: See also B23 and B25. In Ibn Ḥamdūn and al-Ābī phrases from B24 from B25 have been mixed together. The story is discussed in Chapter 2.6.1.

B25 < *al-Madāʾinī* < *Ḥafṣ ibn Muʿāwiya ibn ʿAmr al-Ghalābī*: I once said to Khālid: "O Abū Ṣafwān, I hate the idea that you, one of the richest men in Basra, would die and no one but slavegirls would cry for you."[96] Khālid replied: "Then get me a woman!" I told him: "Describe her to me so that I may find one." He said: "I want her to be a virgin like a widow[97] or a widow like a virgin, neither a skinny young thing nor big and old. She should not have been confined, so that she would yearn,[98] nor should she be (a young girl) kept within, so that she would be shameless.[99] She shall have grown in comfort but difficulties shall have befallen her, so that wealth has educated her and poverty made humble. As to her beauty, it is enough that she looks great from afar, pretty from near. As to her descent, it is enough that she is the pearl of her people. She should be satisfied from my side with (what) the *sunna* (defines). As long as I live, I shall respect her and when I die, she shall inherit me. She shall not raise her head towards the sky haughtily (Q 8: 47) nor let it sink towards earth despondently."

I told him: "O Abū Ṣafwān, people have been searching for such a one since time immemorial[100] but they have never found one!"

---

96 Ibn ʿAsākir reads: "that you do not have an Arab wife."

97 Or divorcée, which in Khālid's time is an equally possible translation for *thayyib*.

98 *Qarraʾa* refers (see Lane 1863–93, s.v.) to a woman kept confined, after divorce, until she menstruates. It might also refer to the end of her periods in menopause. Al-Murtaḍā and Ibn Ḥamdūn (see B24) read *fa-tajbun* "that she would be weak hearted" instead of *fa-taḥnun*. Most versions quietly omit the problematic sentence and abbreviate the story.

99 The point seems to be that she should not be so old that her periods have ended nor so young that she has only just attained puberty. The verb FTW II is used of a girl almost attaining to puberty and confined inside and kept from playing with boys (cf. Lane 1863–93, s.v.).

100 Ibn ʿAsākir reads: "since the time ʿUthmān was murdered."

al-Murtaḍā, *Amālī* II: 262;[101] Ibn ʿAbdrabbih, *ʿIqd* VI: 107;[102] Ibn Qutayba, *ʿUyūn* IV: 6–7 (abbreviated); al-Dajājī, *Safaṭ*, p. 137;[103] Ibn ʿAsākir, *Taʾrīkh* XVI: 112–113;[104] al-Sharīshī, *Sharḥ* III: 134; al-Maqdisī, *Laṭāʾif*, p. 123 (abbreviated).

B25a Khālid ibn Ṣafwān said to a matchmaker (masc.): "Get me a virgin (like a widow)[105] or a widow like a virgin, chaste to her neighbour but enticing to her husband. Wealth shall have educated her and poverty made humble. She shall neither be a skinny young thing nor big and aged. She shall have grown in comfort but poverty shall have befallen her. She should have ample reason, immaculate moral, perceptible beauty, smooth forehead and bridge of the nose, black eyes,[106] large shanks, and stout legs. She should be of a noble abode and origin and have a melodious voice. No arrogance shall have entered her and her face shall not have been disfigured by freckles. Her scent must be fragrant and her face radiant. She should have tender fingers and heavy haunches. Her colour should be that of (white) parchment and her breasts like jars, her upper part a leafless palm branch and her lower part a sandhill. She should have a lank belly and a fine waist, a long neck and a full chest. She shall bend like reed and (while walking) swing like a drunkard. She has to have beautiful eye corners like al-Burāq. She should neither be ridiculously tall nor too short." The matchmaker replied: "Knock on the door of the Paradise and you will find her!"
(ps.-al-Jāḥiẓ, *Maḥāsin*, pp. 220–221).

COMMENTARY: Cf. B23 and B24. It should be noted that the text has several masculine forms (like *ibghinī*), which show that in the original the interlocutor of Khālid was not a female matchmaker. In Ibn ʿAbdrabbih, *ʿIqd* VI: 107, the beginning and the end read:

---

101 "With the previous *isnād*," cf. B98 < al-Madāʾinī < Ḥafṣ ibn Muʿāwiya ibn ʿAmr al-Ghalābī.

102 Abbreviated and modified. The penultimate sentence is an allusion to a *ḥadīth*, see Lane (1863–93), s.v. *rafīq*. The version of al-Sharīshī roughly agrees with that of Ibn Qutayba. See also Marzolph (1992) II: 95, no. 380 (about al-Fuḍayl ibn ʿAbd al-Raḥmān).

103 < Ibn Qutayba, *ʿUyūn*.

104 With variants < Abū Manṣūr ʿAbd al-Raḥmān ibn Muḥammad ibn ʿAbd al-Wāḥid < Abū Bakr Aḥmad ibn ʿAlī *al-khaṭīb* < Abū l-Ḥasan ʿAlī ibn ʿAbd al-ʿAzīz al-Ṭāhirī < Abū Muḥammad ʿAlī ibn ʿAbdallāh ibn al-Mughīra al-Jawharī < Aḥmad ibn Saʿīd al-Dimashqī < al-Zubayr ibn Bakkār < "my uncle" Muṣʿab ibn ʿAbdallāh < al-Haytham ibn ʿAdī < Ḥafṣ ibn Ghalāth [sic].

105 Missing from the edition, but the emendation is obvious in the light of the parallel tradition.

106 Or: eyes lined with black.

> Khālid ibn Ṣafwān saw some people in the mosque of Basra and asked: "What is this crowd?" He was answered: "People (have gathered) around a woman who makes matches." Khālid went to her and said (…)."
>
> He [sic] answered: "I have found her for you!" Khālid asked: "Where is she then?" He [sic] said: "Among the highest companions of Paradise! Strive for her!"

The suffix *-hā* in the last sentence might also be understood as a reference to Paradise ("strive for it"), but in, e.g., B25a the reference is to the woman, i.e., a Houri.

In a note to Ibn Qutayba's *ʿUyūn*,[107] the editor identifies the interlocutor of Khālid, here *dallāl*, as Dallāl al-Mukhannath, but in the light of the other versions and the fact that Dallāl was active in Medina, not Basra, this is improbable.

Al-Jāḥiẓ tells a similar story where al-Ḥajjāj writes to al-Ḥakam ibn Ayyūb to procure for his son ʿAbd al-Malik ibn al-Ḥajjāj a woman, described roughly in Khālidian terms. Al-Ḥakam later replies that he has found one, with the only blemish that she has big breasts. Al-Ḥajjāj writes back that a woman should have big breasts.[108] In a story transmitted by Jirāb al-Dawla, al-Ḥasan ibn Rajāʾ asks a *nakhkhās* to get him a donkey, which he describes in unrealistic terms, and the *nakhkhās* advises him to wait until God will transform a *qāḍī* into a donkey.[109]

B26 Khālid used to say: What would a man be without tongue but a loose-running beast or a painted picture?

al-Jāḥiẓ, *Bayān* I: 170, 353;[110] al-Maydānī, *Majmaʿ* III: 294 (no. 3958, anonymous); al-Thaʿālibī, *Yawāqīt*, p. 169 (anonymous); al-Jurjānī, *Asrār*, p. 23.[111] *Longer versions*:[112] al-Jāḥiẓ, *Ṣināʿat al-quwwād* I: 380; Ibn ʿAbd al-Barr, *Bahja* I: 55; al-Waṭwāṭ, *Ghurar*, p. 185; al-Balawī, *Alif-Bāʾ* I: 34 (anonymous).

---

107 Ibn Qutayba, *ʿUyūn* IV: 6–7.

108 Al-Jāḥiẓ, *Bayān* IV: 8.

109 Jirāb al-Dawla, *Tarwīḥ*, p. 104.

110 < Abū l-Ḥasan < Ibrāhīm ibn Saʿd, inverted: *ṣūra mumaththala aw bahīma muhmala*.

111 Translated by Ritter (1959): 18–19.

112 *Ḍālla muhmala aw bahīma mursala aw ṣūra mumaththala* "a neglected camel astray, a loose-running beast, or a painted picture" (in various orders).

COMMENTARY: Cf. the Aristotelian definition of man as a talking/rational (*nāṭiq*) animal. The comparison of men without knowledge (*ʿilm*) to beasts is not infrequent. Among others, it is found among Khālid's older contemporary's, al-Ḥasan al-Baṣrī's sayings.[113] A similar anonymous verse[114] is quoted by al-Waṭwāṭ: "The tongue of a young man is half of him, the heart the other half / all the rest is only a picture in flesh and blood."[115]

B27 < *al-Haytham ibn ʿAdī and Abū l-Ḥasan al-Madāʾinī*: When Khālid ibn Ṣafwān was sitting in the mosque of Basra, a Bedouin from Banū l-ʿAnbar joined his company. Khālid was just saying to his companions: "The best woman is one who is old enough to be wise and whose understanding has become solid. Her belly is slender and her neck is long, the side of her neck (*līt*)[116] is beautiful, and her buttocks are large. Her hairless cunt shall fill the hand of her spouse."

The ʿAnbarī said to this: "Never mind those whose understanding has become solid! Take an inexperienced girl, whose breasts have (newly) become round[117] and who does not yet know what is wanted of her!" Then he recited:[118]

> If you want to marry, O Abū Ṣafwān, then take
> a young woman,[119] who wears a shirt (*itb*) and drawers (*miʾzar*).
>
> She shall have protruding buttocks and a wrinkled belly,
> and a pussy (*ajthamu*)[120] of hairless, cup-like shape.

---

113 E.g., Ibn al-Jawzī, *Ādāb*, pp. 42, 58. Cf. also Marlow (1997): 36–38, al-Fārābī, *Siyāsa*, pp. 57–58, and Ṣāʿid al-Andalusī, *Ṭabaqāt*, p. 146.

114 Variously attributed to al-Aʿwar al-Shannī or Ziyād al-Aʿjam. For al-Aʿwar, see *GAS* II: 196. For Ziyād, see *GAS* II: 373–374.

115 Al-Waṭwāṭ, *Ghurar*, p. 185.

116 See Ibn Manẓūr, *Lisān* XII: 373a, s.v.

117 Al-Tijānī's version seems here better: *ḥīna akʿabat ilā an anhadat*.

118 The poem is attributed to al-ʿUshsh ibn Kaʿb al-ʿAnbarī addressing Khālid ibn Ṣafwān in al-Marzubānī, *Muʿjam* I: 221–222.

119 Vocalised in the text as *inās*, but I read *fatāta unāsin* (as also in al-Marzubānī). In his note to the edition of al-Balādhurī, the editor, Ramzī Baʿlabakkī, suggests with some hesitation reading *īnās* for *inās*. This seems improbable, though, since *fatāt unās* is often found in poetry, cf., e.g., al-Aʿshā Maymūn, *Dīwān* XLI: 5.

120 *Jāthim* refers to an animal, such as hare (cf. the use of "beaver" in English), lying low, or a hill, both of which would give a suitable meaning, even though *ajtham* does not seem to be listed in dictionaries. Al-Marzubānī and al-Tijānī read *akhtham*. The root KhThM is not found in Lane (1863–93). In Ibn Manẓūr, *Lisān*, s.v., *akhtham* is explained as *al-jahāz al-murtafiʿ al-ghalīẓ*. A verse by al-Nābigha, quoted in Ibn Manẓūr, *Lisān* IV: 28, s.v. KhThM reads: *wa-idhā lamasta, lamasta akhthama jāthimā*, etc., but in the *Dīwān* recension *akhthama* is replaced by *ajthama* (al-Nābigha, *Dīwān* 7: 30). *Ajtham* is used for

If you get such a one, you will be a lord.
Flee like a frightened ostrich from the other,

who is experienced in sex and has gone through the limit,[121]
becoming a bold woman, not asking for protection.[122]

She is a matching opponent (*qirn*), like a lion of the thicket when she attacks,
or nagging, if lying low for fear.

al-Tijānī, *Tuḥfa*, pp. 193–194 (no. 416).[123]

COMMENTARY: A similar story is told by al-Qālī involving a group of Tamīm, sitting in the Friday mosque of Basra and talking about women, but their words are only referred to, not quoted. A Bedouin from Banū l-ʿAnbar arrives and recites a poem, different from that in al-Balādhurī. After hearing the poem, Khālid exclaims: "By God, you are good! You have said what we had in mind!"[124] Al-Bakrī gives a better version of the poem, attributed to Ḍamra ibn Ḍamra.[125] A prose saying on woman's age by ʿUmar ibn al-Khaṭṭāb resembles this poem,[126] as does a poem by Abū Dulaf al-ʿIjlī (d. 225/840 or 226/841) on the ages of men.[127]

B28 Khālid used to say: If manliness (*muruwwa*)[128] were easy to carry and light to bear, the base would not leave an inch of it for the noble.[129] Yet it is

---

female genitals in al-Jāḥiẓ, *Qiyān* II: 151, in a famous *rajaz* by Ḍubāʿa. See also Beeston (1980): 46.

121 I.e., from virginity to womanhood.

122 Al-Marzubānī reads this verse as: "who is experienced in sex and whom her womenfolk have taught / the ways to make perish a stout inexperienced boy." After this, he adds another verse: "she makes it a joke if you make a mistake or if you say other than / what she likes. But if you do right, she is not thankful."

123 Abbreviated < ʿAṭāʾ ibn Muṣʿab; translated in [al-Tijānī], *Glory*, pp. 169–170. ʿAṭāʾ is indicated as an eyewitness to the encounter.

124 Al-Qālī, *Dhayl*, pp. 33–34 (< Abū ʿUthmān). The poem has been translated in Hämeen-Anttila (1994): 120 (no. 132).

125 Al-Bakrī, *Simṭ*, pp. 18–19.

126 Ibn Ḥabīb, *Adab*, p. 153 (no. 32, with further references on p. 410).

127 Al-Thaʿālibī, *Mirʾāt*, p. 56. For Abū Dulaf, see GAS II: 632–633

128 Al-Murtaḍā, *Amālī* II: 262, reads erroneously *al-marʾa*.

129 Literally: the victuals for a single night (*bītata layla*).

heavy to bear and formidable to carry. Hence, the noble have taken it on themselves, but the base have turned away from it.

al-Murtaḍā, *Amālī* II: 262; al-Washshā', *Muwashshā*, p. 51; Ibn ʿAsākir, *Ta'rīkh* XVI: 113;[130] Ibn Manẓūr, *Mukhtaṣar* VIII: 363.[131]

B29 < *al-Madā'inī*: A woman said to Khālid ibn Ṣafwān: "You are beautiful." Khālid replied: "How can you say so? By God, I do not have the pillar of beauty, nor its robe or cloak! The pillar of beauty is tallness, but I am not tall. Its robe is fairness, but I am not fair. Its cloak is black and curly hair, but I am bald.[132] You should say instead: 'You are sweet'!"

al-Jāḥiẓ, *Bayān* I: 340;[133] Ibn Qutayba, *ʿUyūn* IV: 23–24; Ibn ʿAbdrabbih, *ʿIqd* VI: 116; al-Ḥuṣrī, *Zahr*, pp. 953–954; Ibn ʿAsākir, *Ta'rīkh* XVI: 109;[134] Ibn al-ʿAdīm, *Bughya* VII: 66–67;[135] al-Thaʿālibī, *Thimār*, p. 600; al-Thaʿālibī, *Tawfīq*, p. 113; al-Tijānī, *Tuḥfa*, p. 251 (no. 574);[136] al-Suyūṭī, *Nuzha*, p. 18;[137] al-Rāghib, *Muḥāḍarāt* III: 281.

COMMENTARY: In most versions, the speaker is the wife of Khālid. In many, there is an intervening question by her: "What is the pillar of beauty?"

B30 Khālid said to al-Farazdaq, with whom he used to jest: "O Abū Firās, you are not the one 'whom the women admired when they saw him and cut their hands'."[138] Al-Farazdaq replied: "Neither are you, O Abū Ṣafwān, the one concerning whom the girl said to her father: 'O father, hire him. Surely the best man you can hire is the one strong and trusty'."[139]

---

130 < Abū Naṣr ibn Riḍwān < Abū Muḥammad al-Jawharī < Abū ʿUmar ibn Ḥayyawayhi < Abū Bakr Muḥammad ibn Khalaf ibn al-Marzubān < Abū Jaʿfar al-Thumāmī < Abū l-Ḥasan al-Madā'inī.

131 In al-Thaʿālibī, *Mir'āt*, p. 72, this saying, in an abbreviated form, is ascribed to Ibn ʿĀ'isha al-Qurashī, for whom, see commentary to A89, and for other persons of this name, see al-Thaʿālibī, *Bard*, p. 31, note 1.

132 In the version of al-Jāḥiẓ, Khālid is said to be grey-haired (*ashmaṭ*), though after narrating the story al-Jāḥiẓ adds that Khālid was bald.

133 Al-Jāḥiẓ prefaces this by telling us that Khālid was beautiful (using the very word Khālid tells the woman not to use), but that he was not tall.

134 < Abū l-Qāsim ʿAlī ibn Ibrāhīm < Rasha' ibn Naẓīf < al-Ḥasan ibn Ismāʿīl < Aḥmad ibn Marwān < Muḥammad ibn Dā'ūd < Muḥammad ibn Sallām.

135 < Aḥmad ibn Marwān < Muḥammad ibn Dā'ūd < Muḥammad ibn Sallām.

136 Fragments of the story also on pp. 237 and 271 (nos. 521, 621). Translated in [al-Tijānī], *Glory*, p. 204, cf. also p. 194.

137 < Ibn ʿAsākir.

138 The quotation comes from Q 12: 31. For the topos of an ugly poet, cf., e.g., Abū Nuwās, *Dīwān* IV: 51 (*mu'annathāt*, no. 63).

139 The quotation comes from Q 28: 26.

al-Balādhurī, *Ansāb* (ed. ʿAẓm) XI: 89–90;[140] Ibn Qutayba, *ʿUyūn* I: 435; Ibn Qutayba, *Shiʿr*, p. 293; al-Tawḥīdī, *Imtāʿ* III: 168; al-Tawḥīdī, *Baṣāʾir* IX: 136–137 (no. 433); Ibn ʿAbdrabbih, *ʿIqd* IV: 42; al-Waṭwāṭ, *Ghurar*, p. 261; al-Marzubānī, *Nūr*, p. 204; Ibn abī ʿAwn, *Ajwiba*, p. 24 (no. 109); al-Ḥuṣrī, *Jamʿ*, p. 171; Ibn ʿĀṣim, *Ḥadāʾiq*, p. 236; Ibn Hudhayl, *Maqālāt*, pp. 136–137; al-Rāghib, *Muḥāḍarāt* III: 283.

B31 Khālid once said of a man: He really is a man whom God has made extraordinary by nature and whose behaviour He has set upright. Whom wealth makes haughty and immoderate, him does it leave and lower.

B32 Khālid used to say: Jesting is the reviling of the stupid.[141] Yet there is no objection to a joke (*fukāha*) by which a man's face is brightened in his social gathering and which draws him out of gloom.
al-Zamakhsharī, *Mustaqṣā* I: 346 (no. 1487); Rāghib, *Muḥāḍarāt* I: 282.

COMMENTARY: *Al-mizāḥ sibāb al-nawkā* is also attested as an anonymous saying in several collections of proverbs.[142] Al-Māwardī relates an anonymous saying "jesting is reviling, except that the speaker smiles."[143] Cf. B84.

B33 Khālid said to a man: "God bless your father! He used to feast the eye with his beauty and the ear with his eloquence."
al-Qālī, *Amālī* II: 172;[144] Ibn Qutayba, *ʿUyūn* II: 185; ibn al-Muʿtazz, *Badīʿ*, p. 6; al-Washshāʾ, *Fāḍil*, p. 183; al-Zamakhsharī, *Rabīʿ* IV: 162;[145] Ibn ʿAsākir, *Taʾrīkh* XVI: 114;[146] al-Būnisī, *Kanz*, p. 79.

B33a It was said to someone, I think it was Khālid ibn Ṣafwān: "A friend of yours has died!" He replied: "God bless him! He used to fill the eye with his beauty and the ear with his eloquence. He was a man who was sought after but

140 < al-Madāʾinī.
141 This has found its way to Lane (1863–93), s.v. SBB III. Ammann (1993): 174–175, 213, 223, ties this saying by Khālid into its context, with reference to Abū ʿUbayd's *Kitāb al-amthāl* (see Ammann, p. 170), where there is a chapter on jesting, *al-Duʿāba wa'l-muzāḥ*, where Khālid's saying is cited and then commented upon by ʿUmar ibn ʿAbd al-ʿAzīz.
142 E.g., Abū Hilāl al-ʿAskarī, *Dīwān*, p. 334; al-Maydānī, *Majmaʿ* III: 286 (no. 3914).
143 Al-Māwardī, *Adab*, p. 298.
144 < Abū Bakr [Ibn Durayd] < Abū Ḥātim < al-Aṣmaʿī < al-ʿAlāʾ ibn al-Faḍl ibn ʿAbd al-Malik.
145 Al-Zamakhsharī introduces this with the words "Khālid ibn Ṣafwān lauded Ibrāhīm ibn al-Ahtam." Biographical sources do not mention any Ibrāhīm to whom this could refer in the family of al-Ahtam. Al-Washshāʾ's version also seems to refer to a relative of Khālid's, as we should delete "*ibn*" after "Ṣafwān" to make the sentence flow properly: *dhakara Khālid ibn Ṣafwān* [[*ibn*]] *ʿAbdallāh ibn al-Ahtam fa-qāla* (…).
146 < al-Aṣmaʿī < al-Faḍl ibn ʿAbd al-Malik.

was not afraid. He did not visit but was visited and gave and was not given to. Rarely was he there when something bad was done, and his mind was sound towards his friends."

(al-Jāḥiẓ, *Bayān* IV: 92)

COMMENTARY: Cf. B89. Many versions use here, as in B89, the verb *yamlaʾ* (for *yaqrī*), but those that only contain the brief saying are listed here, irrespective of whether they use *yaqrī* or *yamlaʾ*.

B34 Khālid said: I came to Syria and went to a bathhouse there. Abū Miḥjan,[147] the servant of Hishām ibn ʿAbd al-Malik, entered the bath at the same time, but I did not know him. He said: "Glory be to God, who has favoured us over many of his creations!" I said: "There is not a creature on earth with two testicles, but is better than you." He asked me who I was and I told him. He left the bath before me and gave orders to a servant of his to stay behind. When I left, the servant took me to his house where Abū Miḥjan treated me hospitably and let me near him and fulfilled all my needs.

B35 Khālid used to make mistakes (*yalḥan*) in his speech. Someone said to him: "What if you took a look in grammar (*al-naḥw*)?" He replied: "I am afraid lest I might lose the Arabness (*iʿrāb*) of my speech and my tongue would break." It is also said that he replied: "I am afraid lest when I exert myself with inflection (*iʿrāb*) my tongue would break."

B36 He (al-Madāʾinī?) said: Khālid once heard a man recite the following verse:

When your soul tells you that you are capable
of taking what other men hold, then try!

Khālid exclaimed: "Nay, by God, but call it a lie!"

COMMENTARY: The verse and the story behind it are transmitted by, e.g., ps.-al-Jāḥiẓ and al-Bayhaqī. In both, the rhyming word is *fa-kadhdhibī*, as suggested by Khālid in this story.[148]

147 According to al-Ṭabarī, *Taʾrīkh* II: 1823/XXVI: 179, and al-Iṣfahānī, *Aghānī* VI: 140, Abū Miḥjan was a freedman (*mawlā*) of Khālid al-Qasrī. After the murder of the Caliph al-Walīd in 126/743, he lampooned the dead Caliph, who earlier in the year had had Khālid al-Qasrī executed. According to al-Iṣfahānī, he further mocked the dead body of al-Walīd by repeatedly inserting his sword into al-Walīd's anus.

148 Ps.-al-Jāḥiẓ, *Maḥāsin*, p. 94, and al-Bayhaqī, *Maḥāsin*, p. 281.

B37 One day Abū l-ʿAbbās al-Saffāḥ ordered Khālid to be brought to him. Entering, Khālid said to Abū l-ʿAbbās: "You have been commissioned to the Caliphate and you are the man for it and its rightful place. You tend the right in its pasture and bring it to its watering place. You have given everybody his due of your attention, justice, politeness (*adab*), and company (*majlis*) so that it is as if you belonged to everyone (i.e., to every tribe) or to none." This pleased Abū l-ʿAbbās, who ordered money to be given to him.

al-Balādhurī, *Ansāb* III: 167;[149] al-Qālī, *Amālī* I: 213 (abbreviated);[150] Ibn Qutayba, *ʿUyūn* I: 172; Ibn ʿAbdrabbih, *ʿIqd* II: 135; al-Bakrī, *Simṭ*, p. 502;[151] al-Ḥuṣrī, *Zahr*, pp. 916, 1079; al-Rāghib, *Muḥāḍarāt* I: 195; Ibn ʿAsākir, *Taʾrīkh* XVI: 105.[152]

COMMENTARY: In most versions Khālid's interlocutor is an anonymous governor (*wālī*).[153]

B38 Khālid has said: I came in a delegation (*wafadtu*) to Hishām ibn ʿAbd al-Malik and found him having come forth to the desert (*badā*) to enjoy the rain.[154] This happened in a year when first spring rains had fallen early and thereafter more rain had come (*tatābaʿa waliyyuhu*). Earth had put on its ornaments and various adornments.[155] It was like carpets outspread[156] and Egyptian clothes[157] unfolded. The earth was like camphor: if a piece of meat (*baḍʿa*) had fallen there, it would not have become dusty.[158] Pavilions of striped

149 < Abū Masʿūd al-Kūfī < ʿAbd al-Jabbār al-Kātib.

150 < Abū ʿAbdallāh Nifṭawayhi < Abū l-ʿAbbās Aḥmad ibn Yaḥyā < Ḥammād ibn Isḥāq < "his father" < "my uncle" Ṣabbāḥ ibn Khāqān.

151 < Abū ʿAlī [al-Qālī].

152 < al-Mubarrad. In Ibn ʿAsākir, *Taʾrīkh* XVI: 105, this is combined with B90, where a more detailed *isnād* is given.

153 E.g., al-Qālī, *Amālī* I: 213.

154 *Duhn* "weak rain," see Lane (1863–93), s.v. Ps.-Ibn Qutayba, *Imāma* II: 143, and ʿAwfī, *Jawāmiʿ* I/2: 16, locate this somewhere near al-Ruṣāfa.

155 Cf. Q 10: 24, *akhadhat-i l-arḍu zukhrufahā wa-zzayyanat*. The verse is pregnant with meaning for Khālid's sermon: the Qurʾānic scene comes from a parable of worldly life awaiting imminent disaster. Note, however, that this part of the text is not part of the sermon, but the background story narrated on the authority of Khālid. The composer of the text has anticipated the pious sermon by describing the scene in Qurʾānic terms that hint at the passing away of all earthly beauty, which is the theme of the sermon, too.

156 Q 88: 16.

157 For *qubāṭī*, see Ibn Manẓūr, *Lisān* XI: 15b, s.v.

158 Because the soil was so moist and luxuriant with plants. Ps.-Ibn Qutayba, *Imāma* II: 143, reads *qiṭʿat dīnār*.

linen (*surādiqāt ḥibara*), which Yūsuf ibn ʿUmar had sent for him from Yemen,[159] had been erected for him and they glistened like pure gold.

Maslama mentioned me to Hishām, who sent for me. When I entered, he lied on four embroidered carpets, with as many hassocks and cushions. He wore a silken *jubba* and a silken turban. I renewed my invocations for him and kept standing until he told me to sit down. He looked at me as if wishing me to speak,[160] and I said: "O Commander of the Believers, may God make complete his blessings to you and may He defend you from his vengeances! This is a position with which God has embellished my cause and raised my worth and reputation and made sweet the perfume of my fame by letting me see the face of the Commander of the Believers. I will never be able to see a more suitable way to recompense my being here than by drawing the attention of the Commander of the Believers to how God has favoured him so that he would praise God for what He has commissioned and given him. Further, I can see no more concise exhortation than telling a story about an ancient king.[161] If the Commander of the Believers allows me, I will tell him the story."[162] Hishām sat up and said: "Go ahead, O son of al-Ahtam."

I said: In ancient times there was a king who had youth, the splendour of adolescence, soundness of nature, plenty of wealth, and wide kingdom. One day he was in al-Khawarnaq looking at all he had. He was pleased with himself and said to those around him: "Have you ever heard of anyone who had all that I have?"

People remained silent. Among them there was a man belonging to the remnants of those who carry the decisive argument.[163] He said to the king: "If you allow me, I will speak." The king told him to do so, and he said: "Consider all this that God has given you. Is it something that has always been yours and will always remain so? Or is it something that belonged to others before you, which they lost and it came to you and you, too, will one day lose it?" The king replied: "It is indeed something that belonged to others before me and that I will one day lose." The man continued: "I think you are enchanted with something

---

159 Ibn Ḥabīb adds: *wa-huwa lladhī yunsab ilayhi l-washy al-Yūsufī*. For the standard comparison of a meadow full of flowers to, usually Yemeni, clothes, cf., e.g., Schoeler (1974): 27.

160 This was the usual court etiquette, cf., e.g., al-Thaʿlabī, *Tāj*, p. 15. Ps.-Ibn Qutayba, *Imāma* II: 144, adds: "I was adorned (in his opinion) by oratorical talent, understanding, and wisdom."

161 "Of Persians," adds Ibn Qutayba. Al-Ḥimyarī wishes to go beyond this and explains, p. 227, that this king was al-Nuʿmān ibn Imriʾ al-Qays, the grandfather of al-Nuʿmān ibn al-Mundhir. For the Lakhmid kings, see Toral-Niehoff (2014a): 223–224.

162 The story belongs to the type "This too will pass". Another story of this type gives Solomon as the king thus admonished, see, e.g., Taylor (1968): 345–350.

163 I.e., a holy man.

the pleasure of which you will lose but the consequences of which shall remain. You enjoy it for a short while but you shall be held responsible for it for a long time."

The king burst in tears and asked: "How may I escape this? To what should I take recourse!" The man answered: "Either you must retain your kingship and work in the obeisance of thy Lord or else you must throw on your back a coarse cloth and take to mountains where you may worship your Lord until your time comes and you will enjoy a life after which there will be no death and a health with which there will be no disease." The king threw a coarse cloth on himself and devoted himself to the service of God on a mountain until he died.

Khālid has said: Then I recited him the verses by ʿAdī ibn Zayd al-ʿIbādī:[164]

Where is Kisrā, the Kisrā of kings, Anūshirwān?
Where Sābūr, who was before him?

Or the man who built al-Ḥaḍr[165] and the taxes
of Tigris and Khabur were brought to him?

The uncertainties of destiny did not stand in his awe:
his kingship ended, and his gate is now deserted.

Think of the lord of al-Khawarnaq, who one day
looked (at what he had) – guidance is to make one think!

What he had, delighted him: how much he ruled,
how the sea was subservient, and al-Sadīr.

Suddenly he saw and repented, saying:
"What meaning has the bliss for one destined to die?

After prosperity, kingship, and leadership
tombs covered them there.

They became like dry leaves,
winds driving them east and west."

164 This is one of the most famous examples of Arabic *ubi sunt* motif. Cf. Kilpatrick (2003): 255, and 206, who calls ʿAdī's verses "the classic example" of the motif. See also Fowden – Fowden (2004): 191. Al-Ḥimyarī, p. 227, defines ʿAdī as *akhū Banī Tamīm*, thus linking the poet to Khālid's tribe.

165 Hatra.

Hishām cried and sobbed. Then he stood up as a man in anger, and everyone in the assembly stood up with him. The chamberlain[166] said to me: "You there, how incompetent you are! You have drawn evil upon yourself. The Commander of the Believers called for you to tell him stories and delight and entertain him. You should have known that because of the malady he suffers he came here so as not to hear anything or see anything that would displease or annoy him. Yet you did not fail to announce him his own death and you rendered his life turbid!"

Khālid has said: I stayed some days awaiting something unpleasant to happen. The Syrians started asking: "Where is that stupid Iraqi who angered the Commander of the Believers?" Hishām started to say: "O Maslama, you always bring me things I dislike." Then the chamberlain met me and said: "The Commander of the Believers has mentioned you and said: 'How excellent the son of Ahtam is!' He has ordered a present and given you permission to leave."

Ibn Qutayba, *'Uyūn* II: 368–370; Yāqūt, *Irshād* III: 276–279; al-Balādhurī, *Ansāb* (ed. 'Aẓm) VII: 335–336 (major variants);[167] Ibn Ḥamdūn, *Tadhkira* I: 157–159 (no. 347); Ibn 'Asākir, *Ta'rīkh* XVI: 96–99 (a longer version);[168] Ibn 'Asākir, *Ta'rīkh* XL: 106–109 (with variants);[169] Ibn al-'Adīm, *Bughya* VII: 50–53 (with variants);[170] Ibn Manẓūr,

---

166 Ps.-Ibn Qutayba, *Imāma* II: 144, calls him al-Rabī', i.e., al-Rabī' ibn Sābūr, on whom see al-Ṭabarī, *Ta'rīkh* II: 1614/XXV: 149 and note 537.

167 < Abū 'Adnān < Hishām ibn Muḥammad and al-Haytham ibn 'Adī < 'Awāna.

168 < Abū l-Su'ūd Aḥmad ibn 'Alī ibn Muḥammad < Abū l-Ḥusayn ibn al-Muhtadī < al-Sharīf Abū l-Faḍl Muḥammad ibn al-Ḥasan ibn Muḥammad ibn al-Faḍl al-Hāshimī < Abū Bakr Muḥammad ibn al-Qāsim ibn Bashshār al-Anbārī < "my father's paternal uncle" Abū l-'Abbās Aḥmad ibn Bashshār ibn al-Ḥasan ibn Bayān < Isḥāq ibn Bahlūl ibn Ḥassān ibn Sinān al-Tanūkhī al-Anbārī < "his father" Bahlūl ibn Ḥassān < Isḥāq ibn Ziyād from Banū Sāma ibn Lu'ayy < Shabīb ibn Shayba.

169 < Abū l-Qāsim 'Alī ibn Ibrāhīm < Rasha' ibn Naẓīf < al-Ḥasan ibn Ismā'īl < Aḥmad ibn Marwān < Muḥammad ibn 'Abd al-'Azīz < "my father" < Hishām ibn Ḥassān < Isḥāq ibn Ziyād of (read min for the edition's *ibn*) Banū Sāma ibn Lu'ayy (*'an* or (*ḥaddatha*)*nā* after the tribe's name is missing) < Shabīb ibn Shayba. Ibn 'Asākir, *Ta'rīkh* XVI: 96–99, also offers a variant *isnād* (< Abū l-Qāsim 'Alī ibn Ibrāhīm < Abū l-Fatḥ 'Abd al-Karīm ibn Muḥammad ibn Aḥmad ibn al-Qāsim al-Maḥāmilī "in his letter to us from Baghdād") and then gives a variant version (*Ta'rīkh* XVI: 99–102) with the following *isnād*: Abū Ghālib ibn al-Bannā < 'Abd al-Karīm ibn Muḥammad al-Maḥāmilī < Abū l-Ḥasan al-Dāraquṭnī al-Ḥāfiẓ < Abū Bakr al-Azraq Yūsuf ibn Ya'qūb ibn Isḥāq ibn al-Bahlūl < "my grandfather" < Isḥāq ibn Ziyād from Banū Sāma ibn Lu'ayy < Shabīb ibn Shayba < Khālid ibn Ṣafwān ibn al-Ahtam. Ibn 'Asākir, *Ta'rīkh* XL: 109, gives variant *isnāds* for the story: 1) < Ja'far ibn Muḥammad al-Faryābī and Aḥmad ibn 'Abd al-'Azīz ibn al-Ja'd al-Washshā' < Isḥāq ibn al-Buhlūl al-Anbārī < "his father"; 2) < Yūsuf ibn Ya'qūb ibn Isḥāq al-Buhlūlī < "his grandfather" < "his father." The editor has taken this from al-Suyūṭī, *Ta'rīkh*, pp. 239–240, to Ibn 'Asākir, *Ta'rīkh* LXXIV: 32.

170 < Abū Ḥafṣ 'Umar ibn Muḥammad ibn Mu'ammar al-Baghdādī in Aleppo < Abū Bakr Muḥammad ibn 'Abd al-Bāqī al-Anṣārī < *al-sharīf* Abū l-Ḥusayn Muḥammad ibn 'Alī

Mukhtaṣar VII: 353–357; Sibṭ Ibn al-Jawzī, *Kanz*, pp. 84–86; Sibṭ ibn al-Jawzī, *Jalīs*, pp. 255–257;[171] Ibn Ḥabīb, *Taʾrīkh*, pp. 120–122;[172] al-Suyūṭī, *Taʾrīkh*, pp. 239–240; Ibn Nāqiyā, *Jumān*, pp. 348–352;[173] al-Ḥimyarī, *Rawḍ*, pp. 226–227; Ibn al-Sarrāj, *Jawāhir*, pp. 834–836; ps.-Ibn Qutayba, *Imāma* II: 143–146;[174] al-Iṣfahānī, *Aghānī* II: 35–36;[175] *Alf layla wa-layla* (Būlāq 1252) I: 178–179 (Night 66);[176] ʿAwfī, *Jawāmiʿ* I/2: 16–17 (no. 17, Persian translation).

COMMENTARY: Yāqūt's version, like some of the others (e.g., Ibn Ḥamdūn), adds that Khālid was there in an embassy of Iraqis, sent by Yūsuf ibn ʿUmar al-Thaqafī.

Yāqūt's version contains many variants. It follows the general lines of al-Balādhurī's version, but in a more polished and artistic manner. It definitely seems to be a later revised version. E.g., the mention of *ḥujja* leads the author of Yāqūt's version onto a theological discussion of God's arguments. Appropriately, Yāqūt quotes 13 verses from the poem to al-Balādhurī's 8 verses.

Ibn al-Jawzī simplifies the story by letting Khālid tell it without any context. The description of spring is here transposed to the original narrator of the story, and Khālid takes the role of a transmitter only. Ibn al-Jawzī's version shows the mechanisms of Mediaeval narrative at work.

Ibn Nāqiyā refers to this story simply as "*khabar Khālid ibn Ṣafwān*," implying that it was famous in his time, which is also shown by the numerous attestations. This story obviously belongs to the literary canon of early ʿAbbāsid literature.

---

ibn al-Muhtadī bi'llāh < Abū l-Faḍl Muḥammad ibn al-Ḥasan ibn al-Faḍl ibn al-Maʾmūn < Muḥammad ibn al-Qāsim al-Anbārī < "the paternal uncle of my father" Abū l-ʿAbbās Aḥmad ibn Bashshār ibn al-Ḥasan ibn Bayān < Isḥāq ibn Buhlūl ibn Ḥassān ibn Sinān al-Tanūkhī al-Anbārī < "my father" al-Buhlūl ibn Ḥassān < Isḥāq ibn Ziyād of Banū Sāma ibn Luʾayy < Shabīb ibn Shayba < Khālid ibn Ṣafwān al-Ahtam.

171 < "My grandfather" < Yaḥyā ibn ʿAlī al-Mudabbir (the text reads: al-Mudīr) < ʿAbd al-Ṣamad ibn al-Maʾmūn < al-Dāraquṭnī < Ibn Ṣāʿid < Muḥammad ibn Hishām al-Marwazī < Abū Muʿāwiya. Note that in one place, p. 257, Sibṭ ibn al-Jawzī, *Jalīs*, reads Ṣafwān for Khālid ibn Ṣafwān, but this seems a mere error, as Khālid's father is otherwise never linked to Hishām.

172 Ibn Ḥabīb explicitly locates this in al-Ruṣāfa and gives his *isnād* as < Abū l-Qāsim < Abū ʿAbd al-Raḥmān < ʿAbdallāh ibn ʿAbd al-Wahhāb ibn Muḥammad ibn Ṣāliḥ.

173 < ʿAbdallāh ibn Bakr al-Wāʿiẓ and Muḥammad ibn ʿAlī al-Muhtadī bi'llāh < Ibn al-Anbārī.

174 Longer and with variants but without verses < Shabīb ibn Shayba.

175 < Jaʿfar ibn Muḥammad al-Faryābī and Aḥmad ibn ʿAbd al-ʿAzīz ibn al-Jaʿd al-Washshāʾ < Isḥāq ibn al-Buhlūl al-Anbārī < "my father" al-Buhlūl ibn Ḥassān al-Tanūkhī < Isḥāq ibn Ziyād of Banū Sāma ibn Luʾayy < Shabīb ibn Shayba.

176 Within the *Story of ʿUmar al-Nuʿmān*. Translated in Lyons (2008) I: 380, and Littmann (1953) I: 618–619.

Al-Balādhurī also relates another brief story with some resemblance to B38:[177]

> Umm Salama, the wife of Abū l-ʿAbbās, said: "O Commander of the Believers, how nice kingship would be if it only lasted!" Abū l-ʿAbbās replied: "If it lasted, it would have done so with those before me and never come to me."[178]

B39 Someone asked Khālid, and he gave the man one dirham. The man said: "Good God! Do you give me a single dirham?" Khālid replied: "You stupid man, do you not know that a dirham is a tenth part of ten dirhams and ten dirhams is a tenth part of a hundred, and a hundred dirhams is a tenth parth of a thousand, and a thousand dirhams is a tenth part of the bloodmoney of a Muslim!"

al-Jāḥiẓ, *Bukhalāʾ*, p. 150;[179] al-Jāḥiẓ, *Bayān* II: 202 (anonymous); al-Murtaḍā, *Amālī* II: 262; al-Zamakhsharī, *Rabīʿ* IV: 148; al-Khaṭīb al-Baghdādī, *Bukhalāʾ*, p. 259;[180] Ibn ʿAsākir, *Taʾrīkh* XVI: 115;[181] Ibn al-ʿAdīm, *Bughya* VII: 67; Ibn Manẓūr, *Mukhtaṣar* VII: 364;[182] al-Balawī, *Alif-Bāʾ* I: 127 (anonymous);[183] Ibn Durayd, *Jamhara*, p. 710 (s.v. RMZ, anonymous); al-Waṭwāṭ, *Ghurar*, p. 378.[184]

COMMENTARY: Ibn Nubāta tells a similar story about Sahl ibn Hārūn:[185]

> Sahl (ibn Hārūn) was one of the most avaricious people. Fine anecdotes are told about his avarice and other characteristics. Al-Jāḥiẓ has said: Someone met Sahl ibn Hārūn and said: "Give me what does not

177 Al-Balādhurī, *Ansāb* III: 160 (< al-Madāʾinī).

178 For a similar story about Khusraw and Shīrīn in Persian, see Salemann – Shukovski (1947): 50*. Cf. also Marzolph (1983), no. 98. For a similar story where Ardashīr converts to asceticism, see Askari (2016): 211–212.

179 Translated in Serjeant (1997): 130.

180 Combined with B17. Al-Khaṭīb begins his version with *qāla*, which seems to refer back to al-Jawālīqī, the authority of the previous anecdote.

181 Introduced by *qāla*, referring back to al-Madāʾinī in B60, which Ibn ʿAsākir combines with B17.

182 Combined with B17.

183 < al-Khaṭṭābī.

184 Al-Waṭwāṭ has "a tiny little dinar (*dunaynīran*)" instead of dirham and respectively stops at "a thousand dinars is your blood money!" In his version, Khālid starts his reply with "You belittled a grand thing, may God belittle you," playing with the technical and non-technical meanings of *ṣaghghara* "to belittle; to form a diminutive."

185 Ibn Nubāta, *Sarḥ*, p. 243.

damage you." Sahl asked: "What is that, O brother?" The beggar replied: "A dirham." Sahl said: "You have despised the dirham! Yet it obeys God on His earth without disobedience. It is a tenth of ten and ten is a tenth of a hundred and a hundred is a tenth of a thousand and a thousand is a tenth of the blood money of a Muslim! Can't you see where a dirham ends up? And yet you despise it! Are not treasuries merely a dirham upon a dirham?" Here the man went away. Had he not, Sahl would have never stopped.

B40 Khālid ibn Ṣafwān has said: I came in a delegation to Hishām and entered upon him. This happened after he had dismissed Khālid ibn ʿAbdallāh al-Qasrī. I found him sitting on a chair in a pond with water up to his ankles. He ordered a chair to be brought for me, and I sat down. Then he asked me questions, and I told him stories for a long time. Finally he bowed his head in silence, then raised it and said: "O Khālid, there was another Khālid sitting where you now sit, who was closer to my heart and dearer to me than you are." I replied: "O Commander of the Believers, your clemency is not too narrow for him. What if you forgive him his crime?" He replied: "O Khālid, that Khālid was bold and annoyed me, he troubled and exhausted (*aʿjafa*) me without leaving a way to return."

Ibn Qutayba, *ʿUyūn* I: 78;[186] Ibn ʿAbdrabbih, *ʿIqd* IV: 446; al-Ḥuṣrī, *Zahr*, p. 874; al-Dajājī, *Safaṭ*, p. 42.

B40a < *al-Madāʾinī* < *Shabīb ibn Shayba*: Khālid ibn Ṣafwān ibn al-Ahtam said: Khālid (ibn ʿAbdallāh al-Qasrī) continued to act in it (Iraq) until Hishām discharged him of his office, punished him, and killed his son Yazīd ibn Khālid. I saw him with a rope around his foot, children pulling it. One day I came to Hishām and spoke with him for a long time. Finally he sighed and said: "Khālid, there was another Khālid whose presence was dearer to me and whose speech was more pleasant to me than yours." By this he meant Khālid al-Qasrī.

I used the opportunity and wished to intervene on Khālid al-Qasrī's behalf so that he would owe me a favour, so I said: "O Commander of the Believers, why don't you take him back into your favour? Surely you have taught him the lesson for exceeding his boundaries." He answered: "Oh no! He took liberties and wearied me with them; he troubled me and made me exhausted. He went too far in his wrongdoings, and we have gone too far in punishing him. The hide has been spoilt by worms, the wound has festered, the flood has reached

186 Introduced by *wa-fī akhbār Khālid ibn Ṣafwān*.

the hills, and the belt has passed beyond the teats.[187] There is no good left in him and there is no way for him to return to office. Continue with your stories!"

(al-Iṣfahānī, *Aghānī* XIX: 63); Ibn Ḥamdūn, *Tadhkira* III: 104 (no. 263); al-Nuwayrī, *Nihāya* III: 374.

COMMENTARY: See also B98. Ibn ʿAbdrabbih notes that Hishām had given Khālid al-Qasrī into the hands of his governor on Iraq, Yūsuf ibn ʿUmar. Khālid al-Qasrī was first dismissed in 120/738 and imprisoned for about a year and a half, after which he was freed, but at his accession in 125/743 the Caliph al-Walīd ibn Yazīd delivered him into the hands of the governor of Kufa Yūsuf ibn ʿUmar al-Thaqafī, who tortured him to death in 126/743.[188]

B41 Khālid ibn Ṣafwān said to Umayya ibn ʿAbdallāh ibn Khālid ibn Asīd when he came to Basra, fleeing from Abū Fudayk: "Glory be to God who has preferred us to you and not you to us! You were eager to attain martyrdom, but God refused that in order to adorn our city with you, calm our anxiety by you, and drive away our distress by you!"

al-Balādhurī, *Ansāb* (ed. al-ʿAẓm) VI: 558;[189] al-Washshāʾ, *Fāḍil*, pp. 92–93;[190] Ibn Munqidh, *Lubāb*, p. 341; Ibn ʿAsākir, *Taʾrīkh* XVI: 104;[191] Ibn Manẓūr, *Mukhtaṣar* VII: 359;[192] al-Tawḥīdī, *Baṣāʾir* IX: 204 (no. 693);[193] Ibn al-Sarrāj, *Jawāhir*, p. 865.[194]

COMMENTARY: Abū Hilāl al-ʿAskarī tells a similar story about Aslam ibn Zurʿa who, with his 2,000 men, was put to flight by Mirdās al-Khārijī with his 40 men. A woman of his tribe similarly consoles Aslam.[195]

Abū Hilāl also relates another version of the story, in which people remain dumbfounded, not knowing what to say to Umayya, until Ṣafwān ibn

---

187 See al-Maydānī, *Majmaʿ* I: 295 (no. 871: *jāwaza l-ḥizāmu l-ṭubyayn*).

188 See *EI2*, s.v. (G. Hawting).

189 The story of Abū Fudayk is told *in extenso* in *Ansāb* (ed. al-ʿAẓm) VI: 552ff.

190 Indirectly from al-Madāʾinī (*wa-khubbirtu ʿan al-Madāʾinī*). The story does not come to al-Washshāʾ through al-Balādhurī as shown by the final comment, missing from the *Ansāb*: *qāla l-Madāʾinī: fa-hādhā min aḥsani kalāmin yulqā bihi mahzūm.*

191 With variants < Rashaʾ ibn Naẓīf < Abū l-Qāsim ʿAlī ibn Ibrāhīm and Abū l-Waḥsh Subayʿ al-Musallam from him < Abū l-Fatḥ Ibrāhīm ibn ʿAlī ibn Ibrāhīm ibn Sībakht al-Baghdādī < Abū Bakr Muḥammad ibn Yaḥyā al-Ṣūlī < Abū l-ʿAynāʾ < al-Aṣmaʿī.

192 < al-Aṣmaʿī, with variants.

193 Significant variants.

194 Abbreviated, with "an Emir of ʿAbd al-Malik's" as the other protagonist.

195 Abū Hilāl al-ʿAskarī, *Dīwān*, p. 1047 < al-Ghalābī < ʿAbdallāh ibn al-Ḍaḥḥāk < al-Haytham ibn ʿAdī < ʿAwāna.

ʿAbdallāh ibn al-Ahtam, further defined as "the father of Khālid ibn Ṣafwān," steps forth and delivers a speech similar, but not identical, to that of Khālid in al-Balādhurī's version.[196] Ibn Qutayba features ʿAbdallāh ibn al-Ahtam as the speaker.[197]

As Abū Fudayk won the battle of Bahrain against Umayya in 72/691 and died a year after,[198] the story would better fit Khālid's father or grandfather.[199]

B42 < *al-Madāʾinī* < *Ḥafṣ ibn Muʿāwiya*: Khālid said: "Maid, bring me cheese because it gives a good appetite and strengthens the stomach, being one of the sour foods (*ḥamḍ*) of the Arabs!" The maid told him that there was no cheese in the house. To this Khālid said: "No matter, I did not know that. It is bad for teeth, causes constipation (*yūkī l-baṭn*), and makes your breath bad. Moreover, it is produced by the people of *dhimma*."

Ibn Qutayba, *ʿUyūn* III: 254; Ibn Ḥamdūn, *Tadhkira* IV: 80 (no. 216); al-Zamakhsharī, *Rabīʿ* II: 724; Ibn ʿAsākir, *Taʾrīkh* XVI: 109;[200] al-Rāghib, *Muḥāḍarāt* II: 616.

B42a The saying by Abū ʿUbayda has already been mentioned in the article on Ḥumayd al-Arqaṭ that Khālid ibn Ṣafwān was, despite his excellence and sublimity, one of the four Arab misers.[201] It is said that one day when he was eating bread and cheese a Bedouin saw him and greeted him. Khālid replied: "Have some bread and cheese! They are the sour food of the Bedouins. They are good appetisers and go well down, and it is lovely to drink something thereafter." The Bedouin sat down and ate heartily until nothing was left. Then Khālid said: "Girl, bring us some more bread and cheese!" The girl answered: "But we have run out of them." Khālid replied: "Thank God who turned from us its harm and protected us from its burden! By God, they are so harmful to teeth and irritate the throat, swell in the stomach and are hard to push out." The Bedouin said: "By God, I have never seen blame coming so soon after praise!"

(Yāqūt, *Irshād* III: 279); Ibn al-ʿAdīm, *Bughya* VII: 64–65.[202]

---

196 Abū Hilāl al-ʿAskarī, *Dīwān*, pp. 1047–1048 < al-Qāsim ibn Ismāʿīl < Rafīʿ ibn Salama < Abū ʿUbayda.

197 Ibn Qutayba, *ʿUyūn* I: 295.

198 Cf. *EI3*, s.v. Abū Fudayk (K. Lewinstein).

199 Cf. Chapter 1.3.2.

200 < Abū l-Ḥasan Rashaʾ ibn Naẓīf and Abū l-Qāsim ʿAlī ibn Ibrāhīm and Abū l-Waḥsh al-Muqriʾ from him < Ibrāhīm ibn ʿAlī ibn Ibrāhīm al-Baghdādī < Muḥammad ibn Yaḥyā al-Ṣūlī < Abū Ḥātim Sulaymān ibn Aḥmad al-Mādaraʾī < "my father" < "my grandfather."

201 See A52.

202 < Abū Naṣr Muḥammad ibn Hibatallāh < Abū l-Qāsim ibn abī Muḥammad < Abū l-Ḥasan Rashaʾ ibn Naẓīf and Abū l-Qasim ʿAlī ibn Ibrāhīm and Abū Waḥsh al-Muqriʾ < Ibrāhīm

COMMENTARY: Cf. B43. Al-Rāghib gives a twist to the story at the end:[203]

> His friend asked him: "Which of the two shall we transmit from you?" Khālid replied: "The former if there is cheese, the latter if there is not."

Al-Jāḥiẓ refers to the story of Khālid, but without telling it, which implies that he assumed the reader to be familiar with it.[204] Both he and Ibn Ḥamdūn tell before this another story of *madḥ wa-dhamm* featuring Ghaylān ibn Kharasha al-Ḍabbī,[205] who crossed the river Nahr-ʿAbdallāh in Basra in the company of two different Emirs and was equally quick to elaborate on their opinions of the river, whether good or bad.[206]

For cheese, see Cook (1984): 449–467. Both Ibn Qutayba and al-Zamakhsharī read *yastawlī ʿalā l-baṭn*, which in all probability is a corruption of *yastawkī*.[207] A similar story concerning aubergine is told about a courtier and Maḥmūd the Ghaznavid in Persian literature.[208]

B43 He (al-Madāʾinī) said: Once Khālid passed by a man who was eating cheese and said to him: "Don't eat it! It goes down easily but comes out with difficulty." Later, the man saw Khālid eating cheese and asked: "O Abū Ṣafwān, didn't you forbid me from eating it?" Khālid replied: "It draws forth the appetite and goes well with bread. And it also is one of the sour foods of the Arabs."

Ibn al-ʿAdīm, *Bughya* VII: 64.[209]

COMMENTARY: Cf. B42.

B44 Maslama ibn ʿAbd al-Malik said to Khālid ibn Ṣafwān: "Tell me about al-Ḥasan."[210] Khālid answered: "His secret self resembled his public self more than anybody's. Of all people he was himself the most eager to observe what he

---

ibn ʿAlī ibn Ibrāhīm al-Baghdādī Muḥammad ibn Yaḥyā al-Ṣūlī < Abū Ḥātim Sulaymān ibn Aḥmad al-Mādarāʾī < "my father" < "my grandfather."

203 Al-Rāghib, *Muḥāḍarāt* II: 616.

204 Al-Jāḥiẓ, *Bayān* I: 395.

205 On whom, see Donner (1993): 96, note 632.

206 Al-Jāḥiẓ, *Bayān* I: 394–395; Ibn Ḥamdūn, *Tadhkira* IV: 79–80 (no. 215).

207 For which see Ibn Manẓūr, *Lisān* XV: 390a, s.v.

208 See Salemann – Shukovsky (1947): 52*.

209 < ʿAlī ibn ʿAbd al-Munʿim ibn ʿAlī < Yūsuf ibn Ādam < Abū Bakr Muḥammad ibn Manṣūr al-Samʿānī < Abū Bakr Muḥammad ibn ʿAbdallāh ibn Muḥammad al-Sājī < Abū Ṭāhir Muḥammad ibn Aḥmad ibn ʿAbd al-Raḥīm < ʿAbdallāh ibn Muḥammad ibn Jaʿfar < Abū l-ʿAbbās al-Jammāl < Abū Ghassān < al-Aṣmaʿī.

210 The text reads al-Ḥusayn, but the emendation is obvious.

commanded others to do and to leave what he forbade others from. He kept his soul under control better than anyone. He never took up ruling nor was ever seen trading in the market. He had no need of other people's wealth, but they needed him for religious matters." Maslama said: "How could a people perish with such a person among them!"

Ibn ʿAbdrabbih, *ʿIqd* II: 230.

B44a < *ʿUrābī ibn al-Ḥusayn* < *ʿAbdallāh ibn Bakr al-Sahmī* < *Muḥammad ibn Dhakwān*: Khālid ibn Ṣafwān said: I met Maslama ibn ʿAbd al-Malik in al-Ḥīra after the defeat of Ibn al-Muhallab. Maslama said to me: "Khālid, tell me about the Ḥasan of the Basrans." I replied: "I was his neighbour by his side and his companion in his circle of *ḥadīth* and I am better informed about him than those before me (i.e., those older than me). His secret self resembled his public self more than anybody's. His words resembled his deeds more than anybody's. If he sat down with something, he rose up with the same, and if he rose up with something, he sat down with it, too. If he ordered (others) to do something, he, more than anyone, was doing the same. If he forbade (others) from something, he was the first to leave that. I found that he did not need others but others needed him." Maslama exclaimed: "That is enough, that is enough! How could a people among whom there was this man go astray?" With this he referred to them having followed Ibn al-Muhallab.

(Wakīʿ, *Akhbār*, p. 239/II: 12)

B44b < *Aḥmad ibn ʿAlī* < *Ṣalt ibn Masʿūd* < *Ibrāhīm ibn Saʿd*: I heard Khālid ibn Ṣafwān reply when he was asked about al-Ḥasan: "I am the man to know about him. His house was my playground when I was young and my *majlis* when I was older." They asked him to tell them about al-Ḥasan, and he replied: "He was the keenest of men to do what he ordered (others) to do. I never saw him elbow his way to anything in the world."

(Wakīʿ, *Akhbār*, p. 239/II: 12); Ibn ʿAsākir, *Taʾrīkh* XVI: 116.[211]

B44c Hishām asked Khālid ibn Ṣafwān: "Did you know al-Ḥasan?" Khālid replied: "I have heard that when he was young, he was in his house, and when old, he was in his circle's *majlis*."[212] Hishām asked: "What was he like?" Khālid

---

211 < ʿAlī ibn ʿAbdallāh Yaḥyā ibn al-Ḥasan < Abū Tammām ʿAlī ibn Muḥammad < Abū ʿUmar ibn Ḥayyawayhi < Muḥammad ibn al-Qāsim al-Kawkabī < Ibn abī Khaythama < al-Ṣalt ibn Masʿūd < Ibrāhīm ibn Saʿd. Ibn ʿAsākir's version is slightly corrupt.

212 This seems to be a corruption, and we should probably read: "I (the author) have heard that he (Khālid) was in his (al-Ḥasan's) house as a child and in his circle's *majlis* when he was old(er)," cf. B44a and B44b.

replied: "He was the first to do what he ordered (others) to do and to refrain from what he forbade (others) from doing.[213] If he sat down to a task, he rose only when it was done, and if he rose to a task, he sat down only when it was done. By day he was a teacher and by night an ascetic."

(al-Tawḥīdī, *Baṣāʾir* VIII: 110, no. 419).

COMMENTARY: Cf. B45 and A61, A61a.

B45 Maslama[214] ibn ʿAbd al-Malik said to Khālid: "Tell me about al-Aḥnaf." Khālid replied: "If you wish, I will tell you about three of his characteristics, or two if you wish, or just one." Maslama said: "Tell me about three of his characteristics." Khālid said: "He was neither ignorant nor covetous and when an obligation came to him he did not push it aside." Maslama asked: "And the two?" Khālid said: "He prepared the way for good and obviated the bad." Maslama asked: "And the one?" Khālid replied: "He kept his soul under control better than anyone."

Ibn ʿAbdrabbih, *ʿIqd* II: 278;[215] al-Waṭwāṭ, *Ghurar*, p. 27; al-Ṭurṭūshī, *Sirāj*, p. 340; al-Salawī, *Kawkab*, p. 755; Ibn ʿAsākir, *Taʾrīkh* XXIV: 317;[216] Ibn ʿAdīm, *Bughya* III: 379–380.[217]

B45a Khālid ibn Ṣafwān has told: I was in al-Ruṣāfa with Hishām ibn ʿAbd al-Malik when al-ʿAbbās ibn al-Walīd[218] came. People flooded upon him. When I came to al-ʿAbbās, he said to me: "Tell me about how you took al-Aḥnaf as your lord and came to be led by him." I answered: "If you wish, I will tell you (about him) one characteristic which made him a lord, or if you wish two, or three, or I can tell you the whole evening till it ends without you noticing that you are fasting" – it was a Thursday and he was fasting. He replied: "Tell me the

213 The edition vocalises these as passive voices ("He was the first to do what he was ordered to, etc."). This is not an impossible reading, but in light of the other versions it seems better to read the verbs as active voices and to translate as above.

214 In all other sources the interlocutor is Hishām ibn ʿAbd al-Malik. Al-Waṭwāṭ roughly follows Ibn ʿAbdrabbih, al-Ṭurṭūshī is somewhat of a mix between Ibn ʿAbdrabbih's and al-Balādhurī's versions.

215 With major variants.

216 < Ibn Marwān < Aḥmad ibn Dāʾūd < al-Māzinī < al-Aṣmaʿī.

217 < ʿAbd al-Ghanī Sulaymān ibn Banīn < Abū ʿAbdallāh Muḥammad ibn Ḥamd al-Artāḥī < Abū l-Ḥasan al-Farrāʾ < Abū l-Qāsim ʿAbd al-ʿAzīz ibn al-Ḥasan ibn Ismāʿīl < Abū Muḥammad ibn al-Ḥasan ibn Ismāʿīl al-Ḍarrāb < Abū Bakr al-Mālikī < Aḥmad ibn Dāʾūd < al-Māzinī < al-Aṣmaʿī.

218 Ibn ʿAsākir adds: ibn ʿAbd al-Malik.

first!" I said: "He kept his soul under control better than anyone we have seen or heard about when he wanted to make it undergo something or when he turned it aside from something." Then I came to my mind again and added: "except for the Caliphs."

He said: "That's a grand and sufficient one! But what about the second characteristic?" I said: "A man may have great control over his soul, but yet be unable to discern what is good and what is bad. Yet we never saw or heard about anyone who could better discern between good and bad. He used his ability only for good and turned it away from bad."

Al-ʿAbbās said: "You have brought something that links with the first, something that only suits the first. Now what is the third?" I said: "A man may have great control over his soul and be able to discern what is good and what is bad, yet he may be unlucky so that his fame does not spread, but al-Aḥnaf was well known among people."

Al-ʿAbbās replied: "By your father, that one joined well with the earlier ones! What about the rest that should entertain me through the evening so that I forget my fasting?"

I said: (Take, for example,) his earlier battle days, like the conquest of Khurāsān, when Persians assembled against him in Marw al-Rūdh. He was against something which he could not cope with. He was in a perilous place when the matters had come to this. He prayed the last evening prayers and added a private prayer, imploring God to help him. Then he went and walked among the troops, like a worried man would do. He was in disguise so that he could hear what people were talking about. He went by a slave, who was kneeding and saying to his friend: "I wonder at the Emir! He lets the Muslims stay in a perilous place where enemies have surrounded us from every side and are taking aim at us, even though he would be able to change his place!" Al-Aḥnaf started saying (in his mind): "O God, help me! O God, guide me!" The other slave asked what he should do, and the first continued: "He should summon (the army) to set moving. Between us and a thicket there is only a mile (*farsakh*). He should set that at his back so that God would protect him through it. When the back is protected, he should send out his (army's) two wings (*mujannibatayhi*), the right and the left, so that God would protect his sides through them. Then he could face the enemy from just one direction."

Al-Aḥnaf kneeled down and then summoned from that very place the army to set moving. When they came to the thicket, he camped in front of it. In the morning the enemy came, but could not find their way except from one direction. They had four war drums, which they were drumming. Al-Aḥnaf mounted, took the flag, and himself attacked one of the drums, breaking it and killing the drummer, saying:

Every leader has a responsibility:
to dye the slope or to be crushed![219]

Then he broke the remaining drums. When the Persians lacked the sound of their drums, they took to flight. The Muslims pursued them and won.

After that Khālid kept telling stories for the whole day until the end of the day.

(Ibn Nubāta, *Sarḥ*, pp. 107–108); al-Jarīrī, *Jalīs* IV: 77–79;[220] Ibn ʿAsākir, *Taʾrīkh* XXIV: 317–321.[221]

COMMENTARY: Cf. B46. Ibn Manẓūr mentions this story, giving an interesting *isnād* and setting the scene:[222]

> < *Muḥammad ibn Aḥmad ibn Yaʿqūb* < *"my grandfather" Yaʿqūb, who said*: I found (the following) in the book by Ḥujayn ibn al-Muthannā al-Yamāmī,[223] who said: We have heard that Khālid ibn Ṣafwān once came to Hishām ibn ʿAbd al-Malik, who asked him to come closer. Muʿāwiya ibn Hishām, who was the lord of the children of Hishām, asked Khālid: "O Khālid, how did al-Aḥnaf ibn Qays attain to what he attained among you?"

Ibn ʿAsākir and al-Jarīrī continue for much longer, letting Khālid tell two further stories about al-Aḥnaf.[224] Ibn al-ʿAdīm refers to the same story,[225] but only gives its *isnād*[226] and says that he has told the story in the article on al-Aḥnaf.[227] There he does give a version of this story, B45,[228] but the *isnād*

219 I.e., either dye the ground with enemy blood or be killed in the attempt.

220 < al-Ḥusayn ibn al-Qāsim al-Kawkabī < Muḥammad ibn Zakariyyā al-Ghalābī < al-ʿAbbās ibn Bakkār < Shabīb ibn Shayba.

221 < Abū l-ʿIzz ibn Kādish < Abū ʿAlī Muḥammad ibn al-Ḥusayn < al-Muʿāfā ibn Zakariyyā < al-Ḥusayn ibn al-Qāsim al-Kawkabī < Muḥammad ibn al-Qāsim ibn Zakariyyā al-Ghalābī < al-ʿAbbās ibn Bakkār < Shabīb ibn Shayba.

222 Ibn Manẓūr, *Mukhtaṣar* V: 155.

223 Baghdadi *ḥadīth* scholar (d. ca. 220/835), cf. al-Ṣafadī, *Wāfī* XI: 325 (no. 478).

224 Ibn ʿAsākir, *Taʾrīkh* XXIV: 317–321; al-Jarīrī, *Jalīs* IV: 77–79.

225 Ibn al-ʿAdīm, *Bughya* VII: 49–50.

226 The same as Ibn ʿAsākir, *Taʾrīkh* XXIV: 317–321.

227 Ibn al-ʿAdīm, *Bughya* III: 367–394

228 Ibn al-ʿAdīm, *Bughya* III: 379–380.

would imply that he should be speaking about B45a. For the incident during al-Aḥnaf's campaign, see al-Ṭabarī.[229]

Ibn al-Jawzī relates a story similar to B45, where people ask ʿAbd al-Wāḥid, the *ṣāḥib* of al-Ḥasan al-Baṣrī, to tell them about al-Ḥasan (cf. B44).[230]

B46 One of the governors (*ʿummāl*) of Basra said to him: "Describe al-Aḥnaf for me." He answered: "If you wish, I will tell you about him for a month, or for ten (days), or, if you wish, I will condense the story." He said: "Condense it." Khālid replied: "He kept his soul better under control than anyone."

COMMENTARY: Cf. B45.

B47 < *Abū l-Ḥasan al-Madāʾinī ʿAlī al-Qurashī*:[231] Khālid used to say: Do not invest kindness in a vicious, stupid, or villainous person. The vicious one will think that you do so because you are weak and afraid of his evil. The stupid one does not acknowledge the kindness you are conferring on him. The villainous one is a salt marsh, which does not produce crop or if it does, it does not grow well and properly. But when you see a noble person, do a good deed to him and sow kindness so that you may reap thankfulness. I will pledge and guarantee that for you.

al-Jāḥiẓ, *Bayān* II: 109 (anonymous);[232] Ibn Munqidh, *Lubāb*, p. 354. *Other versions*: Ibn Ḥamdūn, *Tadhkira* III: 248 (no. 733); Yāqūt al-Mustaʿṣimī, *Asrār*, p. 103 (no. 218); al-Ābī, *Nathr* IV: 189 (abbreviated); Ibn al-Sarrāj, *Jawāhir*, p. 852.

B48 < *al-Madāʾinī* < *ʿAbdallāh ibn Salm*: Khālid used to mention the al-Muhallab family and say: "Blessings wander on earth restlessly until they come to the al-Muhallab family and there they rest."

B49 Khālid used to say about Shabīb ibn Shayba: Shabīb does not have secret friends nor open enemies.

---

229 Al-Ṭabarī, *Taʾrīkh* I: 2900–2901/XV: 104–105. See also Haug (2019): 84–85 (with further references).

230 Ibn al-Jawzī, *Ādāb*, p. 30.

231 The text reads Abū l-Ḥasan al-Madāʾinī *ʿan* ʿAlī al-Qurashī. However, Dr. Ilkka Lindstedt (Helsinki) has suggested to me that the word *ʿan* should be deleted, although it remains disturbing that the name ʿAlī only comes after al-Madāʾinī.

232 Attributed to *baʿḍ al-ḥukamāʾ*.

al-Jāḥiẓ, *Bayān* I: 47,[233] I: 340;[234] al-Jāḥiẓ, *Ḥayawān* V: 592; Ibn al-ʿAdīm, *Bughya* VII: 76;[235] Ibn Qutayba, *ʿUyūn* III: 84; Ibn abī l-Ḥadīd, *Sharḥ* V: 500; al-Zamakhsharī, *Rabīʿ* I: 439–440; al-Ḥuṣrī, *Zahr*, p. 953; Ibn ʿAsākir, *Taʾrīkh* LXXIII: 137;[236] Ibn Jinnī, *Fasr* III: 692–693;[237] Ibn Shuhayd, *Dīwān*, p. 182 = Ibn Bassām, *Dhakhīra* I: 237;[238] al-Tawḥīdī, *Ṣadāqa*, p. 193;[239] al-ʿAskarī, *Ṣināʿatayn*, p. 310.

B49a Khālid ibn Ṣafwān was asked about Shabīb ibn Shayba, and he said: There we have a man who has been mixed with envy and moulded upon it. He does not have secret brethren nor open enemies.

(al-Jāḥiẓ, *Faṣl* I: 357).

COMMENTARY: As a saying by Shabīb about Khālid this is found in a large number of sources.[240]

The attribution of this saying to Shabīb, speaking about Khālid, seems to have risen from unvocalised script. E.g., Ibn ʿAbdrabbih, *ʿIqd* II: 270, begins with "Shabīb ibn Shayba mentioned Khālid ibn Ṣafwān and said," reflecting expressions such as "*dhukira Shabīb ibn Shayba ʿinda Khālid ibn Ṣafwān fa-qāla Khālid*"[241] where the deletion of *ʿinda* would result in an inversed

233 Al-Jāḥiẓ adds: "and Shabīb did not oppose him (*lam yuʿāriḍhu*)." He also comments on this saying, adding: "Khālid's saying shows that he well knew how to insult in the way of the nobility." The saying is also given as an example of *sabb al-ashrāf* in Ibn Shuhayd, *Dīwān*, p. 182 = Ibn Bassām, *Dhakhīra* I: 237. It seems that Ibn Shuhayd may have misunderstood al-Jāḥiẓ, who is not speaking about insulting nobles but about insulting in the way of the nobles. However that may be, Ibn Shuhayd says that the Arabs appreciated this saying by Khālid for his ability to use *sabb al-ashrāf*.

234 Here al-Jāḥiẓ introduces the passage as "Khālid used to exchange mutual comments (*yuqāriḍu*) with Shabīb ibn Shayba because they were related and neighbours and shared the same profession" – *yuqāriḍu* (for which see Lane 1863–93, s.v.) should perhaps be accepted as a *lectio difficilior*. Al-Jāḥiẓ further comments on the saying: "This is a saying which can be (truly) valued only by those firmly rooted (*al-rāsikhūn*) in this profession," – echoing Q 3:7 and Q 4: 162.

235 < al-Jāḥiẓ, *Bayān*.

236 < Aḥmad ibn ʿAlī al-Muqriʾ < al-Aṣmaʿī.

237 Vol. III of the edition, vol. IV of the series < ʿAlī ibn al-Ḥusayn al-Kātib < ʿAlī ibn Sulaymān < Abī l-ʿAbbās al-Mubarrad.

238 Quoting Ibn Shuhayd.

239 Khālid about "some man."

240 E.g., in Ibn ʿAbdrabbih, *ʿIqd* II: 270, where Ibn ʿAbdrabbih comments on the saying: "This is a saying which can be (truly) valued only by people of this profession" (cf. al-Jāḥiẓ, *Bayān* I: 340), *ʿIqd* II: 337, *ʿIqd* III: 105, where Ibn ʿAbdrabbih explains this saying: "He means that they cajole him because (they fear) his evil, yet in their heart they hate him;" Ibn Ḥamdūn, *Tadhkira* IV: 370 (no. 963).

241 Al-Jāḥiẓ, *Ḥayawān* V: 592.

sense with DhKR then read in the active voice (*dhakara*). It is probably to avoid the possible confusion that al-Jāḥiẓ adds the subject "Khālid" after *fa-qāla*.[242]

B50 Ḥafṣ ibn Muʿāwiya ibn ʿAmr al-Ghalābī wanted to go to Ahwāz and asked Khālid for counsel. Khālid said: "Fear God, thy Lord, and behave well. You should recite the Qurʾān because it is a remedy to heart's maladies. Do not be boisterous nor full of blame, do not curse a lot nor slander. While speaking (do not ask, but) only be an answerer because you will come to people who do not know you. The way you meet them will be the way they know you and it will be what they attribute you to."

B51 < *al-Madāʾinī and al-Haytham ibn ʿAdī* < *ʿAwāna*: Bilāl ibn abī Burda said to Khālid ibn Ṣafwān when they were travelling down to Basra: "Do you think ʿUkāba al-Numayrī is hard to bear?" Khālid replied: "O, you almost break my heart! Do you ask this as we approach the thickets of al-Baṭāʾiḥ and the heat of Basra and the hot vapour of the sea![243] By God, he is harder for me to bear than drinking Theodorean medicine[244] with hot water in a hot and moist day after overeating at the time of cupping!"

al-Ḥuṣrī, *Jamʿ*, p. 44; Ibn ʿAsākir, *Taʾrīkh* XVI: 109–110.[245]

COMMENTARY: Al-Ḥuṣrī continues by telling another story about this ʿUkāba ibn Ghayla al-Numayrī, who is here depicted thoughtless and ignorant. "Ghayla" is probably an error for Numayla (in Arabic script almost identical with Ghayla).[246] Cf. also B79.

B52 A Yemeni man boasted to Khālid at the door of al-Ḥajjāj. Khālid replied: "From among us come the Prophet, who was sent, and the Caliph, who is hoped for. Among us is the revealed (*munzal*) Book and the House towards which one prays."

COMMENTARY: Cf. B82.

242 See also Werkmeister (1983): 81.

243 For *wamad*, see Ibn Manẓūr, *Lisān* XV: 408, s.v.

244 For this purgative, see al-Zabīdī, *Tāj*, s.v. *idhrīṭūs*. The same medicine is mentioned in A13, here written *shurb al-TYʾDR bi-Ṭūs*. Al-Ḥuṣrī and Ibn ʿAsākir read *sharāb/shurb al-ayārij*.

245 < Abū l-Ḥasan ibn Qubays < Abū l-Ḥasan ibn abī l-Ḥadīd < "my grandfather" Abū Bakr < Abū Muḥammad ibn Zabr < Muḥammad ibn Sulaymān ibn Dāʾūd al-Minqarī < Abū ʿUthmān al-Māzinī < al-Aṣmaʿī < ʿAwāna.

246 For ʿUkāba ibn Numayla, see al-Ṭabarī, *Taʾrīkh* II: 1723/XXVI: 63.

B53 < *al-Madāʾinī*: The Commander of the Believers Abū l-ʿAbbās said to Khālid: "Is it not wonderful that the Prophet of a people died and before he was buried they were already disagreeing!" Khālid replied: "O Commander of the Believers, more wonderful is the case of Adam. God created him with his very hand and set him in his own Paradise freely to eat from where he wanted forbidding him just one tree.[247] He even warned him of his enemy and said: 'Let him not oust you from Paradise so that you will become wretched.'[248] Not withstanding, Adam desired to leave the Paradise and all that was in it. He ate from that tree and committed a sin, yet after all this God, He is exulted, turned to him!"

B54 < *al-Madāʾinī* < *Abū Muḥammad ibn Saʿd*: Khālid sat down in Mecca beside a man[249] from the tribe of ʿAbd al-Dār. The man asked: "Who are you?" Khālid replied: "I am Khālid ibn Ṣafwān from Banū l-Ahtam." The ʿAbdarī commented: "You, Khālid, are like a man who is eternally (*khālid*) in Hellfire.[250] You are the son of Ṣafwān, but God has said: 'a rock (*ṣafwān*) covered with earth.'[251] Finally, you are the son of al-Ahtam, yet a sound one is better than a toothless one (*ahtam*)."

Khālid replied: "O brother from ʿAbd al-Dār, how dare you speak! Hāshim has smashed (*hashama*) you and Umayya hit (*amma*) you on the head. Makhzūm has bridled (*khazama*) you and Jumaḥ overcome (*jamaḥa*) you. You are the domestic slave of Quraysh (*ʿabd dār Quraysh*), opening the door when they enter and closing it when they leave."

al-Jāḥiẓ, *Bayān* I: 336; ps.-al-Jāḥiẓ, *Maḥāsin*, pp. 23–24 (variants); Ibn ʿAbdrabbih, *ʿIqd* IV: 39; al-Murtaḍā, *Amālī* I: 295;[252] Abū Ṭāhir al-Baghdādī, *Qānūn*, p. 31; al-ʿAskarī, *Ṣināʿatayn*, p. 323; al-Khafājī, *Sirr*, pp. 188–189; Ibn al-Sarrāj, *Jawāhir*, p. 767 (variants); Jirāb al-Dawla, *Tarwīḥ*, p. 96.[253]

---

247 Cf. Q 2: 35.

248 Cf. Q 20: 117.

249 A note in Ibn al-Kalbī, *Jamhara* I: 72, identifies this person as ʿAbdallāh ibn Shayba ibn abī Ṭalḥa. The text of Ibn al-Kalbī only mentions that he "was the one who replied to Khālid ibn Ṣafwān."

250 Cf. Q 47: 15.

251 Cf. Q 2: 264. The context is a parable referring to hypocrites.

252 In al-Murtaḍā's version the ʿAbdarī is specified as one of those who inhabit al-Yamāma. There are slight variants in this version.

253 Jirāb al-Dawla adds that the ʿAbdarī suddenly died when he had returned to his house and that his slavegirls lamented him as having been slain by Khālid (*wā qatīla Ṣafwānāh*). The same idea is found in al-Waṭwāṭ's version, see B54a.

B54a It is said that a Qurashī asked Khālid ibn Ṣafwān ibn al-Ahtam al-Tamīmī, who he was, and Khālid gave him his genealogy. The Qurashī said: "Your name is a lie: no one lives in this life forever (*khālid*)! Your father was an arid stone, far from moisture. Your grandfather was toothless, and a sound one is better than a toothless one." Khālid said to him: "You asked me, and I answered. Now, from which tribe are you?" The man answered that he was from Quraysh, and Khālid asked from which part of Quraysh, to which the man replied: "From Banū ʿAbd al-Dār."

Then Khālid said: "You have not accomplished a thing (with your blame)! Would someone like you be permitted to revile Tamīm in its glory and nobility? Hāshim has smashed you and Umayya hit you on the head, Jumaḥ has overcome you and Fihr[254] has shattered your head. Makhzūm has bridled your nose, Luʾayy has turned (*lawat*) you away, Ghālib has vanquished you (*ghalabatka*), and Manāf expelled (*nafat*) you. Zuhra has outshone you and Quṣayy has driven you away and made you his domestic slave and the utmost limit of his shame: you open the doors when they enter and close them when they exit."

The man fell down dead of rage. Later his wife went around on the streets of Basra crying: "Khālid killed my husband with his tongue!" The man's family claimed his blood money from Khālid as he had died because of his words.

(al-Waṭwāṭ, *Ghurar*, p. 259)

B54b A man envied Khālid and asked: "Where are you from?" Khālid replied that he was from Iraq, and the man asked: "From which part of Iraq?" Khālid replied that he was from Basra, and the man did not pursue this any further but stopped asking. Khalid then said to him: "You asked me and I answered. Now, where are you from?" The man answered that he was from Hijaz, to which Khālid commented: "Good, good, the country of the Arabs and the place where people of *adab* have grown. From which part of Hijaz?" The man replied he was from Mecca, and Khālid said: "Good, good, the sacred town of God and his asylum, where Abraham and Ishmael took refuge. Which group of people in Mecca?" The man replied he was from Banū ʿAbd al-Dār.

Then Khālid said: "You have not accomplished a thing,[255] O ʿAbdarite! Hāshim has smashed you and Umayya hit you on the head, Luʾayy has turned you away, Ghālib has vanquished you, Manāf expelled you, and Zuhra has outshone you. You are their slave and the son of their slave. You close the doors

254 Lane (1863–93), s.v.: "a stone such as fills the hand."

255 This outburst remains rather unwarranted in the text, which has dropped the attempts of the man to ridicule Khālid's family, cf. B54a.

when they exit and open them when they enter. Leave, your name will (henceforth) be al-ʿAbqarī,[256] the plant of the hills!"

This was the reason why this ʿAbdarī fled from Syria.

(Ibn al-ʿAdīm, *Bughya* VII: 57)

COMMENTARY: al-Balādhurī is the only one to set the scene in Mecca. Al-Waṭwāṭ (B54a) sets it in Basra. Ibn al-ʿAdīm (B54b) does not mention where this confrontation took place, but gives it as the reason why the ʿAbdarī fled from Syria, thus implicitly situating it in Syria. The use of *figura etymologica* in this saying by Khālid is noticed in various sources.[257]

B55 < *al-Madāʾinī* < *Abū Isḥāq ibn Fāʾid*: Ḥafṣ ibn Muʿāwiya proposed to Arwā bint Khālid. Khālid said: "I am not satisfied with you for her nor with her for you. You are a divorcer and speak bluntly while she is sharptongued. You do not fit together."

B56 Khālid said: Do not ask from wrong persons nor at wrong times. Do not ask for what you do not deserve. Whoever asks for what he does not deserve, deserves to be deprived of what he asks for.

Ibn Qutayba, *ʿUyūn* III: 135; Ibn ʿAbdrabbih, *ʿIqd* I: 241;[258] Yāqūt, *Irshād* III: 280; Ibn ʿAbd al-Barr, *Bahja* I: 320; Ibn abī l-Ḥadīd, *Sharḥ* V: 377; Ibn ʿAsākir, *Taʾrīkh* XVI: 115;[259] Ibn al-ʿAdīm, *Bughya* VII: 63;[260] Ibn al-ʿAdīm, *Bughya* VII: 69;[261] Ibn Manẓūr, *Mukhtaṣar* VII: 365; al-ʿĀmilī, *Mikhlāt*, p. 78 (no. 109).

COMMENTARY: Cf. B75. Ibn ʿAsākir transmits two further versions of the story.[262]

---

256 "The one from the land of the Jinnīs," playing with the phonetic similarity with ʿAbdarī.

257 E.g., Ibn Khalaf, *Mawādd*, p. 180 (from Qudāma ibn Jaʿfar). Independently, such figures are used in, e.g., Ibn Nubāta, *Sarḥ*, p. 345 (in a verse): *man rāma Hāshiman hushimā*. The same figure of speech was used to attack the Umayyad Caliph Hishām, see Cook (2002): 43.

258 Here the saying ends: "What you need is asked with the hope (of getting) but it is (only) reached by fate (*qaḍāʾ*)."

259 < Abū l-Qāsim al-ʿAlawī < Abū l-Ḥasan al-Muqriʾ < Abū Muḥammad al-Ḥasan ibn Ismāʿīl < Aḥmad ibn Marwān < Abū Bakr ibn abī l-Dunyā < Abū Zayd < Abū ʿUbayda.

260 < Aḥmad ibn Marwān < Ibrāhīm ibn Naṣr < Muḥammad ibn Sallām.

261 < Ibn Marwān < Abū Bakr ibn abī l-Dunyā < Abū Zayd < Abū ʿUbayda.

262 Ibn ʿAsākir, *Taʾrīkh* XVI: 115–116 < Ibrāhīm ibn Naṣr < Muḥammad ibn Sallām, and < Abū l-Ḥasan ibn Qubays < Abū l-Ḥasan ibn abī l-Ḥadīd < "my grandfather" Abū Bakr < Abū Muḥammad ibn Zabr < al-Ḥasan ibn ʿUlayl < Masʿūd ibn Bishr < al-Aṣmaʿī.

B57 They say: Khālid vied with some Kufans and said (about Basra): "Its lower part is reeds, its middle part is wood, and its higher part is fresh dates. Everything comes there willingly, but leaves reluctantly."

COMMENTARY: Cf. B81.

B58 Khālid said to his servant: "Buy us some bananas, but do not buy them hard and green nor black and withered." When the servant brought him some, he said: "If I did not know that you have already eaten some, I would give you one."

B58a A servant came to Khālid ibn Ṣafwān with a trayful of plums. Either it was a present or the servant brought them from a garden. When he put them in front of him, Khālid said: "If I did not know that you have already eaten some, I would give you one."

(al-Jāḥiẓ, *Bukhalāʾ*, p. 147)[263]

B59 Khālid used to say: Earn dirhams and keep them because they clothe you in soft clothes (*narmaq*), feed you with white bread (*jarmaq*),[264] and preserve you from (the shame of) asking.

Ibn Manẓūr, *Lisān* IV: 338 (s.v. DRMQ), XV: 444 (s.v. YRMQ);[265] al-Azharī, *Tahdhīb* IX: 412 (s.v. DRMQ and s.v. YRMQ); al-Zamakhsharī, *Fāʾiq* I: 411; al-Ṣaghānī, *Takmila* V: 48b; Ibn Qutayba, *Gharīb al-ḥadīth* I: 74.

COMMENTARY: Ibn Manẓūr refers to this saying as *fī ḥadīth Khālid ibn Ṣafwān*, of which he knows more than one *riwāya* (*hākadhā jāʾa fī riwāya*).[266] S.v. DRMK,[267] a Khālid is furthermore quoted as an authority for *darmak* "finely powdered," but whether this refers to Khālid ibn Ṣafwān is unclear.

263 Translated in Serjeant (1997): 128.

264 Not in Ibn Manẓūr, *Lisān*, Lane (1863–93), or Dozy (1881). The translation is based on the Persian word *garme*, cf. Steingass (1892), s.v. Both Ibn Manẓūr, *Lisān* IV: 338, and *Lisān* XV: 444, read *darmaq*. In IV: 338, Ibn Manẓūr explains the Q in *darmaq* as an *ibdāl* for *darmak*.

265 The whole article consists only of Khālid's saying and its commentary. While mentioning the variant *narmaq*, Ibn Manẓūr here has *yarmaq*, which he is at pains to explain, offering possible Turkish etymologies.

266 Ibn Manẓūr, *Lisān* XV: 444.

267 Ibn Manẓūr, *Lisān*, IV: 338.

B60 When he received his stipend (*jā'iza*) Khālid used to say to dirhams: By God, you have travelled long days in various countries and on highlands. Now, by God, I will make you lie down and repose for a long time.

al-Murtaḍā, *Amālī* II: 262; Ibn ʿAsākir, *Ta'rīkh* XVI: 114–115;[268] Ibn al-ʿAdīm, *Bughya* VII: 67;[269] Ibn Manẓūr, *Mukhtaṣar* VII: 364; Ibn Ḥamdūn, *Tadhkira* II: 320 (no. 827); al-Khaṭīb al-Baghdādī, *Bukhalā'*, p. 259;[270] al-Nuwayrī, *Nihāya* III: 297+300.[271]

B60a When he got a dirham, Khālid ibn Ṣafwān used to say: "O vagrant, for how long have you been travelling far and wide (*yā ʿayyār kam taʿīr wa-kam taṭūfu wa-taṭīr*)! I will make you lie down for a long time." Then he would throw it into a chest and lock it in there.

(al-Zamakhsharī, *Rabīʿ* III: 706); al-Zamakhsharī, *Fā'iq* II: 139; *Shurūḥ Saqṭ*, p. 482 (al-Khwārizmī); al-Ibshīhī, *Mustaṭraf* I: 252.[272]

COMMENTARY: The same anecdote also circulated in a more elaborate form, without the mention of Khālid. ʿAwfī narrates an elaborated anonymous version in Persian.[273] There is also an anonymous version with major differences.[274]

B61 Khālid said to Yaḥyā ibn Ḥabīb: "Do you have a free wife?"[275] Yaḥyā replied: "Two actually." Khālid said: "I thought that you would have been satisfied with less than that and abstained from more than that."

---

268 < Abū l-Faraj Ghayth ibn ʿAlī < Abū Bakr al-Khaṭīb < Abū l-Ḥasan ibn al-Jawālīqī in his book < Aḥmad ibn ʿAlī al-Khazzāz < ʿAbdallāh ibn Baḥr < ʿUmar ibn Muḥammad ibn ʿAbd al-Ḥakam < Muḥammad ibn ʿUmar al-Warrāq < ʿAlī ibn Muḥammad al-Qurashī al-Madā'inī.

269 < Saʿīd ibn Hāshim ibn Aḥmad < Masʿūd ibn al-Ḥasan al-Thaqafī < Aḥmad ibn ʿAlī < Abū l-Ḥasan ibn al-Jawālīqī in his book < Aḥmad ibn ʿAlī al-Khazzāz < ʿAbdallāh ibn Baḥr < ʿUmar ibn Muḥammad ibn ʿAbd al-Ḥakam < Muḥammad ibn ʿUmar al-Warrāq < ʿAlī ibn Muḥammad al-Qurashī al-Madā'inī.

270 < Abū l-Ḥasan al-Jawālīqī in his book < Aḥmad ibn ʿAlī al-Khazzāz < ʿAbdallāh ibn Baḥr < ʿUmar ibn Muḥammad ibn ʿAbd al-Ḥakam < Muḥammad ibn ʿAmr al-Warrāq < ʿAlī ibn Muḥammad al-Qurashī al-Madā'inī.

271 Discussed in Malti-Douglas (1985): 91.

272 Al-Ibshīhī, *Mustaṭraf* I: 252, continues with A67.

273 ʿAwfī, *Jawāmiʿ* III/1: 270 (no. 13) < Kitāb Khalq al-insān. The book is by al-qāḍī Bayān al-Ḥaqq Maḥmūd ibn Abī l-Ḥasan Aḥmad (ibn al-Ḥusayn) al-Nīsābūrī, see Ḥājjī Khalīfa, *Kashf* I: 722, and Ahmed (2000): 30, 33.

274 Cf., e.g., al-Balawī, *Alif-Bā'* I: 127, who narrates one version, adding other similar stories about misers.

275 Baʿlabakkī vocalises *muhayra* (not in the dictionaries). The translation is based on reading *mahīra*, a wife who has received her *mahr*, i.e., a free woman (cf. Lane 1863–93, s.v.).

B62 Khālid disputed with ʿAbdallāh ibn Ḥakīm ibn abī Umayya ibn al-ʿĀṣ al-Thaqafī, who said: "I am the son of the white lady of Thaqīf!" Khālid retorted: "It was her whiteness that betrayed her."

B63 They say: Khālid heard Shabīb ibn Shayba speak well in Wāsiṭ and said: "You have announced to me my death. We belong to a family where a speaker does not die until there is another to replace him."

Shurūḥ Saqṭ, p. 1348 (al-Khwārizmī); Ibn Ḥamdūn, *Tadhkira* VIII: 25–26 (no. 32); al-Ṣūlī, *Akhbār*, p. 70; Ibn ʿAsākir, *Taʾrīkh* LXIII: 191;[276] Ibn Manẓūr, *Mukhtaṣar* XXVI: 326; Ibn Khallikān, *Wafayāt* VI: 24; al-Khaṭīb al-Baghdādī, *Taʾrīkh* XIII: 478.[277]

B63a Shabīb ibn Shayba said: "I know something which when two people meet each other and both have it, there will be a successful outcome between them." Khālid ibn Ṣafwān asked: "What is it?" Shabīb said: "Reason. A reasonable man neither asks what is not appropriate nor denies what is possible." Khālid said: "You have announced to me my death. We belong to a family where a speaker does not die until he sees another one, who replaces him."

(Ibn Qutayba, *ʿUyūn* III: 135); Ibn ʿAbdrabbih, *ʿIqd* I: 242, II: 251.

COMMENTARY: According to Ibn Ḥamdūn and Ibn Khallikān, Abū Tammām (d. ca. 232/845) narrated this story a year before his death after having heard a verse by al-Buḥturī.[278]

The same idea is also found in a story involving Ruʾba and his son ʿUqba.[279] One of Ibn ʿAbdrabbih's versions drops Khālid's last comment, thus shifting the focus onto the witty saying by Shabīb and making him the protagonist of the story, instead of leaving the last word to Khālid and focusing on him.[280]

B64 Khālid used to say: Beware the mangonels of the poor – by which he meant their prayers (*duʿāʾ*). He also quoted a verse by ʿAmr ibn al-Ahtam:

> If you want to take something unjustly, go to
> the highest of people and beware of the listless and slandered.

al-Jāḥiẓ, *Bayān* I: 352, III: 274; ps.-al-Jāḥiẓ, *Maḥāsin*, p. 51; Ibn al-Sarrāj, *Jawāhir*, p. 852.

---

276 < Ibn al-Muẓaffar < al-Marzubānī < Muḥammad ibn Yaḥyā < al-Ḥusayn ibn ʿAlī al-Kātib.

277 In a story about al-Buḥturī and Abū Tammām. The story is also told without reference to Khālid in, e.g., Ibn Nubāta, *Sarḥ*, pp. 326–327.

278 Ibn Ḥamdūn, *Tadhkira* VIII: 25–26; Ibn Khallikān, *Wafayāt* VI: 24.

279 See, e.g., al-Jāḥiẓ, *Bayān* I: 68. Cf. *Bayān* I: 205 and I: 207.

280 Ibn ʿAbdrabbih, *ʿIqd* I: 242.

COMMENTARY: In *Bayān* III: 274, al-Jāḥiẓ adds: "He said: Only the prayers of the sincere or the wronged will be answered." It is not clear whether this is to be taken as a separate saying by Khālid or the continuation of this saying. All sources other than al-Balādhurī lack the verse by ʿAmr.

B65 Khālid used to say: No one takes me to task for a misdeed more heinous to me than a misdeed against someone who has no refuge but God.

B66 Khālid said: Eloquence lies not in an easy tongue and a lot of blabbering, but in hitting the mark and getting at the right argument.

Ibn ʿAbdrabbih, *ʿIqd* IV: 190; Ibn Rashīq, *ʿUmda*, p. 424; al-Waṭwāṭ, *Ghurar*, p. 230;[281] Ibn al-Mudabbir, *al-Risāla al-ʿadhrāʾ*, p. 46 (= *Rasāʾil al-Bulaghāʾ*, p. 251); al-Bayhaqī, *Maḥāsin*, p. 427.

B66a Khālid ibn Ṣafwān heard somebody speaking and lengthening his speech and said: "God have mercy on you! Know that eloquence does not mean having an easy tongue and lots of blabbering. It lies in hitting the point and getting at the right argument." The man answered: "O Abū Ṣafwān, there seems to be no more heinous crime than sharing the same profession!"

(Ibn ʿAbdrabbih, *ʿIqd* II: 261); al-Tawḥīdī, *Baṣāʾir* VIII: 102 (no. 370); Ibn ʿAbd al-Barr, *Bahja* I: 71; al-Zamakhsharī, *Rabīʿ* IV: 254.[282]

COMMENTARY: Versions of this story and B91 have partly been contaminated with each other. Cf. also A36.

B67 < *al-Madāʾinī*: Abū l-ʿAbbās, the Commander of the Believers, asked Khālid ibn Ṣafwān whether he knew they had arrested Sulaymān ibn Ḥabīb. Khālid asked where he was found, and Abū l-ʿAbbās replied: "He was found hiding in a well." Khālid ibn Ṣafwān said to this: "He is one who came out[283] dancing, but fell in a cage and died on the spot."

al-Balādhurī, *Ansāb* II:75.

---

281 In al-Waṭwāṭ, *Ghurar*, p. 213, eloquence is defined by a Bedouin as "paucity of words and reaching (the goal)." Similar definitions are common in Arabic literature.

282 Al-Tawḥīdī, *Baṣāʾir* VIII: 102 (no. 370); Ibn ʿAbd al-Barr, *Bahja* I: 71; and al-Zamakhsharī, *Rabīʿ* IV: 254, drop the reply by Khālid's interlocutor, thus focusing on Khālid and giving him the last word.

283 I.e., rebelled.

COMMENTARY: Al-Balādhurī tells the whole story of Sulaymān ibn Ḥabīb: After fleeing to Iran, he went to Oman, where he rebelled. The attempt did not take fire and he returned to Basra, hiding there. When his capture was imminent, he hid himself in a well.[284]

B68 Khālid ibn Ṣafwān said: If a man came to me running, just wishing to do me honour, and I did not acknowledge his rights, then I would be going over from noble to ignoble features.

B69 Hishām ibn ʿAbd al-Malik said to Khālid: "Admonish me but be brief!" Khālid replied: "O Commander of the Believers, you are above other people, since God has made you so. There is none above you, except for God and to God you are proceeding."[285]

COMMENTARY: The same advice is found in a sermon delivered by Khālid's great-grand-uncle in front of ʿUmar ibn ʿAbd al-ʿAzīz.[286] See also A11.

B70 Khālid said: "We have seen no place like al-Ubulla which would be closer, of a sweeter draught, or a better hideout for a servant of God." Durust ibn Ribāṭ said to this: "Why, then, are distances traversed towards Mecca?"

al-Akhfash al-Aṣghar, *Ikhtiyārayn*, p. 66 (variants).[287]

B70a Khālid ibn Ṣafwān has said: We have seen no place like al-Ubulla which would be closer, of a more pleasant draught, easier to reach, more profitable to a merchant, or a better hideout for a servant of God.

(al-Jāḥiẓ, *Bayān* II: 297); Ibn Qutayba, *ʿUyūn* I: 322; Yāqūt, *Muʿjam* I: 77.[288]

B71 Khālid spoke well. When someone present lavishly praised him, Khālid said: "By God, I wish I were dumb."

B72 Someone litigated with Khālid in front of Bilāl and said: "You blame me every day." Bilāl said: "You blame him, too. In this you share the guilt."

---

284 Al-Balādhurī, *Ansāb* II: 75.

285 Fowden (2004): 138 (= Fowden – Fowden 2004: 53) connects Khālid's admonition with the royal ideology, visible in a picture of Adam set over mankind in Quṣayr ʿAmra. Cf. also B90.

286 See Chapter 1.3.2.

287 Here the interlocutor is a Bedouin from Banū Numayr.

288 The edition reads *ʿāʾidh* for *ʿābid*. This, too, would make good sense: it is a good place for a refugee to hide in.

B73 Khālid passed by some people who said: "Why don't you sit down?" Khālid replied: "Sitting down comes after things have been taken care of."

B74 A Bedouin spoke. Someone said to Khālid: "Why don't you answer him?" He replied: "How could we debate with them, since we are only imitating them? Or how could we seek to surpass them, since we grow from their root?"

B75 Khālid used to say: It is better to lose an opportunity than to ask for something from a person not worthy of it. Harder than the misfortune are its bad consequences.

Ibn Qutayba, *ʿUyūn* III: 150; Ibn ʿAbdrabbih, *ʿIqd* I: 241; Ibn Hudhayl al-Fazārī, *Fukāhāt*, p. 318; Ibn ʿAsākir, *Taʾrīkh* XVI: 115–116;[289] Ibn al-ʿAdīm, *Bughya* VII: 60;[290] Ibn Manẓūr, *Mukhtaṣar* VII: 365; al-Balawī, *Alif-Bāʾ* I: 170; Nakhshabī, *Gulrīz*, p. 36 (anonymous).[291]

COMMENTARY: Cf. B56. Ibn ʿAsākir and Ibn Manẓūr add:

> Then he recited a verse by a female descendant of Ḥassān ibn Thābit on the same theme:
>
> Ask a boon from the people of ancient boon, do not ask
> a youth who has tasted the life but recently.

B76 Khālid said: If a good deed goes without thanks, the indebtedness is all the greater.

B77 Khālid said: It would please me better to have a son fond of wine than of meat, because when he wants meat, he will find it, but wine is sometimes lacking.

al-Murtaḍā, *Amālī* II: 263.

289 < Aḥmad ibn Yaḥyā < Ibn al-Sikkīt.

290 < Abū l-Ḥasan Muḥammad ibn Aḥmad ibn ʿAlī < Abū l-Maʿālī ʿAbdallāh ibn ʿAbd al-Raḥmān ibn Ṣābir < *al-sharīf al-nasīb* Abū l-Qāsim ʿAlī ibn Ibrāhīm < Rashaʾ ibn Naẓīf < al-Ḥasan ibn Ismāʿīl < Aḥmad ibn Marwān al-Mālikī < Aḥmad ibn Yaḥyā < Ibn al-Sikkīt.

291 Nakhshabī leaves the last sentence out.

B78 Someone said to Khālid: "I love you." Khālid replied: "Why should you not? You are not my cousin, nor my neighbour, nor sharing the same profession."
Ibn ʿAbdrabbih, *ʿIqd* II: 327; Ibn ʿĀṣim, *Ḥadāʾiq*, p. 90.[292]

B79 They say: Khālid said to Ḥafṣ ibn Muʿāwiya: "What would you say to some fine bread made of Maysān wheat, some mustard sauce (*ṣināb*) of Ḥulwān, and inbetween a chicken, fat as a Kaskarī duck, which has been fattened until it has grown blind and its skin has withdrawn from its flesh. It yields clear white flesh and bright yellow grease, which will take away the weakness (*fuhūha*) of a hungry man." Ḥafṣ replied: "By my life, I would love it!" (Khālid said):[293] "Then your appointed time will be next Saturday in the garden."

Hafṣ has told: When I arrived, Khālid called for his cook (*khabbāz*), who brought a table on which there was everything that he had described. When the table was set, there suddenly appeared a Bedouin who came to us without permission. – Or Ḥafṣ said: there appeared a man who forced his way into the garden.[294] – When he saw him approaching Khālid said: "By God, this damned visitor is more painful to me than drinking *turunjubīn*[295] in the moist heat of the summer after overeating and having been cupped. Take the tray away, boy!"

Ḥafṣ said: I never saw it again. But it is also said that it was brought back after the intruder had gone, but its freshness was gone.

COMMENTARY: In certain aspects, the story resembles al-Hamadhānī's *al-Maqāma al-Maḍīriyya*,[296] where delicious food evades the victimised guest after his appetite has been awakened. For drinking *turunjubīn*, cf. B51.

B80 Khālid said: "Let no one covet one of these four from me: a loan, a share of my property, listening to a petition,[297] or that I would go with him to a ruler in a business not my own." He was asked what, then, could be hoped of him, and he said: "Chilled water and weighty words."[298]

292 Ibn ʿAbdrabbih and Ibn ʿĀṣim have a slightly different version, in which they explain the saying by adding that the closer one is the more he is given to envy.

293 Ed. al-ʿAẓm XI: 364, has here "*qāla*" and the sense more or less demands this.

294 For *khuṣṣ*, cf. also al-Samawʾal al-Maghribī, *Nuzha*, p. 203, which mentions *aṣḥāb al-khuṣṣ*.

295 Cf. Dozy (1881) I: 146a, s.v. *Turunjubīn* is made of spartium.

296 Al-Hamadhānī, *Maqāmāt*, pp. 121–143.

297 I translate according to the *Maʿārif* (*qarḍ*, *farḍ*, *ʿarḍ*). The edition of al-Balādhurī reads *al-farṣ*, *al-qarḍ*, and *al-hars*, thus missing the rhyme and not quite making sense. Ibn ʿAsākir reads *al-qarḍ*, *al-qarṣ*, and *al-hars*.

298 For the expression *lā yunādā walīduhu*, see Abū ʿUbayda as quoted in note 5 in Ibn Qutayba, *Maʿārif*, p. 404.

Ibn Qutayba, *Maʿārif*, p. 404; Ibn ʿAsākir, *Taʾrīkh* XVI: 114;[299] Ibn al-ʿAdīm, *Bughya* VII: 63.[300]

B81 They say: Khālid once described Basra: "Two hunters of ours go out. One returns with carp (*shabbūṭ*) and *shīm*,[301] the other with gazelles and ostriches. We have the largest supply of ivory, teak, brocade, ambling mounts, and amorous slavegirls. Our river is a wonder. Its origin produces fresh dates, its middle part grapes, and its end reeds. We have dates on their branches, like olives of Syria on their branches. The date palm pushes out its inferior dates ripe to fall[302] and its medium-class dates[303] and then it bursts open showing rods of silver, on which lustruous pearls are set. Then they become rods of gold, on which are set green emeralds, then yellow sapphires and red rubies, and finally the dates become honey.

The water of our wonderful river flows briskly and floods copiously, washing clean our city's plants. It first comes to us at the time of our thirst and it leaves us at the time of our satiation. We get of it what we need whilst lying on our beds. Its water comes to us in floods and torrents (*ubāb*).[304] Nothing separates us from it and there is no rivalry caused by its scarceness and it is not detained from us for any reason."

Maslama asked: "How come you have all this and it has not been taken forcibly from you nor have others found it before you?" Khālid replied: "We have inherited it from our fathers and we will leave it as an inheritance to our sons whilst the Lord of Heaven defends it for us." Then he recited:

Whatever good there is, we have
inherited it since time immemorial.

We pass it on to our sons, when we die,
like we inherited it from our fathers.

299 < Aḥmad ibn Yaḥyā < Muḥammad ibn Sallām al-Jumaḥī.

300 < Aḥmad ibn Marwān < Aḥmad ibn Yaḥyā < Muḥammad ibn Sallām al-Jumaḥī.

301 Cf. Persian *shīm* "a small, spotted scaly fish," see Steingass (1892), s.v. The word is not attested in major Arabic dictionaries, but seems to come from the Arabic root ShYM, cf. *shāma*.

302 For *asqāṭ*, see al-Sijistānī *Nakhl*, p. 84.

303 For *awsāṭ*, see al-Sijistānī *Nakhl*, p. 87.

304 For *ubāb*, see Ibn Manẓūr, *Lisān* I: 40a, s.v.

Ibn al-Faqīh, *Mukhtaṣar*, pp. 121–122 = Ibn al-Faqīh, *Buldān*, pp. 169–170; al-Jarīrī, *Jalīs* II: 43–45;[305] Ibn ʿAsākir, *Taʾrīkh* XVI: 102–104;[306] Ibn al-ʿAdīm, *Bughya* VII: 53–56;[307] Ibn Manẓūr, *Mukhtaṣar* VII: 357–359.[308] *Excerpts only*: al-Jāḥiẓ, *Bayān* II: 93–94;[309] al-Jāḥiẓ, *Ḥayawān* VII: 232; Ibn Qutayba, *ʿUyūn* I: 317; al-Rāghib, *Muḥāḍarāt* IV: 587, 592.[310]

B81a < *al-Minqarī* < *Muḥammad ibn abī l-Sarī* < *Hishām ibn Muḥammad ibn al-Sāʾib* < *Abū ʿAbdallāh al-Nakhaʿī*: When al-Ḥajjāj was through (the battle he won) at Dayr al-Jamājim, he went to ʿAbd al-Malik in an embassy, taking with him the nobles of the two cities and let them enter into the presence of the Caliph. One day they began speaking about various places in his presence. Muḥammad ibn ʿUmayr ibn ʿUṭārid said: "May God preserve the Commander of the Believers! Kufa is (located) higher than Basra with its heat and depth, yet lower than Syria with its plagues and cold. It lies next to the Euphrates, its water is sweet, and its fruit tasty."

Khālid ibn Ṣafwān replied: "May God preserve the Commander of the Believers! Our country (*barriyya*) is larger and our detachments quicker than theirs.[311] We have more sugar, ivory, and teak than they. Our water is a clear boon and from us come only generals, commanders, and leaders (*nāʿiq*)."[312]

305 < "my father" < Abū Aḥmad al-Khuttalī < Abū Ḥafṣ al-Nasāʾī < Muḥammad ibn ʿAmr < al-Haytham ibn ʿAdī.

306 < Abū l-ʿIzz Aḥmad ibn ʿUbaydallāh < Abū ʿAlī Muḥammad ibn al-Ḥusayn < *al-qāḍī* Abū l-Faraj al-Muʿāfā ibn Zakariyyā < "my father" < Abū Aḥmad al-Khuttalī < Abū Ḥafṣ al-Nasāʾī < Muḥammad ibn ʿAmr < al-Haytham ibn ʿAdī.

307 < Abū l-Ḥajjāj Yūsuf ibn Khalīl ibn ʿAbdallāh < Abū l-Qāsim Yaḥyā ibn Asʿad ibn Bawsh < Abū l-ʿIzz Aḥmad ibn ʿUbaydallāh ibn Kādish < Abū ʿAlī Muḥammad ibn al-Ḥusayn al-Jāzirī < *al-qāḍī* Abū l-Faraj al-Muʿāfā ibn Zakariyyā < "my father" < Abū Aḥmad al-Khuttalī < Abū Ḥafṣ al-Nasāʾī < Muḥammad ibn ʿAmr < al-Haytham ibn ʿAdī.

308 In Ibn ʿAsākir's and Ibn Manẓūr's version the interlocutors of Khālid are Maslama and Hishām ibn ʿAbd al-Malik.

309 Introduced by "Khālid ibn Ṣafwān was asked about Kufa and Basra." Khālid only speaks one line, after which al-Aḥnaf and Abū Bakr al-Hudhalī have their lines, the latter speaking here, as in *Bayān* I: 357, the line *naḥnu aktharu minkum sājan wa-ʿājan wa-dībājan wa-kharājan wa-nahran ʿajjājan*. In al-Jāḥiẓ, *Ḥayawān* VII: 232, the saying is given as *naḥnu aktharu minkum ʿājan wa-sājan wa-dībājan wa-kharājan* and primarily attributed to al-Aḥnaf ibn Qays, boasting against Kufans, but al-Jāḥiẓ adds that the saying is also attributed to Khālid and to Abū Bakr al-Hudhalī.

310 Abbreviated and modified (*naḥnu manābitunā qaṣab wa-anhārunā ʿajab wa-thimārunā ruṭab wa-arḍunā dhahab*). The interlocutors are al-Aḥnaf and Abū Bakr al-Hudhalī, the latter saying the line on teak, etc.

311 In al-Jāḥiẓ, *Bayān* II: 93, this is said by al-Aḥnaf.

312 For *nāʿiq*, see Ibn Manẓūr, *Lisān* XIV: 205b, s.v. The verb *naʿaqa* refers to the voice of the shepherd urging his flock.

Al-Ḥajjāj said: "May God preserve the Commander of the Believers! I know the two countries, having tread on both." ʿAbd al-Malik said to him: "Speak, we believe in you(r verdict)!" Al-Ḥajjāj said: "Basra is a stinking, foul-smelling grey old woman, who has jewels and ornaments, whereas Kufa is a beautiful pretty young girl, who has neither jewels nor ornaments." ʿAbd al-Malik said: "Kufa has taken the first rank over Basra!"

(al-Masʿūdī, *Murūj* §2102)

B81b Describing date palms Khālid ibn Ṣafwān said: They are firmly set in mud and feed (people) during famine. They push out their big inferior dates ripe to fall[313] and their medium-class dates, just as they are full of dry, sticky dates.[314] Then they are split open showing rods of silver, on which white pearls are set. These become then rows of red gold with green emeralds. Then they become bags of honey hung in mid-air, neither in skins nor waterskins, far from dust. Flies approach them not, driven away by spears. Finally, they become pieces of silver in the purses of men, giving protection to families.

(al-Tawḥīdī, *Baṣāʾir* III: 37, no. 82).

COMMENTARY: Ibn al-Faqīh gives the context of Khālid's speech, as well as its beginning:[315]

> ʿAlī ibn Muḥammad al-Madāʾinī has said: Khālid ibn Ṣafwān went in an embassy to ʿAbd al-Malik ibn Marwān. At the time there were delegations from all the cities. Maslama had erected some establishments (*maṣāniʿ*)[316] and he asked permission from ʿAbd al-Malik to take them with him to these. ʿAbd al-Malik gave his permission. When they saw the establishments, Maslama turned to the embassy of Mecca and asked: "O Meccans, do you have anything suchlike?" They replied: "Nay, but we have the House of God towards which people pray." Then Maslama asked the embassy of Medina: "Do you have anything suchlike?" They answered: "Nay, but we have the grave of the Prophet of God, who was sent (to humankind)." Then he turned to the embassy of Kufa and asked: "Do you have anything suchlike?" They answered: "Nay, but we have the recitation of the Noble Qurʾān." Then Maslama

313 The text reads *asfāṭ*, which does not make good sense and seems to be a mistake for *asqāṭ*, as in B81.

314 I read, with some hesitation, *ribāṭan* for *riyāṭan*, cf. al-Sijistānī *Nakhl*, p. 82.

315 Ibn al-Faqīh, *Mukhtaṣar*, p. 192 (= Ibn al-Faqīh, *Buldān*, p. 235). Cf. Ibn ʿAsākir, *Taʾrīkh* XVI: 102–104.

316 The passage seems to allude to Q 26:129, *wa-tattakhidhūna maṣāniʿa laʿallakum takhludūn*.

turned to the embassy of Basra and asked: "Do you have anything suchlike?" Khālid ibn Ṣafwān started speaking: "May God preserve the Emir, these have admitted a decision against their countries. But if there was present someone who knew their countries, he would have been able to answer in their stead." Maslama asked: "Do you have more to say than they about your country?" Khālid replied: "Yes, I do, if I may describe our country to you." Maslama said: "Go ahead!"

The rest of the story is told in Ibn al-Faqīh, *Mukhtaṣar*, pp. 121–122, with many major variants.[317] The version there relates that Hishām (sic) ibn ʿAbd al-Malik asked Khālid about Basra. Yāqūt and Ibn ʿAsākir tell the same story as Ibn al-Faqīh.[318] Yāqūt adds one verse before the two quoted by al-Balādhurī and attributes the poem to Maʿn ibn Aws.[319] Al-Jarīrī also sets this at the time of Hishām ibn ʿAbd al-Malik.[320]

Note how the subject matter changes from version to version as well as the informing drive of the passage: it may be told as a pure descriptive tour-de-force, or as a debate between Basra and Kufa or, finally, as a debate between dates and raisins. Cf. also A59 and al-Ābī, *Nathr* VI/1: 44, 48.

Interestingly, al-Balādhurī quotes the last verse in a story narrated by "a member of Banū l-Ahtam" and dated to the Caliphate of ʿAbd al-Malik.[321]

B82 They say: The Commander of the Believers Abū l-ʿAbbās summoned Ibrāhīm ibn Makhrama al-Kindī, some people from Banū l-Ḥārith ibn Kaʿb, who were maternal uncles to Abū l-ʿAbbās, and Khālid ibn Ṣafwān. They started boasting.

Ibn Makhrama said: "The people of Yemen are the kings of the Arabs. In the age of the Jāhiliyya, the Bedouinship and the kingship belonged to them and they passed these on as an inheritance, one mighty man inheriting from another, the latter from the former, and the (now) bygone from his ancestors. To them belonged the Nuʿmāns, the Mundhirs, and the Qābūses,[322] to them belonged ʿIyāḍ, the lord of the sea,[323] as well as the one whose flesh was protected

317 = Ibn al-Faqīh, *Buldān*, pp. 169–170.

318 Ibn al-Faqīh, *Mukhtaṣar*, pp. 192, 121–122 = Yāqūt, *Muʿjam* I: 438–439 (< al-Madāʾinī); Ibn ʿAsākir, *Taʾrīkh* XVI: 102–104.

319 Cf. Maʿn, *Dīwān*, p. 115 (addition taken from Yāqūt).

320 Al-Jarīrī, *Jalīs* II: 43.

321 Al-Balādhurī, *Futūḥ*, p. 366.

322 Kings of al-Ḥīra, see Toral-Niehoff (2014a): 223–224.

323 Ibn al-Faqīh, *Mukhtaṣar*, p. 39 (= Ibn al-Faqīh, *Buldān*, p. 96), reads *ghāṣib al-baḥr*, which would be a reference to Q 18: 79. Ibn Ḥamdūn, *Tadhkira* III: 412, reads *ʿIyāḍ ṣāḥib al-siḥr*.

by bees.[324] To them belonged the one whose body the angels washed,[325] and the one on whose death the Throne shook.[326] To them belonged the one spoken to by the wolf[327] and the one who used to take every ship by force.[328] There is nothing important that is not attributed to them, neither a fine horse nor a cutting sword, neither strong armour nor a valuable garment. When they were asked, they gave, and when a guest alighted by them, they received him hospitably. No one can vie with them nor boast to them. They are the real Arabs whilst others just want to pass as Arabs!"

Abū l-ʿAbbās said: "I do not think the Tamīmī will agree on this." Khālid said: "The rash fellow has erred without knowledge and spoken amiss when he boasted to Muḍar, to whom belonged the Messenger of God (may God bless him and greet him) as well as the Caliphs and the members of his family. How can he boast to Muḍar of people who ride asses,[329] weave clothes, train monkeys,[330] and tan hides? A hoopoe led (Solomon) to them and a rat drowned them."

Then he turned to al-Kindī and said: "Are you boasting of fine horses, sharp swords, and strong armours? What glory is there greater than Muḥammad, the best of mankind and the most noble of the nobles? God has bestowed him graciously on both us and you. They[331] were his followers and they were known and respected because of him. To us belong the Chosen Prophet and

324 ʿĀṣim ibn Thābit al-Anṣārī, see, e.g., Ibn Hishām, *Sīra*, p. 639, translated in Guillaume (1955): 427.

325 Ḥanẓala ibn abī ʿĀmir al-Anṣārī, see, e.g., Ibn Hishām, *Sīra*, p. 568, translated in Guillaume (1955): 377–378.

326 Saʿd ibn Muʿādh al-Anṣārī, see, e.g., Ibn Hishām, Sīra, p. 698, translated in Guillaume (1955): 468.

327 In note 10, the editor, Ramzī Baʿlabakkī, identifies this as Uhbān ibn al-Akwaʿ al-Aslamī or Rāfiʿ ibn ʿUmayra (or ʿAmīra, cf. Blankinship 1993, Index) al-Ṭāʾī. For the former, see Ibn Qutayba, *Maʿārif*, p. 323. A further possibility is Uhbān ibn Aws, also called by this nickname, see Ibn Qutayba, *Maʿārif*, p. 324, and al-Thaʿālibī, *Thimār*, pp. 386–387 (no. 606). Baʿlabakkī vocalises *mukallim*, the one who spoke to wolves.

328 Cf. Q 18: 79. This probably refers to al-Julandā (d. 134/752), see *EI2*, s.v. al-Djulandā (W. ʿArafat). Cf. also al-Ṭabarī, *Taʾrīkh* III: 78–79/XXVII: 201–202.

329 The passage is not as innocent as it might first seem, as there is an obscene connotation in the word *ʿard* "ass," which also means "erect penis." For examples of this word in the latter sense, see, e.g., ps.-al-Jāḥiẓ, *Maḥāsin*, p. 352, and al-Qālī, *Amālī* II: 106 (a verse by one of the daughters of Humām ibn Murra).

330 For the association of Yemen with monkeys, see, e.g., al-Damīrī, *Ḥayāt* II: 201 ("The Yemenis teach their monkeys to serve them so that a butcher or a greengrocer may teach his monkey to take care of the shop until its master has returned from his errands"); al-Thaʿālibī, *Kināyāt*, p. 32 ("If a man is ugly and repulsive, one may allude to this by saying that he has relatives in Yemen – for there are many monkeys there").

331 I.e., the Northern Arabs.

the Accepted Caliph, the lordship and the nobility. To us belong the founded Temple, the raised roof, and the *minbar* whence he preached. To us belong the Zamzam, its (Mecca's) lowlands,[332] and the office of giving water (to pilgrims). Can anyone be equal to us? Do anyone's words reach our glory? To us belongs Ibn ʿAbbās, the learned among people, whose stories are sweet and whose sayings are followed. To us belongs the Lion of God[333] and the Sword of God,[334] to us belongs the Veracious One[335] and the Distinguisher[336] and ʿAlī ibn abī Ṭālib (may God, He is exalted, be pleased with him). He never disbelieved in God or swerved from truth to vanity. To us belongs the man of Two Lights, the martyred ʿUthmān."

Then the son of al-Ahtam continued: "How about your knowledge of your people's language? What do they call fingers among you?" Al-Kindī replied: "*Shanātir.*" Khālid asked: "What about the ear?" He replied: "*Ṣinnāra.*" Khālid asked: "And the beard?" He replied: "*Zubb.*"[337] Khālid said: "God, He is praised and exalted, has spoken 'in a clear Arabic tongue.' Yet have you heard Him say: 'Put your *shanātir* into your *ṣinnārāt*?' (cf. Q 2: 19) Or: 'Do not take me by the *zubb*?' (cf. Q 20: 94)"[338]

Abū l-ʿAbbās (may God be pleased with him) said: "What have you, Yemeni, to do with the men of Muḍar?" Then he ordered Khālid to be rewarded, giving him money and property in Basra.

al-Zubayr ibn Bakkār, *Muwaffaqiyyāt*, pp. 112–117 (no. 57);[339] Ibn al-Faqīh, *Mukhtaṣar*, pp. 39–41 = Ibn al-Faqīh, *Buldān*, pp. 96–98;[340] Ibn Ḥamdūn, *Tadhkira* III: 411–413 (no. 1102); al-Jarīrī, *Jalīs* III: 42–44;[341] Ibn ʿAsākir, *Taʾrīkh* XVI: 105–107;[342] Ibn

---

332 For the *baṭḥāʾ* of Mecca, see Yāqūt, *Muʿjam* I: 446.

333 Ḥamza ibn ʿAbd al-Muṭṭalib.

334 Khālid ibn al-Walīd.

335 Abū Bakr al-Ṣiddīq.

336 ʿUmar al-Fārūq.

337 Ibn Fāris, *Ṣāḥibī*, p. 55, tells a similar story, but evades any obscenity by merely saying that "they have another word for *al-liḥya*."

338 Cf. *Kitāb al-ʿAyn* VII: 353, and al-Iskāfī, *Mukhtaṣar*, p. 1056, where *al-zubb* is explained as *al-ḥayya* (read: *al-liḥya*) in the language of Yemen (Wild 1965: 54, vocalizes this as *zibb*).

339 < Muṣʿab ibn ʿAbdallāh < "his grandfather" ʿAbdallāh ibn Muṣʿab < "a companion of Abū l-ʿAbbās."

340 < al-Madāʾinī.

341 < Aḥmad ibn al-ʿAbbās al-ʿAskarī < ʿAbdallāh ibn abī Saʿd < Abū Jaʿfar Muḥammad ibn Ibrāhīm ibn Yaʿqūb ibn Dāʾūd < al-Haytham ibn ʿAdī.

342 < Abū l-ʿIzz al-Sulamī < Abū ʿAlī Muḥammad ibn al-Ḥusayn < Abū l-Faraj al-Muʿāfā ibn Zakariyyā *al-qāḍī* < Aḥmad ibn al-ʿAbbās al-ʿAskarī < ʿAbdallāh ibn abī Saʿd < Abū Jaʿfar Muḥammad ibn Ibrāhīm ibn Yaʿqūb ibn Dāʾūd < al-Haytham ibn ʿAdī.

al-ʿAdīm, *Bughya* VII: 57–60;[343] Ibn Manẓūr, *Mukhtaṣar* VII: 359–362; al-Bayhaqī, *Maḥāsin*, pp. 98–100; Yāqūt, *Muʿjam* V: 448 (abbreviated); al-Itlīdī, *Iʿlām*, pp. 114–117.[344]

COMMENTARY: The version of al-Zubayr ibn Bakkār differs essentially from both that of al-Balādhurī and that of Ibn al-Faqīh and his followers. Al-Zubayr's version is most probably a later elaboration. In it, there is a change of focus in the discussion on single words and their South Arabic equivalents. In al-Zubayr's version, Khālid asks about South Arabic words (starting with *fa-akhbirnī ʿan al-shanātir*) and Ibrāhīm answers by giving their North Arabic equivalents.

Ibn al-Faqīh gives a somewhat more elaborate version. He (and his followers) end their versions by letting Khālid ask about four things from Ibrāhīm, who either has to admit Khālid's point or be guilty of unbelief: to which of them belong the Prophet, the Qurʾān, the House (of God), and the *minbar* (i.e., the office of Friday preaching, or in other words, the Caliphate). Ibrāhīm has to admit that all these belong to Northern Arabs, after hearing which Khālid concludes: "So begone, and let everything else freely belong to you!" The very famous sentence of Khālid about the Yemenis being trainers of monkeys, etc. is here reserved as the parting shot by Khālid after his final victory and its approval by al-Saffāḥ.

Al-Zubayr's version also ends with four questions, but these are somewhat different (to whom does the Prophet belong?; to whom does the Caliph belong?; to whom was the Qurʾān revealed?; and, finally, to whom does the House[345] of God belong?). Here the parting shot of Khālid is "what would equal these features?" (*fa-ayyu shayʾin taʿdilu hādhihi l-khiṣāl?*), after which the Caliph gives his final verdict and rewards (only) Khālid – in Ibn al-Faqīh's version both receive a reward, though Khālid a more generous one.

Khālid's last question has a deliberately obscene connotation (Arabic *zubb* "penis"). The version of Ibn al-Faqīh and those following him continues with the word for wolf (*kutaʿ*), which flattens the obscene climax. The obscenity is further underlined in al-Zubayr's version, where, besides *zubb*,

343 < Abū l-Ḥajjāj Yūsuf ibn Khalīl < Abū l-Qāsim Yaḥyā ibn Asʿad ibn Bawsh < Abū l-ʿIzz ibn Kādish < Abū ʿAlī al-Jāzirī < Abū l-Faraj al-Muʿāfā ibn Zakariyyā al-Jarīrī < Aḥmad ibn al-ʿAbbās al-ʿAskarī < ʿAbdallāh ibn abī Saʿd < Abū Jaʿfar Muḥammad ibn Ibrāhīm ibn Yaʿqūb ibn Dāʾūd < al-Haytham ibn ʿAdī.

344 < al-Haytham ibn ʿAdī. Ibn Ḥamdūn, Ibn Manẓūr, and al-Itlīdī mainly follow the version given by Ibn al-Faqīh. The apparent length of al-Zubayr ibn Bakkār's and al-Itlīdī's versions is caused by the layout of the editions.

345 In the edition wrongly *kitāb*.

Khālid asks the last but one question about *faqḥa* (North Arabic "anus") and receives the answer that it means *al-rāḥa* in South Arabic. Khālid's reference to Q 20: 94, though, shows that one should here read *al-raʾs*. The final question concerns the *kutaʿ* (wolf), which again falls apart for semantic reasons, as all the other questions concern body parts.[346]

See also B86 and B101, as well as B52.

B83 < *al-Madāʾinī*: Khālid contested with ʿAmr ibn ʿUbayd al-Anṣārī, who was foulmouthed and reviled those who did not give him when he asked. He was called Ibn Umm Ḥakīm. Umm Ḥakīm was his mother and had remarried after having had him (*qāmat ʿanhu*). ʿAmr said: "You are like what God has said: 'When fear overtakes them, you see them looking to you, their eyes rolling as though they were on the point of death. But once they are out of danger they assail you with their sharp tongues'."[347]

Khālid replied: "Woe upon you, Ibn Umm Ḥakīm, you have taken recourse to two things, unbelief and baseness. You stretch out your hands, the left open (for gifts), the right full of excrement and then you say: 'Fill my open hand or I shall smear you with my excrement!' Woe upon you, Ibn Umm Ḥakīm! God, He is praised and exalted, has also said: 'Those who defame chaste but careless believing women shall be cursed in this world and the next!'[348] Umm Ḥakīm, God bless her soul, was a chaste believer, yet I am not so sure about her carelessness when she touched the tip of the penis of Kuthayyir the oil seller!"[349]

B83a Khālid did not use to compose verses. It is told that he had promised al-Farazdaq something but had postponed fulfilling the promise – Khālid was one of the (famous) misers. Once al-Farazdaq went by him and threatened him. Khālid refrained from (answering) until al-Farazdaq had passed. Then Khālid turned to his friends and said: "This man has opened one of his hands and filled the other with excrement and then he says: 'Grease my open hand or I shall disgrace you with my excrement!'"

(al-Mubarrad, *Kāmil* II: 44); al-Zamakhsharī, *Rabīʿ* II: 156–157 (abbreviated).

B83b < *Abū l-ʿAbbās* < *ʿUmar ibn Shabba* < *al-Zaʿil ibn al-Khaṭṭāb*: Abū Nukhayla built a house. Khālid ibn Ṣafwān happened to pass by and stopped

346 For the Yemeni words, see Piamenta (1990–1991) I: 195, 288; Al Selwi (1987): 57, 125–126.

347 Q 33: 19.

348 Q 24: 23.

349 The editor, Ramzī Baʿlabakkī, suggests in note 8 that the passage is corrupt, which it may well be. In any case, the allusion evades us.

by him. Abū Nukhayla asked him: "O Ibn Ṣafwān, what do you think?" Khālid replied: "I think you are asking importunately[350] and spending extravagantly. You have opened one of your hands and filled the other with excrement and then you say: 'Either put something in my open hand or I shall throw upon you my excrement!'" With this Khālid continued his way. People asked Abū Nukhayla: "Are you not going to satirise him?" He replied: "Then he would sit a whole year in gatherings, describing my nose, and he would do so without repeating a single expression!"

(Thaʿlab, *Majālis*, p. 416); Ibn ʿAsākir, *Taʾrīkh* VII: 304;[351] Ibn al-ʿAdīm, *Bughya* VII: 70;[352] Ibn Ḥamdūn, *Tadhkira* VIII: 189 (no. 595); Yāqūt, *Irshād* III: 275–276;[353] al-Iṣfahānī, *Aghānī* XVIII: 141.[354]

B83c < *Abū Isḥāq al-Nawfalī*: Abū Nukhayla had built a house he was selling. He came to Khālid ibn Ṣafwān and said to him: "I would like you to come with me to see how my house has been built." Khālid went with him. When they entered and Khālid had seen the house, Abū Nukhayla asked him: "Now how do you find it, Abū Ṣafwān?" Khālid replied: "If I tell you the truth, Abū Nukhayla, you will be angered." Abū Nukhayla said: "I am not one to do so!" Then Khālid, who was one of the most eloquent men, said: "I think you are asking importunately and spending extravagantly. You have filled one of your hands with excrement and opened the other and then you say: 'If you do not grease my open hand I shall cover you with my excrement!'" Abū Nukhayla was ashamed and did not reply a word.

(Ibn al-Muʿtazz, *Ṭabaqāt*, p. 86)

---

350 For *saʾalta ilḥāfan*, cf. Q 2: 273 (*lā yasʾalūna l-nāsa ilḥāfan*). Also the rhyming *isrāfan* has Qurʾānic connotations (e.g., Q 4: 6).

351 < 1. Abū ʿAlī Muḥammad ibn Saʿīd ibn Ibrāhīm ibn Nabhān and Abū l-Faḍl ibn Nāṣir < Aḥmad ibn al-Ḥasan ibn Aḥmad and Abū l-Ḥasan Muḥammad ibn Isḥāq ibn Ibrāhīm ibn Makhlad al-Bazzāz and Abū ʿAlī ibn Nabhān; and 2. < Abū l-Qāsim ibn al-Samarqandī < Aḥmad ibn al-Ḥasan (from here on the *isnād* to both is the same) < Abū ʿAlī ibn Shādhān < Abū Bakr Muḥammad ibn al-Ḥasan ibn Muqsim < Abū l-ʿAbbās Thaʿlab < ʿUmar ibn Shabba < al-Zaʿil (in the text al-Daghl) < ibn al-Khaṭṭāb.

352 "I read in the handwriting of Ibrāhīm ibn Muḥammad al-Ṭabarī in the *Amālī* of Abū ʿAmr Muḥammad ibn ʿAbd al-Wāḥid, the companion of Thaʿlab by dictation in 328" < Thaʿlab < ʿUmar ibn Shabba < al-Zaʿil, or al-Ziʿl, ibn al-Khaṭṭāb.

353 < ʿUmar ibn Shabba.

354 < Ḥabīb ibn Naṣr al-Muhallabī < ʿUmar ibn Shabba < al-Zaʿil (in the text al-Raʿl) ibn al-Khaṭṭāb.

COMMENTARY: Yāqūt reads the end of B83b as follows: "By God, then he would ride his mule and go around the gatherings of Basra describing my daughter (*ibnatī*) in a way that would dishonour her." It seems that this is a mistake for **arnabatī* "the tip of my nose," which is Ibn Ḥamdūn's version (for Thaʿlab's *anfī*). Ibn Ḥamdūn's version ends: "By God, then he would ride his mule and go around the gatherings of Basra describing the tip of my nose in a way that would dishonour it – yet what might it hurt one that the tip of his nose be described? – for a whole year without repeating a word."[355]

The story seems to have grown around a saying by Khālid and the context, as well as the interlocutors, have been freely invented, as long as the story has remained within the framework of early 8th-century Basra. A somewhat similar story is told on the authority of al-Aṣmaʿī by Yāqūt about Shabīb ibn Shayba and Abū Nukhayla, who are said to have been friends. In this story, Shabīb promises to give a garment to Abū Nukhayla. When the gift is late in coming, Abū Nukhayla satirises Shabīb in three *rajaz* verses:

> O people, do not make Shabīb your lord,
> that traitor, son of traitor, the liar!
> Yet would a she-wolf give birth but to a wolf?

Shabīb quickly sends him the garment and is rewarded with four verses of *rajaz*.[356] Shabīb is also elsewhere shown to have been in contact with Abū Nukhayla.[357] A similar story about al-Farazdaq and al-Ḥasan al-Baṣrī is told by al-Rāghib.[358]

The identity of ʿAmr ibn ʿUbayd al-Anṣārī, mentioned in this story, is not clear. Elsewhere (A101, A106)[359] it is the famous Muʿtazilite theologian ʿAmr ibn ʿUbayd that is meant, but here the question is more tangled. As is well known,[360] the theologian's genealogy is obscure and although the more common version claims that he was descended from a Persian grandfather Bāb, taken as prisoner close to Kabul, there are also variant versions. However, it seems that in none of these is the theologian ʿAmr called either al-Anṣārī or Ibn Umm Ḥakīm, which makes his identification with the ʿAmr in this story precarious. There is also a marked discrepancy between the images of the foulmouthed blackmailer ʿAmr ibn ʿUbayd al-Anṣārī in B83 and

355 Yāqūt, *Irshād* III: 275–276.
356 Yāqūt, *Irshād* III: 407.
357 See Chapter 1.3.2.
358 Al-Rāghib, *Muḥāḍarāt* II: 80.
359 See Chapter 1.3.2.
360 Cf. van Ess (1991–97) II: 280–285.

of the humble and ascetic ʿAmr ibn ʿUbayd in A101 and A106. Such discrepancies are by no means lacking in anecdotal literature, but combined with the problems in the names of ʿAmr ibn ʿUbayd al-Anṣārī Ibn Umm al-Ḥakīm it seems improbable that this story refers to the theologian.

It is quite possible that the ʿAmr ibn ʿUbayd of this story is an otherwise little known Basran. The genealogical literature knows a number of Umm Ḥakīms,[361] but none of them can be identified as the mother of this ʿAmr ibn ʿUbayd. The virtual anonymity of ʿAmr ibn ʿUbayd al-Anṣārī might explain why Khālid's interlocutor in B83 is changed into a better-known person in the variants.

B84 Khālid mentioned joking and said: You strike your friend with something harder than stone and make him inhale something more pungent than mustard and empty upon him something more scathing than a (boiling) kettle and then you say: "I was just joking!"

al-Zamakhsharī, *Rabīʿ* IV: 169; al-Tawḥīdī, *Baṣāʾir* V: 31 (no. 82); al-Ābī, *Nathr* IV: 181 (variants); Ibn ʿAbd al-Barr, *Bahja* II: 570; al-Rāghib, *Muḥāḍarāt* I: 283; al-Ḥuṣrī, *Zahr*, p. 522; al-Ḥuṣrī, *Jamʿ*, p. 50; al-Māwardī, *Adab*, p. 299.

COMMENTARY: Cf. B32.

B85 They say: A man belonging to Banū Tamīm came to Khālid and asked him for some money. Khālid gave him one *dānaq*, and the man said: "Good God, do you give a man like me just one *dānaq*!" Khālid replied: "If every man of Banū Tamīm gave you as much as I did, by the end of the day you would be immensely rich."

al-Murtaḍā, *Amālī* II: 262.

B86 They say: Khālid came to Abū l-ʿAbbās, may God, He is exalted, have mercy on him. Abū l-ʿAbbās said to him: "O Khālid, how well do you know my maternal relatives?" Khālid asked: "Which of them, O Commander of the Believers? I know them all." Abū l-ʿAbbās said: "Those who are the closest to me and have the strongest claim on me, the offspring of al-Ḥārith ibn Kaʿb." Khālid said: "O Commander of the Believers, they are the height of nobility and the trunk of generosity! They have features which have never been combined in any other of their people. Among their people they have the best condition

361 See especially Juwayriya bint Qāriẓ, on whom see, e.g., al-Masʿūdī, *Murūj*, Index, VI: 252–253. She is known to have married several times and one of his husbands was ʿUbaydallāh ibn al-ʿAbbās ibn ʿAbd al-Muṭṭalib.

and the noblest disposition. They keep their covenant best and they have the furthest aspirations. In war they are a firebrand and under duress a support. They are the heads while others are but tails." Abū l-ʿAbbās said: "How excellent you are, O son of Ṣafwān. You have well described them!"

al-Balādhurī, *Ansāb* III: 167; al-Washshāʾ, *Fāḍil*, pp. 80–81 (variants); al-Ḥuṣrī, *Zahr*, pp. 872, 1079; al-Ābī, *Nathr* VI: 37–38; al-Sharīshī, *Sharḥ* IV: 135.[362]

COMMENTARY: Cf. B82 and B101.

B87 Khālid said: Do not make fun with a noble man, lest he resent you. Do not make fun with an ignoble man, lest he become bold towards you. – Abū l-Ḥasan (al-Madāʾinī) has said: It is also said that this was said by Saʿīd ibn al-ʿĀṣ. – He (Khālid) recited:

Leave both jest and quarrel,
features I like not in a friend.

It is said that it was Misʿar ibn Kidām,[363] who used this verse as a proverb.

B88 Khālid mentioned Abū Muslim[364] and said: Can't you see how this man began with harshness and continued with stupidity after oppressing people.

B89 He (Khālid) said about man: Damn him, by God, his rhymes are like necklaces and his nicknames are like straps (that stick). He fills the ear with his eloquence and the eye with his beauty.

al-Tawḥīdī, *Baṣāʾir* VIII: 13 (preface).[365]

COMMENTARY: For the last sentence, cf. B33.

B90 Khālid used to say: The best speech is that which is in neither (excessively) strange Bedouin language nor defective village language, but such that its elements are noble and its meanings intricate, sweet in the speakers' mouth, and pleasing to the hearers. When years pass it only grows in beauty.

362 Al-Ḥuṣrī, *Zahr*, p. 872, al-Ābī, and al-Sharīshī link this story with B101. Al-Ḥuṣrī, *Zahr*, p. 1079, gives an abbreviated version of B86 only.

363 On whom, see al-Ṭabarī, *Taʾrīkh* III: 2513/XXXIX: 253–254.

364 D. 137/755, see *EI3*, s.v. (S.S. Agha).

365 From a book by Aḥmad ibn al-Ṭayyib.

Transmitters (*ruwāt*) pick it up and travellers acquire it, and it is like the treasures of famous verse and stories you cannot forget.

Ibn ʿAsākir, *Taʾrīkh* XVI: 104–105;[366] al-Dhahabī, *Siyar* VI: 226; Ibn al-Mudabbir, *al-Risāla al-ʿadhrāʾ*, pp. 35–36 (= *Rasāʾil al-bulaghāʾ*, p. 244); al-Dhahabī, *Siyar* VI: 226. *Short versions:*[367] Ibn Manẓūr, *Lisān* VIII: 145b (s.v. ṬRF); Ibn ʿAbd al-Barr, *Bahja* I: 72; Ibn Munqidh, *Lubāb*, p. 349.

B91 Khālid heard a Qurashī speaking well and eloquently. He became jealous, stood up against him, and started attacking him. The Qurashī said: "Abū Ṣafwān, I am not aware of having committed any sin against you, except for sharing the same profession."

B91a It is told that Khālid ibn Ṣafwān spoke in some matter and a Medinese man answered him in words the like of which Khālid had not thought him to possess. When the session was prolonged, Khālid insinuated something, and the Medinese said: "Abū Ṣafwān, my only fault seems to be that we have the same profession." This was narrated by al-Aṣmaʿī.

(al-Jāḥiẓ, *Bayān* I: 173).

COMMENTARY: Cf. B66c.

B92 Khālid gave a speech in the desert, saying: "O people of the desert, how rough your country is, how rude your life, and how coarse your manners. You do not attend Friday prayers nor do you follow a (religious) storyteller (*qāṣṣ*)." A Bedouin stood up and said: "The roughness of our country and the coarseness of our manners is as you said. But you, O people of the settled country, break into houses, rob graves, and have sex with males." Khālid said: "Be quiet, may God make ugly what you brought up!"

B93 They say: People said to Khālid about his son: "You are worth (*yaduka tashtamilu*) thirty thousand (dirhams), yet you give your son a mere dirham a day. He is at his wit's end, as you know." Khālid replied: "Two *dānaqs* for his bread, two for a chicken, and two for fruit. That makes a good dinner."

COMMENTARY: Cf. B22.

---

366 < Abū Bakr al-Salmāsī < Abū ʿAbdallāh Muḥammad ibn Fattūḥ < Abū l-Qāsim Manṣūr ibn al-Nuʿmān in Egypt < *al-sharīf* Abū ʿAbdallāh Muḥammad ibn ʿUbaydallāh < Abū l-ʿAbbās ʿAbdallāh ibn ʿUbaydallāh al-Ṣafarī < Abū Bakr al-Ṣanawbarī < ʿAlī ibn Sulaymān al-Akhfash < Muḥammad ibn Yazīd al-Mubarrad < Ibn ʿĀʾisha < "his father."

367 Consisting only of the definition of the best speech as that the elements of which are noble and the meanings intricate and which pleases the ears of the hearers, with slight variants.

B94 He said: Khālid mentioned a man and said: By God, he was a great speaker (*farīgh al-manṭiq*),[368] with a swift tongue, easy flow, and ample words. The root of his tongue was firm and its sides fine. He had nimble lips, his mouth never dried, and his mind was wide. He made few gestures, but good allusions. He was of sweet character and beautiful grace. He was quiet or loquacious (as need be), he healed the mange, treated the sores, and hit the mark.[369] He was not babbling in his speech nor scanty in his manliness. He was not confounded in his nature. He did not follow but was followed, "like a roadmark with a fire on its top."[370]

Ibn ʿAbdrabbih, *ʿIqd* II: 136, 220–221; al-Ḥuṣrī, *Zahr*, p. 916; al-Tawḥīdī, *Baṣāʾir* VIII: 102–103 (no. 371); al-Waṭwāṭ, *Ghurar*, p. 189 (abbreviated).

B95 He (Khālid) mentioned someone and said: By God, he used to be a frequent host, not a frequent guest, always a giver, never a taker, a man to be followed, not to follow.

B95a Khālid mentioned someone and said: By God, he used to be a frequent host, not a frequent guest, always a giver, never a taker, the man to speak among understanding men, steadfast, fierce in a fight.

(al-Tawḥīdī, *Baṣāʾir* VIII: 103, no. 372)

B96 He (Khālid) mentioned a man and said: How sweet was his mind, how far his fame travelled! How great was his worth, how exalted his nobility and how many did praise him, both those who knew him and those who did not! His courtyard was wide, his cooking vessel large, and his forefathers noble!

B97 He (Khālid) mentioned a man and said: (Now that he is gone), where are the comely, luminous faces, sound, superior minds, eloquent, momentous tongues, noble, unadulterated lineages, wide and spacious minds, and lucrative, precious, noble traits!

B98 < *al-Haytham*: When Khālid came to Hishām, Khālid al-Qasrī happened to be mentioned. Hishām said: "Khālid was bold and annoyed me, he troubled and exhausted (*aʿjafa*) me without leaving a way to return or means to come back." Then he said: "Would you not like me to tell you about him, O son of Ṣafwān?" I replied: "Please do, O Commander of the Believers." He

---

368 Other versions read *qarīʿ* or *badīʿ*. For *farīgh* "wide," cf. Lane (1863–93), s.v.

369 Literally, "he hit the joints." As a metaphor for hitting the mark in a speech, see Ibn ʿAbdrabbih, *ʿIqd* II: 261.

370 The verse is by al-Khansāʾ, *Dīwān*, p. 386.

said: "Since he came to Iraq he never asked me anything before I took the matter up."

Khālid said: I said: "Then it is even more appropriate for you to turn back to him." Hishām replied by quoting a verse:

> When my soul turns away from something, it
> hardly ever advances again towards it.[371]

He said: Then Hishām asked: "What do you want, O son of Ṣafwān?" I replied: "That you would add ten dinars to my stipend." He kept silent for a while and then asked: "What for? For a religious deed you have done and we should help you in it? Or have you suffered something on behalf of the Commander of the Believers? Why, O son of Ṣafwān? (If I gave without a valid reason), people would all be asking me and the public treasury could not take it."

He said: I said: "O Commander of the Believers, may God give you success and may He show you the right way! You are, by God, just like the Khuzāʿite who said:

> When the bonds of kinship or those of friendship
> do not oblige you to give away property, you refuse it.
>
> Yet refusing is sometimes but discretion and strength.
> Only those worth it, get some of your property."[372]

When Khālid returned to Basra, people asked him what had made him present avarice to Hishām in favourable terms. He replied: "I wanted him to deny others, too, so that those who blame him would multiply."

Ibn ʿAbdrabbih, *ʿIqd* VI: 175–176 (abbreviated and with variants); al-Zamakhsharī, *Rabīʿ* II: 664–665; al-Tawḥīdī, *Baṣāʾir* III: 119–120 (no. 404); Ibn Ḥamdūn, *Tadhkira* II: 367 (no. 942); Ibn ʿAsākir, *Taʾrīkh* LXXIV: 25–26; al-Murtaḍā, *Amālī* II: 261–262;[373] al-Ābī, *Nathr* III: 63–64 (much abbreviated).

COMMENTARY: For the beginning, cf. B40. Most parallels give only part of the story, often contaminated with B40.

371 The verse is by Maʿn ibn Aws, cf. his *Dīwān*, p. 73.

372 The verses are by Kuthayyir ʿAzza cf. his *Dīwān*, p. 182.

373 < Abū l-Ḥasan ʿAlī ibn Muḥammad al-Kātib < Muḥammad ibn Yaḥyā al-Ṣūlī < Yaḥyā ibn ʿAlī ibn Yaḥyā al-Munajjim < Aḥmad ibn Jābir al-Balādhurī < al-Haytham ibn ʿAdī. Al-Murtaḍā combines B40 and B98. After the story, there is a brief note that "*sayyidunā*," i.e. al-Murtaḍā, held Khālid (ibn Ṣafwān) to have been famous for his eloquence.

B99 Khālid said to a cousin of his: "Your father had the ugliest[374] face of all and your mother had the worst of characters. You combine the bad characteristics of both your parents."

B99a < *Abū l-Qāsim ibn al-Samarqandī and Abū l-Faḍl ibn al-Ḥasan ibn Hibatallāh < Abū l-Khiṭāb ʿAbd al-Malik ibn Aḥmad ibn ʿAbdallāh < Abū ʿAbdallāh al-Ḥusayn ibn Muḥammad ibn Jaʿfar al-Khāliʿ < "my uncle" Abū ʿAmr ʿUthmān ibn Jaʿfar ibn Muḥammad ibn al-Ḥusayn al-Jawālīqī < Abū Muqātil Muḥammad ibn al-ʿAbbās ibn Aḥmad ibn Mujāshiʿ < al-Ḥārith ibn Abī Usāma < al-Ḥanẓalī*: Khālid ibn Ṣafwān said to a man: "Your father was ugly (*damīm*) but intelligent and your mother beautiful but lightheaded. You have combined your father's ugliness with your mother's stupidity, O you combiner of your parents' nobility!"[375]

(Ibn ʿAsākir, *Taʾrīkh* XVI: 115); Ibn Manẓūr, *Mukhtaṣar* VII: 364; al-Ḥuṣrī, *Zahr*, p. 1079.[376]

B99b In early 217/832, Ṣāliḥ ibn Shaykh ibn ʿAmīra ibn Ḥayyān ibn Surāqa al-Asadī fell seriously ill. Ibrāhīm ibn al-Mahdī has said:

I came to see him and found him somewhat better. We started talking and among other topics we spoke about his grandfather ʿAmīra,[377] one of whose full brothers had died. As he left no children, this was a great calamity to ʿAmīra, but then it was found out that one of the slavegirls of the deceased was pregnant. After his death, she gave birth to a girl, and ʿAmīra's grief was somewhat relieved. He took the child into his house and gave her preference over all his children, male and female.

When she came of age, ʿAmīra wanted to find her a husband, equal to her. When someone asked her hand from him, he took it upon himself first to investigate his lineage and then his character. One of those who were drawn to ask her hand was a cousin of Khālid ibn Ṣafwān ibn al-Ahtam al-Tamīmī.

ʿAmīra knew the young man's lineage, so he said to him: "Young man, I do not need to investigate your lineage. You are quite the equal to my brother's daughter in noble descent. But I will not let anyone conclude the marriage with her until I know his character. If you can stay a year in my house, I shall get

---

374 Reading *adamm* for the edition's erroneous *ādam*. Cf. *damīm* in Ibn Manẓūr's version.

375 Al-Ḥuṣrī reads *sharr* "evil" for *sharaf*. If Ibn ʿAsākir's reading is correct it is ironic.

376 In al-Ḥuṣrī, *Zahr*, p. 1079, the roles of the man and Khālid are reversed, and this has become a saying by the anonymous man about Khālid.

377 Briefly mentioned in al-Ṭabarī, *Taʾrīkh* III: 935/XXXI: 208. ʿĀmira was still active in 198/813, and it seems slightly dubious whether he could have been old enough to have had this correspondence with Khālid, who had died some sixty years earlier.

to know your character, like I have got to know that of others. So be welcome to stay in all convenience. Yet if that does not suit you, then go back to your family and we will give orders to prepare your equipment and to bring everything that you might need to take with you." The young man chose to stay.

Ṣāliḥ ibn Shaykh has said: My father has told me from his father that every night ʿAmīra got contradictory evidence of the young man's character. Some gave evidence about best possible manners, some about the worst possible. The contradictions in the reports forced him to disbelieve them all. Finally, he wrote to Khālid: "Your cousin has come to us to ask the hand of my[378] niece. If his character is up to his lineage, he would be a good match for her and it would be suitable for me to write the marriage contract. If you can advise me in this matter about your cousin and my niece according to your view, I wish you to do so, God willing. The one whose opinion is asked is a trusted man."

Khālid wrote back: "I have read and understood your letter. The father of my cousin had the finest character in the family, but he was very ugly. When he was mistreated he was the kindest to forgive. He was the most liberal of them but he was plagued by ugliness and repulsive appearance. My cousin's mother was the most beautiful of God's creatures but she had a bad character. She was miserly and had less sense than anyone I know. My cousin has received the bad characteristics of both his parents but none of their good characteristics.[379] If you wish to marry her to him after what I have told, do so. And if you do not wish, then I hope God will select a husband for your niece, if so He wishes."

Ṣāliḥ has said: When my grandfather had read the letter, he ordered a meal to be prepared for the young man. Then he gave him a *mahrī* camel to ride and gave someone orders to see him out of Kufa.

Ibrāhīm has said: I found the story so pleasing that I learned it by heart.[380]

(Ibn al-Qifṭī, *Ta'rīkh*, pp. 388–390);[381] Ibn abī Uṣaybiʿa, *ʿUyūn*, pp. 228–229.

378 Actually, throughout the rest of the story she is called Khālid's niece (here *ibnat akhīka*, in the Persian translation *dukhtar-e barādar-e tu*). Either this is a mistake or the deceased was Khālid's acquaintance, his "brother."

379 One remains wondering why, then, he should have had a contradictory character.

380 The text continues by telling how Ibrāhīm told the story to Hārūn ibn Sulaymān ibn Manṣūr and Yūḥannā ibn Māsawayh (in whose biography the story is found). Ibn Māsawayhi replied by referring to his own son who had inherited his parents' bad characteristics. If he were free to do so, Ibn Māsawayh said, he would dissect him, like Galenos had done to men and monkeys, to get to know his anatomy and to rid people of him.

381 Translated in the 11th-century AH Persian translation, Qifṭī, *Tārīkh al-ḥukamā'*, pp. 525–526, with negligible variants.

COMMENTARY: Ibn ʿAbdrabbih tells us, on the authority of al-Aṣmaʿī, how a tall but ugly Bedouin married a short but beautiful wife and the child became short and ugly despite the father's wish of the child inheriting his tallness and her beauty.[382] Ibn al-Anbārī relates a somewhat similar story about ʿUmāra ibn ʿUqayl.[383]

B100 Khālid – or, as some say, ʿAbdallāh ibn al-Ahtam – said to some clients (*mawālī*) of Āl Asīd, who disputed with him: "The most proper person to remain silent is the one who neither has a firm root nor a growing branch, who is a tail that follows, a shoe tread underfoot, and an additional excrescence. Women have never remarried after having given birth to another like the son of ʿĀʾisha, may God have mercy on him.[384] He inspected his kith and kin and whitewashed their scum, annexing (to it) their riffraff. These he sent to Iraq as tax collectors and roughians. When its (Iraq's) tax collectors were disloyal toward him and the roughians grew weak, he vexed Iraq with a man without property with him, a separate army, or a drawn sword.[385] This man came to it when the bellygirth had been tightened and hastened away from radiant branches and ravaging lions. He scattered its leaders and profaned its meadows. He broke its difficult terrains and made even its rough ground, not like the one[386] who betrayed properties and shied away from fighting, granting his hindpart to the tips of lances and then presented wine and betrayal and deception as beautiful and faithfulness and courage and loyalty as ugly. To the devil those swollen lips and bloodshot eyes, flat noses, blackened colours, and curly hairs! To the devil those characteristics which brought upon them shame and earned them foul vices. They refused to do any good."

COMMENTARY: Cf. B106. As the story discusses persons of the previous generation(s), it would better fit an older relative of Khālid.

B101 < *Abū l-Ḥasan al-Madāʾinī*: Khālid spent an evening at the court of the Commander of the Believers, Abū l-ʿAbbās. Some people of Banū l-Ḥārith boasted, but Khālid remained silent. The Commander of the Believers said to him: "O son of Ṣafwān, what is the matter? Why do you not say anything?"

382 Ibn ʿAbdrabbih, *ʿIqd* III: 472 = al-Tijānī, *Tuḥfa*, p. 241 < Qāsim ibn Thābit < al-Aṣmaʿī; translated in [al-Tijānī], *Glory*, p. 194.
383 Ibn al-Anbārī, *Nuzhat al-alibbāʾ*, p. 108. Cf. also ʿAwfī, *Jawāmiʿ* III/1: 22–24 (no. 10, about a man called Zakī and a Byzantine slavegirl).
384 Marginal note in a manuscript identifies this as ʿAbd al-Malik ibn Marwān.
385 Marginal note in a manuscript identifies this as al-Ḥajjāj.
386 Marginal note in a manuscript identifies this as Ibn Khālid ibn Asīd.

Khālid replied: "But these are the maternal relatives of the Commander of the Believers!" The Caliph said: "You are my paternal relative. Paternal relatives are not below maternal relatives." Khālid said: "But what should I say to people who weave clothes, train monkeys, and tan hides? A hoopoe led the way to them and a rat drowned them." Abū l-ʿAbbās laughed at this.

al-Balādhurī, *Ansāb* III: 166–167;[387] al-Jāḥiẓ, *Bighāl* II: 273; al-Jāḥiẓ, *Ḥayawān* VI: 152;[388] al-Jāḥiẓ, *Bayān* I: 339; Ibn Qutayba, *ʿUyūn* I: 317; al-Zamakhsharī, *Rabīʿ* II: 185; al-Thaʿālibī, *Thimār*, p. 412;[389] al-Tawḥīdī, *Baṣāʾir* VI: 169 (no. 508); al-Masʿūdī, *Murūj* §1257; al-Waṭwāṭ, *Ghurar*, p. 260; Yāqūt, *Muʿjam* V: 37; Ibn al-Kumaylī, *Nuzha*, p. 857; al-Maqqarī, *Mukhtār*, p. 204;[390] Abū Hilāl al-ʿAskarī, *Dīwān*, p.333.[391]

COMMENTARY: Al-Masʿūdī says that after his famous sentence about tanners and weavers Khālid went on to expostulate on the faults of the South Arabs, finishing with the story of how the Ethiopians conquered their country and how the Persians enslaved them. Though this end to al-Masʿūdī's version may well have been freely invented, it would fit with Khālid's reputation as a transmitter of historical stories, a claim which is often made but seldom substantiated.

In a series of insults al-Azdī quotes this saying of Khālid's: "O you lowlier than a weaver of clothes, tanner of hides, rider of donkeys, and monkey trainer!"[392]

Al-Jāḥiẓ's high opinion of Khālid can be seen in *Bayān* I: 339, where al-Jāḥiẓ adds his own comment, probably thinking about the longer boast of Khālid against Southern Arabs:

> If Khālid had thought and pondered upon this, he was a great transmitter with a good memory and an excellent author (*al-muʾallif al-mujīd*).

---

387 < al-Madāʾinī.

388 In a story about a rat gnawing a hole in the dam of al-ʿArim. Here the interlocutor is given as the Yemeni who boasted against him, and the Caliph in whose presence this takes place is al-Mahdī, whose rule only began in 158/775. The version, though, does not claim that the discussion took place during his Caliphate which, technically, saves it from being anachronistic.

389 As in al-Jāḥiẓ, *Ḥayawān* VI: 152.

390 Al-Maqqarī sets the scene in the court of Hishām ibn ʿAbd al-Malik. Note 3 refers to *Iklīl* where the Yemeni is identified as Ibrāhīm ibn Makhrama.

391 < al-Ṣūlī < al-Ṭayyib ibn Muḥammad al-Bāhilī < Mūsā ibn Saʿīd ibn Muslim < Aḥmad ibn Yūsuf al-Kātib. The protagonist is erroneously given as Khālid ibn Yūsuf al-Tamīmī, but the ed. al-Jīl I: 151, has the correct form.

392 Al-Azdī, *Ḥikāya*, p. 120. The edition reads *rākib qird wa-sāʾis ʿard*, but the emendation is obvious. Al-Azdī also refers to the same insults on p. 140, last two lines.

> If, on the other hand, this was something that just occurred to him when he was incited and given an opportunity, then he had no equal in the whole world!

Al-Ḥuṣrī presents a longer version of this story in which B101 is linked to B86[393] and then refers to al-Jāḥiẓ's opinion in slightly different words:

> Yamūt ibn al-Muzarriʿ has said: I heard my maternal uncle al-Jāḥiẓ mention this speech of Khālid and say: "By God, even if he had thought for a year of all their faults and how to put their defects concisely after this refined praise, that would have been a short time. Yet he extemporized this without exerting his thought!"

Cf. also B82 and B86.

B102 They say: Khālid came to Abū l-ʿAbbās together with Sulaymān ibn ʿAlī, who had with him his two sons, Muḥammad and Jaʿfar. Khālid sat down between them, and Sulaymān said: "Where did you sit down, Abū Ṣafwān?" He replied: "Between Muḥammad and Jaʿfar." Sulaymān asked: "What do you think of them?" Khālid replied:

> Abū Nāfiʿ is her neighbour and Ibn Burthun.
> What humble and lowly neighbours they are!

Sulaymān got angry with this. – The verse is by Ibn Mufarrigh.[394]

al-Mubarrad, *Kāmil* II: 43–44;[395] al-Zamakhsharī, *Rabīʿ* I: 479–481; Ibn Ḥamdūn, *Tadhkira* II: 159 (no. 352); Ibn Aydamur, *Durr* I: 218/*ḥāshiya*; al-Ṣābiʾ, *Hafawāt*, p. 319 (no. 319); al-Rāghib: *Muḥāḍarāt* I: 272; Ibn abī l-Ḥadīd, *Sharḥ* V: 9.

COMMENTARY: Al-Mubarrad dates this to the time when Sulaymān ibn ʿAlī was the governor of Basra in 133–139/751–756,[396] adding that he was the paternal uncle of the Caliph(-to-be) al-Manṣūr. Most authors give this as an example of Khālid's habit of saying what occurred to him without pausing to think about what he was saying.

393 Al-Ḥuṣrī, *Zahr*, pp. 872–873 = Abū Hilāl al-ʿAskarī, *Dīwān*, p. 333.
394 Ibn Mufarrigh al-Ḥimyarī (69/689), cf. *EI2*, s.v. (Ch. Pellat).
395 Al-Mubarrad reads Abū Mālik but adds that the correct version is Abū Nāfiʿ, whom he proceeds to identify as a client of ʿAbd al-Raḥmān ibn abī Bakr al-Ṣiddīq.
396 Al-Mubarrad, *Kāmil* II: 43–44. For Sulaymān ibn ʿAlī, see Pellat (1953): 280.

B103 < *al-Tawwazī* < *al-Aṣmaʿī*: Khālid came to his wives and said: "You are long-necked and of noble manners and stock, but I am a divorcing man, so go! You are divorced."

B104 Khālid said: There has never been a night dearer to me than the one after having divorced my wives. When I came home, curtains[397] were torn down and furniture removed. (One of my ex-wives) sent my little daughter[398] to me with a little basket with my dinner in it and another sent me something to sleep on.

Ibn Qutayba, *ʿUyūn* IV: 123; Ibn Qutayba, *Maʿārif*, p. 404; Ibn Qayyim al-Jawziyya, *Akhbār*, p. 79.

B105 Khālid said to his son: "O son, be outwardly as well off as possible, but inwardly of as little wealth (*mālan*) as possible. A noble man is one whose subsistance is noble even when he is in need, and an ignoble one is one whose food is paltry when he is poor."

al-Zamakhsharī, *Rabīʿ* IV: 387 (with slight differences).

B105a Khālid said to his son: "O son, be outwardly as well off as possible, but inwardly of as little returning (*maʾālan*, i.e., attachment to the world) as possible. Leave those deeds done in secrecy that would not suit you in public.

(Ibn ʿAbdrabbih, *ʿIqd* III: 153); Ibn Shams al-Khilāfa, *Ādāb*, p. 28.

COMMENTARY: Al-Thaʿālibī gives the first part as a saying by the Prophet Muḥammad,[399] and al-Qālī attributes this to ʿAbdallāh ibn Shaddād in a long testament of his to his son.[400]

B106 < *al-Madāʾinī*: Khālid used to say about al-Ḥajjāj: What a wonder! The lad was born in al-Ṭāʾif, but things went on raising and lowering him until he came to Iraq without property with him and without a separate army. He profaned its meadows and set it ablaze. He humbled them, so that men came to

---

397 Of the *ḥaram*. The furniture traditionally comes to the family as dower and remains the wife's property. Hence, in divorce it goes with the divorced wife.

398 The text of B104 actually reads "my little daughter sent me …," but in Ibn Qutayba's version in the *ʿUyūn*, it is one of the divorced wives who sends him his dinner through his daughter, which is what one might expect, and I have translated accordingly.

399 Al-Thaʿālibī, *Tarjama*, pp. 85–86.

400 Al-Qālī, *Amālī* II: 203. The testament covers pages II: 202–204; cf. Ibn Munqidh, *Lubāb*, pp. 22–28.

him in scattered troops.[401] Olive oil from Syria and fish sauce (*ṣīr*) from Egypt were brought posthaste to him.

COMMENTARY: Cf. B100.

B107 Khālid saw Mālik ibn Dīnār, Muḥammad ibn Wāsiʿ al-Azdī, and Farqad al-Sabakhī[402] at some Basran Emir's house. He joined them and asked: "What has brought you to join us at this door? We used to see you shunning away from here. By God, when one of you comes to us, it will lead him to misery, and when one of us enters among you, it will lead him to bliss."[403] Having said this he became afraid that they might think his words offensive so he returned to them and said: "God knows that I love you in my heart. It is only that we have enjoyed this world and it has enjoyed us.[404] I can compare our case to nothing better than a wing attached to a house. People may well say that it does not belong to the house because it is outside of it, or they may say that it does, because it is attached to it."

Ibn abī ʿAwn, *Ajwiba*, p. 79 (no. 469).[405]

B108 < *Abū l-Ḥasan*: Someone sued Khālid, and Bilāl ibn abī Burda judged for the man against Khālid, treating him unjustly. Khālid rose up, saying:

> A summer cloud that will soon disperse.

Bilāl said: "Yet it will not disperse ere it hits you with a downpour of hail!" It is said that he let him be whipped a hundred lashes and then sent him to prison. Khālid asked: "Why do you send me to prison, Bilāl? I have committed no crime." Bilāl answered: "A solid door, heavy chains, and a jailor called Ḥafṣ will tell you."

---

401 Reading *shilālan*.

402 Three Basran preachers/ascetics, who belonged to the same circle (se Pellat 1953: 99) and might well have queued up together to meet a Basran Emir. For Mālik (d ca. 130/748), see *EI2*, s.v. (Ch. Pellat). For Ibn Wāsiʿ, who was called one of the "weepers," although he himself reportedly did not accept the title, see *EI2*, s.v. *bakkāʾ* (F. Meier). For Farqad, who is best known as having been one of Maʿrūf al-Karkhī's teachers, see *EI2*, s.v. Maʿrūf al-Karkhī (R.A. Nicholson–[R.W.J. Austin]).

403 Cf. also Ibn Manẓūr, *Mukhtaṣar* X: 67, and Lecker (1996): 34.

404 Cf. Ibn Manẓūr, *Lisān* XIII: 84b, s.v. MRGh.

405 Much abbreviated. Here the interlocutors of Khālid are Thābit al-Banānī and Muḥammad ibn Wāsiʿ and the scene is set at the door of a Sultan.

Ibn Qutayba, *ʿUyūn* I:150;[406] Ibn Ḥamdūn, *Tadhkira* III:179 (no. 553);[407] al-Ābī, *Nathr* V:152 (abbreviated); al-Waṭwāṭ, *Ghurar*, p. 147; Ibn al-Kumaylī, *Nuzha*, pp. 870–871.

COMMENTARY: Cf. B7–B9.

B109 Khālid was asked: "How far did al-Ḥasan (al-Baṣrī)'s ascetism go?" He replied: "He never turned a dirham around (i.e., inspected one) and he was never seen in a market place except passing by. During the day he was a teacher and at night a worshipper and an ascetic."

COMMENTARY: Cf. B44.

B110 When others left him behind on a military expedition (*wa-huwa ghāzī*) Khālid used to say: "Is this how chiefs and noblemen do?" When he left others behind, he was asked: "Do you prohibit something but commit it yourself?" Khālid answered: "Why would we otherwise spend fortunes on swift horses?"

B110a < *Muḥammad*[408] < *Abū l-ʿAbbās*: One day Khālid ibn Ṣafwān rode with his companions when rain overtook them. Khālid, who rode a donkey, said: "Do you not know that the rider of the short-stepped animal is the prince of the people?" Thus, the others rode with him. The next day Khālid rode a nimble horse and again rain overtook them. Khālid let his horse run on and people said: "Abū Ṣafwān, how well you spoke yesterday!" Khālid replied: "But why would we then pay high prices for nimble horses!"

(Thaʿlab, *Majālis*, pp. 35–36); Ibn ʿAsākir, *Taʾrīkh* XVI: 110;[409] Ibn al-ʿAdīm, *Bughya* VII: 65.[410]

---

406 < Abū ʿUbayda.

407 In the previous story, no. 552, Ibn Ḥamdūn has labelled Bilāl as the first one who "exhibited tyranny in judging."

408 The transmitter of Thaʿlab's *Majālis*, Abū Bakr Muḥammad ibn al-Ḥasan ibn Yaʿqūb ibn Miqsam al-Muqriʾ, who transmitted the text in 344/955 (*Majālis*, pp. 3–4).

409 < Abū l-Qāsim ibn al-Samarqandī and Abū l-Faḍl Muḥammad ibn Nāṣir < Abū Ṭāhir Aḥmad ibn al-Ḥasan and Abū l-Ḥasan Muḥammad ibn Isḥāq ibn Ibrāhīm and Abū ʿAlī ibn Nabhān < Abū ʿAlī ibn Shādhān < Abū Bakr Muḥammad ibn al-Ḥasan ibn Miqsam al-Muqriʾ < Abū l-ʿAbbās Aḥmad ibn Yaḥyā.

410 < Abū Muḥammad ʿAbd al-Raḥmān ibn ʿAbdallāh ibn ʿUlwān < Abū ʿAbd al-Raḥmān Muḥammad ibn Muḥammad al-Kushmayhanī < Abū Bakr Muḥammad ibn Manṣūr al-Simnānī < Abū ʿAlī Muḥammad ibn Saʿīd ibn Ibrāhīm ibn Nabhān < Abū ʿAlī ibn

COMMENTARY: A similar story is told about Shabīb ibn Shayba by al-Khaṭīb al-Baghdādī. While he was travelling with the Caliph Abū Jaʿfar (al-Manṣūr), Shabīb referred to a *ḥadīth* according to which "he who rides a short-stepped animal is the prince among his fellow travellers." Hence he, Shabīb, would be the prince of the Caliph. The Caliph donated him a swift horse to avoid this.[411]

B111 Khālid proposed to a woman of Banū Saʿd[412] and said: "I am Khālid ibn Ṣafwān. My lineage is as you know and my wealth is as abundant as you have heard. There are some traits in me of which I shall tell you so that you will know beforehand. There is no way to my dirhams or dinars. I get easily bored: sometimes there comes a moment when I would throw away my own head if it were in my hand." She answered: "I have understood what you have said. These are traits which not even the daughters of the Devil would be happy with, let alone daughters of man! Good bye and good luck!"

Ibn Qutayba, *ʿUyūn* IV: 16; Ibn abī ʿAwn, *Ajwiba*, p. 50 (no. 286, abbreviated); al-Maghribī *Nuzha*, pp. 174–175; al-Dajājī, *Safaṭ*, p. 139.

COMMENTARY: For throwing away one's head, cf. A77.

B112 Khālid said: "Slavegirls are a bad substitute for free women. Their necks are dirtier and their reason less." It was said to him: "But you yourself marry only slavegirls!" He replied: "Have you not heard it said: 'Obey the priest in what he says, not in what he does'?"

B113 Khālid used to say: There are three things in which I am not sparing with my dirhams: dower for women, presents for relatives, and buying bananas.

B114 Someone was about to spend the wedding night with his wife. Khālid said to him: "May it be with blessing and vehement motion and a victory on the battle ground!"

al-Rāghib al-Iṣfahānī, *Muḥāḍarāt* IV: 634.

Shādhān < Abū Bakr Muḥammad ibn al-Ḥasan ibn Miqsam al-Muqriʾ < Abū l-ʿAbbās Aḥmad ibn Yaḥyā Thaʿlab.

411 Al-Khaṭīb al-Baghdādī, *Taʾrīkh* IX: 274 < ʿUbaydallāh ibn ʿUmar < "his father" < ʿAbdallāh ibn Sulaymān < ʿAlī ibn Khashram < ʿĪsā ibn Yūnus < Shabīb ibn Shayba. Cf. Ibn Khallikān, *Wafayāt* II: 459.

412 Maʿadd in al-Maghribī.

B115 Khālid said: I had a wife, but I am easily bored by nature. She used to make slight of me and say: "I have never heard of a noble lady who would endure as much as I endure from you!" One day I had been riding with Sulaymān ibn ʿAlī. I had new bridles, so my hands got dirty. I started washing them, saying: "Thank God, who created man from dirt!" She said to me: "But not from such dirt as is coming from you!" I divorced her, and she said: "Divorced, but willingly!"

CHAPTER 4

Stories from Other Sources

4.1 Storyteller and Transmitter of Poetry

A1 < *al-Ḥasan ibn ʿAlī al-Ḥirmāzī* < *al-ʿUtbī and others*: Abū l-ʿAbbās used to say: "When we want to know something about Hijaz or Tihāma we go to Saʿīd ibn ʿAmr ibn al-Ghasīl al-Anṣārī.[1] When we want to know something about Tamīm or Persia and the Persians (*ʿulūm Fārs wa'l-ʿajam*)[2] we go to Khālid ibn Ṣafwān. When we want to know something about this world and the next and about Jinnīs and men we go to Abū Bakr al-Hudhalī."[3] These were his nightly companions (*summār*) and his storytellers (*ḥuddāth*).

(al-Balādhurī, *Ansāb* III: 160).

A2 Khālid ibn Ṣafwān said: "When I hear a story I will not pass it forward before seasoning and flavouring it." He also said: "I hear a bare story and I clothe it, and I hear a featherless story and add feathers to it."

(al-Rāghib, *Muḥāḍarāt* I: 123)

A3 Shabath[4] ibn Ribʿī used to clear his throat in his house and it was heard as far away as in al-Kunāsa. When he called out his herdsman, his cry was heard a mile (*farsakh*) away. He was the muezzin of Sajāḥi, the false prophetess. This was told by Khālid ibn Ṣafwān.

(Ibn Qutayba, *ʿUyūn* I: 282–283).

A4 Khālid ibn Ṣafwān ibn ʿAbdallāh ibn ʿAmr ibn al-Ahtam Abū Ṣafwān al-Tamīmī al-Minqarī, one of the eloquent Arabs and their orators. He was a great transmitter (*rāwiya*) of historical stories (*akhbār*) and an eloquent and talented speaker. He used to accompany Hishām ibn ʿAbd al-Malik and Khālid al-Qasrī.

---

1 Briefly mentioned in al-Ṭabarī, *Ta'rīkh* II: 1260/XXIII: 208–209, as an eyewitness for something that took place in 94/712

2 Literally, "of the sciences of Persia and al-ʿAjam." *ʿAjam* usually refers to Persians but may also refer to other non-Arabs. *ʿUlūm* literally means "sciences; fields of scholarship," but in this case it rather obviously (primarily) refers to historical knowledge *about* Persians.

3 This probably refers to Sulmā ibn ʿAbdallāh Abū Bakr al-Hudhalī (d. 159/775), see *EI2*, s.v. al-Madā'inī (U. Sezgin). Cf. also above, Chapter 1.3.2, p. 20, note 75.

4 In the text Shabīb, but cf. al-Ṭabarī, *Ta'rīkh* I: 1919/X: 95 and Index.

 | DOI:10.1163/9789004433977_005

< *al-ʿUtbī*: When he was Emir, Hishām ibn ʿAbd al-Malik said to Shubba[5] ibn ʿIqāl, with al-Farazdaq, Jarīr, and al-Akhṭal present: "Tell me who is the most talented poet among these who have torn their reputations, shattered their decency, and incited their tribes in matters where no good is ensuing, nor godliness, nor profit." Shubba replied: "Jarīr ladles from sea, al-Farazdaq chisels from rock, and al-Akhṭal excels in *madḥ* and *fakhr*." Hishām said: "You have said nothing useful!" Shubba answered: "That is all I have!"

Then Hishām said to Khālid ibn Ṣafwān: "You describe them for me, Ibn al-Ahtam!" Khālid replied: "The greatest of them in *fakhr* is al-Farazdaq. His fame travels widest and he is the best when apologising, but he is the most tilted of them, the least in love poetry, but again the sweetest in giving a second draught, a torrent when he overflows, fiercely hot when he rages, lofty when he is parading. When he bellows he says the right thing and in a serious moment he assaults. He speaks correctly and holds long reins.

The best of them in description in al-Akhṭal. His verses are the best panegyric and he makest the fewest mistakes. When he lampoons he debases, and when he panegyrises he raises.

Yet the most abundant sea of them is Jarīr. His poetry is the most delicate and he tears his enemy to pieces. He is the blazed piebald. When he pursues, he reaches, but when he is pursued he is not caught. However, all of them are pure of heart, lofty of stature, and sparkling firebrands."

Maslama ibn ʿAbd al-Malik said to him:[6] "Never have we heard, Khālid, of anyone among the Ancients like you, nor seen among the Moderns. I testify that you are the best in description, yet the most docile, the chastest in your words, and the most noble in your deeds." Khālid replied: "May God fulfill his favours to you and may He provide you with the amplest of provisions! May He make exile a home through you and may He dispel all worries through you. By God, O Emir, I know you to be of noble origin, knowledgeable of men, generous at the time of famine, smiling when you give, mild even when angered. Standing at the top of Quraysh you are the sap of ʿAbd-Shams, and your present is even better than your past!"

Hishām smiled and said: "O Ibn Ṣafwān, I have never seen such an escape! You praised them all and described them in a way that satisfied them all!"

---

5 Read so, with Ibn Ḥamdūn, against the edition's Subba.

6 Al-Ḥuṣrī's addition (*wa-kāna ḥāḍiran*) shows that, indeed, both Hishām and Maslama are assumed to be present. In other anecdotes, Hishām and Maslama are occasionally confused with each other.

(Yāqūt, *Irshād* III: 274–275); Ibn Ḥamdūn, *Tadhkira* IV: 37–38 (no. 78); al-Ḥuṣrī, *Zahr*, pp. 688–689; al-Iṣfahānī, *Aghānī* VII: 73;[7] al-Bayhaqī, *Maḥāsin*, pp. 458–459.

COMMENTARY: See the discussion of this story in Chapter 1.3.2. Al-Bayhaqī lacks the background story with Shubba ibn ʿIqāl and the end of the story from Maslama's reaction onward. Instead, he has a variant ending:

> He (= Maslama) said: "Describe the ten poets for us." He (= Khālid) replied: "Their case is easily explained. Imru' al-Qays is the best in writing *nasīb*, making love, and exciting. Zuhayr's words are the bravest (*afḥal*), his relatives the most noble, and his deeds the most generous. Aws ibn Ḥajar's words are the weightiest, his position the most noble, and his battle days the most illustrious. Al-Nābigha has the purest language and the most solid basis, and he is the strongest in obedience. ʿAdī ibn Zayd is the best in describing a hunt, the most stubborn in cunning, and the most steadfast in chains. Ibn Muqbil is the best in describing arms and depicting divining arrows and fierce battles. Al-Ḥuṭay'a is the best of all in describing years of famine,[8] earning hundreds, and eulogising. Ṭarafa is the best in composing invectives against men, the vilest in his words, and the best in coining sayings. Salāma ibn Jandal is the chastest as to drinking, the best in inciting to war, and the most truthful according to people.

According to, e.g., al-Ābī, the Prophet asks ʿAmr ibn al-Ahtam about the poet al-Zibriqān, and ʿAmr gives a similar description of him.[9]

A5 < *Yūnus ibn Ḥabīb al-Naḥwī:* Someone said to Khālid ibn Ṣafwān: "ʿAbda ibn al-Ṭabīb[10] did not master invectives." Khālid replied: "Don't say so! By God, he did not refrain from them because of incapacity, but he felt himself to be above invective. He considered it base and leaving it virtuous and noble." Then Khālid recited:

---

7 < "my uncle" < al-Kurānī < al-ʿUmrī < al-ʿUtbī.

8 I prefer the variant *al-sinīn* in note 5, for the text's *al-sayyi'ayn*, which does not properly rhyme with the rest.

9 Al-Ābī, *Nathr* VI/1: 45. For al-Zibriqān, see *GAS* II: 200–201.

10 D. after 20/641, see *GAS* II: 198.

The most insolent, I have seen, blaming
others behind their back are the blameworthy.

(Yāqūt, *Irshād* III: 276); al-Iṣfahānī *Aghānī* XVIII: 165.[11]

A6 Someone said to Khālid ibn Ṣafwān: "Why do I always fall asleep when I hear you telling each other historical stories, studying traditions together, or reciting poetry to each other?" Khālid replied: "Because you are a donkey under your human skin."

(al-Jāḥiẓ, *Bayān* I: 170); Ibn Qutayba, *ʿUyūn* II: 136; al-Zamakhsharī, *Rabīʿ* I: 630; Ibn ʿAsākir, *Taʾrīkh* XVI: 116;[12] Ibn al-ʿAdīm, *Bughya* VII: 68;[13] Ibn al-ʿAdīm, *Bughya* VII: 68–69.[14]

COMMENTARY: A similar story is told about Yūnus ibn Ḥabīb by Ibn ʿĀṣim.[15] Cf. A7.

A7 How well Khālid ibn Ṣafwān put it when he was asked: "Do you never grow bored with stories (*al-ḥadīth*)?" He replied: "One only gets bored with old ones."

(al-Tawḥīdī, *Imtāʿ* II: 24).

COMMENTARY: The saying (cf. A6) plays with the meanings of *ḥadīth* "story; new one." It seems improbable that *ḥadīth* should here be taken in its technical sense of "tradition of the Prophet." The passage has been discussed by Dimitri Gutas.[16] The same word play is, naturally, also found elsewhere, e.g., in a verse by Ibn al-Rūmī ("a *ḥadīth* is always, as its name suggests, new").[17]

---

11 < Muḥammad ibn al-Ḥasan ibn Durayd < Abū ʿUthmān al-Ushnāndānī < al-Tawwazī < Abū ʿUbayda < Yūnus.

12 < Ismāʿīl ibn Isḥāq al-Sarrāj < al-Ziyādī < Muʾarrij.

13 < Abū Hāshim ʿAbd al-Muṭṭalib ibn al-Faḍl al-Hāshimī < Abū Saʿd ʿAbd al-Karīm ibn Muḥammad ibn Manṣūr al-Marwazī < Abū ʿAbdallāh Muḥammad ibn ʿAlī ibn Muḥammad al-Mālikī in Wāsiṭ < Abū Ghālib Muḥammad ibn Aḥmad ibn Bishrān al-Naḥwī < Abū l-Ḥusayn ʿAlī ibn Muḥammad ibn ʿAbd al-Raḥīm ibn Dīnār < Abū Muḥammad ʿAbdallāh ibn Jaʿfar ibn Durustawayhi in *Kitāb ʿUyūn al-akhbār* < Abū Muḥammad ʿAbdallāh ibn Muslim ibn Qutayba.

14 < Abū l-Ḥasan ibn abī Jaʿfar < ʿAbdallāh ibn ʿAbd al-Raḥmān, both < ʿAlī ibn Ibrāhīm al-ʿAlawī < Rashaʾ ibn Naẓīf < al-Ḥasan ibn Ismāʿīl < Aḥmad ibn Marwān < Ismāʿīl ibn Isḥāq al-Sarrāj < al-Ziyādī < Muʾarrij.

15 Ibn ʿĀṣim, *Ḥadāʾiq*, p. 103.

16 Gutas (1975): 459–460.

17 Quoted in Ibn Buṭlān, *Daʿwa*, p. 25.

4.2 Encounters with Caliphs and Governors

A8 Khālid has said: I have promised God that when I am alone with a king, I will always remind him of God, He is noble and mighty.

(al-Ṣafadī, *Wāfī* XIII: 255).

COMMENTARY: This saying is transmitted in conjunction with A9.

A9 ʿUmar (ibn ʿAbd al-ʿAzīz) said to Khālid ibn Ṣafwān: "Admonish me but be brief." Khālid replied: "O Commander of the Believers, some people are beguiled by the fact that God keeps (their weaknesses) covered and they are seduced by being praised, but let not other people's ignorance of you prevail on your own knowledge of yourself.[18] May God help guard both us and you from being beguiled by (our weaknesses) being covered and from rejoicing in people's praise! May He guard us from lagging behind and falling short of what He has imposed upon us and from bending towards our lusts!"

ʿUmar wept and said: "May God preserve both us and you from following our lusts!"

(Ibn Ḥamdūn, *Tadhkira* I: 207, no. 480); Ibn ʿAsākir, *Taʾrīkh* XVI: 96;[19] Ibn al-ʿAdīm, *Bughya* VII: 74;[20] Abū Nuʿaym, *Ḥilya* VIII: 18;[21] Ibn Rajab, *Sīra*, pp. 89–90; Ibn al-Jawzī, *Sīra*, p. 138.[22]

COMMENTARY: The story is translated by Richard Gramlich from Abū Nuʿaym's *Ḥilya*.[23]

A10 Khālid ibn Ṣafwān consoled ʿUmar ibn ʿAbd al-ʿAzīz and congratulated him for the Caliphate, saying: Praise be to God, who has bestowed a favour on people by (raising) you, and praise be to God, who has set your growth as a

---

18 For this sentence, cf. al-Jāḥiẓ, *Bayān* III: 173 (anonymous < Ibn al-Aʿrābī).

19 < Abū l-Qāsim Zāhir ibn Ṭāhir < Abū Bakr al-Bayhaqī < Abū ʿAbdallāh al-Ḥāfiẓ < Jaʿfar ibn Muḥammad < Ibrāhīm ibn Naṣr < Ibrāhīm ibn Bashshār < Ibrāhīm ibn Adʾham. In the text Ibrāhīm ibn Bashshār is erroneously given as Ibrāhīm ibn Yasār, but in the next *isnād* the name is correctly Bashshār. Ibrāhīm ibn Bashshār al-Khurāsānī was a servant of Ibrāhīm ibn Adʾham.

20 < Abū l-Maḥāsin Sulaymān ibn al-Faḍl ibn Sulaymān < ʿAlī ibn abī Muḥammad < Abū l-Qāsim Zāhir ibn Ṭāhir < Abū Bakr al-Bayhaqī < Abū ʿAbdallāh al-Ḥāfiẓ < Jaʿfar ibn Muḥammad < Ibrāhīm ibn Naṣr < Ibrāhīm ibn Bashshār < Ibrāhīm ibn Adʾham.

21 < Jaʿfar < Muḥammad ibn Ibrāhīm < Ibrāhīm ibn Naṣr < Ibrāhīm ibn Bashshār.

22 < Ibrāhīm ibn Bashshār < Ibrāhīm ibn Adʾham.

23 Gramlich (1995–96) I: 236 and (1997): 300.

mercy, your Caliphate as protection, and your misfortunes as an example, and has set yourself as a model.

(al-Ḥuṣrī, *Zahr*, p. 1079).

A11 < *Abū ʿAbdallāh al-Ḥāfiẓ* < *Jaʿfar ibn Muḥammad ibn Nuṣayr* < *Ibrāhīm ibn Naṣr* < *Ibrāhīm ibn Bashshār* < *al-Fuḍayl*: I have heard that Khālid ibn Ṣafwān came to ʿUmar ibn ʿAbd al-ʿAzīz, who said to him: "O Khālid, admonish me!" Khālid replied: "God, He is mighty and majestic, is not pleased to see anyone above you, so be not pleased to see anyone more grateful than you."

He (al-Fuḍayl) said: ʿUmar wept until he fainted. When he had recovered he said: "O Khālid, He is not pleased that anyone should be above me? By God, I will fear Him and beware of Him. I will look forward to Him and love Him, thank Him and praise Him. To all this I will earnestly strive as well as I ever can. I will strive to be just and fair. I will renounce this transitory world, which will vanish, and until I meet God I will strive for the lasting life in the hereafter, which will remain. Perhaps I will be among those who are saved and who will win." Then he wept until he fainted again.

Khālid said: I left him fainted and went away.

(Ibn ʿAsākir, *Taʾrīkh* XVI: 96); Ibn al-ʿAdīm, *Bughya* VII: 74–75;[24] Ibn Manẓūr, *Mukhtaṣar* VII: 353; Ibn Rajab, *Sīra*, pp. 90–91; Ibn al-Jawzī, *Sīra*, pp. 138–139;[25] al-Ṣafadī, *Wāfī* XIII: 255.

COMMENTARY: Cf. B69.

A12 < *Maslama ibn Muḥārib*: Muʿāwiya ibn Sufyān ibn Muʿāwiya ibn Yazīd ibn al-Muhallab was killed in the war between Qutayba and Sufyān ibn Muʿāwiya. When Sufyān was appointed governor of Basra he sent for Khālid ibn Ṣafwān: "Your son was killed and so was mine. I have sent for you so that I might be consoled by you and you by me." Khālid replied: "May God keep the Emir! Me and you, we are like the wailing woman who said:

> Assist me, O sisters –
> yet woe to me, and to you!"

---

24 < Abū ʿAbdallāh al-Ḥāfiẓ < Jaʿfar ibn Muḥammad ibn Nuṣayr < Ibrāhīm ibn Naṣr al-Manṣūrī < Ibrāhīm ibn Bashshār < al-Fuḍayl.

25 < Ibrāhīm ibn Bashshār < al-Fuḍayl.

Sufyān said: "You have revived my grief!" Khālid replied: "May God keep the Emir! May what I revived for you be dispelled by the knowledge that you, too, will not remain."

(al-Mubarrad, *Taʿāzī*, p. 50); al-Balādhurī, *Ansāb* III: 178 (abbreviated).

COMMENTARY: Sufyān ibn Muʿāwiya ibn Yazīd ibn al-Muhallab was the governor of Basra in 132/750 and again in 139–145/757–763.[26] He rebelled in Basra on behalf of Qaḥṭaba in 132/750, but was defeated.

A13 Khālid ibn Ṣafwān was fleeing from Basra when Yazīd (ibn al-Muhallab) met him in Wāsiṭ. There were on Khālid's face signs of smallpox with some medicine on them. Khālid asked him permission (to continue his travel), saying: "I have been prescribed the drinking of *tayādir* in Ṭūs." Yazīd gave him the permission and Khālid retreated (from Basra).

(al-Balādhurī, *Ansāb*, ed. al-ʿAẓm, VII: 264).

COMMENTARY: The "*tayādir* in Ṭūs" is clearly an error for Tiyādurīṭūs, for which see B51.

A14 Yazīd summoned al-Faḍl ibn ʿAbd al-Raḥmān ibn al-ʿAbbās ibn Rabīʿa ibn al-Ḥārith ibn ʿAbd al-Muṭṭalib ibn Hāshim, who paid homage to him, but ʿAbd al-Wāḥid, from among the sons of Ibn ʿĀmir ibn Kurayz, and Khālid ibn Ṣafwān ibn ʿAbdallāh ibn al-Ahtam al-Minqarī, the Orator, as well as some other people from Banū Tamīm and others hid themselves and ran away from him.

(al-Balādhurī, *Ansāb*, ed. al-ʿAẓm, VII: 259).

COMMENTARY: Cf. A13. Yazīd ibn al-Muhallab rose in revolt against the Caliph Yazīd II and was killed in 102/721.[27]

A15 < *Abū Bakr* < *al-ʿUklī* < *"his father"*: ʿAbd al-Malik asked al-Ḥajjāj what faults the latter had. Al-Ḥajjāj hesitated, but ʿAbd al-Malik insisted until he replied: "I am vehement, envious, rancorous, obstinate, and harsh." When he heard this Khālid ibn Ṣafwān said: "He has ascribed to himself every possible evil and every deviation from good. Yet he blamed himself elegantly and was generous in pointing out his ignoble character and in giving evidence of the

26 Pellat (1953): 281; Crone (1980): 134.

27 See also Chapter 1.3.2.

excess of his unbelief and of his leaving the side of his Lord and of his having become most like to his Satan, who has misguided him."

(al-Qālī, *Amālī* II: 111); al-Waṭwāṭ, *Ghurar*, p. 72 (slight variants); Ibn ʿAbdrabbih, *ʿIqd* II: 324 (briefer and without reference to Khālid).

A16 Khālid ibn Ṣafwān said: "That son of a Christian mother has renounced and left all decency." By this he meant Khālid ibn ʿAbdallāh al-Qasrī.

(Ibn Durayd, *Jamhara*, p. 482).

COMMENTARY: Khālid al-Qasrī's Christian mother was a favourite target for ridicule, as, e.g., in the following verses by al-Farazdaq:[28]

> Convey to the Commander of the Believers this message:
> Hasten, may God guide you, to dismiss Khālid.
>
> He has built for his mother a church with its crucifix
> and destroyed mosques for he hates the prayer.

A17 Someone has said: Khālid ibn Ṣafwān stopped at the door of Sulaymān ibn ʿAlī, beware of a mule that stood there. Someone said to him: "It has never kicked anyone!" Khālid replied: "I am afraid that I will be the exception and then it will be said: 'except for Khālid'!"

(Ibn ʿĀṣim, *Ḥadāʾiq*, p. 104).

A18 < *Abū Aḥmad* < *al-Ṣūlī* < *Muḥammad ibn al-Ḥasan al-Ghiyāʾī* < *Abū Ḥātim* < *Abū ʿUbayda*: Khālid ibn Ṣafwān al-Tamīmī advised Sufyān ibn Muʿāwiya al-Muhallabī not to make war on Salm ibn Qutayba al-Bāhilī, who was the Emir of Basra on behalf of Marwān ibn Muḥammad. Abū Salama al-Khallāl had written to Sufyān about the governorship of Basra. Khālid said to Sufyān: "Wait. If things turn for Marwān, you should not make war on his agent (*ʿāmil*). And if they turn for your companions then Salm will seek refuge with you." Sufyān did not accept Khālid's advice but made war on Salm. He was put to flight and his son, Muʿāwiya ibn Sufyān, got killed. Then Khālid said to him: "I am from Ghaziyya."[29] Sufyān asked what he meant and Khālid replied: "I mean the words of Durayd ibn al-Ṣimma:[30]

---

28 Al-Farazdaq, *Dīwān*, p. 145. Cf. also Ibn al-Sikkīt, *Qalb*, p. 29.

29 The story is told to illustrate this saying which, according to al-ʿAskarī, is said of a man advising someone who does not accept his advice.

30 Pre-Islamic poet, see GAS II: 267–268, and *Aṣmaʿiyyāt* 24: 6–8.

At the rind of the dune I gave them my opinion,
but its good sense only dawned on them the next day.

Though they disobeyed me, I remained one of them, though I knew their error and that I was not doing right.

Yet I am but from Ghaziyya: If they err,
I err, and if they do right, so do I."

(Abū Hilāl al-ʿAskarī, *Jamhara*, p. 195).

COMMENTARY: This story is unique in showing Khālid in the role of a political advisor, but it should be noted that Shabīb is also said to have had a role in this.[31]

A19 < *al-Madāʾinī* < *Ziyād ibn ʿUbaydallāh and ʿĀmir ibn Ḥafṣ*: The family of al-Qāsim ibn Salīm[32] and Khālid ibn Ṣafwān quarrelled. They accepted al-Ḥasan (al-Baṣrī) as arbitrator. Al-Ḥasan decided the case but the party against which he had decided refused to comply. Then Mūsā ibn Anas wrote, in the year 102/721, to ʿUmar ibn Yazīd ibn ʿUmayr, who was the chief of police: "From Mūsā ibn Anas to ʿUmar ibn Yazīd. The family of al-Qāsim ibn Sulaymān and Khālid ibn Ṣafwān accepted al-Ḥasan to arbitrate in their quarrel. When he had decided the case they refused to comply. Now, carry out the decision of al-Ḥasan and force them to comply with it."
(Wakīʿ, *Akhbār*, p. 195/I: 309).

COMMENTARY: Khālid seems to have gained the upper hand against al-Qāsim. At least, al-Balādhurī mentions among the *iqṭāʿs* of Basra a Khālidiyya, belonging to Khālid but having earlier belonged to al-Qāsim ibn Sulaymān.[33]

---

31 For Salm ibn Qutayba, see Chapter 1.4 and al-Ṣafadī, *Wāfī* XV: 299–300. For the incident, see al-Ṭabarī, *Taʾrīkh* III: 21–23/XXVII: 143–145.

32 Later Sulaymān.

33 Al-Balādhurī, *Futūḥ*, p. 369.

4.3 *Mufākharas* and *maḥāsin wa-masāwī*

A20 The Debate between Yemen and Muḍar. Al-Abrash al-Kalbī said to Khālid ibn Ṣafwān: "Let us vie in glory!" They were then in the presence of Hishām ibn ʿAbd al-Malik. Khālid asked al-Abrash to begin, and he said: "To us belongs one fourth of the House" – by this he meant the Yemeni Corner of the Kaʿba – "and from among us are Ḥātim of the Ṭayyiʾ as well as al-Muhallab ibn abī Ṣufra." Khālid ibn Ṣafwān replied: "From among us is the Prophet, who was sent, and among us is the Revealed Book and to us belongs the Caliph, who is hoped for." Al-Abrash said: "After this I will never vie with a Muḍarī!"

(Ibn ʿAbdrabbih, *ʿIqd* III: 330); Ibn ʿAbdrabbih, *ʿIqd* IV: 46.

COMMENTARY: Cf. B82, B86, and B101.

A21 One night some Iraqis sat together in the presence of Yazīd ibn ʿUmar ibn Hubayra, who asked: "Which of the two cities has tastier fruits, Kufa or Basra?" Khālid ibn Ṣafwān said: "Ours, O Emir! We have *azādh* and *maʿqilī* dates and so and so."

ʿAbd al-Raḥmān ibn Bashīr al-ʿIjlī replied to this: "I believe, O Emir, that you have already chosen what to send to the Commander of the Believers?" Yazīd said that this was the case, and ʿAbd al-Raḥmān continued: "Then we will be satisfied by your choice, whether for us or against us. Which fresh dates are you sending him?" Yazīd said: "*Mushān*." To this ʿAbd al-Raḥmān said: "There are no *mushān* dates in Basra. Then what?" Yazīd replied: "*Sābirī*." ʿAbd al-Raḥmān said: "There are no *sābirī* dates in Basra." Khālid ibn Ṣafwān interrupted: "Nay, we do have some in Basra!"

Then ʿAbd al-Raḥmān asked: "Which dried dates do you send him?" Yazīd replied: "*Nirsiyān*." ʿAbd al-Raḥmān said: "There are none in Basra. Then what?" Yazīd replied: "*Hayrūnazādh*."[34] ʿAbd al-Raḥmān said: "There are none of them in Basra. Which hard (*qasb*)[35] dates do you send him?" Yazīd replied: "*ʿAnbar*." ʿAbd al-Raḥmān said: "There are none of them in Basra." Now Ibn Hubayra said to Khālid: "He claimed five against you and you could only claim to partake in one and left to him the four remaining. I think he has won you."

(Ibn Qutayba, *ʿUyūn* I: 321); Ibn al-Faqīh, *Mukhtaṣar*, pp. 175–176[36] = Ibn al-Faqīh, *Buldān*, pp. 211–212.

---

34 Ibn al-Faqīh has *hayrūn* and *azādh*, speaking of them as separate types of dates.

35 See Lane (1863–93), s.v.

36 < al-Madāʾinī.

COMMENTARY: Ibn al-Faqīh transmits his version on the authority of al-Madāʾinī, yet it need not come from the Khālid monograph, as Khālid has only a marginal role here as the interlocutor of ʿAbd al-Raḥmān. Al-Madāʾinī is, among scores of other books, credited with a *Kitāb Mufākharāt ahl al-Baṣra wa'l-Kūfa*.[37]

A22 Khālid ibn Ṣafwān has said: If someone has never eaten *rāziqī* (grapes) when the west wind starts to blow,[38] it is right for his family to weep for him.

(Ibn al-Faqīh, *Mukhtaṣar*, p. 126) = Ibn al-Faqīh, *Buldān*, p. 173.

A23 One night the people of Iraq assembled around Yazīd ibn ʿUmar ibn Hubayra for an evening talk (*samar*). Someone asked: "Which city, Kufa or Basra, has better dates?" Khālid ibn Ṣafwān replied: "Nay, our dates are better and sweeter. Against the people of *Kufa[39] we have the excellence of grapes which are *rāziqī* in their taste, *sūnāʾī*[40] in their sweetness, and wine-like in their delicateness."

(Ibn al-Faqīh, *Buldān*, p. 254).

COMMENTARY: The passage continues with several snippets of text where various aspects of Basra and Kufa are discussed, but it does not form a full dialogue and Khālid does not appear anymore, except anachronistically on p. 256, where he is listed as one of the famous orators of Basra.[41] The manuscript of Ibn al-Faqīh's unabbridged *Buldān* is incomplete and the text is partly corrupt.

A24 One day during Abū l-ʿAbbās al-Saffāḥ's Caliphate, Khālid ibn Ṣafwān was alone with him and said:[42] "O Commander of the Believers, I have been thinking about you and the extent of your power. Yet a single woman holds

37 See Lindstedt (2013) I: 22, and, e.g., al-Ṣafadī, *Wāfī* XXII: 47, line 3.

38 See Lane (1863–93), s.v. DBR IV.

39 The text reads here Basra, but the whole text seems to have been corrupted. The passage is missing from Ibn al-Faqīh's *Mukhtaṣar*.

40 From the ancient village of Sūnāyā, see Yāqūt, *Muʿjam* III: 285.

41 Note, though, that while al-Ḥajjāj seems to be the person who mentions Khālid and his younger relative Shabīb ibn Shayba (read so for the edition's Shabba), it is not necessary to read the list of names as still belonging to al-Ḥajjāj's words.

42 Al-Raqīq al-Qayrawānī, *Quṭb*, p. 325, makes Abū l-ʿAbbās introduce the topic (*ilā an aḥrā Abū l-ʿAbbās dhikr al-nisāʾ*), as in B24.

sway over you[43] and you are confined by her. If she is sick, you have to be sick with her, and if she is away,[44] you are yourself away. You have prohibited yourself the pleasures of trying other girls, getting to know them, and enjoying whatever you want of them. Know, O Commander of the Believers, that among them there are the young and delicate with lofty stature, the tender and white, the dark emancipated, the brown slave, the Berber with her heavy buttocks, the half-breed Medinese, who charms you with her conversation and whom you can enjoy in privacy, too. And what about freeborn girls, O Commander of the Believers! To look at what they have and to speak with them! O Commander of the Believers, if you would but see the tall white, the brown and red-lipped, the blond with heavy buttocks! And the half-breed Basrans and Kufans who have a sweet tongue, a slender body, and a slim waist, golden curls, painted eyes, and cup-shaped breasts! Their fine clothes, jewels, and shapes! Now, there is something for you to see!" Khālid excelled in description and went on and on with his sweet words and his excellent description.[45]

When Khālid had finished the Caliph said: "Woe to you, Khālid! By God, I have never heard anything as beautiful as what you just said. Repeat your speech;[46] it has affected me indeed!" Khālid repeated his speech even more beautifully than the first time. Then he departed. Abū l-ʿAbbās was still pondering upon what he had heard when his wife, Umm Salama, entered. When she saw him deep in thought and looking worried, she said: "You look strange, O Commander of the Believers: has something bad happened or have you heard a worrying report?" "Nothing of that sort," he answered, and she asked: "Well, what is it then?" Abū l-ʿAbbās tried to change the subject, but she kept asking him until he had to tell her what Khālid had said. "And what did you say to that son-of-a-bitch!" she cried, but he said: "By God, the man is giving me counsel and you scold him?!" Umm Salama left furious and sent to Khālid some[47] of her

---

43 According to a well-known story, Abū l-ʿAbbās had promised his wife neither to marry another wife nor to take concubines, see al-Masʿūdī, *Murūj* §2326, and al-Tījānī, *Tuḥfa*, pp. 179–180. Cf. also ps.-al-Jāḥiẓ, *Maḥāsin*, p. 232, where al-Saffāḥ's successor al-Manṣūr (r. 136–158/754–775) gives a written document to Umm Mūsā al-Ḥimyariyya promising not to take a second wife. *Murūj* §2326 gives the full name of Umm Salama as Umm Salama bint Yaʿqūb ibn Salama ibn ʿAbdallāh al-Makhzūmiyya.

44 Var. "menstruates." The word *ḥāḍat* was considered improper when addressing a king, see al-Thaʿālibī, *Yatīma* I: 167.

45 The listing of women and their qualities is a common theme in Arabic literature. For an interesting example, see Abū Nuwās, *Dīwān* IV: 132 (*muʾannathāt* no. 172).

46 The repetition of amusing and witty stories to the Caliph is a topos found in similar contexts. Cf., e.g., *Kalīla wa-Dimna*, p. 14.

47 Al-Bayhaqī's version has here the truly gargantuan number of one hundred.

Bukharan slaves with their clubs[48] with orders not to leave a single one of his limbs unbroken or sound.

Khālid himself said: So I left the Caliph and headed homewards. I was glad about the effect my speech had had on him. I did not doubt in the least that his gift would soon reach me. It did not take long until those Bukharans came to me while I was sitting in my doorway. When I saw them draw near, I was positive about the present and the gift. They stopped in front of me and asked about me. "I'm Khālid," I said, but then one of them dashed towards me with the club he was carrying. When I saw him coming I jumped up, entered my house, and locked the doors behind. I then remained hidden for some time without going out. It crossed my mind that the men might have come from Umm Salama.

Meanwhile, Abū l-ʿAbbās kept asking for me urgently. All of a sudden some people rushed in and said to me: "Answer to the Commander of the Believers!" I was sure I was going to die! Still, I mounted and rode, being all jelly and no bones! While on my way to the palace several messengers came to me. When I entered and found him alone, I calmed down a little. I greeted him and he beckoned me to sit down. I looked around and saw behind me a door with curtains drawn across it and I noticed some movement behind it.[49]

Abū l-ʿAbbās said to me: "Khālid, I have not seen you for three days." "I was sick, O Commander of the Believers," I replied, and he continued: "Woe to you, Khālid, last time you described women and slavegirls to me, and I have never heard a speech more beautiful. Now repeat your words to me!" "It is a pleasure, O Commander of the Believers," I replied, "I told you that the Arabs of the olden days derived the word *ḍarra*, 'second wife,' from *ḍarr*, 'harm.'[50] None of them took more than one wife without getting into trouble." "What!" he cried, "that wasn't what you said!" "Oh yes it was, O Commander of the Believers," I insisted, "Moreover, I told you that three wives are like the three stones on

48 The word *kāfirkūb* (see WKAS, s.v.) is often used in connection with al-Saffāḥ, cf., e.g., al-Maqdisī, *Badʾ* VI: 72. On these and other clubs in general, see Zakeri (1995): 216–218 – Zakeri claims, p. 216, that the word is only attested in plural, but one does find the singular, though rarely, see, e.g., al-Jāḥiẓ, *Bayān* I: 142, note 6, for its occurrence in the margin of one manuscript.

49 In al-Raqīq al-Qayrawānī's version, *Quṭb*, p. 326, Khālid explicitly says that he realised that this was a set-up (*amr maṣnūʿ*).

50 The problems inherent in taking a second wife were often described in literature, and the *jinās* between *ḍarrat-* and *ḌRR* did not escape the notice of other authors, e.g., al-Qālī, *Amālī* II: 35–36. For a *ḥadīth* comparing this world and the hereafter to two wives of a man ("if a man pleases the one he will anger the other"), see Ibn ʿAbdrabbih, *ʿIqd* III: 172.

which the cauldron boils, and you, too!"[51] Abū l-ʿAbbās exclaimed: "May I be absolved from my relationship with the Messenger of God if I ever heard you say anything like that!"

I went forth: "Yes, and I told you that four wives are the sum of all evil combined for their husband: they turn his hair grey and make him senile and sick." Abū l-ʿAbbās cried: "Woe to you! By God, I have never heard this from either you or anybody else before this moment." I said: "Yes you have, by God!" "Do you call me a liar?" he asked, and I replied: "And you, do you want to kill me (*turīdu an taqtulanī*),[52] O Commander of the Believers?" "Go on", he said, and I continued: "Then I told you that virgin slavegirls are no more than men without a pair of testicles."[53]

I heard laughter from behind the curtain and went on: "Yes, and I told you also that the tribe Makhzūm is the flower of Quraysh and that you have with you one of these flowers.[54] Still, your eye covets freeborn women and slavegirls thereto!" Then a voice came from behind the curtain: "You have said the truth, dear uncle, and been true. So you told the Commander of the Believers, but he altered your words and changed them and put words in your mouth!" Abū l-ʿAbbās said: "What's the matter with you, may God kill you and put you to shame!"[55]

I left him and went out, sure that I was saved. It was but a moment until the messengers of Umm Salama came to me bringing ten thousand dirhams, a robe of honour, a horse, and a slave.[56]

---

51 The phrase *taghlī ʿalayhinna* is ambivalent in Arabic ("it boils" – "you boil"). In the translation, the double entendre has been opened by translating it both ways.

52 The same expression, reminiscent of Q 28: 19, is used by Abū l-ʿAynāʾ in Jirāb al-Dawla, *Tarwīḥ*, pp. 123–124.

53 Cf. B112.

54 The metaphor *rayḥān* (fragrant basil) for women is very common, cf., e.g., al-Thaʿālibī, *Thimār*, p. 270 (no. 400); al-Jurjānī, *Muntakhab*, p. 17; Ibn ʿAbdrabbih, *ʿIqd* III: 79, lines 14–15, and III: 158, line 8 (< ʿAlī ibn abī Ṭālib). Banū Makhzūm are called the *rayḥān* of the Quraysh in, e.g., al-Thaʿālibī, *Thimār*, p. 298 (no. 449), and Ibn abī l-Ḥadīd, *Sharḥ* V: 395 (+ commentary until p. 411). The Prophet's wife Umm Salama also belonged to Makhzūm (see, e.g., Ibn abī l-Ḥadīd, *Sharḥ* V: 409). For the Banū Makhzūm, see also Cook (2002): 180–181.

55 These are formulaic exclamations also used for admiration, see, e.g., al-Suyūṭī, *Muzhir* I: 331.

56 These were the usual gifts sent by the magnates, cf., e.g., al-Zajjājī, *Majālis*, pp. 54–55 (a story which also contains other similarities with the present story).

(al-Masʿūdī, *Murūj* §§2327–2330); al-Bayhaqī, *Maḥāsin*, pp. 420–422; Ibn Hilāl al-Ṣābiʾ, *Hafawāt*, pp. 101–105 (no. 114);[57] al-Raqīq al-Qayrawānī, *Quṭb*, pp. 325–327;[58] Ibn Badrūn, *Sharḥ qaṣīdat Ibn ʿAbdūn*, pp. 216–218; al-Jarīrī, *Jalīs* II: 456–459;[59] Ibn ʿAsākir, *Taʾrīkh* LXX: 244–247;[60] Ibn al-ʿAdīm, *Bughya* VII: 71–74;[61] Ibn al-Jawzī, *Adhkiyāʾ*, pp. 116–117; Ibn al-Kumaylī, *Nuzha*, pp. 691–693;[62] al-Itlīdī, *Iʿlām*, pp. 108–111; al-Shirwānī, *Nafḥa*, pp. 64–66; al-Sharīshī, *Sharḥ* IV: 134–135; al-Damīrī, *Ḥayāt*, pp. 170–172 (s.v. *birdhawn*); Ibrāhīm al-Aḥdab, *Dhayl* II: 292–296;[63] al-Tijānī, *Tuḥfa*, pp. 176–179 (no. 383).[64]

COMMENTARY: The story has been translated by Weisweiler.[65] It is referred to also by al-Khaṭīb al-Tibrīzī and al-Maʿarrī.[66] The same story is later told about Hārūn al-Rashīd, Lady Zubayda, and Abū Nuwās in several popular *Nawādir Abī Nuwās* collections.[67] Popular stories with some similar features may also be found in folklore collections.[68] Al-Thaʿālibī relates another story

57 < Abū l-ʿAbbās al-Mubarrad.

58 With some significant variants.

59 < al-Ḥusayn ibn al-Qāsim al-Kawkabī < Abū l-Faḍl al-Ribʿī < al-ʿAbbās ibn al-Faḍl < Isḥāq ibn Ibrāhīm al-Mawṣilī < Shabīb ibn Shayba.

60 < Abū l-ʿIzz Aḥmad ibn ʿUbaydallāh < Abū ʿAlī Muḥammad ibn al-Ḥusayn al-Jāzirī < Abū l-Faraj al-Muʿāfā ibn Zakariyyā al-Qāḍī < al-Ḥusayn ibn al-Qāsim < al-Ribʿī Abū l-Faḍl al-ʿAbbās ibn al-Faḍl < Isḥāq ibn Ibrāhīm al-Mawṣilī < Shabīb ibn Shayba.

61 < Abū l-Ḥasan ibn abī ʿAbdallāh ibn al-Muqayyir al-Baghdādī in Cairo < Abū l-Faḍl Muḥammad ibn Nāṣir ibn ʿAlī < Abū Isḥāq Ibrāhīm ibn Saʿīd ibn ʿAbdallāh al-Ḥabbāl < Abū l-Ḥasan Aḥmad ibn Muḥammad ibn al-Qāsim ibn Marzūq < Abū l-Fatḥ Ibrāhīm ibn ʿAlī < Abū Bakr Muḥammad ibn Yaḥyā Abū Aḥmad ʿAbd al-Wāḥid ibn al-Ḥārith < ʿAbdallāh ibn Mawhūb al-Khāzin < Saʿīd al-Ḥājib.

62 < Abū l-Faraj.

63 < Abū l-Faraj, *Nisāʾ* and *Ibn al-Kardabūs, Iktifāʾ*.

64 < Abū l-Faraj, *Nisāʾ* and Ibn al-Kardabūs, *Iktifāʾ*, translated in [al-Tijānī], *Glory*, pp. 162–165. For Abū l-Faraj Ibn al-Jawzī's (d. 597/1200) *Kitāb al-nisāʾ*, see *GAL* S II: 919, 75b. For Ibn al-Kardabūs (d. early 13th century), see Zameño (online). Al-Tijānī mentions that his version is a combination of his two sources, but, in fact, it remains rather faithful to al-Masʿūdī's.

65 Weisweiler (1954), no. 67. A small part of the first speech is also translated in Pellat (1953): 241.

66 Al-Khaṭīb al-Tibrīzī, *Dīwān Abī Tammām* I: 403 (*wa-ḥadīthuhu mashhūr maʿa Umm Salama imraʾat Abī l-ʿAbbās*), and al-Maʿarrī, *Ṣāhil*, p. 360. The editor of al-Maʿarrī's *Ṣāhil*, wrongly identifies Khālid as Khālid ibn Ṣafwān ibn Umayya al-Jumaḥī. See also Marzolph (1992) II: 104–105, no. 420 (< al-Damīrī, *Ḥayāt*, pp. 170–172).

67 E.g., *Nawādir Abī Nuwās* (Silsilat "al-ḍāḥikūn"), pp. 33–40; *Nawādir Abī Nuwās* (Bayrūt n.d.), pp. 3–6; *Dīwān Abī Nuwās*, pp. 21–27; Ingrams (1933): 36–38.

68 See, e.g., in Bushnaq (1987): 274 = Ingrams (1933): 42–43.

of contest between the Caliph and Umm Salama, this version including ʿUmāra ibn Ḥamza instead of Khālid.[69]

Ibn Nubāta relates a structurally similar story involving the Caliph ʿAbd al-Malik, Ibrāhīm ibn Ṭalḥa, and al-Ḥajjāj ibn Yūsuf.[70] Likewise, a story told by Jirāb al-Dawla is structured on the repetition of a story in an inverted way, much to the annoyance of the listener.[71] A further similar story narrated by al-Khālidiyyān involves the Caliph, Umm Salama, and ʿUmāra ibn Ḥamza.[72] The story of Umm Salama is not technically unique although it is uniquely well executed.

The first speech of Khālid does actually not fall too far of what *ḥadīth* collections have to say. Thus, e.g., Ibn Ḥabīb mentions the predilection of the Prophet for women and sex and represents the pious ʿAbdallāh ibn ʿUmar approaching, i.e., having sex with, eleven women in one night.[73] The same book has a chapter on the duties of wife toward her husband, which depicts an ideal wife that is in dire contrast with Umm Salama in her behaviour toward al-Saffāḥ.[74]

For a full analysis of the story, see Chapter 2.5.1.

4.4 *Laḥḥān* and Linguistic Authority

A25 *Abū l-ʿAynāʾ < al-Qaḥdhamī*: Khālid ibn Ṣafwān entered a bath where there was a man with his son. The man wanted to show off his eloquence to Khālid and said: "O my son, begin with your hands and second with your feets (*ibdaʾ bi-yadāka wa-thanni bi-rijlāka*)." Then he turned to Khālid and said: "O Ibn Ṣafwān, this is the language of men who are no more!" Khālid replied: "Nay, this is the language of men never created by God!"

(al-Tawḥīdī, *Baṣāʾir* VI: 223–224 (no. 704); al-Muqriʾ, *Akhbār*, p. 44 (no. 18);[75] al-Ābī, *Nathr* V: 270; al-Waṭwāṭ, *Ghurar*, p. 223; al-Zamakhsharī, *Rabīʿ* I: 629; Ibn ʿAsākir,

69 Al-Thaʿālibī, *Thimār*, pp. 201–202.
70 Ibn Nubāta, *Sarḥ*, pp. 174–176.
71 Jirāb al-Dawla, *Tarwīḥ*, p. 55. Here, there is a *mājin*, who tells a *qāḍī* in Basra in private that he had seen him in a dream outweighing the whole *umma*. The *qāḍī* wishes him to repeat the story next day in public, which the man does, but this time the *qāḍī* merely outweighs a donkey's penis.
72 Al-Khālidiyyān, *Tuḥaf*, pp. 143–145, translated and analysed by Sharlet (2011): 76–82.
73 Ibn Ḥabīb, *Adab*, pp. 176–178 (nos. 64–66); p. 178 (no. 67).
74 Ibn Ḥabīb, *Adab*, pp. 257–266 – cf. the brief chapter, pp. 256–257, on the duties of man toward his wife.
75 < Abū Ṭāhir < Wakīʿ < Muḥammad ibn Khallād < al-Walīd ibn Hishām al-Qaḥdhamī.

Ta'rīkh XVI: 109;[76] Ibn al-ʿAdīm, *Bughya* VII: 68;[77] Ibn al-Jawzī, *Akhbār al-ḥamqā*, p. 119.[78]

COMMENTARY: The version of al-Muqri', Ibn al-Jawzī, and Ibn ʿAsākir, *ibda' bi-yadāka wa-rijlāka*, misses the point,[79] as does al-Waṭwāṭ's version (*ighsil yadāka qabla wajhika*).[80] The other sources read *wa-thanni bi-rijlāka*. The point lies in the use of the not too common verb *thannā* (which Khālid himself uses in B88), in contrast to the gross grammatical mistake in the use of the dual nominative instead of accusative. Without the verb, the joke does not work, as the erroneous use of the dual does not imply a misguided effort to speak eloquent language.

Similar jokes are also told about other eloquent persons and grammarians,[81] and al-Rāghib collected several *laḥn* stories on the wrong forms of the dual in his *Muḥāḍarāt* I: 66–67. In Ibn abī ʿAwn, *Ajwiba*, p. 222 (no. 1340), there is a story about al-Aṣmaʿī and a man who uses a similar expression to which al-Aṣmaʿī gives a witty reply similar to that of Khālid. Cf. also al-Sīrāfī, *Akhbār*, pp. 16–20, for stories about *laḥns* that caused Abū l-Aswad (or others) to start codifying pure Arabic grammar.

A26 Khālid went by some *mawlās* who were discussing Arabic language and said: "Are you discussing Arabic? But you were the first to corrupt it!"

(Ibn ʿAbd al-Barr, *Bahja* I: 66).

---

76 < Abū l-Qāsim ibn al-Samarqandī < Abū ʿAlī Muḥammad ibn Muḥammad ibn al-Maslama and al-Ḥasan ibn ʿAlī ibn al-Bannā and ʿAbd al-Wāḥid ibn Muḥammad ibn Fahd al-ʿAllāf < Abū l-Ḥasan ʿAlī ibn Aḥmad al-Muqri' < Abū Ṭāhir ʿAbd al-Wāḥid ibn ʿUmar ibn abī Hāshim al-Muqri' < Wakīʿ ibn Khalaf < Muḥammad ibn Khallād < al-Walīd ibn Hishām al-Qaḥdhamī.

77 < Abū l-Yumn Zayd ibn al-Ḥasan ibn Zayd al-Kindī in Damascus < *al-imām* Abū Muḥammad ʿAbdallāh ibn ʿAlī al-Muqri' < *al-ḥājib* Abū l-Ḥasan ʿAlī ibn Muḥammad ibn al-ʿAllāf < Abū l-Ḥasan ʿAlī ibn Aḥmad ibn ʿUmar ibn Ḥafṣ al-Ḥammāmī al-Muqri' < Abū Ṭāhir ʿAbd al-Wāḥid ibn ʿUmar < Wakīʿ < Muḥammad ibn Khallād < al-Walīd ibn Hishām al-Qaḥdhamī.

78 < Abū Ṭāhir.

79 Al-Muqri', *Akhbār*, p. 44, Ibn al-Jawzī, *Akhbār al-ḥamqā*, p. 119, and Ibn ʿAsākir, *Ta'rīkh* XVI: 109.

80 Al-Waṭwāṭ, *Ghurar*, p. 223.

81 Cf., e.g., al-Khalīl ibn Aḥmad in a story in Ibn Nubāta, *Sarḥ*, p. 270, also discussed in Talmon (1997): 90 (no. 57).

COMMENTARY: Abū ʿUbayda, as quoted by Ibn ʿAbdrabbih, tells the same story about ʿAbdallāh ibn al-Ahtam.[82] Khālid's averseness towards non-Arabs discussing Arabic, such as Sībawayhi would have been in his eyes, matches well his reputed averseness towards learning grammar (*iʿrāb*). Khālid belonged to the last generation of city-dwellers who could still keep up the illusion of speaking pure Arabic as their mother tongue. Later, and partly already in his time,[83] this was only attributed to the Bedouins of the desert, who, in fact, would by that time have moved from speaking a version of Old Arabic to speaking a form of Modern Arabic.

A27 < *Faḍḍāl al-Azraq* < *a Minqarī*: Once Khālid ibn Ṣafwān spoke concerning a peace agreement (*fī ṣulḥ*)[84] in a way people had never before heard. A Bedouin, clad in a coarse clothes and without shoes, answered him in a way that, by God, I wished I had died before hearing it! When he realised what he was in, Khālid said: "My Minqarī brother, how could we keep up with them, since we merely imitate them? Or how could we beat them, since we merely follow in their footsteps? Calm down, he belongs to Muqāʿis and the Muqāʿis are for you."[85] I replied: "O Abū Ṣafwān, by God, I cannot blame you for the former and I will continue praising you for the latter!"

(al-Jāḥiẓ, *Bayān* I: 173); Ibn ʿAbdrabbih, *ʿIqd* III: 418.

A28 Khālid ibn Ṣafwān made a grammatical mistake (*laḥana*) in the presence of ʿAbd al-Malik, who said: "A mistake in speech is uglier than (scars caused by) smallpox on face."

(al-Zamakhsharī, *Rabīʿ* I: 648); al-Zamakhsharī, *Rabīʿ* III: 241; al-ʿĀmilī, *Mikhlāt*, p. 10 (no. 36).

A29 Khālid ibn Ṣafwān used to say: If one occupies oneself with searching for a *laḥn* and looking for a rhyme, one forgets the argument.

(Miskawayhi, *Ḥikma*, p. 184).

COMMENTARY: *Laḥn* does not, here, refer to linguistic mistakes, as it usually does, but to (premeditated) manner of speech, e.g., the use of tones or idioms.[86]

---

82 Ibn ʿAbdrabbih, *ʿIqd* III: 415.

83 Cf. A27.

84 For the use of the verb *takallama*, cf. van Ess (1991–97) I: 50–51.

85 Muqāʿis is one of the further ancestors of Khālid, see Chapter 1.4, as well as the name of the subtribe of Tamīm descending from him. See also Ibn Manẓūr, *Lisān* XI: 244, s.v.

86 For the term, see Chapter 2.2.1, Fück (1950): 128–135, and Ullmann (1979).

A30 < *Abū l-Qāsim ʿAlī ibn Ibrāhīm and Abū l-Waḥsh Subayʿ al-Muqriʾ < Rashaʾ ibn Naẓīf < Abū Muslim Muḥammad ibn Aḥmad < Abū Bakr Ibn al-Anbārī < "my father" < Abū Manṣūr al-Ṣāghānī < Abū ʿUbayd < Yazīd < Sufyān ibn Ḥusayn < al-Ḥasan concerning God's, He is noble and majestic, words "He has provided a brook* (sarī) *that runs at your feet"* (*Q 19: 24*): al-Ḥasan said: "By God, he was a *sarī*," meaning Jesus, peace be upon him. Khālid ibn Ṣafwān said to him: "O Abū Saʿīd, the Bedouins name a little stream (*jadwal*) '*sarī*'." Al-Ḥasan admitted: "You are right."

(Ibn ʿAsākir, *Taʾrīkh* XVI: 104); Ibn Manẓūr, *Mukhtaṣar* VII: 359.

A31 < *Ibn Kunāsa < Khālid ibn Ṣafwān*: The East wind (*al-ṣabā*) blows from between the rising of the horns of Aries (al-Sharaṭān) until the Pole-Star. The North wind (*al-shamāl*) blows from between the Pole-Star until the setting of the horns of Aries. The West wind (*al-dabūr*) blows from between the setting of the horns of Aries until the Lower Pole-Star. The South wind (*al-janūb*) blows from between the Lower Pole-Star until the rising of the horns of Aries.

(Ibn al-Ajdābī, *Azmina*, p. 116).

COMMENTARY: Al-Bīrūnī refers to this piece of information, taking Khālid as an authority for there being four basic winds, not six as others would have it.[87] The passage in *Āthār* seems to derive from Ibn Kunāsa (d. 207/822 or 209/824), too. The Kufan scholar wrote a *Kitāb al-Anwāʾ*, from which this passage presumably comes.[88]

4.5 Orator and Wit

A32 Khālid used to say: You will not be truly eloquent until you address your black slave girl during a dark night in an urgent matter in the same way as you would speak in the council of your tribe. The tongue is a member which you have to train. If you neglect it, it will grow weak,[89] just as you strengthen your hand by exercise and your body by lifting stones and other weights. It is like your feet, which will walk when you have accustomed them to walk.

---

87 Al-Bīrūnī, *Āthār*, p. 435, translated in Sachau (1879): 339.

88 See *GAS* VII: 342.

89 Al-Mubarrad has *khāra*, Ibn ʿAbdrabbih *lakina*, and al-Zamakhsharī *ḥāra*. Abū Ṭāhir al-Baghdādī reads *ḥarana* "to be obstinate," which is probably an attempt to form a rhyme with *marana*.

(al-Mubarrad, *Kāmil* II: 20); al-Zamakhsharī, *Rabīʿ* IV: 255 (slightly abbreviated); Ibn ʿAbdrabbih, *ʿIqd* II: 269–270; Abū Ṭāhir al-Baghdādī, *Qānūn*, p. 74 (only a part); ps.-al-Jāḥiẓ, *Maḥāsin*, p. 28 (anonymous).

A33 Someone said to Khālid ibn Ṣafwān: "You speak too long." Khālid replied: "I give long speeches for two reasons: either when speaking briefly would not avail or in order to exercise my tongue. Holding your tongue will make you tongue-tied."

(al-Mubarrad, *Kāmil* II: 20); Ibn ʿAbdrabbih, *ʿIqd* II: 269.

A34 < *Muḥammad ibn Saʿd al-Kurānī* < *ʿAbd al-Wāḥid ibn Ghiyāth* < *Muḥammad ibn Muʿāwiya ibn Abān* < *Khālid ibn Abān*: Khālid ibn Ṣafwān said: "When one makes speeches, the parts of his speech need one another, except in the case of al-Ḥasan (al-Baṣrī). A single expression of his is enough." Someone asked: "O Abū Ṣafwān, give us an example." He replied: "His saying: Death has disgraced the earthly life."

(Wakīʿ, *Akhbār*, p. 239/II: 12).

A34a Someone asked Khālid ibn Ṣafwān: "Who is the most eloquent man?" He replied: "Al-Ḥasan, who said: Death has disgraced the earthly life."

(al-Ābī, *Nathr* VII: 113); Ibn abī l-Ḥadīd, *Sharḥ* V: 489 (variants).

COMMENTARY: This saying by al-Ḥasan al-Baṣrī is also transmitted without reference to Khālid.[90]

A35 A Bedouin observed Khālid delivering a speech and said: "How come this man has not become the lord of his people despite all this eloquence!" Khālid replied: "I withhold my property from them and I dislike the sword."

(al-Tawḥīdī, *Baṣāʾir* VIII: 184, no. 674); al-Ābī, *Nathr* IV: 184.

A36 Khālid ibn Ṣafwān has said: The most eloquent speech is that which has few words but lots of meaning. The best speech is that the beginning of which makes you desire to hear its end.

(Ibn al-Naqīb, *Muqaddima*, p. 19); Ibn Khalaf, *Mawādd*, p. 63.

COMMENTARY: Ibn Khalaf, *Mawādd*, p. 63, gives the second sentence separately as an anonymous saying. Cf. B66.

---

90 E.g., al-Jāḥiẓ, *Bayān* III: 135, and al-Rāghib, *Muḥāḍarāt* IV: 483.

A37 Khālid ibn Ṣafwān: There are two cases in which I do not apologise for incapacity:[91] when I address an ignorant person or when I make a request to someone who will not comply.
(al-Thaʿālibī, *Tamthīl*, p. 271).

COMMENTARY: Cf. B56.

A38 He has said:[92] The best speech is that which is far from restricted and useful to hearers. The speech should neither incline towards too much conciseness, so that its argument is weakened, nor towards blabbering, so that its point is lost.
(al-Waṭwāṭ, *Ghurar*, p. 230).

A39 Shabīb ibn Shayba used to say: "I have never seen a speaker who has better memorised what he had composed nor remembered what he had earlier said than Khālid ibn Ṣafwān. He filled his compositions with metaphors, which seemed impossible to come out from, but then he undid the metaphors into clear words, which were lucid and well explained. The listener did not understand what he was aiming at until Khālid had come to the end."
(al-ʿAskarī, *Ṣināʿatayn* II: 442).

A40 < *Ibrāhīm ibn Ayyūb* < *ʿAbdallāh ibn Muslim ibn Qutayba and ʿAlī ibn Sulaymān al-Akhfash* < *Muḥammad ibn Yazīd*: Thābit Quṭna[93] had been appointed governor in some part of Khurasan. He ascended the pulpit on a Friday in order to give a sermon but found himself dumbfounded and unable to speak. Then he said: "God will give facility after difficulty[94] and eloquence after incapability. You need more an Emir who acts than an Emir who speaks.

Though I be not an orator among you,
my sword is eloquent when the battle rages!"

This speech of his came to the ears of Khālid ibn Ṣafwān – or, according to others, al-Aḥnaf ibn Qays – who said: "By God, that pulpit has never been

91 I.e., for not using my rhetorical talent.

92 The preceeding saying is attributed to Khālid, so technically *qāla* should here refer back to him. However, al-Waṭwāṭ is often careless with his *qālas*, so the attribution to Khālid is suspect. The following saying in the *Ghurar* (A89) is also attributed to Khālid, which makes it possible that this is also to be understood as a saying of his.

93 Minor poet, d. 110/728, see *EI2*, s.v. (El Achèche).

94 Q 65: 7.

ascended by a more eloquent preacher than he with these words of his. If any oration could move me from my town to visit an orator I admire these words would have done it." This is more in accordance with Khālid ibn Ṣafwān than with al-Aḥnaf.

(al-Iṣfahānī, *Aghānī* XIII: 51); ʿAbd al-Qādir al-Baghdādī, *Khizāna* IX: 578–579.

COMMENTARY: Thābit's speech is also transmitted without reference to Khālid.[95] Al-Murtaḍā transmits a similar speech attributed to ʿUthmān ibn ʿAffān in his *Amālī*.[96]

A41 < *Muḥammad ibn Ismāʿīl ibn Yaʿqūb* < *Muḥammad ibn Salām* < *ʿAbd al-Qāhir Ibn al-Sarī*:[97] Iyās ibn Muʿāwiya and Khālid ibn Ṣafwān were sitting together. Iyās said: "O Abū Ṣafwān, we should not[98] sit together." [Khālid asked: "And why so, Abū Wāthila?"] He replied: "Because you do not want to be quiet and I do not like to listen!"

(Wakīʿ, *Akhbār*, pp. 217–218/I: 346–347);[99] al-Rāghib, *Muḥāḍarāt* I: 69 (slight variants); al-Mubarrad, *Kāmil* II: 44.

COMMENTARY: Al-Jāḥiẓ and al-Ḥuṣrī give the protagonists as Iyās ibn Muʿāwiya and ʿAbdallāh ibn Shubruma, the latter saying the punch line.[100]

A42 < *Aḥmad ibn Saʿīd al-Dimashqī* < *al-Zubayr* < *Abū l-Ḥasan al-Madāʾinī*: Someone said to Khālid ibn Ṣafwān: "Welcome, Abū Ṣafwān!" He replied: "May your valley be spacious and your company noble and may dark clouds pour rain down upon you!" The man asked: "How was your travel?" Khālid replied:

> In the ample grace of God, of which we only knew increase, until we were in the pass of al-Samāwa[101] when God sent upon us an icy wind, the

---

95 E.g., Ibn Qutayba, *Shiʿr*, pp. 400–401, and Ibn ʿAbdrabbih, *ʿIqd* IV: 147–148 (with some other similar stories).

96 Al-Murtaḍā, *Amālī* II: 103.

97 Wakīʿ adds a short note on Iyās before the story, which shows that the focus of the story is on Iyās, rather than on Khālid.

98 The negation *lā* is missing from both editions. Also the following line by Khālid has been dropped from the editions and is here added from al-Mubarrad, *Kāmil*.

99 Immediately after the story Wakīʿ gives another *isnād* for "a similar story about Iyās and Khālid," narrated by al-Ramadī < Muḥammad ibn Salām < "our friends."

100 Al-Jāḥiẓ, *Bayān* I: 98, and al-Ḥuṣrī, *Zahr*, p. 199. ʿAbdallāh ibn Shubruma was a Kufan *qāḍī* and died in 144/762. See al-Jāḥiẓ, *Bayān* I: 98, note 2. A slightly different version with these characters is also given in al-Jāḥiẓ, *Bayān* II: 315.

101 Al-Washshāʾ has Qubbat al-Sāq. Al-Bakrī, s.v. Bīsha, reads *bīshat* for *thaniyya*.

beasts entered their burrows, and the birds turned[102] to their nests. The horizons became red because of it, and I could neither see a shining road-post nor a rising star. I was like a confused man, not finding his camel.[103] I was like that when there approached to me riders[104] on their horses, which were like branches of *shawḥaṭ*,[105] approaching like falcons upon their prey, noble lords on their backs, like luxurious swords. Behind them were salukis with bent ankles[106] and lean behinds. We then passed by some banana (groves)[107] belonging to ʿAbd al-Malik ibn Marwān, where the bananas were like corpses of jerboas. Their bunches were pitch-black. What a noble place it was to come to, jealously guarded by its owners. We dismounted and then picked and ate, roasted and cooked.[108]

(al-Zubayr ibn Bakkār, *Muwaffaqiyyāt*, pp. 143–144, no. 80); al-Washshāʾ, *Fāḍil*, pp. 193–194;[109] al-Bakrī, *Muʿjam*, p. 294 (only a small part); al-Rāghib, *Muḥāḍarāt* II: 406 (only the beginning); Ibn al-ʿAdīm, *Bughya* VII: 56–57.[110]

COMMENTARY: The whole speech is composed in archaic Bedouin vocabulary.

A43 Khālid ibn Ṣafwān went to the Garden (al-Bustān). When he came back, he was asked: "Where do you come from, O Abū Ṣafwān?" He said he was coming from the Garden, and someone asked: "What did you have?" Khālid replied: "We were brought two bright red loaves with smooth surface and well baked. The wind made them flutter, so thin they were. There was also a jug of water. The bread was as if it had escaped from butter, greese and fat dribbling

---

102 Al-Zubayr reads *infarajat*, but I prefer al-Washshāʾ's *inʿarajat*.

103 Al-Washshāʾ reads: "like a camel in a crowd: if it takes a step forward it will fall down, and if it remains behind it will perish."

104 Al-Washshāʾ reads *fitya min banī Marwān*.

105 Cf. Lane (1863–93), s.v.

106 Al-Washshāʾ adds: "long necks".

107 Al-Washshāʾ reads *bi-mirbad* for *bi-mawz*. Knowing Khālid's fascination with bananas (cf. B17, B58, B113) *bi-mawz* seems the preferable reading. The continuation is somewhat corrupt in al-Washshāʾ.

108 Al-Washshāʾ ends his version with: "Then we left the place. Farewell to all real life after that!"

109 < Muḥammad ibn Mūsā < al-Aṣmaʿī.

110 < Abū Jaʿfar Yaḥyā ibn ʿAbdallāh ibn Muḥammad ibn ʿAlī al-Dāmaghānī < "my father" < Abū Ṭāhir Aḥmad ibn Sawwār < Abū l-Ḥusayn Muḥmmad ibn ʿAbd al-Wāḥid ibn ʿAlī ibn Rizma < Abū Saʿīd al-Sīrāfī < Muḥammad ibn Manṣūr ibn Mazyad < al-Zubayr < ʿUmar ibn abī Bakr al-Mawṣilī < ʿAbdallāh ibn abī ʿUbayda ibn Muḥammad ibn ʿAmmār ibn Yāsir.

from it. There were also vegetables, which had been picked when they were ripe, verdant and radiant, fresh and tender-skinned, with some wine that had settled in an earthen jug, over which the spider had woven her web and the dregs had been lying in peace. The wine was so pure that had you thrown it on the sun, it would have become dark, and if a snake had smelled it, it would have drawn blood from its nose. After that we were brought some dry dates, which fire had done to perfection and farmers had picked. They had fine pits and noble skin. From inside, they were red and their skin was peeling off and when broken they were crisp. That is what I call life!"

(Ibn Ḥamdūn, *Tadhkira* IX: 117, no. 290).

A44 It is said that Khālid ibn Ṣafwān entered on Yazīd ibn al-Muhallab when he was eating. Yazīd said: "Abū Ṣafwān, come closer and have some." Khālid replied: "May God bless the Emir! I have eaten a meal I will never forget!" Yazīd asked what he had eaten, and Khālid replied: "I came to my estate at the time of planting and cultivating. I walked around until the sun was at its hottest and then I decided to take a rest. I went into a well-aired room of mine in a garden. Its doors were open and the soil around had been sprinkled with water. Various flowers covered the ground: fragrant basils, odiferous jasmines, radiant daisies, and verdant roses.

I was brought ricebread, like pieces of carnelian, white-bellied, blue-eyed, and black-sided Bunānī fish,[111] plump and thick, with spices[112] and vinegars, fish-sauce (*mury*) and herbs. Further, I was brought yellow dates, clear, without spots. Hands had not blemished them nor had they been smashed when measured. I ate now from this, now from that."

Yazīd replied: "Ibn Ṣafwān, a thousand *jarībs* of your sayings[113] is better than a thousand *jarībs* of seed!"

(al-Mubarrad, *Kāmil* IV: 112–113); Abū Hilāl al-ʿAskarī, *Dīwān*, p. 563 (variants);[114] Ibn Manẓūr, *Lisān* VI: 391a (s.v. SNSQ);[115] al-Ābī, *Nathr* VI: 42.

---

111 A note in al-Mubarrad's *Kāmil* identifies the fish as fish coming from the Basran area of Bunāna, cf. Yāqūt, *Muʿjam* I: 497. One might also consider an emendation to *bunnī*, for which see Lane (1863–93), s.v.

112 According to Ibn Manẓūr the word is explained by al-Mubarrad himself as *milḥ*. This explanation, however, is not found in the edition of *Kāmil*. For *duqqa*, see Dozy (1881), s.v.

113 Al-Mubarrad adds here *mazrūʿ* "sown", but I prefer to ignore this, as al-Ābī did, too.

114 < Abū Aḥmad < al-Jalūdī < Muḥammad ibn Zakariyyā < Mahdī ibn Sābiq < Shabīb.

115 The whole article in the *Lisān* (< al-Azharī, *Tahdhīb*) consists only of this story, ultimately deriving from al-Mubarrad's version.

COMMENTARY: Al-ʿAskarī's version probably comes from al-Jalūdī's lost monograph. Van Gelder briefly discusses this story.[116]

A45 < Abū l-ʿAynāʾ < al-Qaḥdhamī: Khālid ibn Ṣafwān has said: Yazīd ibn al-Muhallab had imprisoned a nephew of mine. I went to his palace arranging my words, like a young woman arranges the beads of her necklace for a festival. I was given permission to enter. In his presence there was a slave girl, beautiful as a wild cow. In her hand she held a golden censer. When I saw her, I lost all the words I had been preparing and could only think of two sentences, which I said: "I never saw the rust on a helmet or the fragrance of amber suit anyone better than you." Yazīd asked what it was I wanted, and I replied: "There is a nephew of mine in prison." He said: "He will be home before you." When I came home he was already there.

(al-Tawḥīdī, *Baṣāʾir* VI: 88, no. 293); al-Zamakhsharī, *Rabīʿ* II: 279; Ibn abī l-Ḥadīd, *Sharḥ* V: 689 (abbreviated).

4.6 Family

A46 (Al-Farazdaq) said about Khālid ibn Ṣafwān and his mother Arwā bint Sulaym, whose father was one of the cunning Arabs:

> Khālid is just like other Ahtamites
> before him, a farting old goat with thick cheeks.
>
> We are well aware of your (grand)father Sulaym's place,
> and you yourself descend from a short-legged Ḥīran.
>
> Abū l-Zard belongs to us and you know his place,
> like a sword belt with its buckles.
>
> A short-legged ferret is not to be compared
> with someone whose stature is raised on pillars.

(al-Farazdaq, *Dīwān*, ed. al-Ṣāwī, p. 814).

A47 Khālid ibn Ṣafwān was asked about a son of his. He replied: "He spares me my earthly troubles and leaves me free to think of my hereafter."

(al-Ābī, *Nathr* IV: 196).

---

116 Van Gelder (2000): 57–58.

A48 *Abū l-Qāsim Ismāʿīl ibn Aḥmad < Aḥmad ibn Muḥammad ibn al-Naqqūr and ʿAbd al-Bāqī ibn Muḥammad ibn Ghālib < Abū Ṭāhir al-Mukhallaṣ < ʿUbaydallāh ibn ʿAbd al-Raḥmān < Zakariyyā ibn Yaḥyā < al-Aṣmaʿī < Yūnus al-Naḥwī:*[117] We came to Khālid ibn Ṣafwān to console him on the death of his son Ribʿī. We were grieving on his behalf. When we came in he was saying:

It makes it easier to bear this pain
that I will join him in his abode today or tomorrow.

(Ibn ʿAsākir, Taʾrīkh XVI: 114); Ibn Manẓūr, *Mukhtaṣar* VII: 364; al-Marzubān, *Nūr*, p. 53; al-Suyūṭī, *Maqāmāt*, p. 979.

COMMENTARY: The verse is by ʿUmar ibn Ḥafṣ.[118] The verse is also said to have been quoted by Yaḥyā ibn Manṣūr to console Sulaymān ibn ʿAlī.[119]

A49 < *al-Madāʾinī:* A son of Khālid ibn Ṣafwān's, named Abū l-Ḥuṣayn, died, and Khālid said: "God have mercy on Abū l-Ḥuṣayn! By God, I knew him to be dutiful towards his parents, respectful to his kin, and far away from what is loathed in youths." Abū l-ʿAbbās (al-Mubarrad) has said: I have been told this story also in another form, namely:

A son of his, named Nuʿaym, died, and Khālid said: "I will never forget Nuʿaym!" In this version, it is said (that Khālid said): "When he died I remembered the words of the poet" – namely, Abū Khirāsh al-Hudhalī:[120]

By God, I shall never forget the slain I was deprived of
by the side of Qawsā,[121] as long as I will walk on earth.

Then he realized that he would forget him and said:

Nay, traces of wounds will be effaced and we will be
concerned with the closer, although the gone be greater.

(al-Mubarrad, *Taʿāzī*, pp. 208–209).

117 *GAS* IX: 49–51, Yūnus ibn Ḥabīb (d. 182/798).
118 See al-Zajjājī, *Amālī*, p. 9.
119 See al-Jāḥiẓ, *Bayān* IV: 97. See also al-Zawzanī, *Ḥamāsa* I: 224 (no. 71, anonymous).
120 D. before 24/644, see *GAS* II: 257.
121 Cf. Yāqūt, *Muʿjam* IV: 413, where four verses of the eight-verse poem are quoted. Cf. also al-Sukkarī, *Dīwān al-Hudhaliyyīn* III: 1230–1231 (no. 14: 2–3).

A50 The relations between Khālid ibn Ṣafwān and Shabīb ibn Shayba were such as to lead to alienation after competition and mutual envy because they shared the same profession and were relatives and neighbours. It used to be said that were they not the wisest[122] men of Tamīm they would have quarreled with each other like a lion and a leopard.
(al-Jāḥiẓ, *Bayān* I: 47)

4.7 Miser

A51 They say: Dhirāʿ al-Dharrāʿ (Cubit the Measurer) was with Khālid ibn Ṣafwān. A chicken was brought to Khālid whereas Dhirāʿ only got some olives. When he saw his guest staring at the chicken, Khālid asked: "You seem interested in it?" Dhirāʿ replied: "Why shouldn't I?" Khālid said: "But then we would have equal shares in *my* property!"
(al-Jāḥiẓ, *Bukhalāʾ*, p. 151).[123]

A51a A Basran measurer (*dhāriʿ*) has said: Khālid called for me, and I divided some property of his and reckoned it. At noon, he called for lunch. He was brought a chicken whereas I only got some olives and onion. Then he asked: "Would you have liked some of this chicken?" I replied: "Would it hurt you, if I did?" Khālid said: "But then we would have equal shares in *my* property! What would the use of it being mine then be?"
(Ibn Ḥamdūn, *Tadhkira* II: 329–330, no. 860); al-Ābī, *Nathr* III: 278.

COMMENTARY: Ibn Ḥamdūn's *Tadhkira* may retain an earlier form of the story. If so, then it tells us something about al-Jāḥiẓ's way with his material. The original speaks of an anonymous measurer, who in al-Jāḥiẓ's version becomes Cubit the Measurer.

A52 < *al-Aṣmaʿī*: The misers of the Arabs were four, all of them poets: al-Ḥuṭay'a, Ḥumayd al-Arqaṭ al-Saʿdī, Abū l-Aswad al-Du'alī, and Khālid ibn Ṣafwān al-Tamīmī. (…) Once Khālid ibn Ṣafwān fell ill. The doctor prescribed him a chicken, but Khālid said: "Why are you speaking of chickens?" The doctor was adamant, and finally Khālid bought a chicken. When he had eaten some of it, a Qurashī happened to call upon him. Khālid was afraid lest the man might

122 One is tempted to read *aḥlam* "most gentle" for the edition's *aḥkam*.
123 Translated in Serjeant (1997): 131.

want to join him to finish the chicken off and hastened to say: "We are having half of this chicken for lunch and the rest for supper." Then he recited:

> You treat with courtesy the vicious ever-changing fate,
> but who does not treat so his own life is no discerning man.

The Qurashī went his way, reciting:

> At old age, I learned to gaze at eating,
> since Khālid mistreated me, the miser!

(al-Marzubānī, *Nūr*, pp. 146–147); Ibn al-ʿAdīm, *Bughya* VII: 70–71.[124]

COMMENTARY: Al-Iṣfahānī and Yāqūt also mention the four misers.[125]

A53 It was said to Khālid ibn Ṣafwān: "What is the matter with you? You do not spend, although you have a vast fortune." Khālid replied: "Time is vaster than my fortune." They said: "And you think you will live the whole of it?" Khālid said: "I fear I may not die in the very beginning."

(Ibn Qutayba, *ʿUyūn* II: 40); Ibn Ḥamdūn, *Tadhkira* II: 320 (no. 828); Ibn ʿĀṣim, *Ḥadāʾiq*, p. 291; Ibn ʿAbdrabbih, *ʿIqd* VI: 197; Ibn ʿAsākir, *Taʾrīkh* XVI: 113–114;[126] Ibn al-ʿAdīm, *Bughya* VII: 67;[127] Ibn Manẓūr, *Mukhtaṣar* VII: 364. *Only the first question and its reply*: al-Zamakhsharī, *Rabīʿ* IV: 148; Ibn abī ʿAwn, *Ajwiba*, p. 94 (no. 552); al-Tawḥīdī, *Baṣāʾir* III: 184 (no. 662); al-Rāghib, *Muḥāḍarāt* II: 606; al-Ṣafadī, *Wāfī* XIII: 255; al-Ibshīhī, *al-Mustaṭraf* I: 252.[128]

COMMENTARY: For further references, see Marzolph, (1992) II: 143 (no. 160).

124 < al-Sharīf Abū Hāshim ʿAbd al-Muṭṭalib ibn al-Faḍl al-Hāshimī < Abū Shujāʿ ʿUmar ibn Muḥammad ibn ʿAbdallāh al-Bisṭāmī < al-Aṣmaʿī.

125 Al-Iṣfahānī, *Aghānī* II: 46 < Ibn Durayd < Abū Ḥātim < Abū ʿUbayda; Yāqūt, *Irshād* III: 267 and 279. Cf. also Chapter 2.3.3.

126 < Muḥammad ibn Mūsā al-Baṣrī < Muḥammad ibn Sallām al-Jumaḥī.

127 < Ibn Marwān < Muḥammad ibn Mūsā al-Baṣrī < Muḥammad ibn Sallām al-Jumaḥī.

128 Al-Ibshīhī, *al-Mustaṭraf* I: 252, begins with B60a.

4.8 Sayings

A54 Khālid ibn Ṣafwān has said: There are three steps in travelling. The first is decision, the second preparation, and the third departure. The most difficult of the three is the decision.

(al-Thaʿālibī, *Tamthīl*, p. 272); al-Ābī, *Nathr* IV: 154; Ibn ʿAbd al-Barr, *Bahja* I: 226 (slight variants).

A55 Khālid ibn Ṣafwān has said: Various are the medicines of him who does not understand the cause of his malady.

(al-Tawḥīdī, *Baṣāʾir* VIII: 91, no. 310).

A55a Khālid ibn Ṣafwān has said: Various are the mounts of him who does not own one.

(al-Ābī, *Nathr* IV: 165).

COMMENTARY: Both versions are possible as such, but I assume al-Tawḥīdī's version to represent an earlier form of the saying. Al-Ābī's version would then have been born by misreading *dāʾihi* as *dābba* with subsequent modifications in the rest of the story. In any case, one of the versions has been caused by misreading a *written* version of the other.

A56 Khālid ibn Ṣafwān went by a man, who had been crucified by the Caliph, and said: "Obedience made him grow and disobedience reaped him."

(Ibn ʿAbdrabbih, *ʿIqd* II: 269).

A57 Khālid has said: People are of three kinds: scholars, orators, and men of letters (*udabāʾ*). Then there is the riffraff, which causes prices to go up, crowds the marketplaces, and spoils the water.

(Ibn ʿAbdrabbih, *ʿIqd* II: 293).

COMMENTARY: Al-Tawḥīdī narrates how Muʿāwiya asked Ṣaʿṣaʿa ibn Ṣūḥān (d. 60/680) about people, and he replied with five (or four) categories, different from Khālid's, but ending with the same condescending note on the riffraff.[129] Marlow discusses and partly translates this saying. She also refers to variants attributed to al-Faḍl ibn Yaḥyā al-Barmakī and al-Aḥnaf ibn Qays.[130]

---

129 Al-Tawḥīdī, *Baṣāʾir* I: 45 (no. 110).

130 Marlow (1997): 36–38.

A58 Khālid ibn Ṣafwān has said: People are different.[131] Some are like dogs, always growling at others, some like pigs, always dirty and soiled, and some like monkeys, always laughing to themselves.

(al-Rāghib, *Muḥāḍarāt* I: 280); al-Waṭwāṭ, *Ghurar*, p. 589.

A59 Khālid ibn Ṣafwān described dates: They are a gift to old people, a pacifier for babies, and Mary's food after she had given birth to Jesus.

(Ibn Manẓūr, *Lisān* IV: 60, s.v. KhRS); Ibn Durayd, *Jamhara*, p. 584.[132]

COMMENTARY: Al-Ābī has an anonymous man describe raisins in somewhat similar terms in a discussion on the merits of dates and raisins in the presence of the Caliph ʿUmar.[133] Cf. also B81.

A60 Khālid ibn Ṣafwān used to say: To accept the slanderer's report is worse than slandering itself. To slander is to show, but to accept is to allow. The one who shows is not as bad as the one who accepts and allows.

(al-Tawḥīdī, *Imtāʿ* II: 120).

COMMENTARY: A longer version is attributed to Dhū l-Riyāsatayn by al-Ḥuṣrī.[134]

A61 It is said that a Bedouin came to Basra and said to Khālid ibn Ṣafwān: "Tell me who is the lord of this town." Khālid replied: "Al-Ḥasan ibn abī l-Ḥasan." The Bedouin asked: "Is he an Arab or a *mawlā*?" When Khālid told he was a *mawlā*, the Bedouin asked: "By what did he become a lord?" Khālid said: "People need him because of their religious matters whereas he does not need them for their wealth." The Bedouin replied: "This is lordship enough!"

(Ibn Ḥamdūn, *Tadhkira* II: 94, no. 179); Ibn al-Jawzī, *Ādāb*, p. 24; al-Zamakhsharī, *Rabīʿ* III: 178.

A61a Al-Ḥajjāj asked Khālid ibn Ṣafwān: "Who is the lord of the people of Basra?" Khālid replied that it was al-Ḥasan. Al-Ḥajjāj asked: "And how may that be, he being a *mawlā*?" Khālid answered: "People need him because of their

131 Al-Waṭwāṭ reads *ajyāf* "cadavers," but al-Rāghib's reading is better, cf. the proverb *al-nās akhyāf*, e.g., al-Maydānī, *Majmaʿ* III: 394 (no. 4274). The saying is also used, e.g., by ʿAbd al-Ḥamīd al-Kātib, *Rasāʾil*, p. 289 (no. 39).

132 Attributed to "a Bedouin" and with slight variants.

133 Al-Ābī, *Nathr* VI/1: 44, cf. also VI/1: 48.

134 Al-Ḥuṣrī, *Zahr*, p. 355. For al-Faḍl ibn Sahl Dhū l-Riyāsatayn (d. 202/817), see *EI3*, s.v. (H. Yücesoy).

religious matters whereas he does not need them for their wealth. I have seen none among the nobles of Basra who does not wish to join his circle in order to listen to him and write down his teachings." Al-Ḥajjāj said: "By God, that is what I call lordship."

(al-Būnisī, *Kanz*, p. 93).

A62 *Abū l-Qāsim ʿAbd al-Ghanī ibn Sulaymān* < *Abū ʿAbdallāh Muḥammad ibn Ḥamd* < *Abū l-Ḥasan al-Farrāʾ* < *ʿAbd al-ʿAzīz ibn al-Ḥasan* < *Abū Muḥammad al-Ḥasan ibn Ismāʿīl* < *Aḥmad ibn Marwān* < *Muḥammad ibn ʿAbd al-ʿAzīz* < *al-Ziyādī* < *al-Aṣmaʿī*: It was said to Khālid ibn Ṣafwān: "How far did al-Ḥasan (al-Baṣrī)'s knowledge extend?" Khālid replied: "He did not need others."

(Ibn al-ʿAdīm, *Bughya* VII: 62).

A63 Khālid ibn Ṣafwān was asked why al-Aḥnaf became the lord of his people. Khālid replied: "Because of his excellent control of himself."

(Ibn Qutayba, *ʿUyūn* I: 327); al-Zamakhsharī, *Rabīʿ* II: 520.

COMMENTARY: How and why al-Aḥnaf ibn Qays attained his position is a recurrent theme in Arabic literature.[135] See also B45, B45a, and B46.

A64 Khālid ibn Ṣafwān has said: al-Aḥnaf used to run away from nobility, but nobility kept following him.

(Ibn Qutayba, *ʿUyūn* I: 331); al-Zamakhsharī, *Rabīʿ* III: 181; al-Waṭwāṭ, *Ghurar*, p. 35; al-Ṣafadī, *Wāfī* XVI: 357; Ibn ʿAsākir, *Taʾrīkh* XXIV: 317.[136]

A65 Khālid ibn Ṣafwān was asked: "Which one do you love best, your brother or your friend?" Khālid replied: "I only love my brother if he is also my friend."

(al-Zamakhsharī, *Rabīʿ* I: 440); al-Washshāʾ, *Muwashshā*, p. 41 (slightly different); Ibn Nubāta, *Sarḥ*, p. 239 (attributed to ʿAbd al-Ḥamīd); Nakhshabī, *Gulrīz*, p. 66 (variants).

COMMENTARY: A similar saying is attributed to the legendary Sasanian Vizier Buzurjmihr by Ibn Qutayba.[137]

---

135 Cf., e.g., Ibn al-Faraḍī, *Alqāb*, pp. 13–14.

136 < Abū l-Qāsim ibn al-ʿAlawī < Abū l-Ḥasan al-Muʿaddil < al-Ḥasan ibn Ismāʿīl < Aḥmad ibn Marwān < Ismāʿīl ibn Yūnus < al-Riyāshī < al-Aṣmaʿī.

137 Ibn Qutayba, *ʿUyūn* III: 9.

A66 Khālid ibn Ṣafwān said to his son: "O son, I admonish you concerning two things. As long as you keep to them, you will be fine: your money for your subsistance and your religion for your hereafter."

(Ibn ʿAbdrabbih, *ʿIqd* III: 29); al-Zamakhsharī, *Rabīʿ* IV: 147 (slightly different); al-Rāghib, *Muḥāḍarāt* II: 491.

A67 Khālid ibn Ṣafwān used to say: Beware of your eye because it betrays more easily than your tongue.

(Ibn Ḥamdūn, *Tadhkira* III: 155, no. 459); al-Rāghib, *Muḥāḍarāt* II: 402 (anonymous);[138] Ibn ʿAbd al-Barr, *Bahja* III: 181; Ḥamza al-Iṣfahānī, *Durra*, p. 268.[139]

COMMENTARY: Cf. A68.

A68 Khālid ibn Ṣafwān: Many a glance speaks more clearly than the tongue.

(al-Thaʿālibī, *Tamthīl*, p. 250); al-Thaʿālibī, *Tamaththul*, p. 648.

COMMENTARY: Cf. A67.

A69 He (i.e., Khālid) said: The one who should more than anyone else forgive is the one best capable of punishing. The most deficient one in reason is the man who wrongs those below him.

(Yāqūt, *Irshād* III: 280); Ibn ʿAsākir, *Taʾrīkh* XVI: 114;[140] Ibn Manẓūr, *Mukhtaṣar* VII: 364.

COMMENTARY: In Yāqūt, this is listed among a number of wise sayings (*ḥikam*) by Khālid ibn Ṣafwān.

A70 < *Abū Bakr al-Anbārī* < *Aḥmad ibn Yaḥyā al-Naḥwī* < *ʿAbdallāh ibn Shabīb*: Shabīb ibn Shayba said to Khālid ibn Ṣafwān: "Which of your brothers do you love the best?" Khālid replied: "The one who repairs my faults, forgives my slips, and accepts my apologies."

---

138 A longer version, where this is quoted as a proverb.

139 On the saying *rubba ʿayn anamm min lisān*.

140 < Abū l-Qāsim Zāhir ibn Ṭāhir < Abū Bakr al-Bayhaqī < Abū l-Qāsim ʿAbd al-Khāliq ibn ʿAlī *al-muʾadhdhin* < Muḥammad ibn ʿAlī ibn al-Ḥusayn in Bukhara < Aḥmad ibn ʿAbdallāh ibn Naṣr al-Dimashqī < Wurayza ibn Muḥammad < Maʿmar ibn Shabīb < al-Haytham.

(al-Qālī, *Amālī* I: 195); Ibn Qutayba, *ʿUyūn* III: 23; al-Zamakhsharī, *Rabīʿ* I: 445; Ibn ʿAsākir, *Taʾrīkh* XVI: 107–108 (four versions);[141] Ibn al-ʿAdīm, *Bughya* VII: 61;[142] Ibn Manẓūr, *Mukhtaṣar* VII: 362; al-Mubarrad, *Kāmil* II: 167; al-Tawḥīdī, *Baṣāʾir* VIII: 113 (no. 435); al-ʿĀmilī, *Mikhlāt*, p. 256 (no. 5); al-Waṭwāṭ, *Ghurar*, p. 542; Ibn ʿAbd al-Barr, *Bahja* II: 708; Ibn Ḥamdūn, *Tadhkira* IV: 360 (no. 913); Yāqūt al-Mustaʿṣimī, *Asrār*, p. 160 (no. 418); al-Ābī, *Nathr* IV: 170; al-Ābī, *Uns*, p. 50 (no. 10); Ibn al-Buḥturī, *Uns*, p. 172 (no. 388); al-Washshāʾ, *Muwashshā*, p. 33; al-Naḥḥās, *Ṣināʿa*, p. 228 (anonymous);[143] Abū Ṭāhir al-Baghdādī, *Qānūn*, p. 58 (anonymous); al-Dajājī, *Safaṭ*, pp. 28–29; al-Māwardī, *Adab*, p. 179.

A71 Among the sayings of Khālid is: Keep company with persons whose company embellishes you. If you serve them, they protect you, and if you become impoverished, they will provide for you. If they see a good deed, they keep account of it, but if they see a bad one, they hide and veil it. It need not be feared that misfortunes come from them and their manners are not at variance (with yours).

(Ibn ʿAbd al-Barr, *Bahja* II: 707); Ibn ʿAsākir, *Taʾrīkh* XVI: 108 (no. 11).

COMMENTARY: Ibn ʿAsākir and Ibn Manẓūr attribute this to "a sage" (*awṣā ḥakīm waladahu*), and Khālid only transmits his words.[144] Similar admonitions are attributed to various sages.[145]

---

141 1) < Abū l-Qāsim Ismāʿīl ibn ʿAlī ibn al-Ḥusayn al-Ḥammāmī < Abū ʿAlī al-Ḥasan ibn ʿUmar ibn al-Ḥasan ibn Yūnus < Abū l-Ḥasan ʿAlī ibn al-Qāsim ibn al-Ḥasan al-Najjād < Abū Rawq Aḥmad ibn Muḥammad ibn Bakr < ʿAbdallāh ibn Shabīb al-Makkī; 2) Abū l-Qāsim ibn al-Mustamlī < Abū Bakr al-Bayhaqī < Abū Zakariyyā ibn Abī Isḥāq < Muḥammad ibn Muḥammad *al-adīb* < al-Ṣūlī < Abū Qilāba al-Raqāshī < al-Aṣmaʿī; 3) Abū l-Qāsim ibn ʿAlī ibn Ibrāhīm < Rashaʾ ibn Naẓīf < al-Ḥasan ibn Ismāʿīl < Aḥmad ibn Marwān < Ibrāhīm al-Ḥarbī < Abū Naṣr < al-Aṣmaʿī; and 4) Abū Saʿd Muḥammad ibn Muḥammad ibn Aḥmad al-Muṭarriz and Abū l-Qāsim Maḥmūd ibn Aḥmad ibn al-Ḥasan from him in Tabriz < Abū Bakr Aḥmad ibn Jaʿfar ibn Muḥammad al-Faqīh < Abū l-Ḥasan ʿAlī ibn ʿAbdallāh ibn Muḥammad < Aḥmad ibn Muḥammad ibn Bakr < al-ʿAbbās ibn al-Faraj < ʿAbdallāh ibn Shabīb al-Makkī.

142 < Abū l-Ḥasan ʿAlī ibn ʿAbd al-Munʿim ibn ʿAlī ibn Barakāt ibn al-Ḥaddād < Yūsuf ibn Ādam al-Marāghī < Muḥammad ibn Manṣūr al-Samʿānī < *al-shaykh* Abū Saʿd Muḥammad ibn Muḥammad ibn Muḥammad al-Muṭarriz < Abū Bakr Aḥmad ibn Jaʿfar ibn Muḥammad al-Faqīh < Abū l-Ḥasan ʿAlī ibn ʿAbdallāh ibn Muḥammad < Aḥmad ibn Muḥammad ibn Bakr < al-ʿAbbās ibn al-Faraj < ʿAbdallāh ibn Shabīb al-Makkī.

143 But shortly before there is another saying by Khālid.

144 Ibn ʿAsākir, *Taʾrīkh* XVI: 108; Ibn Manẓūr, *Mukhtaṣar* VII: 362.

145 Cf., e.g., al-Thaʿālibī, *Tarjama*, p. 108 (ʿAlī ibn abī Ṭālib admonishing al-Ḥārith al-Hamadhānī in a lengthy speech), and Ibn Qutayba, *ʿUyūn* III: 6–7 (ʿAlqama ibn Labīd al-ʿUṭāridī admonishing his son).

A72 He (Khālid) has said: Be generous with your property to your friends, with your joyful countenance and greeting to your acquaintances, with your help and friendly appearance to common people, and with your justness to your enemies, but be stingy with your religion and reputation to each and everyone!

(Ibn ʿAsākir, *Taʾrīkh* XVI: 112);[146] Ibn Manẓūr, *Mukhtaṣar* VII: 363; Ibn al-Muqaffaʿ, *Adab*, p. 65 (slight variants, anonymous); Yāqūt, *Irshād* III: 280.

A73 Someone said to Khālid: "Teach me how to greet my friends." Khālid replied: "Neither overdo it to hypocrisy nor fail to give them their due."

(al-Tawḥīdī, *Baṣāʾir* VII: 152, no. 473); Ibn Ḥamdūn, *Tadhkira* IV: 365 (no. 937); al-Zamakhsharī, *Rabīʿ* II: 298; al-Naḥḥās, *Ṣināʿa*, p. 228; al-Naḥḥās, *ʿUmda*, p. 322 (no. 1048); Yāqūt al-Mustaʿṣimī, *Asrār*, p. 80 (no. 163); al-Ābī, *Nathr* IV: 211 (anonymous); Ibn Shams al-Khilāfa, *Ādāb*, p. 28.

COMMENTARY: Cf. A96.

A74 Two friends passed by Khālid ibn Ṣafwān. One of them turned to him while the other passed him by (without turning to him). Someone asked him about their behaviour and Khālid replied: "The one turned to me for his own excellence, whilst the other passed me by, being certain of our love."

(al-Tawḥīdī, *Baṣāʾir* IX: 158, no. 521); al-Tawḥīdī, *Ṣadāqa*, p. 58;[147] al-Zamakhsharī, *Rabīʿ* I: 449; al-Ābī, *Uns*, p. 82 (no. 107); al-Dajājī, *Safaṭ*, p. 39.

A75 Khālid ibn Ṣafwān has said: The most impotent of men is the one who falls short of getting friends. Yet even more impotent is the man who loses those he had won.

(al-Māwardī, *Adab*, p. 162); al-Thaʿālibī (attr.), *Tarjama*, p. 64 (anonymous).

A76 Khālid ibn Ṣafwān has said: The tongue of man is his best intercessor and his most effective weapon against his enemies. Through it he attains love and cuts off hatred.

(al-Tawḥīdī, *Baṣāʾir* II: 165, no. 513); al-Waṭwāṭ, *Ghurar*, p. 185.[148]

---

146 Implicitly with the same *isnād* as A80a.

147 With a variant mentioned in a marginal addition to the manuscript.

148 Anonymous, but the previous saying is attributed to Khālid.

A77 Khālid ibn Ṣafwān has said: I am sometimes so weary that I am sick of myself and would hope that my head be taken from me and returned to me only once every week.

(Ibn Ḥamdūn, *Tadhkira* II: 252, no. 654); al-Rāghib, *Muḥāḍarāt* I: 280.

COMMENTARY: Cf. B111.

A78 Khālid ibn Ṣafwān has said: If a governor makes you his brother, make him your lord. Let not your familiarity with him cause any inadvertence or negligence.

(al-Tawḥīdī, *Baṣāʾir* V: 154, no. 509); Yāqūt, *Irshād* III: 279–280; Ibn Razīn, *Ādāb*, p. 119 (no. 170); Ibn ʿAsākir, *Taʾrīkh* XVI: 111;[149] Ibn Manẓūr, *Mukhtaṣar* VII: 363.

COMMENTARY: Cf. Ibn al-Muqaffaʿ, *Adab*, p. 35.

A79 Khālid has also said: If you accompany a governor, do it on the basis of previous love. If you can, accompany someone who has known your sincere love before his governorship.

(Ibn Razīn, *Ādāb*, p. 119, no. 171); Ibn ʿAsākir, *Taʾrīkh* XVI: 111.[150]

COMMENTARY: Cf. Ibn al-Muqaffaʿ, *Adab*, p. 36.

A80 Khālid ibn Ṣafwān has said: If you see someone telling a *ḥadīth* you have heard or a story you know, do not join him in telling it, desiring to let others know that you know it. That is slighting and bad behaviour.

(Ibn ʿAsākir, *Taʾrīkh* XVI: 112);[151] Ibn Manẓūr, *Mukhtaṣar* VII: 363.

A80a *Abū l-Qāsim ibn al-Samarqandī < Abū (l-Ḥusayn ibn)*[152] *al-Naqqūr and Abū Manṣūr < Abū Ṭāhir al-Mukhallaṣ < ʿUbaydallāh ibn ʿAbd al-Raḥmān al-Sukkarī < Zakariyyā ibn Yaḥyā al-Minqarī < al-Aṣmaʿī < al-ʿAlāʾ ibn Jarīr*: Khālid ibn Ṣafwān said: When a governor asks someone other than you, do not answer him yourself. That would be slighting both the one who asks and the one who is asked.

(Ibn ʿAsākir, *Taʾrīkh* XVI: 112); Ibn Manẓūr, *Mukhtaṣar* VII: 363.

---

149 < al-Aṣmaʿī < ʿAbd al-Ṣamad ibn Shabīb.

150 < ʿAbd al-Ṣamad ibn Shabīb.

151 Implicitly with the same *isnād* as A80a.

152 Addition by the editor of Ibn ʿAsākir's *Taʾrīkh*.

COMMENTARY: Ibn al-Muqaffaʿ gives an almost identical version of the saying.[153]

A81 Khālid has said: If one accompanies the Sultan with veracity and sincerity he will have more enemies than if he accompanied him with deception and falseness because both the enemy of the governor and his friend will hate and envy him. The friend will vie with him as to position and the enemy will hate him for his sincere advice.

(al-Tawḥīdī, *Baṣāʾir* v: 154, no. 510); Ibn ʿAbdrabbih, *ʿIqd* i: 11; al-Zamakhsharī, *Rabīʿ* iv: 217; Ibn ʿAsākir, *Taʾrīkh* xvi: 111;[154] Ibn Manẓūr, *Mukhtaṣar* vii: 363; Ibn Shams al-Khilāfa, *Ādāb*, p. 44.

A82 Khālid ibn Ṣafwān has said: Do not attach yourself to a ruler before you have trained yourself. Join them if you can take care of what they have assigned to you, if you are trustworthy when they trust you, if you are cautious when they allow you to come nearer, if you are humble when they drive you away, and if you are content when they irritate you. You teach them as if it were you who is learning from them, and you refine their manners as if it were you who is refining his manners through them. Otherwise, you had better stay as far from them as possible, and beware of them as much as you can.

(Ibn Shams al-Khilāfa, *Ādāb*, p. 43).

COMMENTARY: Cf. Ibn al-Muqaffaʿ, *Adab*, pp. 60–62.

A83 < al-Aṣmaʿī:[155] Khālid ibn Ṣafwān has said: In search of benefit even a great person is considered little, but facing perils even an insignificant person is considered great.

(Ibn ʿAsākir, *Taʾrīkh* xvi: 112); Ibn Manẓūr, *Mukhtaṣar* vii: 363; al-ʿAskarī, *Maṣūn*, pp. 130–131.[156]

A84 Khālid ibn Ṣafwān has said: If your hand is too short to recompensate for a good deed, then let at least your tongue be long in giving thanks.

(al-Thaʿālibī, *Tamthīl*, p. 245); al-Thaʿālibī, *Tamaththul*, p. 636.

---

153 Ibn al-Muqaffaʿ, *Adab*, p. 50.

154 < Abū l-Qāsim ibn al-Samarqandī < Abū l-Ḥusayn ibn al-Naqqūr and Abū Manṣūr ibn al-ʿAṭṭār < Abū Ṭāhir al-Mukhallaṣ < ʿUbaydallāh ibn ʿAbd al-Raḥmān < Zakariyyā ibn Yaḥyā al-Minqarī.

155 Implicitly with the same *isnād* as A80a.

156 < Muḥammad ibn al-Ḥasan ibn Durayd < ʿAbd al-Awwal < ibn Murayd < Ibn abī Suwayya < al-ʿAlāʾ ibn Jarīr.

A85 Khālid ibn Ṣafwān was rebuked because he rode mules. He said: "This mount is lower than the conceit of horses (*khuyalāʾ al-khayl*) but loftier than the lowness of donkeys. It is in between and the best of things is the middle one."

(al-Thaʿālibī, *Tawfīq*, pp. 59–60); al-Thaʿālibī, *Tamthīl*, p. 206; al-Thaʿālibī, *Tamaththul*, p. 541; al-Thaʿālibī, *Thimār*, p. 357 (anonymous); al-Shimshāṭī, *Anwār* I: 350 (attributed to al-Faḍl ibn ʿAbdallāh); al-ʿAskarī, *Awāʾil*, p. 17 (anonymous).

COMMENTARY: According to Ibn Qutayba, this was said by al-Faḍl ibn al-Rabīʿ.[157] The final saying is a famous *ḥadīth*. Cf. also B10 and B10a.

A86 Khālid ibn Ṣafwān said to his son: "O son, *adab* is the splendour of kings and the feathers of the mob and all people between these two. Learn it and you will find it with you whenever you want."

(Abū Naṣr al-Maqdisī, *Laṭāʾif*, p. 43).

A87 Khālid ibn Ṣafwān has said: I rejoice more in being of profit to a student than profiting from a teacher.

(al-Māwardī, *Adab*, p. 88).

A88 Khālid ibn Ṣafwān: Three things cannot be helped: poverty mixed with lazyness, quarrel contaminated by envy, and sickness united with old age.

(al-Thaʿālibī, *Bard*, p. 31).

A89 He (= Khālid)[158] said: Three things are only known in three situations: A gentle man (*ḥalīm*) when he is angered, a friend in need, and a courageous man in an encounter.

Ibn ʿAsākir, *Taʾrīkh* XVI: 108; Ibn Manẓūr, *Mukhtaṣar* VII: 362; al-Dhahabī, *Siyar* VI: 226.

A90 Khālid ibn Ṣafwān has said: The best thing fathers can put aside for their sons are good deeds done to persons of noble descent.

(Ibn ʿAsākir, *Taʾrīkh* XVI: 112);[159] Ibn Manẓūr, *Mukhtaṣar* VII: 363.

---

157 Ibn Qutayba, *ʿUyūn al-akhbār* I: 250.

158 Cf. note 941 to A38.

159 Implicitly with the same *isnād* as A80a.

A91 Khālid ibn Ṣafwān has said: In merchants, you will find vileness of character, incapacity of tongue, a dead heart, evil manners, shortness of aspiration, and union of all calamities.

(Ibn ʿAbd al-Barr, *Bahja* I: 134)

A92 < *Ibn ʿĀʾisha* < *"my father:"* I was sitting one day in the congregational mosque of Basra when I saw Khālid ibn Ṣafwān al-Ahtamī come towards us. I moved from the best place and made place for him. He came and sat down. Then he turned towards me and asked: "Whose son are you?" I replied: "I am Muḥammad ibn Ḥafṣ." He said: "Then you are the nephew of Mūsā?" I said I was, and he said: "By God, your father was a place of constant return (*wa'llāhi in kāna abūka la-mathāba*)."

He (Muḥammad ibn Ḥafṣ) said: I have been told by several of the shaykhs then present in the mosque that they had never heard a eulogy in one word better than this.

(al-Tawḥīdī, *Baṣāʾir* V: 175, no. 594).

COMMENTARY: The conciseness of the original is lost in translation.[160]

A93 < *Zabr* < *ʿAbdallāh ibn ʿAmr ibn abī Saʿd* < *Aḥmad ibn Muʿāwiya* < *al-Aṣmaʿī*: Khālid ibn Ṣafwān said: Nothing is more beautiful than a good deed except for its reward, but not everyone who is able to do it, has the desire (*niyya*) to do so and not everyone who has the desire to do it, will be allowed to do so. When desire, ability, and allowing coincide, only then a good deed comes to be.

(Ibn ʿAsākir, *Taʾrīkh* XVI: 108); Ibn Manẓūr, *Mukhtaṣar* VII: 362; al-Maqdisī, *Muntaqā*, p. 84 (no. 67).[161]

A94 It is told that Khālid-e Ṣafwān was one of the ascetics and pious men of his time. One day, he came to the Commander of the Believers Mahdī to visit him. When he came back he was asked to describe Mahdī's *majlis*. He replied: "I saw that those who entered were hopeful and those who came out were satisfied."[162] Those who were present lauded this saying and acknowledged its merit.

(ʿAwfī, *Jawāmiʿ* I/2: 76–77, no. 62).

---

160 For Muḥammad ibn Ḥafṣ ibn Maʿmar al-Taymī, see references in Popovkin (2007): 348, s.v. For Ibn ʿĀʾisha ʿUbaydallāh ibn Muḥammad ibn Ḥafṣ (d. 228/843), see al-Ṭabarī, *Taʾrīkh* III: 149/XXVIII: 94 and note 446. Ibn ʿĀʾisha is often quoted as a Basran transmitter or historian, and his father is occasionally found in the same role.

161 < al-Aṣmaʿī < Aḥmad < ʿAbdallāh.

162 Khālid's saying is first given in Arabic and then somewhat freely translated into Persian.

A95 < *Abū Bakr Muḥammad ibn Shujāʿ* < *Abū ʿAmr ibn Manda* < *al-Ḥasan ibn Muḥammad al-Madīnī* < *Aḥmad ibn Muḥammad al-Bannānī* < *ʿAbdallāh ibn Muḥammad al-Qurashī* < *al-Ḥusayn ibn ʿAbd al-Raḥmān* < *Shabīb ibn Shayba*: Khālid ibn Ṣafwān has said: "Some men attain to wealth and start speaking and rise to heights." Then he said:

Money has made people speak
after they had been speechless and silent,

but they have not brought any good back to their neighbour
nor have they raised a house for noble deeds.

Thus, money restores blemishes,
but leaves the truly noble silent.

(Ibn ʿAsākir, *Taʾrīkh* XVI: 116–117); Ibn al-ʿAdīm, *Bughya* VII: 69–70).[163]

A96 Khālid ibn Ṣafwān: I spend on friends because I do not want to dissemble to them nor do I give them less than they deserve.
(al-Thaʿālibī, *Tamthīl*, p. 268); al-Thaʿālibī, *Tamaththul*, p. 695; al-Māwardī, *Adab*, p. 166.

COMMENTARY: Cf. A73.

A97 *Abū Yaʿqūb Yūsuf ibn Maḥmūd ibn al-Ḥusayn in Egypt* < *al-Ḥāfiẓ Abū Ṭāhir Aḥmad ibn Muḥammad ibn Aḥmad al-Silafī* < *Abū l-Ḥusayn Muḥammad ibn Aḥmad ibn Mardawayhi al-Mamnābādhī in Isfahan* < *Abū Bakr Muḥammad ibn ʿAlī ibn Iṣbahbadh al-Iṣbahānī* < *Abū Bakr Aḥmad ibn ʿAbdān ibn Muḥammad al-Shīrāzī al-Ḥāfiẓ in Tustar* < *ʿAbdallāh ibn abī Dāʾūd* < *Isḥāq ibn Ibrāhīm* < *al-Qaḥdhamī* < *"his father"*: Khālid ibn Ṣafwān has said: Kindness is an easy thing, just a cheerful face and some soft words.
(Ibn al-ʿAdīm, *Bughya* VII: 61).

A98 < *Abū l-Qāsim ʿAbdallāh ibn al-Ḥusayn al-Ḥamawī* < *Abū Ṭāhir Aḥmad ibn Muḥammad al-Ḥāfiẓ* < *Abū l-Ḥusayn ibn al-Ṭuyūrī* < *ʿAbd al-ʿAzīz ibn ʿAlī*

---

163 < Abū l-ʿAbbās Aḥmad ibn ʿAbdallāh al-Asadī < Masʿūd ibn al-Ḥasan al-Thaqafī < Abū ʿAmr ibn Manda < al-Ḥasan ibn Muḥammad al-Madāʾinī < Aḥmad ibn Muḥammad al-Lunbānī < ʿAbdallāh ibn Muḥammad al-Qurashī < al-Ḥusayn ibn ʿAbd al-Raḥmān < Shabīb ibn Shayba. The editor adds that al-Lunbānī is the correct form of the *nisba* (in the text al-Lubnānī).

ibn Aḥmad al-Azajī < Abū Ṭālib al-Makkī < ʿAbdallāh ibn Yaḥyā al-Qurashī < Muḥammad ibn al-Ḥusayn al-Lakhmī < Abū l-ʿAynāʾ al-Sulamī < al-Walīd ibn Hishām al-Qaḥdhamī: Khālid ibn Ṣafwān has said: Do not ask a favour from three kinds of men. Do not ask a liar because he will claim that what is far away is close by and will push far away that which is close by. Do not ask a stupid person, because he may want to help you, but he, in fact, harms you. Do not ask a man who needs something from your friend, because he will use your asking to get his own need.

(Ibn al-ʿAdīm, *Bughya* VII: 62).

A99 Khālid ibn Ṣafwān saw an ignoble young man, whose parents had been noble, and said:

> Let people not wonder at you and your parents:
> dross from silver, there is nothing to be wondered at.

(al-Rāghib, *Muḥāḍarāt* I: 337).

A100 Khālid ibn Ṣafwān: Be honest in small matters even though they might bring you some harm, so that you can lie in great matters which will profit you.

(al-Rāghib, *Muḥāḍarāt* I: 122).

A101 Shabīb has said: I envied ʿAmr ibn ʿUbayd for two sentences I heard him say. Someone insulted him while he remained silent. When the man had come to an end, ʿAmr replied: "May God reward you for what right you said and may He forgive you the wrong you said." It is also said that it was Khālid ibn Ṣafwān who said this.

(al-Balādhurī, *Ansāb* VII/1: 91–92); Miskawayhi, *Ḥikma*, p. 129; Abū Hilāl al-ʿAskarī, *Jamhara* I: 140.

COMMENTARY: Both Miskawayhi and Abū Hilāl al-ʿAskarī present Khālid as an eye-witness (*shahidtu*) to this saying,[164] so al-Balādhurī's comment has to be taken to refer to the story about ʿAmr, not ʿAmr's saying. In many stories, Shabīb transmits from Khālid, and this is also possible in this case, which would explain why in one version the transmitter is Shabīb, while in the others it is Khālid.

164 Miskawayhi, *Ḥikma*, p. 129, and Abū Hilāl al-ʿAskarī, *Jamhara* I: 140.

A102 It was said to al-Aḥnaf, who was wearing a certain garb of his: "Don't you grow weary of wearing it?" He replied: "There are many whom you have grown weary with but whom you cannot leave." This is also attributed to others.
(al-Balādhurī, *Ansāb* VII/1: 137); Ibn ʿAbdrabbih, *ʿIqd* III: 210 (attributed to Khālid).

A102a Khālid ibn Ṣafwān said to Iyās ibn Muʿāwiya:[165] "You do not seem to care what you are wearing." Iyās replied: "I prefer wearing clothing to protect myself to wearing clothing I myself have to protect."
(al-Māwardī, *Adab*, pp. 340–341)

COMMENTARY: The same story in a slightly different and longer form is told about Abū l-Aswad al-Du'alī.[166]

4.9 Various Stories

A103 < Yaḥyā ibn Saʿīd al-Umawī: I heard al-Aʿmash say to Khālid ibn Ṣafwān: "Do you know that your house is only known through mine? People say you live close to the house of al-Aʿmash." Khālid replied: "You are right, just like they say 'close to the bath of ʿAntara, or *Rawwās,[167] or Bayṭār-ḥayyān'!"
(Ibn Qutayba, *ʿUyūn* II: 232).

COMMENTARY: The references are to various places in Kufa, known by the names of famous cuppers, ʿAntara, Rawwās, and Bayṭār-ḥayyān.[168] The joke is on al-Aʿmash: other people's houses are known for their proximity to baths where these cuppers used to work, cuppers, of course, lying as low as one ever could in the hierarchy of the Mediaeval society.

Al-Aʿmash (d. 147 or 148/764–765) was a Kufan traditionist[169] and the places mentioned are all located in Kufa. A104 relates that Khālid did meet al-Aʿmash when passing through that city, but this would be the only reference to Khālid owning a property in Kufa. Likewise, al-Aʿmash is not known to have owned property in Basra.

---

165 For Iyās (d. 121/739 or a year later), see *EI2*, s.v. (Ch. Pellat), al-Ṣafadī, *Wāfī* IX: 465–468.
166 E.g., al-Rāghib, *Muḥāḍarāt* IV: 367.
167 The text reads: Wardān, but cf. commentary.
168 See al-Balādhurī, *Futūḥ*, p. 282.
169 See *EI3*, s.v. (G.H.A. Juynboll).

A104 < *Abū Muḥammad ibn al-Akfānī* < *ʿAbd al-ʿAzīz ibn Aḥmad* < *ʿAbd al-Wahhāb ibn Jaʿfar* < al-qāḍī *Abū ʿAbdallāh Muḥammad ibn ʿAbdallāh* < *Ibn abī Shaykh Muḥammad ibn Aḥmad al-Rāfiqī* < *Abū Shuʿayb* < *Abū Zayd* < *al-Ḍaḥḥāk*: When the delegation of Basra went to Ibn Hubayra they passed by Kufa, where al-Aʿmash secluded himself from them (in his house). Khālid ibn Ṣafwān said: "I will drag him out." They shouted at his door: "Aʿmash, ho! Aʿmash!" Aʿmash came out angry and asked who they were, to which Khālid said: "We are from among those about whom God has said: 'Most of those who call you from behind the partments do not understand'."[170] When al-Aʿmash recognised him, he sat long with them.

(Ibn ʿAsākir, *Taʾrīkh* XVI: 110).[171]

COMMENTARY: Al-Aʿmash is reported to have been "an ill-natured man."[172]

A105 A *mawlā* said to Khālid ibn Ṣafwān: "Give me your slave girl so-and-so as wife." Khālid replied: "I have married her to you." The *mawlā* asked: "May I invite the tribe to hear the marriage sermon?" Khālid gave permission to this. When they entered, he said: "God is too majestic and mighty to be mentioned in the marriage of these two dogs. So, now I give this bitch as wife to this son-of-a-bitch."

(al-Jāḥiẓ, *Bayān* II: 250); Ibn ʿAbdrabbih, *ʿIqd* IV: 151;[173] Ibn ʿĀṣim, *Ḥadāʾiq*, p. 135.[174]

COMMENTARY: In Ibn ʿAbdrabbih's and Ibn ʿĀṣim's version, Khālid's interlocutor is a slave (*ʿabd*) of his, not a *mawlā* as in al-Jāḥiẓ's version.

A106 Khālid ibn Ṣafwān asked ʿAmr ibn ʿUbayd: "Why do you not accept money from me to pay your debts, if you have any, or to give to your relatives?" ʿAmr replied: "Debts I have none, and to give to relatives is not incumbent. Moreover, I do not have anything to give." Khālid said: "But why not accept something from me?" ʿAmr said: "Because one does not accept anything without humbling himself in front of the donor. By God, I would hate to humble myself in front of you!"[175]

---

170 Q 49: 4.

171 Ibn ʿAsākir also relates this story from Abū ʿAlī Muḥammad ibn Saʿīd ibn Ibrāhīm ibn Nabhān.

172 See *EI3*, s.v. (G.T.A. Juynboll).

173 < al-Aṣmaʿī, with slight differences.

174 As Ibn ʿAbdrabbih's version, no mention of al-Aṣmaʿī.

175 The version of Ibn Ḥamdūn and al-Zamakhsharī has "in front of anyone, except God."

(al-Murtaḍā, *Amālī* I: 170); Ibn Ḥamdūn, *Tadhkira* III: 137 (no. 400); al-Zamakhsharī, *Rabīʿ* IV: 370; Ibn ʿAsākir, *Taʾrīkh* XVI: 116.[176]

COMMENTARY: Ibn Ḥamdūn and al-Zamakhsharī set the story in context by adding a couple of lines before and after the story itself:

< *ʿAbbād ibn Manṣūr*: There were people in Basra who were more correct in language than ʿAmr ibn ʿUbayd and more learned in *fiqh*, but he was the most patient of them as to dirhams and dinars, which is why he became the leader of the Basrans. (…) He lived on the revenues of a house, which brought him a dinar in a month.

A107 Khālid ibn Ṣafwān al-Minqarī has said:

If you need must marry then take
those of shining teeth and wide eyes,

slim waist, agile body,
short steps, heedless of evil, and of ample reason.

(Ibn Ḥamdūn, *Tadhkira* V: 315, no. 855); al-Zamakhsharī, *Rabīʿ* IV: 288; al-Ibshīhī, *Mustaṭraf* II: 293 (only the first verse).

A108 Relating something to something to which it does not belong. That is when you describe something by a description that does not fit. To this belongs Khālid ibn abī (sic) Ṣafwān's saying:

Though a form might please you, yet put it to test.
The taste of aloes may be bitter though it be green.

In this, Khālid alluded to green aloes being sweet, instead of bitter, which is not necessarily so because green aloes does not have a specific taste.
(Ibn Khalaf, *Mawādd*, p. 266); Ibn al-ʿAdīm, *Bughya* VII: 69.[177]

---

176 < Ibn abī Khaythama < Sulaymān ibn abī Shaykh < Ṣāliḥ ibn Sulaymān.

177 < Yaḥyā ibn Manṣūr al-Baghdādī < "my father" < Abū Ṭāhir Aḥmad ibn Sawwār < Abū l-Ḥusayn ibn Rizma < Abū Saʿīd al-Sīrāfī < Muḥammad ibn Manṣūr ibn Mazyad < al-Zubayr < Muḥammad ibn Sallām.

COMMENTARY: Ibn al-ʿAdīm has two verses before the verse quoted by Ibn Khalaf:[178]

> What makes a man is only the two small ones, his tongue
> and his reason, whereas the body is merely a painted thing.
>
> Beauty lies not in the garment you see, but
> a man is adorned or made inadequate by what he knows.

The poem has most probably been misattributed to Khālid, on the basis of its resemblance to his famous saying B26.

The verse is found anonymously in al-Jurjānī, *Asrār*, p. 154.[179] Ritter gives a few anonymous attestations of the verse and refers to Qudāma, who attributes it to Khālid ibn Ṣafwān. Most sources read *ṭurra* "forelock" for Ibn Khalaf's *ṣūra* in the first hemistich.

---

178 Ibn al-ʿAdīm, *Bughya* VII: 69.

179 Translated in Ritter (1959): 131. See also Ritter's note 91.

CHAPTER 5

Stories Excluded from the Corpus

C1 A Bedouin came to Khālid ibn Ṣafwān and said: "May God keep the Emir and may the Emir give an order to fill my bag with wheat." He said (to his servants): "Fill it with dirhams." This was done, and when the Bedouin came back to other people they asked: "What did you do, asking such a thing?" He replied: "I asked the Emir according to what suited me, and he gave his order according to what suits him."

(al-Dajājī, *Safaṭ*, p. 93).

COMMENTARY: This story has most probably been misattributed. Khālid is nowhere else pictured as an Emir. Although the Bedouin's language could always be interpreted as hyperbolic, the tenour of the story would fit a higher-ranking official than Khālid. It may be that the original interlocutor of the Bedouin was Khālid al-Qasrī.

C2 They say: al-Aḥnaf went by Ṣafwān, *the father of*[1] Khālid ibn Ṣafwān, who said to him: "Abū Baḥr, sit down and let us discuss blameworthy features and speak about noble deeds!"

This came to the ears of the father of Ṣafwān (Abū Ṣafwān), who, according to al-Kalbī, was ʿAbdallāh ibn ʿAmr ibn al-Ahtam and, according to others, ʿAbdallāh ibn ʿAbdallāh ibn al-Ahtam, and he became angry with his son and said: "I will not be appeased with you until Abū Baḥr speaks in your favour!" Al-Aḥnaf came to him, and he pleaded with him to appease his father, which he agreed to do.

(al-Balādhurī, *Ansāb* VII/1: 137–138).

COMMENTARY: The names are confused in the story. As al-Aḥnaf ibn Qays died in 67/686, during al-Mukhtār's revolt,[2] the story cannot feature Khālid, but relates to his father Ṣafwān as a young man.

---

1 The original reads Ṣafwān ibn Khālid ibn Ṣafwān, for which I suggest reading Ṣafwān, *abū Khālid ibn Ṣafwān.

2 See *EI2*, s.v. (Ch. Pellat).

 | DOI:10.1163/9789004433977_006

C3 And he said: Long-enduring patience is the key to attaining one's need and the lack thereof is laxity before attaining it.
(Ibn ʿAbdrabbih, *ʿIqd* I: 241).

COMMENTARY: I have not been able to locate this saying attributed to Khālid elsewhere. It seems that Ibn ʿAbdrabbih has here loosely used *wa-qāla*, which technically refers back to the speaker in the previous story (B56), Khālid, and the saying should most probably not be attributed to Khālid.

Bibliography

1 Abbreviations

EI2 = *The Encyclopaedia of Islam. New Edition.* I–XI. Ed. C.E. Bosworth et al. Leiden: Brill 1960–2007. [online version]

EI3 = *The Encyclopaedia of Islam – Three.* Iff. Ed. Kate Fleet et al. Leiden: Brill, 2007ff. [online version]

GAL, GAL S = Carl Brockelmann, *Geschichte der arabischen Literatur.* I–II + *Supplementbände* I–III. Leiden: Brill 1936–1944.

GAS = Fuat Sezgin, *Geschichte des arabischen Schrifttums.* I–IX. Leiden: Brill 1967–1984.

WKAS = *Wörterbuch der klassischen arabischen Sprache.* I–III. Ed. Manfred Ullmann et al. Wiesbaden: Harrassowitz 1957–2001.

2 Arabic and Persian Sources

ʿAbd al-Ḥamīd, *Rasāʾil* = Iḥsān ʿAbbās, *ʿAbd al-Ḥamīd wa-mā tabqā min rasāʾilihi wa-rasāʾil Sālim ibn al-ʿAlāʾ*. ʿAmmān: Dār al-Sharq 1988.

ʿAbd al-Qādir al-Baghdādī, *Khizānat al-adab*. Ed. ʿAbd al-Salām Muḥammad Hārūn. I–XI. Al-Qāhira: al-Hayʾa al-miṣriyya al-ʿāmma liʾl-kitāb 1979–1983.

ʿAbd al-Qādir al-Baghdādī, *Ḥāshiya ʿalā Sharḥ "Bānat Suʿād"*. Ed. N. Hoca. I–IIa and b. Bibliotheca Islamica 27. 1980–1990.

al-Ābī, *Nathr al-durr*. Ed. ʿAlī Muḥammad al-Bajāwī et al. I–VII. Al-Qāhira: al-Hayʾa al-miṣriyya al-ʿāmma liʾl-kitāb, 1981–1991.

al-Ābī, *al-Uns waʾl-ʿurs*. Ed. Īflīn Farīd Yārid. Dimashq: Dār al-Namīr 1999.

Abū Nuʿaym, *Ḥilyat al-awliyāʾ wa-ṭabaqāt al-aṣfiyāʾ*. I–VIII. Miṣr: Maktabat al-Khānjī – Maṭbaʿat al-Saʿāda 1356/1937.

Abū Nuwās, *Dīwān*. Ed. Ewald Wagner (I–III, V) and Gregor Schoeler (IV). I–V. Bibliotheca Islamica 20a–e. Wiesbaden – Stuttgart: Franz Steiner (V: Berlin: Klaus Schwarz) 1958–2003.

Abū Ṭāhir al-Baghdādī, *Qānūn al-balāgha fī naqd al-nathr waʾl-shiʿr*. Ed. Muḥsin Ghayyāḍ ʿAjīl. Bayrūt: Muʾassasat al-Risāla 1409/1989.

Abū Tammām, *Dīwān* = *Sharḥ Dīwān Abī Tammām*. Ed. Shāhīn ʿAṭiyya. Bayrūt: Dār al-Kutub al-ʿilmiyya 1407/1987.

Abū ʿUbayd al-Qāsim ibn Sallām, *Kitāb al-Nasab*. Ed. Maryam Muḥammad Khayr al-Dirʿ. Al-Qāhira: Dār al-Fikr 1410/1989.

Abū ʿUbayda, *Naqāʾiḍ Jarīr waʾl-Farazdaq*. I–III. Ed. A.A. Bevan, repr. Bayrūt Dār al-Kitāb al-ʿarabī n.d.

al-Aḥdab (Ibrāhīm), *Dhayl Thamarāt al-awrāq*. In the margins of al-Ibshīhī, *al-Mustaṭraf fī kull fann mustaẓraf*. I–II. Bayrūt: Dār al-Fikr n.d.

al-Akhfash al-Aṣghar, *Kitāb al-Ikhtiyārayn*. Ed. Fakhr al-Dīn Qabāwa. Bayrūt: Mu'assasat al-Risāla 1394/1974.

Alf layla wa-layla. I–II. (Būlāq 1252 AH), repr. Bayrūt: Dār Ṣādir n.d.

al-ʿĀmilī (Bahā' al-Dīn), *al-Mikhlāt*. Ed. Muḥammad ʿAbd al-Karīm al-Nimrī. Bayrūt: Dār al-Kutub al-ʿilmiyya 1418/1997.

al-Aʿshā Maymūn, *Dīwān* = Rudolf Geyer, *Gedichte von (...) al-ʾAʿshā*. E.J.W. Gibb Memorial, New Series VI. London: E.J.W. Gibb Memorial 1928.

al-ʿAskarī, *al-Maṣūn fī l-adab*. Ed. ʿAbd al-Salām Muḥammad Hārūn. Al-Kuwayt 1960.

al-ʿAskarī (Abū Hilāl), *al-Awā'il*. Ed. ʿAbd al-Razzāq Ghālib al-Mahdī. Bayrūt: Dār al-Kutub al-ʿilmiyya 1417/1997.

al-ʿAskarī (Abū Hilāl), *Dīwān al-maʿānī*. 1) I–II. Ed. Aḥmad Salīm Ghānim. Bayrūt: Dār al-Gharb al-islāmī 1424/2003; 2) I–II. Bayrūt: Dār al-Jīl n.d.

al-ʿAskarī (Abū Hilāl), *Jamharat al-amthāl*. I–II. Ed. Muḥammad Abū l-Faḍl Ibrāhīm and ʿAbd al-Majīd Quṭāmish. 2nd edition. Bayrūt: Dār al-Jīl n.d.

al-ʿAskarī (Abū Hilāl), *Kitāb al-Ṣināʿatayn*. Ed. ʿAlī Muḥammad al-Bajāwī and Muḥammad Abū l-Faḍl Ibrāhīm. Dār Iḥyā' al-kutub al-ʿarabiyya: ʿĪsā al-Bābī al-Ḥalabī wa-shurakā'uhu 1371/1952.

Aṣmaʿiyyāt = W. Ahlwardt, Sammlungen alter *arabischer Dichter* I. Repr. Bayrūt: Dār al-Āfāq al-jadīda 1401/1981.

ʿAwfī, *Jawāmiʿ al-ḥikāyāt wa-lawāmiʿ al-riwāyāt*. I/2. Ed. Amīr Bānū Muṣaffā (Karīmī). Tihrān: Piszhūhishgāh-e ʿulūm-e insānī wa-muṭālaʿāt-e farhangī 1387 AHSh.

ʿAwfī, *Jawāmiʿ al-ḥikāyāt wa-lawāmiʿ al-riwāyāt*. III/1. Ed. Bānū Muṣaffā Karīmī. Intishārāt-e Bunyād-e farhangī-ye Īrān 162. Tihrān: Bunyād-e farhangī-ye Īrān 1352 AHSh.

(*Kitāb*) *al-ʿAyn* = al-Khalīl ibn Aḥmad. *Kitāb al-ʿAyn*. I–VIII. Ed. Mahdī al-Makhzūmī and Ibrāhīm al-Sāmarrā'ī. Qum: Dār al-hijra 1405.

al-Azdī, *Ḥikāyat Abī l-Qāsim* = A. Mez, *Abulḳasim, ein baǵdâder Sittenbild*. (Heidelberg: Carl Winter's Universitätsbuchhandlung 1920), repr. Baghdād: Maktabat al-Muthannā n.d.

al-Azharī, *Tahdhīb al-lugha*. Ed. ʿAbd al-Salām Muḥammad Hārūn et al. I–XV. Al-Qāhira: al-Dār al-miṣriyya li'l-ta'līf wa'l-tarjama 1384–1387/1964–1967; XVI. Ed. Rashīd ʿAbd al-Raḥmān al-ʿUbaydī. Al-Qāhira: al-Hay'a al-miṣriyya al-ʿāmma li-l-kuttāb 1975.

al-Bakrī, *Muʿjam mā staʿjam min asmā' al-bilād wa'l-mawāḍiʿ*. I–IV (in two vols.). Ed. Muṣṭafā al-Saqqā. Al-Qāhira: Maktabat al-Khānjī 1417/1996.

al-Bakrī, *Simṭ al-la'ālī fī sharḥ Amālī l-Qālī*. I–III. Ed ʿAbd al-ʿAzīz al-Maymanī. (N.p. 1936), repr. Dār al-Kutub al-ʿilmiyya n.d.

al-Balādhurī, *Ansāb al-ashrāf*. III. Ed. ʿAbd al-ʿAzīz al-Dūrī. Bibliotheca Islamica 28c. Wiesbaden: Franz Steiner Verlag 1398/1978.

al-Balādhurī. *Ansāb al-ashrāf.* VII/1. Ed. Ramzī Baʿlabakkī. Bibliotheca Islamica 28i. Beirut: al-Sharika al-muttaḥida li-l-nashr wa-l-tawzīʿ 1417/1997.

al-Balādhurī, *Ansāb al-ashrāf.* I–XXIV. Ed. Maḥmūd al-Firdaws al-ʿAẓm. Dimashq: Dār al-Yaqaẓa al-ʿarabiyya 1997–2003.

al-Balādhurī, *Futūḥ* = M.J. de Goeje (ed.), *Liber expugnationis regionum auctore (...) al-Beládsorí.* Lugduni Batavorum: Brill 1866.

al-Balawī, *Kitāb Alif-Bāʾ fī anwāʿ al-adab wa-funūn al-muḥāḍarāt waʾl-lugha.* I–II. Ed. Khālid ʿAbd al-Ghanī Maḥfūẓ. Bayrūt: Dār al-Kutub al-ʿilmiyya 2008.

Bashshār ibn Burd, *Dīwān.* I–IV. Ed. Ṣalāḥ al-Dīn al-Hawārī. Bayrūt: Dār wa-maktabat al-Hilāl 1998.

al-Bayhaqī, *al-Maḥāsin wa-l-masāwī.* Ed. Friedrich Schwally. Giessen: Ricker'sche Verlagshandlung 1902.

al-Bīrūnī, *al-Āthār al-bāqiya ʿan al-qurūn al-khāliya.* Ed. Parvīz Adhkāʾī. Mīrāth-e maktūb 91. Tihrān: Mīrāth-e maktūb 1380 AHSh/2001.

al-Bukhārī. *Ṣaḥīḥ.* Ed. Muḥammad Nizār Tamīm and Haytham Nizār Tamīm. Beirut: Dār al-Arqam n.d.

al-Bukhārī, *Kitāb al-Taʾrīkh al-kabīr.* I–IV (in 8 vols.). Ed. Muḥammad ʿAbd al-Muʿīd Khān et al. (Hyderabad 1358–1362/1941–1945), repr. Bayrūt: Dār al-Kutub al-ʿilmiyya n.d.

al-Būnisī, *Kanz al-kuttāb wa-muntakhab al-ādāb.* Ed. Ḥayāt Qāra. Abū Ẓaby: al-Majmaʿ al-thaqāfī 1425/2004.

al-Dajājī, *Safaṭ al-mulaḥ wa-zawḥ al-taraḥ.* Ed. Khālid Aḥmad al-Mullā al-Suwaydī. 2nd ed. Dimashq: Dār al-Kinān 1430/2009.

al-Damīrī, *Ḥayāt al-ḥayawān al-kubrā.* I–II. 5th edition. Al-Qāhira: Maktabat wa-maṭbaʿat Muṣṭafā al-Bābī al-Ḥalabī 1398/1978.

al-Dhahabī, *Siyar aʿlām al-nubalāʾ.* I–XXV. Ed. Ḥusayn al-Asad et al. Bayrūt: Muʾassasat al-risāla 1417/1996.

Dīwān Abī Nuwās, ḥayātuhu, tārīkhuhu, nawādiruhu, shiʿruhu. Bayrūt: al-Maktaba al-ahliyya n.d.

al-Fārābī, *Siyāsa* = Fuat Sezgin (ed.), *Abū Naṣr Muḥammad ibn Muḥammad al-Fārābī, Various Philosophical Treatises.* Islamic Philosophy 16. Frankfurt: Institute for the History of Arabic-Islamic Science at the Johann Wolfgang Goethe University 1999.

al-Farazdaq, *Dīwān.* 1) Ed. ʿAlī Fāʿūr. Bayrūt: Dār al-Kutub al-ʿilmiyya 1407/1987; 2) = ʿAbdallāh al-Ṣāwī, *Sharḥ Dīwān al-Farazdaq.* I–II. Maṭbaʿat al-Ṣāwī n.d.

al-Fīrūzābādī, *al-Qāmūs al-muḥīṭ.* I–IV. Ed. (and reorganised according to the first radical) al-Ṭāhir Aḥmad az-Zāwī. 3rd edition. Al-Qāhira: Al-Dār al-ʿarabiyya liʾl-kitāb 1980.

Ḥājjī Khalīfa, *Kashf al-ẓunūn ʿan asāmī l-kutub waʾl-funūn.* I–II. Ed. Serefettin Yaltkaya and Rifat Bilge. (Maarif matbaasi 1941), repr. Bayrūt: Dār al-Kutub al-ʿilmiyya 1413/1992.

al-Hamadhānī, *Maqāmāt* = Muḥammad Muḥyī al-Dīn ʿAbd al-ḥamīd, *Sharḥ maqāmāt Badīʿ al-Zamān al-Hamadhānī*. Bayrūt: Dār al-Kutub al-ʿilmiyya n.d.

al-Hamadhānī, *Rasāʾil* = Ibrāhīm al-Aḥdab, *Kashf al-maʿānī wa'l-bayān ʿan Rasāʾil Badīʿ al-Zamān*. Bayrūt: al-Maṭbaʿat al-kāthūlīkiyya li'l-ābāʾ al-yasuʿiyyīn 1890.

Ḥamza al-Iṣbahānī, *al-Durra al-fākhira fī l-amthāl al-sāʾira*. Ed. Quṣayy al-Ḥusayn. Mawsūʿat al-amthāl. Bayrūt: Dār wa-maktabat al-Hilāl 2003.

al-Ḥimyarī, *Kitāb al-Rawḍ al-miʿṭār fī khabar al-aqṭār*. Ed. Iḥsān ʿAbbās. 3rd edition. Bayrūt: Muʾassasat nāṣir al-thaqāfa 1980.

al-Ḥuṣrī, *Jamʿ al-jawāhir fī l-mulaḥ wa'l-nawādir*. Ed. Riḥāb ʿUkāwī. Bayrūt: Dār al-Manāhil 1413/1993.

al-Ḥuṣrī, *Zahr al-ādāb wa-thamar al-albāb*. Ed. Zakī Mubārak and Muḥammad Muḥyī al-Dīn ʿAbd al-Ḥamīd. 4th edition. Bayrūt: Dār al-Jīl 1972.

Ibn ʿAbbād, *al-Muḥīṭ fī l-lugha*. I–II. Ed. Muḥammad Ḥasan Āl-Yāsīn. Bayrūt: ʿĀlam al-kutub 1414/1994.

Ibn ʿAbd al-Barr, *Bahjat al-majālis wa-uns al-mujālis*. I–III. Ed. Muḥammad Mursī al-Khūlī. Bayrūt: Dār al-Kutub al-ʿilmiyya 1402/1982.

Ibn ʿAbd al-Ḥakam, *al-Khalīfa al-ʿādil ʿUmar ibn ʿAbd al-ʿAzīz* (*riwāyat ibnihi*). Ed. Aḥmad ʿUbayd. Al-Qāhira: Dār al-Faḍīla n.d.

Ibn ʿAbdrabbih, *al-ʿIqd al-farīd*. Ed. Aḥmad Amīn et al. I–VII. 3rd edition. Al-Qāhira: Maṭbaʿat lajnat al-taʾlīf wa'l-tarjama wa'l-nashr 1384/1965.

Ibn abī ʿAwn, *al-Ajwiba al-muskita*. Ed. Mayy Aḥmad Yūsuf. Al-Qāhira: ʿAyn li'l-dirāsāt wa'l-buḥūth al-insāniyya wa'l-ijtimāʿiyya 1996.

Ibn abī l-Ḥadīd, *Sharḥ Nahj al-balāgha*. I–V. Ed. Ḥasan Tamīm. Bayrūt: Dār Maktabat al-ḥayāt 1979.

Ibn abī Uṣaybiʿa, *ʿUyūn al-anbāʾ fī ṭabaqāt al-aṭibbāʾ*. Ed. Muḥammad Bāsil ʿUyūn-al-Sūd. Bayrūt: Dār al-Kutub al-ʿilmiyya 1419/1998.

Ibn al-ʿAdīm, *Bughyat al-ṭalab fī taʾrīkh Ḥalab*. I–XII. Ed. al-Mahdī ʿĪd al-Rawāḍiya. London: Muʾassasat al-Furqān li'l-turāth al-islāmī 1438/2016.

Ibn al-Ajdābī, *al-Azmina wa'l-Anwāʾ*. Ed. ʿIzzat Ḥasan. Al-Rabāṭ: Dār Abī Raqrāq 2006.

Ibn al-Anbārī, *Nuzhat al-alibbāʾ fī ṭabaqāt al-udabāʾ*. Ed. Atiyya Amer. Stockholm Oriental Studies 2. Stockholm: Almqvist & Wicksell 1963.

Ibn ʿAsākir, *Taʾrīkh Madīnat Dimashq*. I–LXXX. Ed. Muḥibb al-Dīn Abū Saʿīd ʿUmar ibn Gharāma al-ʿAmrawī et al. Bayrūt: Dār al-Fikr 1415–1421/1995–2000.

Ibn ʿĀṣim, *Ḥadāʾiq al-azāhir*. Ed. ʿAfīf ʿAbd al-Raḥmān. Bayrūt: Dār al-Masīra 1407/1987.

Ibn Aydamur, *Durr* = Fuat Sezgin (ed. [in facs.]), *The Priceless Pearl a Poetical Verse*. I–VII. Publications of the Institute for the History of Arabic-Islamic Science. Facsimile editions 45. Frankfurt am Main: Institute for the History of Arabic-Islamic Science at the Johann Wolfgang Goethe University 1997.

Ibn Badrūn, *Sharḥ qaṣīdat Ibn ʿAbdūn*. Ed. R. Dozy. Leyde: Luchtmans 1846.

Ibn Bassām, *al-Dhakhīra fī maḥāsin ahl al-Jazīra*. I–IV (in 8 vols.). Ed. Iḥsān ʿAbbās. Lībiyā – Tūnis: al-Dār al-ʿarabiyya li'l-kitāb 1398–1399/1978–1979.
Ibn al-Buḥturī, *Uns al-masjūn wa-rāḥat al-maḥzūn*. Ed. Muḥammad Adīb al-Jādir. Bayrūt: Dār Ṣādir 1997.
Ibn Durayd, *Jamharat al-lugha*. I–III. Ed. Ramzī Munīr Baʿlabakkī. Bayrūt: Dār al-ʿIlm li'l-malāyyīn 1987–1988.
Ibn al-Faqīh, *Kitāb al-Buldān*. Ed. Yūsuf al-Hāwī. Bayrūt: ʿĀlam al-kutub 1416/1996.
Ibn al-Faqīh, *Mukhtaṣar* = M.J. de Goeje (ed.), *Ibn al-Fakīh al-Hamadhānī, Compendium libri Kitāb al-Boldān*. Bibliotheca Geographorum Arabicorum V. (Lugduni Batavorum: Brill 1885), repr. Beyrūt: Dār Ṣādir 1967.
Ibn al-Faraḍī al-Andalusī, *Kitāb al-Alqāb*. Ed. Muḥammad Zaynhum Muḥammad ʿAzab. Bayrūt: Dār al-Jīl 1412/1992.
Ibn Fāris, *al-Ṣāḥibī fī fiqh al-lugha wa-sunan al-ʿarab fī kalāmihā*. Ed. Muṣṭafā ash-Shuwaymī (Moustafa el-Chouémi). Bibliotheca Philologica Arabica 1. 1383/1964.
Ibn Ḥabīb (ʿAbd al-Malik), *Kitāb Adab al-nisā' al-mawsūm bi-Kitāb al-Ghāya wa'l-nihāya*. Ed. ʿAbd al-Majīd Turkī. Bayrūt: Dār al-Gharb al-islāmī 1412/1992.
Ibn Ḥabīb (ʿAbd al-Malik), *Kitāb al-Ta'rīkh*. Ed. Sālim Muṣṭafā al-Badrī. Bayrūt: Dār al-Kutub al-ʿilmiyya 1420/1999.
Ibn Ḥamdūn, *Tadhkira*. I–X. Ed. Iḥsān ʿAbbās and Bakr ʿAbbās. Bayrūt: Dār Ṣādir 1996.
Ibn Hishām, *al-Sīra al-nabawiyya*. I–V. Eds. Jamāl Thābit, Muḥammad Maḥmūd and Sayyid Ibrāhīm. Al-Qāhira: Dār al-Ḥadīth 1996.
Ibn Hudhayl al-Fazārī, *Fukāhāt al-asmār wa-mudhahhabāt al-akhbār wa'l-ashʿār*. Ed. ʿAbdallāh Ḥammādī. Al-Kuwayt: Mu'assasat jā'izat ʿAbd al-ʿAzīz Suʿūd al-Bābṭayn li'l-ibdāʿ al-shiʿrī 2004.
Ibn Hudhayl al-Fazārī, *Maqālāt al-udabā' wa-munāẓarāt al-nujabā'*. Ed. ʿAbd al-Raḥmān ibn ʿUthmān al-Halīl. Maṭbaʿat al-Narjis 1426/2005.
Ibn al-Jawzī, *Ādāb al-Ḥasan al-Baṣrī wa-zuhduhu wa-mawāʿiẓuhu*. Ed. Sulaymān al-Ḥarash. Bayrūt: Dār al-Ṣiddīq 1426/2005.
Ibn al-Jawzī, *Kitāb al-Adhkiyā'*. Bayrūt: al-Maktab al-tijārī li'l-ṭibāʿa wa'l-tawzīʿ wa'l-nashr n.d.
Ibn al-Jawzī, *Kitāb Akhbār al-ḥamqā wa'l-mughaffalīn*. Bayrūt: Dār al-Āfāq al-jadīda 1979.
Ibn al-Jawzī, *Akhbār al-nisā'*. Ed. Barakāt Yūsuf Habbūd. Ṣaydā – Bayrūt: al-Maktaba al-ʿaṣriyya 1421/2000.
Ibn al-Jawzī, *Sīrat ʿUmar ibn ʿAbd al-ʿAzīz*. Ed. Muḥibb al-Dīn al-Khaṭīb. Miṣr: Maṭbaʿat al-Mu'ayyad 1331 AH/1291 AHSh.
Ibn Jinnī, *al-Fasr. Sharḥ Ibn Jinnī al-kabīr ʿalā Dīwān al-Mutanabbī*. I–V (in 6 vols.). Ed. Riḍā Rajab. Dimashq: Dār al-Yanābīʿ 2004.
Ibn al-Kalbī, *Jamhara* = Werner Caskel, *Ğamharat an-nasab. Das genealogische Werk des Hišām ibn Muḥammad al-Kalbī*. I–II. Leiden: Brill 1966.

Ibn Kathīr, *Qiṣaṣ al-anbiyāʾ*. I–II. Ed. ʿAbd al-Qādir Aḥmad ʿAṭā. Bayrūt: al-Maktaba al-islāmiyya n.d.

Ibn Khalaf, *Mawādd al-bayān*. Ed. (in facs.) Fuat Sezgin. Publications of the Institute for the History of Arabic-Islamic Science. Series C: Facsimile editions 39. Institute for the History of Arabic-Islamic Science 1986.

Ibn Khallikān, *Wafayāt al-aʿyān*. I–VI. Ed. Iḥsān ʿAbbās. Bayrūt: Dār Ṣādir n.d.

Ibn al-Kumaylī, *Nuzhat al-albāb al-jāmiʿa li-funūn al-ādāb*. I–II. Ed. ʿAbd al-Qādir Suʿūd. Bayrūt: Dār al-Kutub al-ʿilmiyya 1433/2012.

Ibn Mākūlā, *al-Ikmāl fī rafʿ al-irtiyāb*. I–IV. Ed. ʿAbd al-Raḥmān ibn Yaḥyā al-Muʿallimī al-Yamānī. 2nd edition. (Hyderabad: The Dairatu'l-maʿarifil-Osmani 1965), repr. Bayrūt: Muḥammad Amīn Damaj n.d.

Ibn Manẓūr, *Lisān al-ʿarab*. I–XVIII. Ed. (and reorganised according to the first radical) ʿAlī Shīrī. Bayrūt: Dār Iḥyāʾ al-turāth al-ʿarabī 1408/1988.

Ibn Manẓūr, *Muhktaṣar Taʾrīkh Dimashq li-Ibn ʿAsākir*. I–XXIX. Edited by various editors. Dimashq: Dār al-Fikr 1404–1408/1984–1988.

Ibn al-Mudabbir, *al-Risāla al-ʿadhrāʾ*. Ed. Zakī Mubārak. (Al-Qāhira: Maṭbaʿat Dār al-kutub al-miṣriyya 1350/1931), 2nd edition. Dimashq: Dār Saʿd al-Dīn 1422/2002.

Ibn Munqidh (Usāma), *Lubāb al-ādāb*. Ed. Aḥmad Muḥammad Shākir. Bayrūt: Dār al-Jīl 1411/1991.

Ibn al-Muqaffaʿ, *al-Adab al-kabīr wa'l-adab al-ṣaghīr*. Bayrūt: Dār al-Jīl n.d.

Ibn al-Murtaḍā, *Bāb* = T.W. Arnold, *Al Muʿtazilah: Being an Extract from the Kitābu-l Milal wa-n niḥal by (...) B. al Murtadā*. Part I: Arabic Text. (Leipzig: Harrassowitz 1902), repr. Bayrūt: Dār Ṣādir n.d.

Ibn al-Muʿtazz, *Kitāb al-Badīʿ*. Ed. Ignatius Kratchkovsky. (E.J.W. Gibb Memorial Series N.S. X. London 1935), repr. Bayrūt: Dār al-Masīra 1402/1982.

Ibn al-Muʿtazz, *Ṭabaqāt al-shuʿarāʾ. Ṭabaqāt al-shuʿarāʾ al-muḥdathīn*. Ed. ʿUmar Fārūq al-Ṭabbāʿ. Bayrūt: Dār al-Arqam 1419/1998.

Ibn an-Nadīm, *Fihrist*. Ed. Riḍā Tajaddud. Intishārāt-e asāṭīr 348. Tihrān: Asāṭīr 1381 AHSh.

Ibn al-Najjār, *Dhayl Taʾrīkh Baghdād*, printed as volumes 16–20 of al-Khaṭīb, *Taʾrīkh*.

Ibn al-Naqīb, *Muqaddimat tafsīr Ibn al-Naqīb* (formerly also known as Ibn Qayyim al-Jawziyya, *al-Fawāʾid*). Ed. Zakariyyā Saʿīd ʿAlī. Al-Qāhira: Maktabat al-Khānjī 1415/1995.

Ibn Nāqiyā, *al-Jumān fī tashbīhāt al-Qurʾān*. Ed. Muḥammad ibn Riḍwān al-Dāya. Bayrūt – Dimashq: Dār al-Fikr al-muʿāṣir – Dār al-Fikr 1423/2002.

Ibn Nubāta al-Miṣrī, *Sarḥ al-ʿuyūn fī sharḥ risālat Ibn Zaydūn*. Ed. Muḥammad Abū l-Faḍl Ibrāhīm. Ṣaydā – Bayrūt: al-Maktaba al-ʿaṣriyya 1419/1998.

Ibn Qayyim al-Jawziyya, *Kitāb Akhbār al-nisāʾ*. Ed. Nizār Riḍā. Bayrūt: Dār Maktabat al-ḥayāt 1405/1985.

Ibn al-Qifṭī, *Taʾrīkh al-ḥukamāʾ*. Ed. Julius Lippert. Leipzig: Dieterisch'sche Verlagsbuchhandlung (Theodor Weicher) 1903.

Ibn Qutayba, *Faḍl* = Ibn Qutaybah, *The Excellence of the Arabs*. Ed. James E. Montgomery and Peter Webb, translated by Sarah Bowen Savant and Peter Webb. Library of Arabic Literature. New York: New York University Press 2017.

Ibn Qutayba, *Gharīb al-ḥadīth*. I–II. Ed. Naʿīm Zarzūr. Bayrūt: Dār al-Kutub al-ʿilmiyya 1408/1988.

Ibn Qutayba, *al-Maʿārif*. Ed. Tharwat ʿUkāsha. Dhakhāʾir al-ʿarab 44. 2nd edition. Al-Qāhira: Dār al-Maʿārif bi-Miṣr 1969.

Ibn Qutayba, *Kitāb al-Shiʿr waʾl-shuʿarāʾ*. Ed. M.J. de Goeje. (Lugduni Batavorum 1904), repr. Dār Ṣādir n.d.

Ibn Qutayba, *ʿUyūn al-akhbār*. I–IV. Ed. Yūsuf ʿAlī Ṭawīl. Bayrūt: Dār al-Kutub al-ʿilmiyya 1406/1986.

ps.-Ibn Qutayba, *Kitāb al-Imāma waʾs-siyāsa al-maʿrūf bi-Taʾrīkh al-khulafāʾ*. I–II. Ed. ʿAlī Shīrī. Qum: Amīr 1371/1413.

Ibn Rajab, *Sīrat ʿAbd al-Malik ibn ʿUmar ibn ʿAbd al-ʿAzīz*. Ed. ʿIffat Wiṣāl Ḥamza. Bayrūt: Dār Ibn Ḥazm 1414/1994.

Ibn Rashīq, *al-ʿUmda fī maḥāsin al-shiʿr wa-ādābihi wa-naqdihi*. Ed. Muḥammad Qarqazān. Second edition. Dimashq: Maṭbaʿat al-Kātib al-ʿarabī 1414/1994.

Ibn Razīn al-Kātib, Ādāb *al-mulūk*. Ed. Jalīl ʿAṭiyya. Bayrūt: Dār al-Ṭalīʿa 1421/2001.

Ibn Rustah, *Kitāb Aʿlāq al-nafīsa*. Ed. M.J. de Goeje. Bibliotheca Geographorum Arabicorum VII. (Lugduni Batavorum: Brill 1892), repr. Bayrūt: Dār Ṣādir 1967.

Ibn al-Sarrāj, *Jawāhir al-adab wa-dhakhāʾir al-shuʿarāʾ waʾl-kuttāb*. I–II. Ed. Muḥammad Ḥasan Qarqazān. Dimashq: Wizārat al-thaqāfa 2008.

Ibn Shams al-Khilāfa, *Kitāb al-Ādāb*. Ed. Yāsīn al-Ayyūbī. Ṣaydā – Bayrūt: al-Maktaba al-ʿaṣriyya 1422/2001.

Ibn al-Shajarī, *Amālī*. I–III. Ed. Maḥmūd and Muḥammad al-Ṭanājī. Al-Qāhira: Maktabat al-Khānjī 1413/1992.

Ibn Shuhayd, *Rasāʾil* = *Dīwān Ibn Shuhayd wa-rasāʾiluhu*. Ed. Muḥyī al-Dīn Dīb. Ṣaydā – Bayrūt: al-Maktaba al-ʿaṣriyya n.d. (1996?).

Ibn as-Sikkīt, *Kitāb al-Qalb waʾl-ibdāl*. Ed. A. Haffner, *Texte zur arabischen Lexikographie*. Leipzig: Harrassowitz 1905, pp. 3–65.

al-Ibshīhī, *al-Mustaṭraf fī kull fann mustaẓraf*. I–II. Bayrūt: Manshūrāt Dār maktabat al-ḥayāt 1986.

al-Iṣfahānī (Abū l-Faraj), *Kitāb al-Aghānī*. I–XX. (Būlāq 1285), repr. Bayrūt: Dār Ṣaʿb n.d.

al-Iskāfī, *Mukhtaṣar Kitāb al-ʿAyn*. I–III. Ed. Hādī Ḥasan Ḥammūdī. Masqaṭ: Wizārat al-turāth al-qawmī waʾl-thaqāfa 1998.

al-Itlīdī, *Iʿlām an-nās*. Bayrūt: Dār Ṣādir 1410/1990.

al-Jāḥiẓ, *al-Bayān waʾl-tabyīn*. Ed. ʿAbd al-Salām Muḥammad Hārūn. I–IV. Bayrūt: Dār al-Jīl n.d.

al-Jāḥiẓ, *Bighāl*. See al-Jāḥiẓ, *Rasāʾil* II: 211–378.

al-Jāḥiẓ, *Kitāb al-Bukhalāʾ*. Ed. Ṭāhā al-Ḥājirī. 6th edition. Dhakhāʾir al-ʿarab 23. Al-Qāhira: Dār al-Maʿārif n.d.

al-Jāḥiẓ, *Kitāb Faṣl mā bayna l-ʿadāwa wa'l-ḥasad*. See al-Jāḥiẓ, *Rasā'il* I: 333–373.

al-Jāḥiẓ, *Kitāb al-Ḥayawān*. I–VIII. Ed. ʿAbdallāh Muḥammad Hārūn. 2nd edition. Al-Qāhira: al-Bābī al-Ḥalabī wa-awlādihi 1384–1387/1965–1969.

ps.-al-Jāḥiẓ, *Maḥāsin* = Gerlof van Vloten, *Le Livre des beautés et des antithèses attribué à al-Djahiz*. (Leyde 1898), repr. Amsterdam: Oriental Press n.d.

al-Jāḥiẓ, *Qiyān*. See al-Jāḥiẓ, *Rasā'il* II: 211–378.

al-Jāḥiẓ, *Rasā'il*. I–II. Ed. ʿAbd al-Salām Muḥammad Hārūn. Cairo: Maktabat al-Khānjī 1384/1964.

al-Jāḥiẓ, *Ṣināʿat al-quwwād*. See al-Jāḥiẓ, *Rasā'il* I: 375–393.

[ps.]-al-Jāḥiẓ, *Kitāb al-Tāj*. Ed. Fawzī ʿAṭawī. Bayrūt: al-Sharika al-lubnāniyya li'l-kitāb 1970.

al-Jahshiyārī, *al-Wuzarāʾ wa'l-kuttāb*. Ed. Ibrāhīm Ṣāliḥ. Abū Ẓaby: National Library Abu Dhabi Authority for Culture & Heritage Cultural Foundation n.d.

al-Jarīrī, *al-Jalīs al-ṣāliḥ al-kāfī wa'l-anīs al-nāṣiḥ al-shāfī*. I–IV. Ed. Muḥammad Mursī al-Khūlī (vols. I–II) and Iḥsān ʿAbbās (vols. III–IV). Bayrūt: ʿĀlam al-kitāb 1413/1993.

Jirāb al-Dawla (Aḥmad ibn Muḥammad), *Min Kitāb Tarwīḥ al-arwāḥ wa-miftāḥ al-surūr wa'l-afrāḥ*. Ed. Ibrāhīm al-Sāmarrā'ī. ʿAmmān: Dār al-Karmil 1997.

al-Jurjānī, *Asrār al-balāgha*. Ed. Muḥammad Rashīd Riḍā and Usāma Ṣalāḥ al-Dīn Munaymina. Bayrūt: Dār Iḥyāʾ al-ʿulūm 1412/1992.

al-Jurjānī (Aḥmad), *al-Muntakhab min kināyāt al-udabāʾ wa-ishārāt al-bulaghāʾ*. Ed. Muḥammad Shams al-Ḥaqq Shamsī. Ḥaydarābād: Dā'irat al-maʿārif al-ʿuthmāniyya 1403/1983.

Kalīla wa-Dimna = L[ouis] Cheikho, *La version arabe de Kalîlah et Dimnah*. Beyrouth: Imprimerie catholique 1905.

al-Khafājī, *Sirr al-faṣāḥa*. Ed. Dā'ūd Ghaṭāsha al-Shawābika. ʿAmmān: Dār al-Fikr 1427/2006.

al-Khālidiyyān, *al-Tuḥaf wa'l-hadāyā*. Ed. Sāmī Dahhān. Al-Qāhira: Dār al-Maʿārif 1956.

al-Khansāʾ, *Dīwān*. Ed. Anwar Abū Suwaylim. ʿAmmān: Dār ʿAmmār 1409/1988.

al-Khaṭīb al-Baghdādī, *al-Bukhalāʾ*. Ed. Abū ʿAbdallāh Sayyid ibn ʿAbbās al-Julaymī. Bayrūt: Mu'assasat al-kutub al-thaqāfiyya 1420/2000.

al-Khaṭīb al-Baghdādī, *Ta'rīkh Baghdād*. I–XIV. Bayrūt n.d.

Kuthayyir ʿAzza, *Dīwān*. Ed. ʿAdnān Zakī Darwīsh. Bayrūt: Dār Ṣādir 1994.

al-Maʿarrī (Abū l-ʿAlāʾ), *Risālat al-Ṣāhil wa'l-shāḥij*. Ed. ʿĀ'isha ʿAbd al-Raḥmān (Bint al-Shāṭiʾ). Dhakhā'ir al-ʿarab 51. 2nd edition. Al-Qāhira: Dār al-Maʿārif 1404/1984.

al-Maghribī (al-Samaw'al ibn Yaḥyā), *Nuzhat al-aṣḥāb fī muʿāsharat al-aḥbāb*. Ed. Kisrawī Ḥasan. Bayrūt: Dār al-Kutub al-ʿilmiyya 1429/2008.

Maʿn ibn Aws al-Muzanī, *Dīwān*. Ed. Ḥātim Ṣāliḥ al-Ḍāmin. Bayrūt: Dār Ṣādir 1433/2012.

al-Maqdisī (al-Muṭahhar ibn Ṭāhir), *Kitāb al-Badʾ wa't-ta'rīkh*. I–VI. Ed. Clément Huart. (Paris 1899–1907), repr. [of the Arabic text only] Bayrūt: Dār Ṣādir n.d.

al-Maqdisī (Abū Naṣr), *al-Laṭāʾif waʾl-ẓarāʾif* (*jamaʿa fīhi kitābay Abī Manṣūr al-Thaʿālibī, al-Laṭāʾif waʾl-ẓarāʾif fī l-aḍdād, waʾl-Yawāqīt fī baʿḍi l-mawāqīt*). Ed. ʿAbd al-Raḥīm Yūsuf al-Jamal. Al-Qāhira: Maktabat al-ādāb n.d.

al-Maqdisī (Ḍiyāʾ al-Dīn), *al-Muntaqā min akhbār al-Aṣmaʿī*. Ed. ʿIzz al-Dīn al-Tanūkhī. (Maṭbūʿāt Majmaʿ al-Lugha al-ʿArabiyya bi-Dimashq 1354/1936), 2nd edition Dimashq: al-Bayyina 1432/2011.

al-Maqqarī, *al-Mukhtār min nawādir al-akhbār*. Ed. Anwar Abū Suwaylim. Min ʿuyūn al-turāth al-ʿarabī. Bayrūt – al-Batrāʾ: Muʾassasat al-Risāla – Dār ʿAmmār 1409/1989.

al-Marzubānī, *Muʿjam al-shuʿarāʾ* (and *Tatimmat Muʿjam al-shuʿarāʾ*). I–II. Ed. ʿAbbās Hānī al-Charākh. Bayrūt: Dār al-Kutub al-ʿilmiyya 2010.

al-Marzubānī, *al-Muwashshaḥ fī maʾākhidh al-ʿulamāʾ ʿalā l-shuʿarāʾ*. Al-Qāhira 1343.

al-Marzubānī, *Kitāb Nūr al-qabas al-Mukhtaṣar min al-Muqtabas*. I [text]. Ed. Rudolf Sellheim. Bibliotheca Islamica 23a. Wiesbaden: Franz Steiner 1964.

al-Masʿūdī, *Murūj al-dhahab*. I–VIII. Ed. Barbier de Meynard and Pavet de Courteille. Revised by Charles Pellat. l'Université Libanaise. Section des études historiques XI. Beyrouth: l'Université Libanaise 1966–79.

al-Māwardī, *Adab al-dunyā waʾl-dīn*. Ed. Muṣṭafā al-Saqqā. Bayrūt: Dār al-Kutub al-ʿilmiyya 1398/1978.

al-Maydānī, *Majmaʿ al-amthāl*. I–IV. Ed. Muḥammad Abū l-Faḍl Ibrāhīm. (Maṭbaʿat ʿĪsā al-Ḥalabī wa-shurakāʾihi), repr. Dār al-Kutub 1977–1979.

Miskawayhi, *al-Ḥikma al-khālida*. Ed. ʿAbd al-Raḥmān Badawī. Intishārāt-e Dānishgāh-i Tihrān 1695. Tihrān: Muʾassasat intishārāt-o chāp-e dānishgāh-e Tihrān 1377 AHSh.

Miskawayhi, *Tajārib al-umam wa-taʿāqub al-himam*. I–VII. Ed. Sayyid Kisrawī Ḥasan. Bayrūt: Dār al-Kutub al-ʿilmiyya 1424/2003.

al-Mubarrad, *al-Kāmil*. I-IV. Ed. Muḥammad Abū l-Faḍl Ibrāhīm. Miṣr: Dār Nahḍat Miṣr n.d.

al-Mubarrad, *Kitāb al-Taʿāzī waʾl-marāthī*. Ed. Muḥammad al-Dībājī. (Maṭbūʿāt Majmaʿ al-lugha al-ʿarabiyya bi-Dimashq. 2nd edition), repr. Bayrūt: Dār Ṣādir 1412/1992.

al-Muqriʾ, *Akhbār al-naḥwiyyīn*. Ed. Yaḥyā Fatḥī al-Sayr. Ṭanṭā: Dār al-Ṣaḥāba liʾl-turāth 1410/1989.

al-Murtaḍā (al-Sharīf), *Amālī* = *Ghurar al-fawāʾid wa-durar al-qalāʾid*. I–II. Ed. Muḥammad Abū l-Faḍl Ibrāhīm. Al-Qāhira: Dār al-Fikr al-ʿarabī 1998.

al-Nābigha, *Dīwān* = W. Ahlwardt, *The Divans of Six Ancient Arabic Poets*. (1879), repr. Osnabrück: Biblio Verlag 1972: 2–32.

al-Naḥḥās, *ʿUmdat al-kuttāb*. Ed. Bassām ʿAbd al-Wahhāb al-Jābī. Bayrūt: Dār Ibn Ḥazm 1425/2004.

al-Najāshī, *Kitāb al-Rijāl*. Bayrūt: Sharikat al-aʿlamī liʾl-maṭbūʿāt 1431/2010.

Nakhshabī, *Gulrīz* = Agha Muhammad Kazin Shirazi, *Gulriz*. Bibliotheca Indica NS 1327. Calcutta: Baptist Mission Press 1912.

Nawādir Abī Nuwās. Silsilat "al-ḍāḥikūn". Bayrūt: Maktabat al-maʿārif n.d.

Nawādir Abī Nuwās. Bayrūt: Maktabat al-taʿāwun n.d.

al-Nuwayrī, *Nihāyat al-arab*. I–XXXI. Al-Qāhira: Wizārat al-thaqāfa n.d.

al-Qālī, *Afʿal min kadhā*. Ed. ʿAlī Ibrāhīm Kurdī. Dimashq: Dār Saʿd al-Dīn 1421/2000.

al-Qālī, *Kitāb al-Amālī*. I–II. Bayrūt: Dār al-Fikr n.d.

al-Qālī, *Dhayl al-Amālī* and *Kitāb an-Nawādir* [bound together]. [Bayrūt:] Dār al-Fikr n.d.

Qifṭī, *Tārīkh al-ḥukamāʾ. Tarjuma-e fārsī az qarn-e yāzdahum-e hijrī*. Ed. Bahīn Dārāʾī. Intishārāt-e Dānishgāh-e Tihrān 1174. Tihrān: Dānishgāh-e Tihrān 1347.

al-Rāghib al-Iṣbahānī, *Muḥāḍarāt al-udabāʾ*. I–IV. Bayrūt: Dār Maktabat al-ḥayāt 1961.

al-Raqīq al-Qayrawānī, *Quṭb al-surūr fī awṣāf al-anbidha wa'l-khumūr*. Ed. Sāra al-Barbūshī Ibn Yaḥyā. Freiberg a.N.: Al-Kamel Verlag 2010.

Rasāʾil al-bulaghāʾ. Ed. Muḥammad Kurd ʿAlī. 4th edition. Al-Qāhira: Maṭbaʿat Lajnat al-taʾlīf wa'l-tarjama wa'l-nashr 1374/1954.

al-Ṣābiʾ (Ibn Hilāl), *al-Hafawāt al-nādira*. Ed. Ṣāliḥ al-Ashtar. Dimashq: Majmaʿ al-lugha al-ʿarabiyya bi-Dimashq 1387/1967.

al-Ṣafadī, *Kitāb al-Wāfī bi'l-wafayāt*. I–XXX. Ed. H. Ritter et al. Bibliotheca Islamica 6a–ze. Wiesbaden – Bayrūt: Franz Steiner 1962–2008.

al-Ṣafadī, *Nukat al-himyān fī nukat al-ʿumyān*. Ed. Aḥmad Zakī Bey. (Al-Maṭbaʿa al-jamāliyya bi-Miṣr 1329/1911), repr. Dār al-Madaniyya n.d.

al-Ṣaghānī, *al-Takmila wa-l-dhayl wa-l-ṣila*. I–VI. Ed. ʿAbd al-ʿAlīm al-Ṭaḥāwī and ʿAbd al-Ḥamīd Ḥasan. Cairo: Dār al-Kutub 1970–1979.

Ṣāʿid al-Andalusī, *at-Taʿrīf bi-ṭabaqāt al-umam*. Ed. Ghulām-Riḍā Jamshīdnizhād-e Avval. Mīrāth-e maktūb 40. Tihrān: Muʾassasa-ye Intishārāt-e Hijrat 1376 AHSh.

al-Salawī (ʿAbd al-Qādir ibn ʿAbd al-Raḥmān), *al-Kawkab al-thāqib fī akhbār al-shuʿarāʾ wa-ghayrihim min dhawī l-manāqib*. I–III. Ed. ʿAbdallāh al-Yāsimī. Manshūrāt wizārat al-awqāf wa'l-shuʾūn al-islāmiyya. Al-Rabāṭ: Dār Abī Raqrāq 1427/2006.

al-Sharīshī, *Sharḥ maqāmāt al-Ḥarīrī*. I–IV. Bayrūt: Dār Maktabat al-thaqāfiyya n.d.

al-Shimsāṭī (al-ʿAdawī), *Kitāb al-Anwār wa-maḥāsin al-ashʿār*. I–II. Ed. Muḥammad Yūsuf and ʿAbd al-Sattār Aḥmad Farrāj. Al-Turāth al-ʿarabī 19–20. Al-Kuwayt: Maṭbaʿat ḥukūmat al-Kuwayt 1397–1399/1977–1978.

al-Shirwānī, *Nafḥat al-Yaman*. Ed. Kabīr al-Dīn Aḥmad. Calcutta 1278.

Shurūḥ Saqṭ al-zand. I–V. Ed. Muṣṭafā al-Saqqā et al. Al-Qāhira: al-Hayʾa al-miṣriyya li'l-kitāb 1408/1987.

Sibṭ ibn al-Jawzī, *al-Jalīs al-ṣāliḥ wa'l-anīs al-nāṣiḥ*. Ed. Fawwāz Ṣāliḥ Fawwāz. London: Riyāḍ al-rayyis li'l-kutub wa'l-nashr 1989.

Sibṭ ibn al-Jawzī, *Kanz* = Gösta Vitestam, *Kanz al-mulūk fī kayfiyyat al-sulūk. The Treasure of Princes on the Fashion of Behaviour ascribed to Sibṭ ibn al-Djawzī*. Acta Reg. Societatis Humaniorum Litterarum Lundensis LXVI. Lund: Berlingska Boktryckeriet 1970.

al-Sijistāni, *Kitāb al-Nakhl*. Ed. Ibrāhīm al-Sāmarrāʾī. Bayrūt: Dār al-Liwāʾ 1405/1985.

al-Sīrāfī, *Akhbār* = F. Krenkow, Biographies des *grammairiens de l'école de Basra*. Paris – Beyrouth: Paul Geuthner – Imprimerie catholique 1936.

al-Sukkarī, *Sharḥ Dīwān al-Hudhaliyyīn* I–III. Ed. ʿAbd al-Sattār Aḥmad Farrāj and Maḥmūd Muḥammad Shākir. Kunūz al-shiʿr 3. Al-Qāhira: Maṭbaʿat al-Madanī n.d.

al-Ṣūlī, *Akhbār al-Buḥturī*. Ed. Ṣāliḥ al-Ashtar. Dimashq: al-Majmaʿ al-ʿilmī al-ʿarabī bi-Dimashq 1378/1958.

al-Suyūṭī, *al-Muzhir fī ʿulūm al-lugha*. I–II. Ed. Muḥammad Aḥmad Jād al-Mawlā Beg, Muḥammad Abū l-Faḍl Ibrāhīm and ʿAlī Muḥammad al-Bijāwī. Ṣaydā – Bayrūt: al-Maktaba al-ʿaṣriyya 1406/1986.

al-Suyūṭī, *Shaqāʾiq al-utrujj fī raqāʾiq al-ghunj*. Ed. Muḥammad Sayyid al-Rifāʿī. Dimashq: Dār al-Kitāb al-ʿarabī n.d.

al-Suyūṭī, *Taʾrīkh al-khulafāʾ*. Ed. ʿAbdallāh Masʿūd. Ḥalab: Dār al-Qalam al-ʿarabī 1413/1993.

al-Ṭabarī, *Taʾrīkh al-rusul waʾl-mulūk* = Michael Jan de Goeje et al. (eds.), *Annales quod scripsit (...) al-Ṭabarî*. I–XV. Leiden: Brill 1879–1901. Translation, see sub Rosenthal et al. (1987–2007).

al-Tanūkhī, *Kitāb al-Faraj baʿd al-shidda*. I–V. Ed. ʿAbbūd al-Shāljī. Bayrūt: Dār Ṣādir 1398/1978.

al-Tawḥīdī (Abū Ḥayyān), *al-Baṣāʾir waʾl-dhakhāʾir*. I–IX. Ed. Wadād al-Qāḍī. Bayrūt: Dār Ṣādir 1408/1988.

al-Tawḥīdī (Abū Ḥayyān), *Kitāb al-Imtāʿ waʾl-muʾānasa*. I–III. Ed. Aḥmad Amīn and Aḥmad al-Zayn. Bayrūt – Ṣaydā: al-Maktaba al-ʿaṣriyya 1373/1953.

al-Tawḥīdī (Abū Ḥayyān), *Risālat al-Ṣadāqa waʾl-ṣadīq*. Ed. Ibrāhīm al-Kīlānī. 2nd edition. Dimashq – Bayrūt: Dār al-Fikr – Dār al-Fikr al-muʿāṣir 1416/1996.

al-Thaʿālibī, *Bard al-akbād fī l-aʿdād*. Ed. Iḥsān Dhunnūn al-Thāmirī. Bayrūt: Dār Ibn Ḥazm 1427/2006.

al-Thaʿālibī, *Ghurar* = Hermann Zotenberg, *Histoire des Rois des Perses*. (Paris 1900), repr. Amsterdam: Oriental Press n.d.

al-Thaʿālibī, *al-Kināya waʾl-taʿrīḍ*. In ʿAlī al-Khāqānī, *Rasāʾil al-Thaʿālibī*. Baghdād – Bayrūt: Maktabat Dār al-Bayān – Dār Ṣaʿb n.d.

al-Thaʿālibī, *Mirʾāt al-murūʾāt*. Ed. Iḥsān Dhunnūn al-Thāmirī. ʿAmmān: Dār Ward 2007.

al-Thaʿālibī, *al-Tamaththul waʾl-muḥāḍara*. Ed. Zahiyya Saʿdū. Bayrūt: Dār Ibn Ḥazm 1431/2010.

al-Thaʿālibī, *al-Tamthīl waʾl-muḥāḍara*. Ed. Quṣayy al-Ḥusayn. Bayrūt: Dār wa-maktabat al-Hilāl 2003.

al-Thaʿālibī (attr.), *Tarjamat al-kātib fī ādāb al-ṣāḥib*. Kitāb al-shahr 17. Ed. ʿAlī Dhīb Zāyid. ʿAmmān: Wizārat al-thaqāfa 2001.

al-Thaʿālibī, *Kitāb al-Tawfīq liʾl-talfīq*. Ed. Ibrāhīm Ṣāliḥ. Bayrūt – Dimashq: Dār al-Fikr al-muʿāṣir – Dār al-Fikr 1410/1990.

al-Thaʿālibī, *Thimār al-qulūb fī l-muḍāf wa'l-mansūb*. Ed. Muḥammad Abū l-Faḍl Ibrāhīm. Dhakhā'ir al-ʿarab 57. Al-Qāhira: Dār al-Maʿrifa 1965.

al-Thaʿālibī, *Yatīmat al-dahr.* I–IV. Beirut: Dār al-Kutub al-ʿilmiyya 1399/1979.

al-Thaʿālibī, *Kitāb al-Yawāqīt fī baʿḍ al-mawāqīt fī madḥ al-shay' wa-dhammihi*. Ed. Muḥammad Jāsim al-Ḥadīthī. Baghdād: Dār al-Shu'ūn al-thaqāfiyya al-ʿāmma 1990.

Thaʿlab, *Majālis*. I–II. Ed. ʿAbd al-Salām Muḥammad Hārūn. Dhakhā'ir al-ʿarab 1. Al-Qāhira: Dār al-Maʿārif 1948 (vol. II: 4th edition 1400/1980).

al-Thaʿlabī, *Tāj*, see sub ps.-al-Jāḥiẓ, *Tāj*.

al-Tijānī, *Tuḥfat al-ʿarūs wa-mutʿat al-nufūs*. Ed. Jalīl al-ʿAṭiyya. London-Cyprus: Riad el-Rayyes Books 1992. Trans.: Anon., *The Glory of the Perfumed Garden*. London: Neville Spearman 1975.

al-Ṭurṭūshī, *Sirāj al-mulūk*. I–II. Ed. Shawqī Ḍayf. Al-Qāhira: al-Dār al-miṣriyya al-lubnāniyya 1414/1994.

al-Ṭūsī, *Fihrist kutub al-shīʿa*. Ed. A. Sprenger and Abd al-Haqq Mawlavy. Bibliotheca Indica 19. Calcutta 1853–1855.

Wakīʿ ibn Ḥayyān, *Akhbār al-quḍāt*. 1) Ed. Saʿīd Muḥammad al-Laḥḥām. Bayrūt: ʿĀlam al-kutub 1422/2001; 2) Ed. ʿAbd al-ʿAzīz Muṣṭafā al-Marāghī. Al-Qāhira: Maṭbaʿat al-istiqāma 1366–1369/1947–1950.

al-Washshā', *Kitāb al-Fāḍil fī ṣifat al-adab al-kāmil*. Ed. Yaḥyā Wahīb al-Jabbūrī. Bayrūt: Dār al-Gharb al-islāmī 1411/1991.

al-Washshā', *al-Muwashshā aw al-ẓarf wa'l-ẓurafā'*. Bayrūt: Dār Bayrūt 1400/1980.

al-Waṭwāṭ, *Ghurar al-khaṣā'iṣ al-wāḍiḥa wa-ʿurar al-naqā'iṣ al-fāḍiḥa*. Ed. Ibrāhīm Shams al-Dīn. Bayrūt: Dār al-Kutub al-ʿilmiyya 1429/2008.

Yāqūt, *Muʿjam al-buldān*. I–VII. Bayrūt: Dār Ṣādir 1995.

Yāqūt, *Irshād al-arīb ilā maʿrifat al-adīb*. I–VI. Ed. Aḥmad Shams al-Dīn. Bayrūt: Dār al-Kutub al-ʿilmiyya 1411/1991.

Yāqūt al-Mustaʿṣimī, *Kitāb Asrār al-ḥukamā'*. Ed. Ibrāhīm Ṣāliḥ and Samīḥ Ṣāliḥ. Dār al-Bashā'ir 1994.

al-Zabīdī, *Tāj al-ʿarūs*. I–XL. Ed. ʿAbd al-Qādir Farrāj et al. Kuwait City: Maṭbaʿat ḥukūmat al-Kuwayt 1965–2001.

al-Zajjājī, *Majālis al-ʿulamā'*. Ed. ʿAbd al-Salām Muḥammad Hārūn. Al-Turāth al-ʿarabī 9. Al-Kuwayt: Wizārat al-irshād wa-l-inbā' fī l-Kuwayt 1962.

al-Zamakhsharī, *al-Fā'iq fī gharīb al-ḥadīth*. I–IV (in one vol.). Ed. ʿAlī Muḥammad al-Bijāwī and Muḥammad Abū l-Faḍl Ibrāhīm. Ṣaydā – Bayrūt: al-Maktaba al-ʿaṣriyya 1426/2005.

al-Zamakhsharī, *al-Mustaqṣā fī amthāl al-ʿarab*. I–II. Bayrūt: Dār al-Kutub al-ʿilmiyya 1408/1987.

al-Zamakhsharī, *Rabīʿ al-abrār wa-nuṣūṣ al-akhbār*. I–IV. Ed. Salīm al-Nuʿaymī. N.p. & n.d.

al-Zawzanī, *Ḥamāsat al-ẓurafāʾ min ashʿār al-muḥdathīn waʾl-qudamāʾ*. I–II. Ed. Muḥammad Bahī al-Dīn ibn Muḥammad Sālim. Al-Qāhira – Bayrūt: Dār al-Kutub al-miṣrī – Dār al-Kutub al-lubnānī 1420/1999.
al-Zubaydī, *Ṭabaqāt al-naḥwiyyīn waʾl-lughawiyyīn*. Ed. Muḥammad Abū l-Faḍl Ibrāhīm. 2nd edition. Al-Qāhira: Dār al-Maʿārif.
al-Zubayr ibn Bakkār, *al-Akhbār al-muwaffaqiyyāt*. Ed. Sāmī Makkī al-ʿĀnī. 2nd edition. Bayrūt: ʿĀlam al-kutub 1416/1996.
al-Zubayrī, *Nasab Quraysh*. Ed. É[variste] Levy-Provençal. Dhakhāʾir al-ʿarab 11. Al-Qāhira: Dār al-Maʿārif 1953.

3 Studies

Aarne, A. – S. Thompson (1961), *The Types of the Folktale. A Classification and Bibliography*. Second Revision. Folklore Fellows Communications 184. Helsinki: Academia Scientiarum Fennica.
Ahmed, Shahab (2000), "Mapping the world of a scholar: regional tradition in Medieval Islamic scholarship as reflected in a bibliography." *Journal of the American Oriental Society* 120: 24–43.
Akar, Sylvia (2006), *But if You Desire God and His Messenger. The Concept of Choice in Ṣaḥīḥ al-Bukhārī*. Studia Orientalia 102.
Al-Selwi, Ibrahim (1987), *Jemenitische Wörter in den Werken von al-Hamdānī und Našwān und ihre Parallelen in den semitischen Sprachen*. Marburger Studien zur Afrika- und Asienkunde. Serie B: Asien. Band 10.
Ammann, Ludwig (1993), *Vorbild und Vernunft. Die Regelung von Lachen und Scherzen im mittelalterlichen Islam*. Hildesheim – Zürich – New York: Olms.
Armstrong, Lyall R. (2017), *The Quṣṣāṣ of Early Islam*. Islamic History and Civilization. Studies and Texts 139. Leiden – Boston: Brill.
Askari, Nasrin (2016), *The Medieval Reception of the Shahnāma as a Mirror for Princes*. Studies in Persian Cultural History 9. Leiden – Boston: Brill.
Baalbaki, Ramzi (2014), *The Arabic Lexicographical Tradition from the 2nd/8th to the 12th/18th Century*. Handbook of Oriental Studies I/107. Leiden – Boston: Brill.
Beeston, A.F.L. (1980), *The Epistle on Singing-Girls by Jāḥiẓ*. Approaches to Arabic Literature 2. Warminster: Aris & Phillips.
Beeston, A.F.L. (1983), "The role of parallelism." In A.F.L. Beeston, T.M. Johnstone, R.B. Serjeant and G.R. Smith (eds.), *Cambridge History of Arabic Literature. Arabic literature to the end of the Umayyad period*. Cambridge: Cambridge University Press, pp. 180–185.
Blachère, Régis (1952–66), *Histoire de la littérature arabe des origines à la fin du XV*^{e} *siècle de J.-C.* I–III. Paris: Jean Maisonneuve successeur.

Blankinship, Khalid Yahya (1993) = Rosenthal et al. (1987–2007), vol. XI.

de Blois, François (1990), *Burzōy's Voyage to India and the Origin of the Book of Kalīlah wa Dimnah*. Prize Publication Fund XXIII. (The Royal Asiatic Society), repr. Abingdon, Oxon: Routledge 2011.

Borrut, Antoine (2010), *Entre mémoire et pouvoit. L'espace syrien sous les derniers Ommeyades et les premiers Abbassides (v. 72–193/692–809)*. Islamic History and Civilization. Studies and Texts 81. Leiden – Boston: Brill.

Bray, Julia (2019), *al-Muḥassin ibn ʿAlī al-Tanūkhī, Stories of Piety and Prayer. Deliverance Follows Adversity*. Library of Arabic Literature. New York: New York University Press.

Brinner, William M. (1987), = Rosenthal et al. (1987–2007), vol. II.

Bushnaq, Inea (1987), *Arab Folktales*. Penguin Folklore Library. London: Penguin Books.

Cook, David (2002), *Studies in Muslim Apocalyptic*. Studies in Late Antiquity and Early Islam 21. Princeton, New Jersey: The Darwin Press.

Cook, Michael (1984), "Magian cheese: an archaic problem in Islamic law." *Bulletin of the School of Oriental and African Studies* 47: 449–467.

Crone, Patricia (1980), *Slaves on Horses. The Evolution of the Islamic Polity*. Cambridge: Cambridge University Press.

Dähne, Stephan, *Reden der Araber: die politische ḫuṭba in der klassischen arabischen Literatur*, Frankfurt: Peter Lang 2001.

Dawood, N.J. (1956), *The Koran*. Penguin Books. London: Penguin.

Donner, Fred M. (1993) = Rosenthal et al. (1987–2007), vol. X.

Dozy, R. (1881), *Supplement aux dictionnaires arabes*. I–II. (Leyde: Brill), repr. Beyrouth: Librairie du Liban 1991.

Eisener, Reinhard (1987), *Zwischen Faktum und Fiktion. Eine Studie zum Umayyadenkalifen Sulaimān b. ʿAbdalmalik und seinem Bild in den Quellen*. Wiesbaden: Harrassowitz.

van Ess, Josef (1991–97), *Theologie und Gesellschaft im 2. und 3. Jahrhundert Hidschra. Eine Geschichte des religiösen Denkens im frühen Islam*. 1–6. Berlin and New York: Walter de Gruyter.

Fähndrich, Hartmut (1987–88), "A propos d'une compilation de la sagesse arabe: *ʿUnwān al-ḥikma* d'al-Muḥassin at-Tanūḫī." *Quaderni degli Studi Arabi* 5–6: 241–250.

Farah, Caesar E. (1990), "The prose literature of Ṣufism." In M.J.L. Young, J.D. Latham, and R.B. Serjeant (eds.), *Religion, Learning and Science in the ʿAbbasid Period*. Cambridge History of Arabic Literature. Cambridge: Cambridge University Press, pp. 56–75.

Forster, Regula (2017), *Wissensvermittlung im Gespräch. Eine Studie zu klassisch-arabischen Dialogen*. Islamic History and Civilization. Studies and Texts 149. Leiden – Boston: Brill.

Fowden, Garth (2004), *Quṣayr ʿAmra. Art and the Umayad Elite in Late Antique Syria.* The Transformation of the Classical Heritage 36. Berkeley – Los Angeles – London: University of California Press.

Fowden, Garth – Elizabeth Key Fowden (2004), *Studies on Hellenism, Christianity and the Umayyads.* MELETEMATA 37. Athens: Research Centre for Greek and Romas Antiquity, National Hellenic Research Foundation.

Fück, Johann (1950), *Arabiya. Untersuchungen zur arabischen Sprach- und Stilgeschichte.* Abhandlungen der Sächsischen Akademie der Wissenschaften zu Leipzig. Philologisch-historische Klasse 45/1. Berlin: Akademie-Verlag.

van Gelder, Geert Jan (2000), *Of Dishes and Discourse. Classical Arabic Literary Representations of Food.* Curzon Studies in Arabic and Middle-Eastern Literatures. Richmond, Surrey: Curzon.

Geries, Ibrahim (1977), *Un genre littéraire arabe: al-Maḥāsin wa-l-masāwī.* Publications du Département d'islamologie de l'Université de Paris-Sorbonne (Paris IV) IV. Paris.

Gramlich, Richard (1995–96), *Alte Vorbilder des Sufitums.* I–II. Veröffentlichungen der Orientalischen Kommission der Akademie Mainz 42/1–2. Wiesbaden: Harrassowitz.

Gramlich, Richard (1997), *Weltverzicht. Grundlagen und Weisen islamischer Askese.* Veröffentlichungen der Orientalischen Kommission der Akademie Mainz 43. Wiesbaden: Harrassowitz.

Guillaume, A. (1955), *The Life of Muhammad* (A translation of Ibn *Ishaq's Sirat Rasul Allah*). (Oxford: Oxford University Press), repr. Karachi: Oxford University Press 1982.

Gutas, D. (1975), *Greek Wisdom Literature in Arabic Translation. A study of the Graeco-Arabic gnomologia.* American Oriental Series 60. New Haven, Connecticut: American Oriental Society.

Hämeen-Anttila, Jaakko (1993a), "Unity and Variation in a Mediaeval Anecdote." *In Heikki Palva and Knut S. Vikør (eds.), The Middle East: Unity and Diversity: Papers from the Second Nordic Conference on Middle Eastern Studies, Copenhagen 22–25 October 1992.* Nordic Proceedings in Asian Studies 5: 153–164.

Hämeen-Anttila, Jaakko (1993b), *Lexical Ibdāl. Part I: Introduction. Source studies.* Studia Orientalia 71.

Hämeen-Anttila, Jaakko (1994), "Khālid ibn Ṣafwān – The Man and the Legend." *Studia Orientalia* 73: 69–166.

Hämeen-Anttila, Jaakko (1999), "John the Baptist and early Islamic polemics concerning Jesus." *Acta Orientalia* 60: 72–87.

Hämeen-Anttila, Jaakko (2002), *MAQAMA. A History of a Genre.* Diskurse der Arabistik 5. Harrassowitz: Wiesbaden.

Hämeen-Anttila, Jaakko (2009), "Short Stories in Classical Arabic Literature: The Case of Khālid ibn Ṣafwān and Umm Salama." In Lale Behzadi and Vahid Behmardi (eds.), *The Weaving of Words: Approaches to Classical Arabic Prose*. Beiruter Texte und Studien 112. Beirut: Ergon Verlag, pp. 35–54.

Hämeen-Anttila, Jaakko (2013a), "Dukayn: One Poet or Two?" *Zeitschrift der Deutschen Morgenländischen Gesellschaft* 163: 365–382.

Hämeen-Anttila, Jaakko (2013b), "Khālid ibn Ṣafwān – Between History and Literature." *Orientalia Lovaniensia Analecta* 215: 233–242.

Hämeen-Anttila, Jaakko (2014), "On the Early History of Literary Debate (*munāẓara*) in Islamic Spain." In Mohamed Meouak and Cristina de la Puente (eds.), *Vivir de tal suerte. Homenaje Juan Antonio Souto Lasala*. Series Abacvs 1: 261–273.

Hämeen-Anttila, Jaakko (2017), "Khālid ibn Ṣafwān: An Orator in Umayyad and ʿAbbāsid Courts." In Maurice Pomeranz and Evelyn Birge Vitz (eds.), *In the Presence of Power: Court and Performance in the Premodern Middle East*. New York University Press: New York, pp. 100–118.

Hämeen-Anttila, Jaakko (2018a), *Khwadāynāmag. The Middle Persian Book of Kings*. Studies in Persian Cultural History 14. Leiden – Boston: Brill.

Hämeen-Anttila, Jaakko (2018b), *Al-Maqrīzī's* al-Ḫabar ʿan al-bašar (*Vol. V, section 4) Persia and Its Kings,* Part I. Bibliotheca Maqriziana. Opera Maiora 5. Leiden – Boston: Brill.

Hasson, Isaac (1999), "Ansāb al-ašrāf d'al-Balāḏurī, est-il un livre de ta'rīḫ ou d'adab?" *Israel Oriental Studies* 19: 479–493.

Haug, Robert (2019), *The Eastern Frontier: Limits of Empire in Late Antique and Early Medieval Central Asia*. London – New York: I.B. Tauris.

Hillenbrand (1989) = Rosenthal et al. (1987–2007), vol. XXVI.

Horst, Heribert (1987), "Besondere Formen der Kunstprosa." In Helmut Gätje (ed.), *Grundriss der arabischen Philologie*. Band II*: Literaturwissenschaft*. Wiesbaden: Harrassowitz, pp. 221–227.

Ingrams, W.H. (1933), *Abu Nuwas in Life and Legend*. Port-Louis, Mauritius: M. Gaud & Cie.

Kennedy, Hugh (1986), *The Prophet and the Age of the Caliphates. The Islamic Near East from the Sixth to the Eleventh Century*. A History of the Near East. London – New York: Longman.

Kennedy, Hugh (1990) = Rosenthal et al. (1987–2007), vol. XXIX.

Kilpatrick, Hilary (2003), *Making the Great Book of Songs. Compilation and the Author's Craft in Abū l-Faraj al-Iṣbahānī's Kitāb al-Aghānī*. Routledge Studies in Arabian and Middle Eastern Literature. London – New York: RoutledgeCurzon.

Klasova, Pamela Marketa (2018), *Empire through Language: al-Ḥajjāj b. Yūsuf al-Thaqafī and the Power of Oratory in Umayyad Iraq*. PhD dissertation, Georgetown University.

Kohlberg, Etan (1992), *A Medieval Muslim Scholar at Work. Ibn Ṭāwūs and His Library*. Philosophy, Theology & Science 12. Leiden: Brill.

Kraemer, Jörg (1961), "Legajo-Studien zur altarabischen Philologie." *Zeitschrift der Deutschen Morgenländischen Gesellschaft* 110: 252–300.
Lane, E.W. (1863–93), *An Arabic – English lexicon*. I–VIII. (London), repr. in 2 vols. Cambridge: The Islamic Texts Society 1984.
Lecker, Michael (1996), "Biographical notes in Ibn Shihāb al-Zuhrī." *Journal of Semitic Studies* 41: 21–63.
Lecker, Michael (2005), "Tribes in Pre- and Early Islamic Arabia." In Michael Lecker, *People, Tribes and Society in Arabia Around the Time of Muḥammad*. Variorum Collected Studies Series CS812. Aldeshot: Ashgate Variorum, no. XI, pp. 1–106.
Leder, Stefan (1988), "Authorship and transmission in unauthored literature." *Oriens* 31: 67–81.
Leder, Stefan (1990), "Features of the Novel in Early Historiography. The downfall of Xālid al-Qasrī." *Oriens* 32: 72–96.
Leder, Stefan (1991), *Das Korpus al-Haiṯam ibn ʿAdī (st. 207/822). Herkunft, Überlieferung, Gestalt früher Texte der aḫbār Literatur*. Frankfurt am Main: Vittorio Klostermann.
Lindstedt, Ilkka (2012–14), "The life and deeds of ʿAlī b. Muḥammad al-Madāʾinī." *Zeitschrift für Geschichte der arabisch-islamischen Wissenschaften* 20–21: 235–270.
Lindstedt, Ilkka (2013), *The Transmission of al-Madāʾinī's Material. Historiographical Studies*. PhD thesis. University of Helsinki.
Littman, Enno (1953), *Die Erzählungen aus den Tausendundein Nächten*. I–VI. Wiesbaden: Insel-Verlag.
Lyall, C.I. (1906), "Ibn al-Kalbī's first day of al-Kulāb." In Carl Bezold (ed.), *Orientalistische Studien Theodor Nöldeke zum 70. Geburtstag gewidmet*. I–II. Giessen: Töpelmann, I: 127–154.
Lyons, Malcolm C. (2008), *The Arabian Nights. Tales of 1001 Nights*. I–III. Penguin Classics. London: Penguin.
Malti-Douglas, Fedwa (1985), *Structures of Avarice. The Bukhalāʾ in Mediaeval Arabic literature*. Studies in Arabic Literature 11. Leiden: Brill.
Marlow, Louise (1997), *Hierarchy and Egalitarianism in Islamic Thought*. Cambridge Studies in Islamic Civilization. Cambridge: Cambridge University Press.
Marzolph, Ulrich (1992), *Arabia Ridens. Die humoristische Kurzprosa der frühen adab-Literatur im internationalen Traditionsgeflecht*. I–II. Frankfurter Wissenschaftliche Beiträge. Kulturwissenschaftliche Reihe 21/1–2. Frankfurt am Main: Klostermann.
Marzolph, Ulrich (1983), *Der weise Narr Buhlūl*. Abhandlungen für die Kunde des Morgenlandes 46:4. Wiesbaden: Franz Steiner.
al-Maymanī, ʿAbd al-ʿAzīz (1937), *al-Ṭarāʾif al-adabiyya*. (Al-Qāhira), repr. Bayrūt: Dār al-Kutub al-ʿilmiyya n.d.
Monroe, James T. (1983), *The Art of Badīʿ az-zamān al-Hamadhānī as Picaresque Narrative*. Papers of the Center for Arab and Middle East Studies 2. Beirut: American University of Beirut.

Müller, K. (1979), *Kritische Untersuchungen zum Dīwan des Kumait b. Zaid.* Islamkundliche Untersuchungen 52. Freiburg: Klaus Schwarz.

Pellat, Charles (1953), *Le milieu Baṣrien et la formation de Ǧāḥiẓ.* Paris: Librairie d'Amérique et d'Orient Adrien-Maisonneuve.

Pellat, Charles (1954), *Le Livre de la couronne. Ouvrage attribué à Ǧāḥiẓ.* Traduction d'auteurs arabes. Paris: Société d'édition "Les belles lettres."

Piamenta, Moshe (1990–91), *Dictionary of Post-Classical Yemeni Arabic.* 1–2. Leiden – New York – København – Köln: Brill.

Popovkin, Alex V. (2007) = Rosenthal et al. (1987–2007), vol. XL.

Qutbuddin, Tahereh (2019), *Arabic Oration: Art and Function.* Handbook of Oriental Studies 1/131. Leiden – Boston: Brill.

Ritter, Hellmut (1959) = *Die Geheimnisse der Wortkunst (Asrār al-balāġa) des 'Abdalqāhir al-Curcānī.* Aus dem arabischen übersetzt von Hellmut Ritter. Bibliotheca Islamica 19. Wiesbaden: Franz Steiner Verlag.

Rosenthal, Franz (1956), *Humor in Early Islam.* Leiden: Brill.

Rosenthal, Franz et al. (1987–2007), *The History of al-Ṭabarī* I–XL. Bibliotheca Persica. Albany: State University of New York Press.

Rotter, Gernot (1982), *Die Umayyaden und der zweite Bürgerkrieg (680–692).* Abhandlungen für die Kunde des Morgenlandes 45/3. Wiesbaden: Franz Steiner.

Sachau, C. Edward (1879), *The Chronology of Ancient Nations.* London: Allen Co.

Saleman, Carl – Valentin Shukovski (1947), *Persische Grammatik.* Porta Linguarum Orientalium XII. Leipzig: Harrassowitz.

al-Sāmarrāʾī, Yūnus Aḥmad (1991), *Khālid ibn Ṣafwān al-Tamīmī. Ḥayātuhu, aqwāluhu, khuṭabuhu, ashʿāruhu.* Bayrūt: Dār al-Nidāʾ wa'l-nashr wa'l-tawzīʿ. [not seen].[1]

al-Sāmarrāʾī, Yūnus Aḥmad (2001), *Khuṭab Shabīb ibn Shayba al-Tamīmī wa-aqwāluhu wa-akhbāruhu.* Bayrūt: Dār al-Shuʾūn al-thaqāfiyya al-ʿāmma.

Schoeler, Gregor (1974), *Arabische Naturdichtung. Die Zahrīyāt, Rabīʿīyāt and Rauḍīyāt von ihren Anfängen bis aṣ-Ṣanaubarī. Eine gattungs-, motiv- und stilgeschichtliche Untersuchung.* Beiruter Texte und Studien 15. Beirut: in Kommission bei Franz Steiner (Wiesbaden).

Schoeler, Gregor (1980), "Verfasser und Titel des dem Ǧāḥiẓ zugeschriebenen sogenannten Kitāb al-Tāǧ." *Zeitschrift der Deutschen Morgenländischen Gesellschaft* 130: 217–225.

Schoeler, Gregor (2002), *The Genesis of Literature in Islam from the Aural to the Read.* Translated by Shawkat M. Toorawa. The New Edinburgh Islamic Surveys. Edinburgh: Edinburgh University Press.

1 The book appeared earlier as *Khuṭab Khālid ibn Ṣafwān wa-aqwāluhu wa-akhbāruhu.* Baghdād: Wizārat al-thaqāfa 1990.

Schoeler, Gregor (2006), *The Oral and the Written in Early Islam*. Translated by Uwe Vagelpohl. Ed. James E. Montgomery. Routledge Studies in Middle Eastern Literatures. Abingdon, Oxon: Routledge.

Schwarzbaum, H. (1961–63), "International folklore motifs in Petrus Alphonsi's 'Disciplina Clericalis'." *Sefarad* 21 (1961): 267–299; 22 (1962): 17–59, 321–344; 23 (1963): 54–73.

Serjeant, R.B. (1997), *The Book of Misers. Al-Jāḥiẓ, al-Bukhalāʾ*. Great Books of Islamic Civilization. Reading: Garnet.

Sezgin, Ursula (1971), *Abu Miḫnaf. Ein Beitrag zur Historiographie der umayyadischen Zeit*. Leiden: Brill.

Sharlet, Jocelyn (2011), "Tokens of resentment. Medieval Arabic narratives about gift exchange and social conflict." *Journal of Arabic and Islamic Studies* 11: 62–100.

Talmon, Rafael (1997), *Arabic Grammar in Its Formative Age: Kitāb al-ʿAyn and Its Attribution to Ḫalīl ibn Aḥmad*. Leiden: Brill.

Taylor, Archer (1968), "This Too Will Pass (Jason 910Q)." In F. Harkort, K.C. Peeters and R. Wildhaber (eds.), *Festschrift Kurt Ranke*. Göttingen: Schwartz, pp. 345–350.

Toorawa, Shawkat M. (2005), *Ibn Abī Ṭāhir Ṭayfūr and Arabic Writerly Culture. A Ninth-Century Bookman in Baghdad*. RoutledgeCurzon Studies in Arabic and Middle-Eastern Literatures. London – New York: RoutledgeCurzon.

Toral-Niehoff, Isabel (2014a), *Al-Ḥīra. Eine arabische Kulturmetropole im spätantiken Kontext*. Islamic History and Civilization. Studies and Texts 104. Leiden – Boston: Brill.

Toral-Niehoff, Isabel (2014b), "Talking about Arab origins: the transmission of the *Ayyām al-ʿArab* in al-Kūfa, al-Baṣra, and Baghdād." In Jens Scheiner and Damien Janos (eds.), *The Place to go: Contexts of Learning in Baghdād, 750–1000 C.E.* Studies in Late Antiquity and Early Islam 26. Princeton, New Jersey: The Darwin Press.

Ullmann, Manfred, *Untersuchungen zur Raǧazpoesie. Ein Beitrag zur arabischen Sprach- und Literaturwissenschaft*. Wiesbaden: Harrassowitz 1966.

Ullmann, Manfred (1979), *Wa-ḫairu l-ḥadīthi mā kāna laḥnan*. Beiträge zur Lexikographie des Klassischen Arabisch 1. Bayerische Akademie der Wissenschaften. Philosophisch-historische Klasse. Sitzungsberichte 1979: 9. München: Verlag der Bayerischen Akademie der Wissenschaften.

Ulrich, Brian (2007), "The sources on the Fitna of Masʿūd b. ʿAmr al-Azdī and their uses for Basran tribal history (poster)." *Proceedings of the Seminar for Arabian Studies* 37: 295–296.

Uther, Hans-Jörg (2004), *The Types of International Folktales. A Classification and Bibliography*. I–III. FF Communications 133–135. Helsinki: Academia Scientiarum Fennica.

Versteegh, Kees (1997), *The Arabic Language*. Edinburgh: Edinburgh University Press.

Wagner, Ewald (1962), *Die arabische Rangstreitdichtung und ihre Einordnung in die allgemeine Literaturgeschichte*. Akademie der Wissenschaften und der Literatur. Abhandlungen der geistes- und sozialwissenschaftlichen Klasse, Jahrgang 1962: 8. Wiesbaden: Verlag der Akademie der Wissenschaften und der Literatur in Mainz in Kommission bei Franz Steiner Verlag.

Weisweiler, M. (1954), *Arabesken der Liebe. Früharabische Geschichten von Liebe und Frauen*. Leiden: Brill.

Wensinck, A.J. (1992), *Concordance et indices de la tradition musulmane. 2nd. edition*. I–VIII (in 4 vols.). Leiden – Boston: Brill.

Werkmeister, Walter (1983), *Quellenuntersuchungen zum Kitāb al-ʿIqd al-farīd des Andalusiers Ibn ʿAbdrabbih (246/860–328/940). Ein Beitrag zur arabischen Literaturgeschichte*. Islamkundliche Untersuchungen 70. Berlin: Klaus Schwarz.

Wild, Stefan (1965), *Das Kitāb al-ʿAin und die arabische Lexikographie*. Wiesbaden: Harrassowitz.

Zakeri, Mohsen (1995), *Sāsānid Soldiers in Early Muslim Society. The origins of ʿAyyārān and Futuwwa*. Wiesbaden: Harrassowitz.

Zakeri, Mohsen (2007), *Persian Wisdom in Arabic Garb. ʿAlī b. ʿUbayda al-Rayḥānī (d. 219/834) and His Jawāhir al-Kilam wa-Farāʾid al-Ḥikam*. 1–2. Leiden – Boston: Brill.

Zameño, Amalia (online) Brill Online Christian Muslim relations 600–1500. https://referenceworks.brillonline.com/browse/christian-muslim-relations-i.

Source References to B1–B115

Ansāb, p. 55: B1–B2
Ansāb, p. 56: B3–B7
Ansāb, p. 57: B8–B9
Ansāb, p. 58: B10–B13
Ansāb, p. 59: B14–B17
Ansāb, p. 60: B18–B22
Ansāb, p. 61: B23–B25
Ansāb, p. 62: B26–B27
Ansāb, p. 63: B28–B31
Ansāb, p. 64: B32–B37
Ansāb, pp. 65–66: B38
Ansāb, p. 67: B39–B40
Ansāb, p. 68: B41–B43
Ansāb, p. 69: B44–B47
Ansāb, p. 70: B48–B51
Ansāb, p. 71: B52–B54
Ansāb, p. 72: B55–B60
Ansāb, p. 73: B61–B67
Ansāb, p. 74: B68–B74
Ansāb, p. 75: B75–B79
Ansāb, p. 76: B80–B81
Ansāb, pp. 77–78: B82
Ansāb, p. 79: B83
Ansāb, p. 80: B84–B87
Ansāb, p. 81: B88–B92
Ansāb, p. 82: B93–B96
Ansāb, p. 83: B97–B98
Ansāb, p. 84: B99–B100
Ansāb, p. 85: B101–B102
Ansāb, p. 86: B103–B107
Ansāb, p. 87: B108–B110
Ansāb, p. 88: B111–B115

Index of Personal Names

This index gives first occurrences in the study (Part 1) and then occurrences in the stories themselves (Part 2). Names in *isnāds* have been ignored, except when the last link takes part in the action. When a name appears both in the story itself and in the following commentary or the footnotes, only the first has been indicated. Names appearing in the footnotes are indicated by n (24n = page 24, footnote) and those appearing in the commentary by k (B2k = B2, commentary).

Index of Place Names

This index also includes tribes, clans, and families.

Index of Topics